Houses of the Horoscope

HOUSES
of the
HOROSCOPE

BILL HERBST

International Standard Book Number 0-917086-98-8

Cover Design by Maria Kay Simms
Illustrations by Bill Herbst

Printed in the United States of America

Published by ACS Publications, Inc.
P.O. Box 16430
San Diego, CA 92116-0430

Table of Contents:

Part One
The Houses in Astrology

Table of Contents:

Part Two
Planetary Delineations

Preface

Introduction

For students of astrology, the houses are the least understood of the major frameworks. There's a wealth of literature on signs of the zodiac, interpreting them through every nook and cranny of possible meaning. Planets are similarly well-covered in many texts. But clear, comprehensive information on the houses has been conspicuously lacking. Too often, houses remain one-dimensional, badly understood, and poorly used.

One reason for this is that houses are not convenient in the astrological mass market. To explore your Sun sign, you need to know only your birthday. To work with the other planets in the signs, you need only the date and year of birth. Even most aspects require no more than the day/month/year. Since almost everyone has that information, it's attractive to write books interpreting those levels, because there's a huge market.

But to work with houses, you must know not only day, month, and year of birth, but the exact time and place of birth as well. This cuts the market potential considerably, because books on the houses can be fully applied only by people who already have birth charts, or are willing to go to the considerable trouble of getting them erected by an individual astrologer or by a company like **Astro Computing Services.**

About this Book

The houses are tremendously important in the overall framework of astrological interpretation. It is not merely an oversight, but a travesty that the literature contains so few works of depth. I hope that **Houses of the Horoscope** will help remedy the situation.

Part One contains five chapters that explore the background of houses in astrology—their origins, logic, and implications—as well as a comprehensive overview of the techniques guiding their use in interpretation.

Part Two consists of delineations for planetary meanings through the twelve houses. Each house is divided into five specific levels of experience, and every planet is interpreted in each house at every level—a total of 600 separate interpretations.

Relative Authority

A natal chart might be considered symbolically "permanent." Each of us gets only one original astrological pattern at birth, rather like the genetic code we carry in our cells. However, deciphering that code is anything but absolute. Charts just sit there, their symbols staring up at us from the page. They don't say a thing, and they sure don't interpret themselves.

Interpretation is very much a human endeavor, and therefore relative to a thousand factors: time, place, convention, style, bias, etc. Every astrologer, no matter how expert, will comprehend certain areas better than others. Some houses will be more interesting or compelling, some planets better understood, some signs more easily assimilated. And though natal charts don't technically change, people do. Our knowledge is very relative, both as astrologers looking at another person's chart, and as human beings living out the lives our own charts symbolize.

It is customary for an author to portray himself as an expert on his subject. Writing conveys information more effectively when the words carry solid authority. But this discounts the very real fact that in any effort such as this, where there are so many different levels of information, no author could possibly claim absolute knowledge. What I've written in this book carries only the relative authority of my current understanding, here and now.

Author's Birth Chart

It's tremendously helpful for a reader to understand the biases of an author—both in conscious inclination, and more importantly, unconscious prejudice. Since our system is uniquely designed to reveal the inner workings of personality in wonderfully shorthand form, it's absurd that so many astrology books are written without the inclusion of the author's natal chart, or at the very least, his or her birth data. So I've included my own birth chart below.

One of the most important points I hope to make with this book is that charts are not the same as people, so just having my chart won't tell you whether or not this book is worth reading. But it will let you better assess my personal orientations—the concerns, interests, and paradoxes that form the structure for my living, the vulnerabilities as well as the strengths.

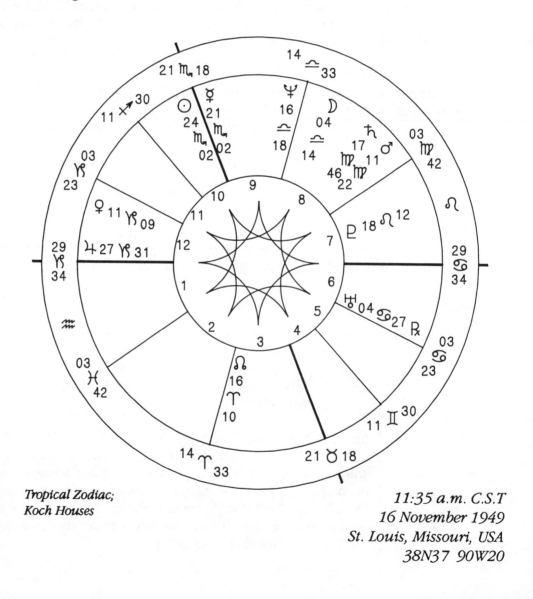

Tropical Zodiac;
Koch Houses

11:35 a.m. C.S.T
16 November 1949
St. Louis, Missouri, USA
38N37 90W20

Production

This book was created entirely on a personal computer. It was initially begun in 1984, using a 128K Apple Macintosh, which became a 512K Macintosh, then a 1-megabyte Mac Plus with a DataFrame 20-megabyte hard drive. Text was written using MacWrite and Microsoft Word. All graphics were created using MacDraw, MacDraft, and SuperPaint, with help from Switcher. Design, layout, and typesetting were composed on PageMaker. The edited files were output directly from a Mac to an Allied Linotype Lintronic 300 laser typesetter, which created the master pages at a resolution of 1,270 dpi.

In an age where "desktop publishing" is fast becoming a reality, I want to thank the people at *ACS Publications* for their vision, support, and cooperation.

Graphic Design

The graphic layout is designed with what are called "glosses," which is the margin in the left column containing the section headings. This space can be used to jot down notes as you read, to record your own ideas as you think about the text.

Books have become sacred cows in our culture, and it would do us good to break the habit of considering them pristine, finished products. If you shelled out hard-earned dollars to buy the book, feel free to use it as the creative tool it should be.

So please write in this book.

Merely a Beginning

In writing the 600 delineations of **Part Two,** I've attempted to make them as complete as space allowed, to offer the best of my experience. But I realize all too well the impossibility of such a task. Far from covering the astrological houses and their use in interpretation, this book represents merely a beginning, a starting point for a subject that has been too long ignored in the literature.

I hope the delineations will provide astrological students with a comprehensive view of planets in houses, as well as a better feel for the the basic thought processes involved in natal interpretation. For professionals, I hope the book offers some original insights and new ways of thinking about the houses that will stimulate greater creativity in working with clients.

Feedback

If you have feedback—ideas, corrections, criticism, or encouragement—please feel free to write me at the post office box listed below.

Thanks for reading.

Bill Herbst

c/o: P. O. Box 24567
Edina, MN 54424-0567

Part One

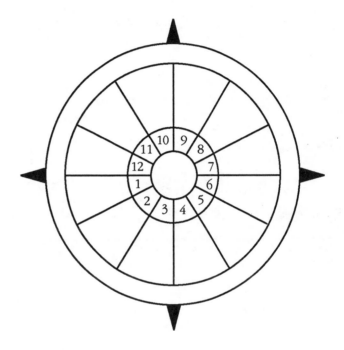

The Houses
in Astrology

The Logic of Houses

The quest for meaning that characterizes astrology and all other human systems begins in the heart. We want to know, to understand, to feel in harmony with our world, at peace with our lives. The yearning of the heart motivates the mind to create ways of seeing and interpreting reality that not only make sense, not only coherently organize the events and experiences of our living, but also satisfy our basic need for order, for beautiful symmetry. It is not enough to simply understand; our sense of myth demands that we also create as we reveal.

Much of the public incorrectly assumes that astrology is just archaic superstition, a false artifact from bygone epochs in human evolution, now degenerated into a parlor game for the mentally infirm. Unfortunately, such a view is in some ways justified, given the popular forms of astrology, the arcane language of the system, and the public visibility of certain astrologers more interested in marketing mysticism than contributing to thoughtful consideration of their profession.

But despite our culture's often hysterical reactions to astrology, the system embodies a graceful sense of logic, even if its conceptual frameworks transcend the ordinary and its technical implications are too comprehensive to be easily grasped.

Astrology versus Science

Astrology is not "science," at least not in the way science is usually understood and used. Each method of interpreting, structuring, and controlling reality has points of contact and convergence with the other, but the two are hardly parallel and should not be considered as having emerged from the same mold.

As a way of knowledge, science is less than 400 years old, a mere babe in the woods, but with a clean freshness because of its youth. It has swept through western culture like wildfire, changing the face of civilization with its power. But that power is still raw and adolescent; science has yet to mature into a discipline of wisdom. Its effect on the world is unquestioned, but its ability to further the consciousness of those who practice it is yet to be demonstrated. In some ways, we stand as a species at the threshold of annihilation because of the urgent momentum of science.

As a way of interpreting reality, astrology originated tens of thousands of years ago before the first agrarian societies. Even parts of the formal system we use today date back over a thousand years. Thus, astrology is not pristine. It has no clean edge, but instead has evolved in harmony with civilization through various stylistic phases of perception and philosophy. As a result, separating the wheat from the chaff, knowing which presumptions to keep and which to shed, is no simple matter.

Although the fundamental principles of astrology are easy enough to learn, ours is not a perfectly logical system. It demands a different approach, for, unlike science, it is neither straightforward nor concrete. Instead, astrology is enigmatically shrouded in the cloak of its own peculiar evolutionary background, and thus more like us than science will ever hope to be. This is both a great strength and a severe weakness. It is so much a reflection of historical human development in the quest for meaning that it becomes as difficult to fully understand astrology as it is to understand ourselves.

*Parents
versus
Children*

But modern times require renewed formulations of the system. Insofar as possible, we strive to make sense of astrology by applying the tools of other, more contemporary methodologies, such as science and psychology. These are in fact the children of astrology, and in their insecure eagerness to establish a unique identity, a firm footing from which to promote their creativity and stature, they do what all adolescent children routinely do—they challenge the history, experience, and spiritual validity of their parents in an attempt to protect themselves from what they do not understand.

They see the inconsistencies of the parents, the peccadilloes of their growth, the psychological scars woven into the fabric of personality. They see how seemingly illogical their parents are, how mistaken are their assumptions. This is the phase through which culture has been moving in the twentieth century. With maturity, the young disciplines of science and psychology may in time come to understand their astrological parent, to venerate its wisdom even as they accept its failings.

Similarly, parents cannot reject their children simply because they pass through a period of rebellious denial. Quite the contrary, it is the responsibility of mature parents to learn from the experience of their children, for it is through their children that they renew their own vitality. In a very real sense, children do not consciously learn; they automatically absorb. Youngsters are downright driven to organize their nervous systems by voraciously establishing relationships to their world, and they certainly assimilate at an amazing pace. But they don't possess the sophisticated awareness to approach learning from a consciously interpretive standpoint. Parents are already the owners of adult awareness—ideally at least, if not in fact. They can learn from their children, however difficult it may be to remain awake to this formidable task.

Therefore, it is natural for astrology to undergo the scrutiny of logical thinking, not solely to gain acceptance in the eyes of a young world, but more importantly, to revitalize itself. If our discipline insists on defending itself by an adamant refusal to question its own assumptions and methods, it risks not only permanent rejection by the world, but worse, it risks the sacrifice of whatever wisdom might be gleaned from its history. It may lose its power to help humankind further develop into psychological and spiritual maturity. This would be a tragedy.

Astrology will never completely make sense through the paradigms of science or psychology, any more than a father can perfectly justify his life through his children's adolescent understanding. There will always be gaps, mysteries, apologies, areas that even the father doesn't truly understand and cannot effectively communicate or explain. But the attempt is worth making in spite of such shortcomings.

This chapter will attempt to explain in rational terms—both scientific and psychological, as well as metaphysical—the derivation of meaning for the twelve houses of an astrological birth chart. Starting from the basic assumptions astrology makes about our world, we'll proceed through step-by-step deductions, increasing the complexity of the system with each further division.

It will not be an entirely linear process; deductions will intersect, parallel, and overlap, resulting in a multi-leveled finished product. And please understand, the analysis cannot be perfectly consistent, since the actual derived meanings at the end of the process already exist in the lexicon of interpretive astrology before we even start. I am admittedly bending the logical method to suit the needs of the system.

The discipline of natal astrology holds that the moment of first breath during the birth of any individual is of profound significance, and that by understanding the positions of the major bodies of the solar system relative to certain background frameworks, we can interpret the symbolic meanings of the birth or natal horoscope to reveal patterns of perception and intention that will shape the development of personality in the individual's life-to-come.

We cannot suggest that the planetary positions at the moment of birth cause any person to be what he or she is and will become. There are other, more obvious factors that clearly shape personality: hereditary genetics, biology, family systems, cultural imprints, free will, etc. So it would be both illogical and absurd to presume that the moment of birth is the primary causal agent in determining life experience. But we could presume—and astrology does—that astronomical factors surrounding the birth environment may correlate with important psychological features of an individual's development within an overall pattern of meaning.

The Nature of Time

Time is the key here. Every moment in time is unique, as has been demonstrated in this century by quantum mechanics, a branch of atomic physics. We can illustrate the principle through the mundane experience of watching a movie.

When we show a film, the images on the screen give the impression of smooth, flowing movement. It is an illusion, however, both optical and psychological. Actually, the film itself is made up of a series of discrete frames, or photos. Each successive frame in the film is slightly different than the previous one. When projected in sequence at fast enough speed—the standard is 25 frames per second—the individual frames appear to blend together into one smooth image of action flowing through time.

They blend for two reasons: first, because our eyes retain images for a brief instant, even after those images have vanished from the screen; and second, because our brains are built to seek continuity of experience, in order to buffer shocks to our consciousness. We provide the sense of flow, but in actual fact, each frame of film is a complete scene, and there's a little "jump" from one scene to the next, a break in the action.

If we release ourselves from the demands of continuity, our tendency to interpret experience through apparently seamless movement, we can interpret each individual frame in isolation, as a still photographer might. Ignoring the ordinary flow of plot or characterization, we could focus instead on abstract qualities such as light and shadow, color, recurring objects, etc. In this way, the salient features of a given film can be compiled into a set of fundamental symbolic elements. The first appearance of a new character at a particular frame in the film would then represent a sudden revelation, an alteration in the pattern of elements in their matrix. It would be almost a spontaneous mutation, a magical appearance, the introduction of a new element that would subtly alter the relationship of everything to everything else.

This is precisely what natal astrology presumes to do with human life. We know that time seems to be a continuous flow, but we also know that in truth it is like a film, an infinite series of separate and unique "instants." If reality embodies a mysterious order beneath its apparent chaos, as everyone from Buddha to Einstein has suggested, then in the "movie of life," the instant something first appears is significant, for it changes the overall pattern.

In natal astrology, that something is a human being, and the significance is that we can understand the meaning of that human being's life by deciphering the meaning of the moment of first appearance. Another way to say the same thing is that any person born in a certain moment of time will naturally be an embodiment of the symbolic meaning for that particular moment in the universe. Understanding this fundamental presumption is crucial if we want to eventually use astrology well, with grace and artistry.

Why Birth?   Why is birth defined as the moment of "first appearance?" Wouldn't it make more sense to use the moment of conception, since that is the instant when genetic selection occurs? The answer is two-fold.

First, if we want to create a workable system, we've got to be able to dependably define a person's "first" moment, and birth—that is to say, the moment of first breath—is the obvious choice. We simply have no method to pinpoint the moment of conception. Pragmatically, we wouldn't get very far with an interpretive system hinged on an initial event that was immeasurable.

But beyond the practical considerations, the birth-moment of first breath is logical because it is the moment at which a human being becomes autonomous. Prior to first breath, the fetus is part of the mother, living off her bloodstream, her oxygen, her nutrients, and—importantly—her experience of the world.

I don't mean to suggest that we are "blank slates" prior to birth, for that philosophy is clearly anachronistic. Much is already determined through conception and in motion throughout gestation. But human life requires more than the genetic information coded in DNA strands. It requires more than the development of physical biology. There may be consciousness in the womb—we do not yet possess the ability to know with absolute certainty—but there is clearly no direct contact with external life, except as it filters through the mother.

Through the nine months of gestation, we are literally fed by our mother. We don't do anything; she does it for us, offering the final product, the distilled essence of food and oxygen. But with birth we have to breathe, to begin the autonomic machinery of cardio-vascular respiration. We force the fluid from our lungs and say good-bye forever to the security of the womb's oceanic oneness. We replace that fluid with air—the raw substance of the external human and earthly environment. We literally breathe in the world for the first time in that moment of birth, inhaling the relationship, saying hello to reality.

At first breath, the whole internal biological system begins to shift over from mother to infant. As we move from an enclosed liquid environment out into the exposed airy world, we are shocked in the most absolute way we are likely to ever experience. Suddenly, we begin to interact with the stimulus of the external environment. There is increasing evidence to suggest that babies learn while in the womb, but this learning is clearly accelerated once we can interact with external life directly. Birth is a critical boundary between the liquidity of prenatal experience and the more rigid imprinting of early infancy.

In the same manner that a photographic print is "stopped" during development by bathing it in a chemical fixative, birth could be considered the fixating experience for many of the changing patterns in prenatal formation, giving each newborn a basic structure through which the innate personality can evolve into a living form.

Breathing establishes rhythms in our brains that are sustained throughout life. Once we start breathing, we're truly alive, and if we stop for more than a few moments, we're dead. Prior to birth, a fetus is both human and being, but it's not fully a human being.

So birth is the moment of first appearance. If we want to reveal the meaning of the individual's nature, the purpose of the life, the root paradoxes of perception that form the very ground of personality and condition its development, we can do so by deciphering the particular instant of first breath, that precise frame in the movie of life where an individual's character initially appeared.

Creating the Astrological System

How do we go about this? How do we design a system to understand the meaning of any given moment in time?

First of all, we remind ourselves of the purpose of what we wish to create. Even though we use the "screen" of the heavens, even though we concern ourselves with the symbolism of the major bodies of the solar system, astrology is not "cosmic" in its implications; the meanings we arrive at are very much human and earthly. That's because we are more psychologists than cosmologists. We're more concerned with our lives here and how to live them well than we are with the ultimate meanings of the universe. So frames of reference in astrology are mainly human- and Earth-centered. We measure everything in our system relative to ourselves and where we are.

What we're doing is observing the solar system from our vantage point as if it were one whole unit, a complete and integrated level of reality. The solar system lends itself well to our purposes, for one of the requirements of any "language" is to keep it simple, and the ten major bodies we observe in our heavens—the **sun,** our own **moon,** and the eight known planets: **Mercury, Venus, Mars, Jupiter, Saturn, Uranus, Neptune, and Pluto**—provide simplicity as well as a sense of wholeness.

Technically, the sun and moon are called **Lights,** for obvious reasons. They are not **planets** according to the astronomical definition. However, astronomy and astrology are distinctly different disciplines, with separate terminologies, and it is conventional in astrology to refer to any major body of the solar system as a "planet."

Of course, there are numerous other bodies from the solar system we could bring into consideration—asteroids, comets, planetoids, etc.—and many astrologers do use these as symbolic indicators. Then too, in addition to literal physical bodies, there are many purely mathematical points of significance—the nodal axes of the moon and other planets, for instance. There are even "imaginary" planets, purely hypothetical bodies, intuitively conceived. But for our purposes, and especially for the beginner in astrology, focusing on the ten major bodies is more than sufficient.

These major astronomical bodies are seen not in their physical context, not as "forces," sending down "rays of influence," but instead, they are understood as symbols revealing the momentary state of the art of evolution in this small sector of the universe, our immediate cosmic "neighborhood."

Yes, we keep it simple, but the complexity of astrology, as well as its relevance and beauty, come from the fact that the planets are constantly moving through our perceptual heavens, each at a different rate of speed. What is crucial is the overall pattern these ten bodies form in relation to us and to one another, for each succeeding moment in time creates a new planetary pattern in the cosmic environment, a quality unique to that moment, never to be duplicated in that precise way.

What we want to do is discover the symbolic nature of each of these ten major bodies, at least as they apply to contemporary human beings. We want to see if they can be interpreted as having specific qualities or functions within the system as a whole.

An automobile has functional systems that work together in a smooth manner—the engine, drive train, brakes, electrical, structural systems, etc. The human body has functional systems that operate in much the same manner—the skeletal, muscular, cardiovascular, digestive, eliminative systems, etc. But what about something more complex and intangible? What about the human psyche? Is it possible that this wellspring of human personality, invisible though it is, might be better understood if we could create a system for defining and interpreting its interrelated parts?

The Historical Evolution of Astrology

Humankind has striven for thousands of years to create systematic ways to understand life. Every culture creates myths, religions, and institutionalized rituals to provide structures to make life feel more secure, predictable, and thus controllable. Astrology is one of the oldest of these endeavors, originating in antiquity as one of the first systems of collective and religious mythology. More recently, the infant science of psychology has attempted to define the components of personality and how they may relate to the course of life-unfoldment.

The so-called primitive people who lived at the dawn of civilization were, in certain ways, much more observant of the natural world than we are today. Their experience of reality was probably fundamentally different than ours, certainly less sophisticated, but then they didn't labor under the weight of 5,000 years of cultural conditioning. Without the distractions of literature, mass media, and the almost unbelievable stimulus of urban life, we might presume them to have been simple souls motivated only by survival. But their nervous systems were functionally the same as ours—10,000 years is a mere drop in the bucket in species evolution—and their brains were basically identical to ours. They would have created complete realities out of their worlds just as we do, likely with the same blend of wisdom and foolishness.

Imagine how vibrant and alive the sky must have been to a hunter-gatherer existing 15,000 years ago. There would be no pollution to haze over the heavens, no city lights to dim the brilliance of the stars illuminating the darkness. Instead, there would have been an ongoing display of celestial fireworks, 7 shows a week, front-row seats guaranteed. These people would have become very familiar with the heavenly lights. They would have realized that these lights appeared to revolve across the sky in the same pattern, night after night. They would also have noticed that within this infinite circle of brilliance, certain points of light were not locked in position relative to all the other points, but actually moved, wandering through the heavenly firmament with regular and predictable motions.

Obviously, the sun and moon would have been of prime importance, since they literally dominate the sky, but there would have been five other, smaller lights that also moved—Mercury, Venus, Mars, Jupiter, and Saturn. (Early humans wouldn't have seen the three outer planets, Uranus, Neptune, and Pluto, since these are not visible with the naked eye.) It would have been obvious that all seven "wanderers" traveled in a cycle through the stationary background of stars in the same general arc, a kind of belt. It would have been equally apparent that each of the seven progressed at separate speeds, completing their trips in different periods of time.

This knowledge of planets and cycles would have been handed down from generation to generation, part of the Great Mystery of Life, and doubtless an inviting subject for every kind of imaginative explanation. As the hunter-gatherers settled and evolved into agrarian farmers, correlations would have arisen between these celestial wanderers and the events happening in the natural world. With the creation of stable societies, planets would become part of the lore of religious rituals, and their cycles would have had great relevance in understanding the timing of natural life.

Cultures once interpreted planets as "Gods ruling human life." They had no relation to individuals, any more than men have relation to ants. They were linked with dominion over the earth, with the control of natural events: the planting of crops, timing of rains, recurrence of floods, etc. This was the first stage; the planets were superhuman deities.

From that totally impersonal basis, planetary symbolism gradually evolved into a social/political system. Human rulers were naturally interested in cementing their power over the people they ruled by claiming identification with "the Gods," so it was inevitable that they would assert that planetary symbols had a connection or relevance to their own lives and decisions they made concerning collective policy; it augmented their authority.

This was the second stage, where the planets were moved into intimate relationship with a specific ruling elite. Their superhuman qualities were beginning to erode, even though they continued to have no personal relation to ordinary individuals.

In aspiring to be like Gods, men necessarily sowed the seeds of the *reverse* correlation, that of pulling the Gods down to the level of common men. Through the ancient cultures of Babylon and Egypt, it remained relatively steadfast. Planets were not linked with any but the most exalted beings. But with the appearance of Christianity at the end of the Greco-Roman period, a change began to assert itself. Though it would take another 1,500 years before Christ's elevation of the common man filtered down far enough to affect social philosophy, the die was cast. Planetary symbolism was headed for stage three, where every person could claim a personal relationship to planetary significance.

More than the writings of social philosophers or the leaps in governmental forms, it was Gutenberg's printing press and the sudden availability of books that opened this third stage. Public access to technical information concerning astronomical data became available in a general way for the first time, and suddenly, anyone who was literate and moderately well-off could study astrology, applying its precepts to his own life. (In this case, "his" is the proper pronoun; women were still shut out at this point.)

Through all the phases of that evolution, the sheer amount of symbolic knowledge about the planets kept growing, amassed through empirical, philosophical, and intuitive associations. But even as it widened in popularity, even as it found a home in the mysticism of the 19th century, astrology was foundering. Theosophy kept it alive, but it was barely a convalescence. The weight of archaic cultural presumptions could not be removed by the Victorian fascination with the eastern mysticism of India, China, and Tibet. This served only to further dilute astrology's power, to reverse the direction of its collective relevance by making it the darling of the disenchanted, a subject more suited to crackpots than to kings.

No, astrology was languishing even as its availability continued to expand. In much the same way that late-19th century physics reached an apparent dead end, astrology appeared destined for a similar fate. But just as physics would soon be turned upside down, revolutionized by the discoveries of Einstein and Heisenberg, so astrology was waiting to be revitalized by Freud, Jung, and other pioneers of modern psychology.

In the 20th century, astrology was reborn because of the ease with which it could be translated from a system of collective and religious myths into a tool for exploring the functional roots of individual personality development. In spite of the seeming leap, this paradigm shift was, in fact, a totally sensible evolution. Given that we already had a mythic base of astrological planetary symbolism existing from these previous cultural epochs, it became a natural source for translation to the contemporary concerns surrounding individual psychology.

It may seem ironic that the planets have devolved from their original position as "Gods" to their current state as mere "components in the machinery of personality," as if they were nothing more than automotive parts, but such is the way of the world and the spiritual evolution of the human species. The more we begin to identify "Godliness" as something existing latently and invisibly within each of us, the more we need every tool at our command to aid in the process of realizing that Godliness, whether it is to achieve the classical state of Enlightenment, or the more humble but equally rare achievement of fulfilled life as a mature and adult human being. And so the planets have been dragged from their lofty pedestals of yore and enlisted as components in a new sense of myth. The Gods of ancient religions have evolved into the archetypes of modern psychology.

Even as the two move closer together in their ever-entwining dance, psychology has begun to overwhelm religion in the advancement of culture. For every "born-again" convert who is saved by Christ, many more people enter therapy and look to psychology for their salvation. Your minister can see you tomorrow; your shrink, however, is booked for two weeks solid. Even the apparent domination of science and technology over every other institution is only a temporary illusion. Technology is a powerful forge for changing the world, but too often it is neither an ethical nor a spiritual path.

Technology will develop for good or evil in the future of mankind depending on the maturity and wisdom of the individuals making the decisions about what to explore and how to develop our resources, and their maturity and wisdom will be guided finally by psychology. In an opportunistic manner, astrology is neatly carving out a niche for itself in the psychological realm.

So no longer are planets considered superhuman deities controlling earthly events. No longer are they the heavenly counsel of kings and princes. No longer are they solely the possession of idiosyncratic occultists. They have evolved into functional, psychological archetypes for understanding the component parts involved in the construction and expression of individual human personality.

Planets finally belong to everyone, for they symbolize urges existing within each of us.

Planetary Urges: Psychological Functions

Planets are the essential backbone of astrology, the most basic level. Without these moving symbols, the system has very little meaning. We currently understand planets in terms of the functional systems that make up the human psyche. We interpret them as **psychological functions,** or **basic human urges.**

Each planet has fundamental, core meanings, and these meanings will be interpreted through the different phases of various types of cycles. In other words, the Sun always has the same basic symbolism, which is to say, it refers to the same basic functions or urges. But its interpreted meaning changes depending on the phase through which it's moving in a given type of cycle. In one phase, its expression takes a certain form, while in another phase of the same cycle, it has a quite different expression. An example is that hunger is a basic human drive, and everybody has the urge to eat. But you don't have the same food for breakfast that you have for lunch or dinner, and you don't approach the meals in the same fashion. Breakfast is preparation for the day, charging up for activity, while dinner is a leisurely repast. So while hunger is the same in each case, the expression of the meals is different.

Planetary qualities may refer to events or external experiences, but they are not the events or experiences themselves. Instead, they denote the urges existing within each human psyche that propel us to create such events and experiences.

Sun

fundamental and central life-purpose; long-term direction and basic goals;
the essence, the most basic level of perceptions and values;
the wellspring of self (but not necessarily of visible, outer expression);
the engine of the human vehicle; the power which fuels the self;
the self's most basic authority; the source of core vitality;
the integrated pattern of total self-expression;
the connection back to the center of the Universe, the pathway home to God.

Moon

emotional patterns and habits; automatic responses to environmental pressure;
the need for security and predictability;
short-term, moment-to-moment emotional needs;
maternal or nurturing energy;
the self-generated feedback loop of daily nourishment;
the formative environment of early life, and early conditioning;
the recent karmic past; what was once consciously learned and is now second nature.

Mercury

mental functioning, the way data is collected and organized;
the process of learning; the urge to communicate;
the nervous system, and one's quality of alertness;
travel or literal movement in the environment, usually short-range;
the desire for diversity; changes of a regular, predictable nature.

Venus

true femaleness; the indicator of active and conscious receptivity to others;
personal love, intimate relatedness;
the type of giving that results in gratification for the self;
the aesthetic sensibilities; harmony, beauty, art; the sense of proportion;
satisfaction, enjoyment, sensual pleasures, and the desire for comfort.

Mars ♂	true maleness; applied energy, spontaneous self-assertion; personal desire, ardency, anger, speed, urgency. the quality and intensity of the sexual drive; the natural, spontaneous approach to the external world; the cutting edge of action; combativeness and the will to fight;
Jupiter ♃	fully expanded worldview; philosophical/moral/ethical considerations; the desire to grow and experience more of life; opportunism; that which seems to come naturally; enthusiasm, optimism, psychological buoyancy; potential excesses, waste; the "religion" of depending on one's luck; wisdom; receptivity to *dharma;* the energy of the guru; willingness to relate socially; cultural integration.
Saturn ♄	the desire to understand consequences; repercussions from the past; limits and definitions; all rigid structures; the composition of the protective ego (both positively and negatively); seriousness and solemnity; the sense of caution or denial; whatever one feels one must not go beyond; that which we can achieve only through gradual effort and pacing; ambition, slow maturation, and the long road of dues-paying; the source of one's greatest potential success; paternal energies, and the authority that comes with achievement.
Uranus ♅	sudden, unpredictable change; revolution and upheaval; psychological awakening through shock; uprooting of habits; electric awareness and experimental consciousness; humanitarian or scientific orientations;the pull of the future; originality; idiosyncrasy; the light bulb over the head *(Eureka!);* independence, individualism, detachment from others; that which is not "normal" in consensus reality.
Neptune ♆	universal love or pure devotion; reunion into cosmic oneness; the sense of transcendence; evaporation of boundaries; true intuition or channelship; knowing what cannot ordinarily be known; true selflessness and spiritual humility; sainthood/martyrdom/victimization; fantasy or dream states, including drugs and their effects; altered consciousness; illusion, deception, and seduction; the irrational; insanity and mental illness; subtle, intangible impressions; sensitivity to image and glamor; the elusive realm where one cannot be concretely pinned down.
Pluto ♇	the urge for self-mastery and self-control; dramatic change, regeneration and renewal, or total destruction; the personal subconscious as it connects with the collective unconscious; obsessions, compulsions, and psychological complexes; confrontation with power; dominance and submission; psychic surgery (given or received); the invisible power buried within the self; amorality, where ethical concerns are irrelevant.

Once we have the planets, the next step in moving toward a system for using those planets to understand the makeup of an individual human personality involves the establishment of precise frames of reference. We need to be able to accurately pinpoint the planets' positions so we can tell how they move in various kinds of cycles.

Technically, there are three basic methods for measuring the exact position of the major bodies in our solar system, three logical frames of reference. Each uses a complete cycle of Earth motion as its essential distinction, and there are three specific Earth motions that lend themselves well to this purpose: 26,500 years (the cycle of the Earth's poles through the fixed stars), one year (the cycle of the Earth around the sun), and one day (the cycle of the Earth revolving on its axis).

Polar Precession

The first method measures the almost imperceptible rotation of the Earth's poles against the background of fixed stars. It is mathematically linked with the 26,500 year period called the **precession of the equinoxes,** during which the Earth's polar axis makes one complete circuit through the fixed stars. Right now, our north pole points toward the star named Polaris (it was given that name for the obvious reason that it is the "polar" star...). However, in 5,000 years, our north pole will no longer aim at that particular star.

The Ecliptic

The second method measures the planets against an abstract, astronomical circle called the **ecliptic**. This frame of reference is based entirely on the cyclic, orbital relationship of our Earth to the sun, and thus corresponds to a time measure of exactly one year. We pinpoint the exact position of the sun relative to the fixed stars as it crosses the Earth's equatorial plane from the southern hemisphere into the northern at the moment of the vernal equinox, the first moment of the spring season here in the northern half of the planet. That becomes the zero point in a frame of reference against which planetary movement can be measured.

Each of these two first frames of reference is associated with its own particular zodiac. The precession of the equinoxes is linked with what is termed the **sidereal zodiac**, which, literally translated, means "zodiac of the stars." The terra-solar ecliptic is linked with the **tropical zodiac**, literally meaning "zodiac of seasons."

Both zodiacs divide the 360° of their respective circles into twelve phases, or *signs,* each of which describes a 30° arc of visual space. Thus, we can pinpoint a certain planet's position in a given moment of its apparent movement through our heavens by using degrees, minutes, and seconds of longitudinal arc. A position at 43° 27' 18" past the zero point translates to the 13th degree of the sign Taurus; 267° 10' 32" equals the 28th degree of the sign Sagittarius.

Sidereal Zodiac

The sidereal zodiac is the less personal of the two. Since it's based on a cycle of such long duration (26,500 years), its symbolism is not especially applicable to an individual life of perhaps 80 years. The time frames are not a natural fit. It is, however, ideally suited to the life of a species. As a result, it is frequently used in astrology is to measure the epochs of humanity's collective evolution by dividing the period of 26,500 years into twelve phases. Each roughly 2,000-year phase is called an **Age**—the Piscean Age, the Aquarian Age, etc.—and is correlated with the precession (backward movement) of the vernal equinox through the signs. The Ages are symbolically linked with the process of cultural growth and change, something gradual enough to be imperceptible to any particular individual, but still relevant to our lives together as a collective, a single species existing through many generations.

The tropical zodiac is more personal, since its reference period is based on the yearly cycle of the Earth around the sun. Linked in its celestial geometry with the regular ebb and flow of Mother Nature's seasonal changes, it has more natural symbolic application to our experiences as human beings living through a particular time in history. The significance of birthdays and the emphasis we place on our age in years are directly tied to the tropical zodiac's meaning.

Most American astrologers use the tropical zodiac in their work with individuals. However, a small and dedicated group of astrologers have embraced the sidereal zodiac even for individuals. Rather than interpreting the twelve signs as symbolic phases of growth related to Earth seasons, siderealists understand the signs as zones of cosmic influence, so they tend to be associated with a somewhat more literal or materialistic cosmology. However, some siderealists would no doubt take offense at such a judgment. More impartially, we could suggest that tropical astrologers are focused on our Earthly relationship to the solar system, while the siderealists are more concerned with our relationship to the galaxy beyond.

Roughly 2,000 years ago, the two zodiacs were in alignment. However, they are currently displaced by roughly 30°, or about one sign (and they continue to shift relative to one another by approximately 50.25 seconds of arc each year), so that a planet moving through the sign Aries in the measurement framework of the tropical zodiac will be located in the sign Pisces of the sidereal zodiac. I use only the tropical zodiac in my work, and this textbook is intended for use with that system.

Each of these zodiacs emphasize the "collective" dimension of astrological interpretation more than the individual. However, there is a third method of pinpointing objects in the heavens, one that references neither the background of fixed stars nor the mundane experience of changing seasons.

This third method involves the period of one day, the time it takes the Earth to make one complete rotation around its own axis. It is the only one of the three frameworks that provides actual reference to a particular human being, to his or her personal sense of space as it relates to the immediate environmental experience of individual reality. **This is the frame of reference that we will eventually call the houses.**

In the semicircular canals of the inner ear, each human being has a biological gyroscope which is tuned to the Earth's gravitational field. It allows us to maintain our vertical homeostasis, our ability to stand erect, by providing us with what we experience as the innate sense of "up" and "down." We learn in infancy to operate this gyroscope, and we tend to forget it thereafter, directing our awareness to the mechanism only if it ever breaks down, if our sense of balance is upset for some reason.

Our human ability to stand erect provides a natural orientation for the symbolic construction of personal space. The most basic experience in this realm is of sky and earth, separated by the line of the horizon. Up is linked with sky, down with earth, and the horizon marks the boundary between the two.

Then we differentiate space more subtly. We learn that two other fundamental human orientations, those of daytime and nighttime, are regulated by the rising and setting of the sun. Daytime begins with the sun rising over the eastern horizon, nighttime starts with the sun setting beneath the western horizon. So we add the sense of east and west.

If we consider personal space a spherical extension outward from the point on the Earth where any individual stands, then these two contrasting pairs of hemispheres give us a way to pinpoint objects in the heavens. At a given moment, from our individual perspective, we can say that the sun is so far above the eastern horizon, or directly overhead, or so far below the western horizon. Naturally, we can't see the sun when it dips below the horizon during nighttime, but we can approximate its position underfoot by the regularity of apparent motion in its daily cycle around the Earth. Marking the position of objects in the heavens in this method—above or below, eastern or western—gives us a relatively precise way of distinguishing the experience of one individual human being from another.

The Importance of Personal Space

If we wish to use astrology as a system for interpreting individual reality, it is not enough to focus on planets and signs of the zodiac. These are generically collective, not truly individual. The position of the planets at any given moment, measured against either the background of fixed stars or the ecliptic of seasonal change, is the same for every person on the Earth at that moment, and therefore no profound distinctions can be made to differentiate one individual from another born around the same time on the same day, month, and year.

How precise a system do we need to recognize differences between individuals? That depends on your definition of "individual." If you know only your Sun's birth sign, then the individuality provided by astrological descriptions includes one-twelfth of the human race. That's approximately 400 million other human beings—not very unique.

If you know only which signs were occupied by the ten planets at your birth, then you are categorized with most of the people born the same day, month, and year as yourself. That's significantly more precise in describing your individuality, but still leaves much to be desired, since you are then grouped with about 200,000 others, all of whom have the same positions.

Even if you know the exact instant of your birth and could calculate very precise positions and interrelationships for the planets in the background of the zodiac, you'd still be linked with approximately 700 other people born at the same moment.

No, the planetary pattern relative to the zodiac is not a sufficient measure for a truly personal system. It's like knowing the chords to a song but not being able to hear the melody. While it may be pleasing to hear the groups of notes that form the tonal background, too many songs have similar chord structures. Without the melody, it would be very difficult, if not impossible, to identify an individual song.

We need a different method of measuring the planetary symbols, a framework that differentiates more substantially one individual birth from another. The year, month, day, even the specific minute of birth—all those are measures of time, and when we simply measure time in astrology we are dealing with symbolic levels that could be considered "psychologically generic." For when we deal with time alone, we are using a measure that applies equally to all persons on the Earth.

To selectively differentiate between individual human beings, we need not only time, but also space. The precise timing of birth is not enough; we need to add the dimension of individual birth space.

At a given moment in time, each planet in the heavens is aligned with a certain degree of the zodiac, the imaginary belt through which the planets apparently move against the background of fixed stars. Further, each planet forms geometric relationships to all the other planets, measured through the 360° of the zodiac, resulting in an overall planetary pattern. These positions apply to every human being on the Earth, since the reference for measurement is the Earth as a whole.

But if I'm in Minneapolis, Minnesota at that moment, and you're in Canton, China, our individual experience of the space surrounding each of us is vastly different. Although the sun occupies the same degree of the zodiac and forms the same interplanetary relationships in both locations, the heavens are hardly the same. If it is daytime in Minnesota, it is nighttime in China, and vice versa. That is to say, when the sun is above the horizon here, it is below the horizon there. If you were born at night, with the sun below the horizon, it symbolizes an essentially different life-meaning than being born during the day, when the sun is above the horizon.

Recognizing this fundamental difference is what houses are all about.

The Analysis of Personal Space

Once we decide to use an individual's personal space as a measuring device to pinpoint planetary positions, we then need to understand how astrology works with that space. What is the difference between being born during the day or during the night? How do we derive meaning out of this? How do we analyze the space of the this sphere we call the houses?

We're looking for a way to comprehend the symbolic meaning of the actual space itself, a method to break that space into pieces conducive to natural meaning.

The very first thing we do is to move from three dimensions down to two. Yes, we could use "birth spheres," but it would be very cumbersome to construct a chart, not to mention the problem with filing. You'd have to have a room to keep your client's birth spheres in—very messy. More seriously, we flatten the space because the planets do not in fact move willy-nilly all over the sphere; they travel in a very limited "belt," the zodiac, and it works more conveniently and naturally to use a flat circle to represent this movement. So the sphere becomes a two-dimensional circle symbolizing the path through our skies of the sun, moon and planets in each daily Earth rotation on its axis.

First there is only the circle, a single unified whole, full, but undifferentiated:

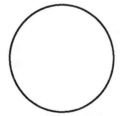

The individual is at the center of the circle, which symbolically contains all possible categories of experience. This is crucial to understand, one of the fundamental orientations in astrological thinking. The circle itself symbolizes all possible life experiences for that particular individual. It is abstract, perfect, and divine.

Since this circle is the one extending outward from you at the moment of your birth, it represents your unique relation to the cosmos, and specifically, to the solar system. Both you and I have perfect circles of individual space, but our circles symbolize a different relationship to the universe, because of the unique way each of our circles are "filled" by planets.

OK. So what now? What do we do with this undifferentiated circle? How do we start breaking it down to get at specific meanings for sections of that space?

To begin the deductive process, we cut the circle in half. It is the simplest thing we can do with the circle. Then we consider what each half might represent, since there is no more fundamental division than by two. We could conceivably place a line through the center of the circle at any angle, but there are two lines out of all the possibilities that fairly "demand" to be drawn: one horizontal and one vertical.

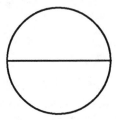 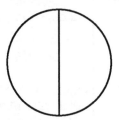

Hemispheres

We now have one circle that has been halved in two different ways, producing four distinct hemispheres: the upper half, the lower half, the left half, and right half. In astrology, we consider these hemispheres as they would appear to an observer facing south. Thus, the upper and lower and lower halves indicate sky above and below the Earth, while the left and right halves indicate eastern and western orientations:

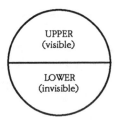 

Horizontal Division:
Upper versus Lower

The horizontal division is the more basic of the two: sky above, earth below. Or, more technically, one hemisphere is the sky above the horizon, the "visible" sky, while the other is the sky below the horizon, the "invisible" sky. How could we divide the range of human experiences to correspond with these two halves?

When the sun is in the upper hemisphere, in the open sky above, it is literally daytime. The world is lit, illumined. Objects on the Earth, in the environment surrounding the individual, are visible. We see the multiplicity surrounding us, the infinite variety of our world. We can measure the size, shape, and distance of things, yet even as we see the differences, we can feel part of a larger whole, a collective.

When the sun is in the lower hemisphere, beneath the horizon, it is literally nighttime. The world is darkened, cloaked in shadows. Objects are no longer clearly visible, nor are they measurable. Distinctions within the environment become impossible; everything blends together seamlessly in the pitch black night. This is the time when most people sleep, entering a state where their own subconscious takes control. A dream world is created out of the archetypes and phantasms within themselves.

Additionally, these hemispheres represent more than visible sky above and invisible sky below. Since our planet is a globe, if everyone on the Earth were to point straight up, then actually we would all be aiming outward, into the larger universe beyond the Earth.

Likewise, if everyone were to point straight down, then together we would all aim inward, toward a single point at the center of the Earth. Thus, up and down are truly outward and inward, and we might symbolize the experience of the upper hemisphere by using the term **macrocosm,** and the lower hemisphere by the term **microcosm.** This distinction serves to reinforce and amplify the collective versus personal natures of the two halves, for in macrocosm we are each a tiny part of an infinitely larger universe—one cell in the "body" of God—while in microcosm we are the center of things—each of us is God.

How might these distinctions be used in interpretation? Imagine that you and I could each represent one of the two types of experience. You are Mr./Ms. Upper Hemisphere, and I am Mr. Lower Hemisphere. While going for a drive in the country, we suddenly see what appears to be a flying saucer streaking across the sky. What is our initial inward reaction to this experience?

As Mr. or Ms. Upper, the very first thing you do is turn to me and say, "Wow! Did you see that?" The upper hemisphere is collective, basing the judgment of reality on group consensus, and since I'm the only other person in our "group" who was present during the experience, you'll naturally check out your perception with me to confirm it. If I say, "Yeah, it looked like a flying saucer!", then you think to yourself, "Wow, I truly did see it—that really was a flying saucer." However, if I say, "See what?" or "You mean that airplane?", then you'll tend to discount the evidence of your own eyes. "Well," you'll conclude sadly, "it probably **was** just an airplane."

As Mr. Lower, my first reaction is much more direct. My judgment as to the reality of the experience is immediate and complete: I saw it, so it was real. Yes, I may ask you if you saw the saucer for any number of different reasons—to share the experience, to convey my astonishment, etc.—but your response won't change my perception of what I saw. If you happen to insist that it was an airplane, I may try to convince you otherwise, or I may back away, filing the experience inside myself for future expression in more sympathetic company. But whatever your reaction, it won't alter my belief that, in fact, I just saw a flying saucer.

Each of the two hemispheres symbolizes a particular way of validating experience: personally, from within one's own perceptions; or impersonally, through collective consensus. In referring to these qualities throughout the book, I'll use the terms **subjective** and **objective** to express the differences in how we interpret experience between the personal and collective approaches. Those aren't the precise dictionary definitions of the words, but I need a shorthand phrase for identifying each one, and these terms come closer than any others I know.

So far so good. The logic seems clear, the intuition sound. But how then do we interpret the division of our circle of symbolic experience in its vertical division, with eastern and western halves? We do so in terms of rising and setting.

The vertical axis (called the **Meridian**) represents the sun's position at its zenith—noon—and its nadir—midnight. From midnight until noon, when the sun appears from our vantage to be moving through the eastern half of the sky, it is rising. At midday, around noon, the sun peaks, reaching its highest point in the sky, and begins its descent through the western hemisphere.

In astrology, the Sun represents the God-force that allows each of us here on the Earth to fuel the self. So when it's rising, the energy available to create a self is on the rise, waxing, increasing in force. When it's setting, the energy for active individuation is on the wane, still present, but lessening in both intensity and urgency.

The middle of the eastern half is the time of breakfast, when people are gearing up for the day to come. They are readying for activity, for doing "business," for facing the world squarely. The middle of the western half is dinner-time, when people are slowing down to relax, reflecting on the events of the day, and preparing for more intimate and less impersonal relating. We might apply Martin Buber's religious terminology and say that the eastern hemisphere emphasizes **"I-It"** interactions, where the I is crucial and the It incidental, while the western hemisphere symbolizes **"I-Thou"** interactions, where the recognition of mutual personhood is paramount.

The eastern (or left) half of the circle symbolizes experiences that are self-motivated, self-directing, or self-actualizing in their basic nature. The western (or right) half represents the opposite, experiences that are relationship-oriented, other-directed, or reflective in their essential meaning. One is active, the other responsive. We might think of the two halves as symbolizing the difference between radiance of self (direct experience) and reflection of self (indirect experience)

One of the areas where traditional astrology fumbles the ball is in the understanding of hemispheres. Too often, this elegant structure is filled with content from archaic philosophies. Older textbooks discuss the eastern hemisphere as the part of the chart symbolizing "control of one's own destiny," while the western hemisphere is defined as "experiences outside or beyond one's control." Even further, the western side was understood as the area where life was "fated."

Such an orientation is not merely untrue, it is downright destructive, especially in this age where the future of our species hangs by a thread. Now more than ever before, it is crucial that individuals be given every encouragement to mature into true adulthood by developing personal integrity. We no longer have the dubious luxury of time. Let's stop the momentum of this unconsciousness, the legacy of belief to future generations that entering into relationships is the same as giving up control of one's life. It is not.

The eastern hemisphere involves mastery of oneself and one's actions; the western hemisphere involves mastery of relatedness to others. Each is mysterious, potentially confusing, and often difficult. But neither is innately beyond our control.

At this point, we're well into the analytic process of differentiating the symbolic space surrounding any individual. We have four hemispheres, two pairs of opposites. If we combine the horizontal and vertical axes in the same circle, the result is a circle with four quadrants, each of which combines elements from two different hemispheres.

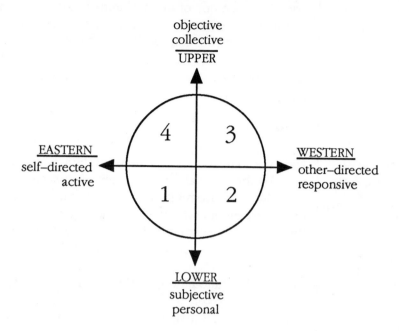

Quadrant #1, in the eastern and lower hemispheres, symbolizes human experience that is self-directed and subjective, or active and personal. Quadrant #2 is also below the horizon, so it too is subjective/personal, but since it is part of the western hemisphere, those qualities combine with other-directedness and responsiveness. Each quadrant shares one quality with its two adjacent quarters, and each is completely dissimilar from the opposite quadrant.

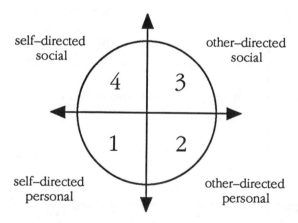

We could conceivably stop here and begin using the system to interpret any individual's particular perception and experience of life. We could calculate the natal positions of the various planets in terms of this fourfold division of personal space, placing them at their appropriate positions on the wheel. Knowing each planet's meaning, understanding its symbolic function in the overall "machinery" of the human drive system, we could interpret its significance in ways that are relevant to day-to-day living.

In addition, we could ignore the planets as individual symbols and use them as a group, counting the number in any particular hemisphere or quadrant, arriving at a feel for the emphasis and the balance in any or all of the four dimensions of experience. Indeed, this type of "wholistic" approach to the interpretation of a natal chart can reap significant benefits, since one of the problems in astrology, especially at the introductory level, is keeping things simple, so as not to overwhelm the mind still working to learn the language and procedures of the system.

But of course, we don't stop there. We continue to subdivide the circle, distinguishing more precisely areas of personal space with specific types of human experience.

Bisecting the Quadrants

Here we come to a wrinkle in the system. So far, we've divided the circle by halves. First we took the circle as a whole, then we bisected it into hemispheres along two different axes. We went from one whole, to two halves, to four quadrants, dividing by two each time. Consistency would dictate that we continue to divide the sections in half, doubling their number again. If we did so, we would arrive at an eightfold division of space, and at one level of astrology, this is precisely how we proceed.

That level is called the **lunation cycle**. It divides the circle into eight equal pieces, or phases. Each phase is a 45° section of the whole. Its symbolism in astrology was introduced by Dane Rudyhar and Marc Robertson, among others, and though it can be used in any way one might wish, the most specific application is in the understanding of cycles that move and evolve through time, rather than the apparently static patterns that indicate basic personality in the natal chart. In other words, the lunation cycle is the archetype used to pinpoint predictable crises in the timing of natural growth.

It's rather like driving a car with a manual transmission. There are various times when we have to change gears—back off the accelerator, clutch, shift, back off the clutch, and reaccelerate—in order to keep the engine working efficiently. We have to know not only how to shift, but when, and what new gear to shift into. The eightfold division of the circle defines the exact points in time during any cycle when a "crisis" will emerge in our growth, demanding that we "shift gears." It also indicates the nature of the shift, the new way we must think, process, or create reality to keep ourselves growing smoothly.

The diagram below shows the eightfold division, with conventional names listed for each phase:

The Lunation Cycle

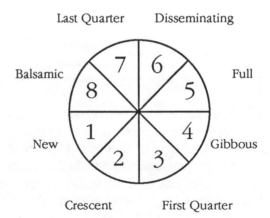

Notice that the names of the phases are those we all use in reference to the monthly cycle of the sun and moon—New Moon, First Quarter, Full Moon, and Last Quarter. Although the other four intermediate phases are little-used and practically unknown by the general public, they are routinely used by astrologers concerned with natural phases of growth and subtler aspects of timing.

Every astrological cycle, regardless of its time frame, can be divided in these eight predictable phases. Whether it is a Moon cycle of 29 days with two and one-half day phases, a Jupiter cycle of 12 years with one and a half year phase changes, or an 84-year Uranus cycle with roughly 10-year phases, we can still use the 45° division of zodiacal space to predict the timing of significant "shocks" in the evolution of any particular growth pattern.

Trisecting the Quadrants

In the structure of houses, the method of subdividing the four quadrants is not a simple repetition of halving them one more time. We don't bisect the quadrants, we **trisect** them, dividing each quarter into three pieces rather than two. In that way, instead of ending up with eight sections in the circle, we end up with twelve.

The reasons for this change in the process of division are both obvious and obscure. On the surface, the most obvious reason is mere convention; that's how it's been done for hundreds of years, so we simply continue to do it in the traditional manner, unquestioningly.

Much of human living is like this, based on quirky rules of precedence. Your mother always puts ginger into her beef stew. One day you ask her why. She answers that she's always done it that way. It's how her mother taught her, and her mother's mother before that. It's a family tradition, and she may talk about the particular flavor that the "secret ingredient" of ginger adds to the dish, about the "healing properties" of the herb, about how it tenderizes the beef chunks, etc.

But as likely as not, sometime way back in the far distant past, one of her maternal ancestors was making beef stew one fine day, when she discovered that ginger was the only fresh spice she had on hand that day, so that's what she used to season her stew. The experiment didn't ruin the dish nor make anyone sick, so the next time she made it, she fine-tuned the amount of ginger to explore the exotic taste further. No one ever asked her why she'd done it that way, and her daughter simply adopted the recipe, followed in turn by the granddaughter, and so on right down to your mother. Presto! Instant tradition, although, in fact, it took a long time to develop.

And all along the way, families kept commenting on the unique flavor, and mothers kept inventing perfectly good but bogus reasons why they used ginger.

The use of a twelvefold division for the houses is similar in some ways. We've done it that way for as long as we can remember, so of course we continue to do so. God knows why. On the other hand, we can and do create various rationales to explain the division into twelve sections rather than eight. It may have little more to do with our discipline than the cooks' explanation of their spices, but it's part of human nature to hunt for reasons. We are, after all, a species of pattern-making, pattern-seeking beings.

First of all, there is a tenet in astrology that all cycles are analogous. One day is the same symbolically as one year, and one year is the same symbolically as 26,500 years. Why? Because each represents a complete Earth cycle. One day is the period of a single Earth rotation around its own axis, sunrise to sunrise. One year is the period of a single Earth rotation around the sun, spring to spring. 26,500 years is the period of a single rotation of the Earth's polar axis around the galaxy, orienting the north pole from one fixed star all way around the galaxy and back to that same star again.

Although their periods differ dramatically, each of these cycles represents one complete "Earth revolution," echoing different levels of the same symbolic implication. So while their concrete meanings are hardly analogous, we should still be able to analyze any one of the cycles and apply that analysis to either of the others.

In mother nature's year, there are four seasons, and each season is composed of three lunation cycles, three revolutions of the moon "around" the sun, three periods of the dark of the moon followed by waxing to full and waning to dark again. We call the three periods of each season "months"—the word itself coming from the Old English term "mona," or satellite of the Earth.

Technically, there are thirteen complete lunar cycles per year, but human beings are very big on symmetry, and thirteen months just won't cut it symmetrically. So we bend things to suit our own sense of form, dividing the year into twelve months—four seasons of three months each. The tropical zodiac is the symbol for this symmetrical year, and its twelve signs of 30° each are precisely aligned with the timing of the four seasons. Each season is symbolized by three consecutive signs, just as each season has three months in the calendar. Since the houses represent one complete Earth day, from sunrise to sunrise, they are symbolically equivalent to the period of one Earth year. So we use the same structure—four quadrants of three sections each, twelve houses total.

The Implications
of Division

Every analysis involves division, for analyzing is a process of separating a whole into its constituent parts in order to better comprehend that whole. But it's not enough to understand the parts; it's also very helpful to understand the nature and the meaning of the scalpels we use to make the divisions.

When we break something in half, we need to understand the nature of division by two. The principles of polarization and complementary opposites come into play. We divide the diurnal rotation of the Earth every 24 hours into the halves of daytime and nighttime, light and dark. Every division by two produces this quality: day/night, black/white, male/female, yang/yin, active and responsive. These are complementary opposites, for the word "light" has no meaning without the relativity of its opposite, "dark."

Certainly the quality "light" could exist without "dark," but if it did—if there were no dark—then we wouldn't name the quality of light. It would be ubiquitous, and therefore tautological. To understand division by two, we need to comprehend the meanings of duality—polarity and complementarity.

But however challenging it is to understand the "two-ness" within any complete whole (or cycle), it is far more difficult to comprehend the "three-ness" of it. Division by three invokes an entirely different process of thinking.

The Meaning of Division by Three

There's an old riddle that may shed light on how three-ness works: "What happens when an irresistible force meets an immovable object?" The answer is that nothing happens; they cannot meet. By definition, the force cannot be resisted, and the object cannot be moved. They exist in two separate worlds, mutually exclusive, one denying the other. They are absolute and cannot interact.

A third force is necessary to allow interaction, something that changes the very nature of the first two from absolute to relative. If an almost irresistible force met an almost immovable object, the force could deflect at a slight angle, and the object could spin on its axis. Here they have relationship to one another; they have impact on each other. Threefold division involves a "something" (a quality), its polar opposite (another quality), and relatedness between them to allow interaction and mutual interpenetration (a process we might term understanding).

Metaphysical Numbers

We're dealing here with the significance of numbers, and while it may seem hopelessly abstract, it is relevant, for numbers carry their own special metaphysical implications.

- **One** is the number of unity—the absolute, God, that which is undifferentiated, out of which everything came, and to which everything will ultimately return.

- **Two** is the leap into differentiation, into relativistic awareness, of this being different from that, opposite but linked. Duality is static, however, for nothing can occur but a perpetual seesaw. There is awareness of relationship, for each defines and reinforces the reality of its opposite, but two-ness exists in a vacuum, with no medium to allow interaction. In the physical universe, time and space provide the medium of interaction, and they are linked with the numbers three and four.

- **Three** is the number of time—the sense of movement, flowing continuity, and duration. Three combines the essential meaning of unity and the awareness of relationship in duality. It provides for interaction, blending through connection, either in the logical flow of ideas or movement through time.

- **Four** is the number of space, or more precisely, matter structured into space. Our material world is based on four-ness, since the Earth is composed largely of carbon-structured elements, and thus the very material of our bodies and our sense of physical existence is perceived through the four-fold nature of carbon. Four is sometimes referred to as the crucifixion of spirit in matter.

Looking at it in another manner, One represents the primordial revelation of life force, Two is the Big Bang at the beginning of our universe, Three symbolizes the creation of time, and Four reveals the crystallization of time into living matter and space. In other words, one and two are the primary factors behind the universe itself, but three and four are the essential numbers of the material world in which we live.

Twelve is the smallest number divisible by one, two, three, and four. It combines all the features of those more primary numbers, so in the houses, the astrological structure that describes all possible human experiences, we use a circle divided into twelve pieces, four quadrants of three sections each.

In the astrological zodiac, threefold division results in what are called **modes**. The three modes are **cardinal, fixed,** and **mutable** (also sometimes called common). Cardinality is rather like the irresistible force. Fixity is like the immovable object, and mutability is the process of understanding that allows relationship between them. There is also modality in the house structure, but the names are different. The first house in any quadrant is called **angular**, the second **succeedent**, and the final house of the quadrant **cadent**. Although the concepts are similar to the modal qualities used to describe the zodiacal signs, the application of meaning varies sufficiently to warrant different names.

Angular
Houses

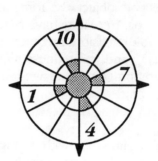

An **angular** house is an area concerned with the establishment of a particular kind of experience (based on the implications of its quadrant). Angular houses symbolize the ongoing process of initiation into new levels of the most basic, fundamental experiences in human living. They tend to be slightly more event-oriented than the other two categories. The angular houses in the horoscope are the 1st, 4th, 7th, and 10th.

Succeedent
Houses

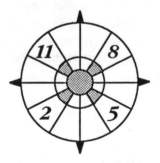

A **succeedent** house is an area concerned with the evaluation or the use of experience. Succeedent houses symbolize a reaction to what was established in the angular houses that precede them. What was set into motion in the angular houses is given solidity through a set of values. The succeedent houses are the 2nd, 5th, 8th, and 11th.

Cadent
Houses

A **cadent** house is an area concerned with understanding the meaning of whatever was established and grounded in the two preceding houses. Cadent houses represent relativity and the perspective necessary for learning. Also, they provide a bridge, a willingness to alter and adjust our experience, preparing for the new tone that will be established in the angular house of the following quadrant. The cadent houses are the 3rd, 6th, 9th, and 12th.

Many chart forms include a listing of planets and or other significant points (angles, asteroids, nodes, etc.) through the three modalities, usually for the signs, and somewhat less frequently for the houses. The purpose of such an analysis is to give a picture of overall emphasis in the chart-as-a-whole, the balance or lack of it.

Most often these are little more than a simple count, especially in computerized charts, with one point for each planet or angle, totalled for each modality. As such, they have little real usefulness, since planets can hardly be considered to have equal importance. The Sun is clearly more significant than Neptune in the general scheme of planetary weighting. In a particular natal chart, the complexity is much greater, since any planet can have dramatically increased importance in the individual's symbolic makeup, for any number of reasons. Then finally, at a given phase in an individual's life, the planetary emphasis may shift again through transit or progression cycles moving through time. So the crude listing found on many chart forms (i.e., 5 angular, 2 fixed, 3 mutable) is basically a useless measure, as misleading as it is revealing.

But the principle behind such lists is valid. There are solidly pragmatic reasons for learning all the abstract categories we've been discussing in this first chapter: the break-down of space into hemispheres, quadrants, modes, etc. We're building systems of understanding from which we will eventually be able to see the directions of symbolic emphasis for any individual, in any situation. We're creating a structure similar to that used in medical diagnosis, for before we can work with any individual to improve the quality of that person's life, we must be able to effectively diagnose the condition by sorting out the matrix of symbolic factors involved. That sorting is one of the basic steps in astrological interpretation. The more we understand the different categories, the better we can see the patterns at work.

Six Axes

More important than the modalities themselves is the concept of *axes*. Houses can be divided in six pairs of opposites, two pairs for each mode. The 1st house is the initial section of the lower hemisphere, while the 7th house, exactly opposite, is the first section of the upper hemisphere. Together, they define the axis of the horizon, so they're naturally linked. It's the same with every other house; each forms a natural axis with its opposite.

The cliché "opposites attract" is not always true, since they can also repel. It might be better to use the macrobiotic principle, **"That which has a front also has a back."** This rule that opposites are connected in bipolar reality is very important in astrology.

Another way to understand this level is to consider that there are four angular houses that form two perpendicular axes. The horizontal axis of the 1st and 7th houses is crossed to the vertical axis of the 4th and 10th houses, and they're all angular. It's the same with succeedent houses, with the 2nd/8th axis being perpendicular to the 5th/11th axis, and with cadent houses, where the 3rd/9th axis is crossed to the 6th/12th axis. We're further differentiating the meanings of the angular, succeedent, and cadent categories, breaking each type into two different, mutually exclusive styles of meaning.

The symbolic meanings of the six axes are graphically displayed in the table on the next page. Naturally, there are many more meanings that could be listed; this conveys only the basic patterns. The third and fourth columns are organized according to house position in the upper and lower hemispheres of the chart, but they could just as easily be formatted to reveal the eastern/western hemisphere orientation.

Table of House Axes

House Axis	Principle	Lower House	Upper House
		1st	**7th**
	action	active	receptive
1st/7th	awareness	self-generated	reflected by others
	boundaries	natural	social
	security	private	public
4th/10th	stability	family	career
	responsibility	for self/loved ones	for world in general
		4th	**10th**
		2nd	**8th**
	values	personal	shared
2nd/8th	judgment	by oneself	through relatedness
	gratification	alone	together
	behavior	involved	detached
5th/11th	creativity	individual	group-oriented
	love	giving	receiving
		5th	**11th**
		3rd	**9th**
	education	pragmatic	ethical
3rd/9th	exploration	local	foreign
	communication	immediate	long-distance
	understanding	of one's literal life	of the universe
6th/12th	healing	outer (physical)	inner (emotional)
	helping	for compensation	for charity
		6th	**12th**

Angular

Succeedent

Cadent

Scope

A convenient way to think of the twelve houses is as a set of twelve concentric circles, the 1st house being the innermost circle and the 12th house being the outer. Since the houses represent all possible experiences available to any human individual, then the 1st house symbolizes not only the most fundamental level of experience, but also the initial experience that defines one as an individual identity. As we move through the cycle, each following house increases the breadth of experience, until finally in the 12th we reach the level where individuality itself is transcended.

Think of the houses as three consecutive groups of four: houses 1-4 are self-interested or self-centered, focusing primarily on the development of a personal identity; houses 5-8 are interactive or one-to-one oriented, carrying personal identity into the realm of one-to-one relationships; and houses 9-12 are social or universal, allowing individual identity to find its place in a larger, group context.

Planetary Linkage

Finally, there is the natural linkage of planets with houses. This is analogous to the concept of planetary rulership in the zodiacal signs. The planet Mars bears a certain tonal similarity to the first sign of the zodiac, Aries. Therefore, it carries that same similarity in its emphasized relationship to the 1st house. Venus is associated with Taurus and the 2nd house, Mercury with Gemini and the 3rd house, and so on.

Many astrologers rely heavily on this natural association of sign rulerships to houses, and it touches on one of the most basic concepts in astrology: the parallel meanings of planets, signs, and houses. Mastery of the subtleties of these parallels is one of the benchmarks of a good astrologer—understanding when and how planets, signs, and houses are symbolically interchangeable, yet also comprehending the clear distinctions that make each component level uniquely different in meaning, tone, and interpretation. Much will be made of this subtle linkage in **Chapter Three: Using the Houses**, but it is enough here to state that there are natural associations of each house with a planet.

Now we have six different value systems through which to understand the symbolic meanings of the experiences associated with each of the twelve houses, the relevant characteristics that help give them their interpretive meanings. We'll go on in **Chapter Two: The Twelve Houses** to a more down-to-earth discussion of each house, comparing the traditional interpretive meanings as given in many textbooks to the more psychologically-oriented meanings I use in my own work with clients.

Clockwise or Counter-Clockwise?

It's significant to note that in terms of daily motion, the planets move through the houses **counterclockwise** (backward), from 12 to 11 to 10, and so on. This may seem illogical, and indeed, a case can be made to support clockwise numbering of the houses, but once again, convention rules. Also, since the house structure of daily motion is in many ways analogous to the zodiacal structure of yearly, seasonal change, there is a logic to the counterclockwise numbering.

The 1st house is symbolically similar to the first sign of the zodiac, Aries; the 2nd house is symbolically parallel to Taurus, the second sign. If we were to reverse the houses to clockwise numbering, the signs and houses would sacrifice their connection, and the whole system would require radical rethinking. Some astrologers would love to see this very change, but for most of us, the system as it currently stands contains sufficient relevance to endure the existing paradoxes.

Before leaving this introductory chapter, let's take one more look at the basic components of natal astrology and how they fit together. There are ways to simplify understanding these various elements, and whether you're a beginner or a professional, keeping it simple is one of the supreme challenges of using astrology.

Planets are **symbolic functions or urges** within the individual psyche; they describe the structure of the human machinery. In an automobile, there are various components—the engine, fuel system, transmission, differential, cooling system, brakes, etc. Each component system has a specific function to perform in the overall operation of the vehicle. It's the same in a human being. There are various functional components at the psychological level, each of which have certain tasks to perform in the overall experience of interacting with Life. The ten planets represent different functions in the operation of a human life by an individualized spirit (that's you).

The purpose of an automobile is narrow and well-defined; the various component functions are relatively simple and direct. For instance, the fuel system performs only a few tasks. It stores the gasoline, filters it, and regulates the flow to the engine. On the other hand, the "human vehicle" has a very broad and complex life-purpose; thus, the component functions are neither simple nor direct. Each planetary symbol has multi-leveled functions, performing a veritable rainbow of tasks even in ordinary living. The list of functions for even a single planet can run into the hundreds, limited only by our ability to perceive different levels of operation within the human psyche.

Happily, though, each planet has a characteristic "tone" of operation, so that all the functions of that planet are linked, no matter how different they may seem at first glance. When learning the meanings for each planetary symbol, try to feel the essence of what the planet represents, for an emotional grasp is more important than any rote memorizing of specifics. Ask yourself how the various meanings could possibly be linked; probe the intuitive heart of each planet.

Signs of the zodiac are a measure of the changing seasons in Mother Nature's year, and as such are a collective factor, representing natural and consecutive phases of growth in the yearly cycle of life on Earth. They are best thought of as **attitudes**—basic methods of approach in manifesting the various planetary functions.

Every automobile has an engine, and every engine performs the same basic function, but how an engine is designed matters a great deal in terms of the type of performance the vehicle requires. A police car demands a very different engine design than the family station wagon, just as a limousine has different engine requirements than a subcompact. In the same way, the Sun in a horoscope (the engine) performs its basic functions differently in Aries (the "hot rod") than in Cancer (the "family station wagon"), Taurus (the "limousine"), or Virgo (the efficient "subcompact").

Houses are the basic structure of individual personhood—individual because they are based on the exact moment and place of birth, not simply the seasonal phase. In the mass-mind understanding of astrology, they are routinely omitted because their use is dependent upon having an accurate birth time, rather than just a birth date, but their importance in any serious and sensitive interpretation is paramount.

They represent the environment, more precisely, our inner relationship to the actual environments within and beyond ourselves, the various "fields" through which we play out our functions and attitudes. They can be seen as **areas of life experience**, the different "arenas of circumstance" where we express ourselves.

Houses delineate the whole range of literal and psychological experiences available to each human being, not merely in the sense of external events, but also internal events. They describe your natural relationship to the worlds around and inside you, revealing how you integrate these different worlds into a single coherent experience of reality.

Houses could be thought of as the road test for any vehicle. On the drawing board, all cars are perfect; in the showroom, each is a shining promise. But the proof of the pudding is in the driving. How does it corner? What's the ride like at 60? Can it brake on wet pavement, handle gravel roads, or start dependably in the winter? Will you spend all your time in the repair shop? Houses reveal the type of environmental challenges your human vehicle will be tested against, the road conditions you naturally tend to "drive" through in discovering and fulfilling your life-purpose.

The Formula

We can condense these three levels to a simple formula: planets reveal what kind of physical, psychological, or spiritual function you're working with; signs show how those functions characteristically express themselves; and houses define where in life they most naturally manifest.

$$
\begin{aligned}
\textbf{Planets} \quad &= \quad \textbf{WHAT} \\
\textbf{Signs} \quad &= \quad \textbf{HOW} \\
\textbf{Houses} \quad &= \quad \textbf{WHERE}
\end{aligned}
$$

As with any such learning device, this simplification is designed as an aid to clarity. It is not hard-and-fast, nor is it the ultimate rule. There is already too much formulaic thinking in astrology, too much rigidity in the way charts are understood and used. Because astrology is so complex, so multileveled, it's a continuing challenge to maintain flexibility and openness, especially when trying to teach the system well.

In grammar, nouns are subjects and verbs are actions. That's the basic structure of the English language. But there are also gerunds, which are verbs acting as nouns. It's the same in the "grammar" of astrology. Planets are certainly more than just urges or functions, signs are much more than mere attitudes, and houses are a great deal more than areas of circumstance. In practice, the clear distinctions between the levels tend to blur as each reflects and absorbs qualities of the others. A good astrologer will weave the levels into a seamless tapestry of individual meaning.

However, a gerund will hardly make sense unless there is first an understanding of the more basic structure of nouns and verbs. In much the same way, comprehension of the interweaving of planets, signs, and houses is unlikely to be clear and correct unless there is first a basic understanding of their structural differences.

That's what this formula offers. When you're looking at charts and everything begins to blend together in a confusing fog, remember: **planets tell you about urges, signs tell you about attitudes, and houses tell you about areas of life experience— what, how, and where.**

Once you're clear, this formula, like every other "rule" in astrology, becomes irrelevant, mere background, like knowing that 2 + 2 = 4. But when you need it, it's there to help.

The various cyclic motions of astrology are sufficiently complex that some astrologers don't attain a real understanding of the movement. It smacks too much of geometry for some, too dry and lifeless for comprehension. Since the birth chart is a "slice out of time," a snapshot of the heavens at a given instant, it appears absolutely motionless, and some astrologers are seduced by that stable image, thinking about charts as if they were fixed and unchanging, as if that were their only reality.

But it's an illusion. **Everything is moving.**

Planets move through their orbits around the sun at different speeds, completing those orbits in different periods of Earth time. We see them apparently move across our heavens, periodically exhibiting retrograde or backward movement as they accelerate and decelerate due to the visual anomalies of parallax.

The zodiac of seasons is slowly, almost imperceptibly shifting in its relation to the fixed stars, which are not really fixed at all, but are themselves moving through the universe over time periods so immense as to be incomprehensible.

The houses of an individual's personal space are revolving once each day because we are on the Earth and it's turning on its axis, and therefore turning us with it, but because we measure everything from a person- and Earth-centered point of view, it appears that the houses remain fixed while the planets and signs rotate clockwise around them once each day. And this occurs while the planets are moving much more slowly counter-clockwise through the signs.

All this confusing motion can be a bit much. Since we are, after all, concerned with the final essence of meaning for any individual, then why fry our brain circuitry and blow mental fuses trying to visualize these motions?

Why?… **Because motion is meaning.**

In other words, the meanings come out of the movements, and the better you can understand the movements, the better you'll be able to understand and apply the meanings. This isn't merely window dressing; it's the basic mechanics behind astrology. If you want to be an astrologer, you should understand what you're looking at, at least well enough to explain it to someone who knows nothings about astrology.

A second reason to visualize the motions we see frozen in charts is to reconstitute our relationship to the natural world around us. Living in modern civilization has its payoffs and costs. One of the costs involves alienation from the natural world. We live in artificial urban environments, little boxes inside of bigger boxes linked by a network of concrete ribbons. We leave the stable box of our home only to enter the moving box of our cars, and we travel in those boxes to other stable boxes—offices, theaters, shops and grocery stores. Out of one box and into another. The sense of infinity, of the astonishing breadth of natural reality is severely restrained. Astrology can help us reconnect to the infinity of our natural universe, if only we allow it to.

With that in mind, the following two pages contain a metaphor that may simplify visualizing these complex motions.

Imagine that you're in a helicopter about 500 feet above the ground. Next, imagine that you can look down directly beneath you to see a circular railroad track. The track is painted twelve different colors, each color filling approximately one-twelfth of the circular arc.

*The Track
= The Houses*

On the track is a train. There are twelve cars in all—the engine, ten Pullman cars, and the caboose—and the length of the train just happens to be exactly the same as the length of the track, so that the front of the engine touches the rear of the caboose.

The track is like the houses with their twelve numbered sections. This circular section of track doesn't move, of course. It just sits there, fixed in the ground. In much the same way, the houses appear to be fixed in the chart form. The 1st house is always on the left (or east,) the 7th always on the right (or west); the 10th is always directly overhead, and the 4th always directly underfoot.

The track is painted in twelve sections to represent each of the twelve houses. If we wanted to get fancy, we could imagine various coordinated color schemes to represent the qualities of each house/section—for instance, we could use reds for the 1st, 5th, and 9th houses, green for the 2nd, 6th, and 10th, yellow for the 3rd, 7th, and 11th, and blue for the 4th, 8th, and 12th. Or we could use different colors, something blending the elemental quality with the modal or axis relationship—pastels might work. But it's your visualization, so hire your own painters, and do it up however you wish.

*The Train
= The Signs*

The train of twelve cars is like the zodiac of twelve signs, with the engine being the sign Aries and the caboose being the sign Pisces.

The train moves continuously around the track at a regular speed, but rather slowly—it's just a "local"—so that once each day it makes a complete circuit of the track. This is what happens from our perspective; as the Earth turns on its axis, we here on the Earth have the experience of remaining stationary, and we perceive the heavens around us turning one complete cycle in a 24-hour period. That's why the sun appears to "rise" and "set," naturally.

So the zodiac train makes one trip around the house track every day. As a rule of thumb, each car (sign) takes roughly two hours to travel over a certain section of track (house), although that varies because the train doesn't travel at a constant speed, instead fluctuating through gradual accelerations and decelerations.

So far so good. Next we add the planets, and here's where it gets interesting.

*The Passengers
= The Planets*

The planets are like passengers on the train. There are ten passengers in all, and they're moving gradually through the train, very slowly changing seats in one car until they run out of seats in one car and have to move to the next. They move back through the train, from the engine toward the caboose and then round again—in a direction **opposite** to the train's movement over the track.

In other words, the train moves over the track in a **clockwise** direction as the passengers are moving much more slowly through the cars of the train **counterclockwise**. All the passengers move through the train, from one car to the next, at different speeds. In fact, they travel through the cars at **vastly** different speeds.

For instance, the Moon is like a little kid who can't sit still, bouncing from one seat to the next, changing cars about every two and a half days, or every two and a half trips of our train round the track. To get through the twelve cars of the whole train takes a month, or roughly 28 trips.

On the other hand, Pluto is like an old man who can barely walk. He takes two steps and has to rest seemingly forever. Currently, it takes him about 15 years just to move from one car to another. That means it would take him over 5,000 complete trips of the train just to get out of one car and into the next one, and to make even a single passage around all twelve cars of the train takes him almost 100,000 trips. He's very slow.

Relationships = Aspects

Since the passengers move through the cars at different speeds, they often pass one another. Sometimes they sit in adjacent seats in the same car, and sometimes they can look out the window and see another passenger moving through the opposite car on the other side of the circular track. The relationships of the individual passengers to one another as they move through the cars are like the geometrical or angular relationships planets form with each other as they move through the zodiac. These relationships are called **aspects**.

Put it all together

Now, imagine all this motion happening together. Everything is constantly moving, shifting, changing relationship to everything else. At any given moment, a certain passenger is in a certain car of the train, which is moving over a certain section of track, and the passengers as a group form a kaleidoscopic pattern; sometimes they're all together, sometimes they're spread out, sometimes they all occupy one half the train, leaving the other half empty. The variations are endless.

Take a photo

If we took a photograph from our helicopter, freezing the various motions, stopping the action like a slice out of time, then we would have a picture of the train, the track, the passengers, and their relationships to one another. Erecting a natal chart is like developing a photo in a darkroom. It takes awhile to calculate the exact positions of all the various motions. Having a computer to do it is like using a polaroid—instant snapshot.

That's essentially what a horoscope is—a picture of all these complex celestial motions and their interrelationships, frozen in time, seen from a specific point of view.

In natal astrology, the point of view is that of an individual human being taking life's first breath. When you look at a natal chart with all those arcane symbols dotted around the circle, all those colored lines drawn inside the circle between the symbols, what you're seeing is an accurate diagram of the different celestial motions as they were actually configured from a particular person's vantage point at birth.

If you understand this and remember it when you look at a natal chart, whether it's your own or someone else's, then you'll have a tremendous head start toward using astrology with reverence as well as savvy.

The Twelve Houses

1st House

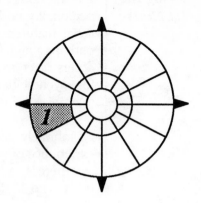

Qualities

hemisphere .... *eastern* .... self-directed and expressive
hemisphere .... *lower* .... subjective and personal
scope .... *initial third* .... self-interested or self-centered
mode .... *angular* .... initiating and establishing
axis .... *1st/7th* .... action, awareness, and boundaries
planet .... *Mars* .... desire, assertion, and thrust

Traditional Meanings

one's personality
the way one appears to others
physical appearance and the vitality of the body
self-image
potential means of self-expression
conditions of birth

Contemporary Meanings

self-expression   natural, spontaneous, unconditioned projection
                       of the self outward into the environment

natural persona   the characteristic face shown to the world;
                       the "name-tag"

self-awareness   spontaneous awareness of the existence
                       of an "I," generated through activity

boundaries   the "bridge" between inner and outer realities;
                       the lens through which we focus

vitality   overall personal energy as it pertains to
                       the general condition of health

The 1st house is the most basic area of life experience. Traditionally, it indicates the personality and the body, with special attention paid to physical characteristics like facial features. For instance, Leo rising supposedly indicates a "regal" appearance, perhaps a high forehead or a mane of red hair. Certainly our appearance influences how others react and respond to us, especially in a culture as image-sensitive as ours, but for psychologically-oriented astrologers, these interpretations lack relevance and depth; they miss the point, condemning astrology to superficial status.

Of infinitely greater relevance is the importance of the 1st house as it describes the experience of individual self-awareness, the fundamental event of becoming conscious that there is an "I" present, linked in mysterious fashion with the existence of the physical body. The 1st is about having a personal human identity.

The seat of self-awareness is usually located behind the eyes. That's where we experience our identity, even though the nervous system is literally diffused throughout the entire body. We know our hands are part of our self, but ordinarily the only time the hands or another part of the body-extension call our attention is through pain or other extreme stimulus. Only in a physical state of emergency do we leave the consciousness in the head, and even then there's a tug-of-war between the momentary site of heightened awareness and our normal center of self-identification. The 1st house is primarily about that sense of "I-ness," that conscious identity we cling to behind the eyes, the one who's observing, feeling, thinking, interacting with life—both the life outside the self and the life emanating from deeper within the self.

The condition of the 1st house by sign quality and planetary associations shows the typical way we create self-awareness. It reveals the automatic way of identifying the "I."

Yes, it does indicate many of the characteristic traits we spontaneously express under the nontechnical heading of "personality," and this is important. But of greater subtlety is its role as an interface, a boundary that defines and maintains individual integrity. The 1st house is a bridge connecting the self with everything outside. It shows the way we protect our inner core while still encouraging interaction with the environment.

Since the 1st house reveals the moment-to-moment experience of personal identity as an individual human being, it is directly involved in every event of our lives. Its implications may be overridden in certain experiences by other specific houses, but its basic significance can't be totally eradicated. Any experience that allows personal expression or self-awareness invokes the 1st; any action we take works through 1st house connections. As a result, it's an area of primary importance in considering our approach to life.

It's for this reason that the ascending sign—the sign on the cusp of the 1st house—commands such importance in astrology. It is one of the four most important interpretive factors in the natal chart. Any question regarding an individual's life requires understanding and consideration of the positions of the Sun, Moon, and Saturn—by sign, house, and interplanetary aspects—along with with the condition of the 1st house.

There are any number of specific indicators we could (and should) assess in addressing specific situations, but every situation demands an understanding of the interrelated working of these four fundamental factors.

2nd House

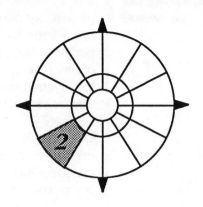

Qualities

hemisphere ....*eastern*..................self-directed and expressive
hemisphere ....*lower*.....................subjective and personal
scope ....*initial third*..........self-interested or self-centered
mode ....*succeedent*............reactive and fixed
axis ....*2nd/8th*..................values, judgments, and gratification
planet ....*Venus*....................appreciation, enjoyment, and comfort

Traditional Meanings

money
possessions and property
attitudes toward possessions, wealth, and property
personal resources
personal values

Contemporary Meanings

self-worth   psychological judgment of the self by the self
(involving basic feelings of liking or disliking)

possession   ownership, personal possessions, property;
the sense of "mine"

money   the experience of personal wealth;
money, especially in its personal use

self-exertion   the experience of effort,
and the style of actual work

sensuality   pure, self-centered, self-involved physicality
and the general capacity for pleasure

Exploring the 2nd House

In almost every traditional astrological textbook, and in many supposedly "humanistic" or "new age" texts as well, the 2nd house is primarily interpreted as money. It's discussed in great detail—the money you earn, how you work to get it, whether you can expect a lot or a little, what you'll do with it, etc.

We live in a culture that places tremendous emphasis on money. The "bottom line" is measured in dollars (the phrase itself comes from accounting spreadsheets), since we are, after all, creatures of survival, and our financial assets have a great deal to do with the levels of comfort and freedom we can achieve as we survive.

But psychologically, interpreting the 2nd house on such a strictly physical level is unsatisfying. Traditional texts attempt to expand the meaning to include other levels by adding the phrase "personal resources," but this is a vague term without clear meaning. Even if they attempt a more psychological approach, many texts end up focusing almost exclusively on money in their 2nd house interpretations.

What the 2nd is really about is substantiation of the self-awareness that was initially gained through 1st house experience. It concerns the evaluation of the self by the self. In a very real sense, you don't identify so much with the awareness of yourself as you do the values and judgments you make about yourself. These are your primary "possessions" in the truest sense—what you feel about yourself.

To be a self is a fluid, spontaneous experience, very kinetic, with very few judgments. To have a self is a quite different experience, for although you cannot really ever have yourself, you do identify with those objects in your world that symbolize your grounded-ness in personal feeling. Everything surrounding you that could be called "yours" helps you define yourself in tangible ways—your car, your house, your toothbrush.

The 1st house is too spontaneous to be considered truly self-centered. Self-actualized or self-focused would be better terms. The 2nd house, however, is the natural arena of self-centeredness—me, my, and mine. It holds a crucial position in the growing awareness of twentieth-century psychology around the issue of self-worth. Shame and guilt are the predominant emotional diseases of modern culture—the inner feeling of worthlessness or inadequacy, often without clear or conscious experience of the feelings. It is in this realm that we need to begin reassessing and restructuring our interpretations of the 2nd.

Money is the predominant cultural symbol of worth, so it has gained prominence in 2nd house interpretations, but we should remember that the headlong, compulsive pursuit of money as a substitute for emotional self-worth usually indicates the presence of blockage such as shame or guilt within the psyche.

The 2nd house shows our characteristic attitudes around the experience of effort. While the 6th will later show the mental approach to organizing work through task orientation, the 2nd provides a more fundamental indication, our basic style of self-exertion.

It also symbolizes the reward we expect for such efforts—the satisfactions that physicality can bring, both through the body and through objects external to the body. Enjoyment of food, the luxury of fine clothing or beautiful surroundings are 2nd house pleasures. This is not the appreciation of art found in the 5th house, nor does it touch on the concerns of surrounding class and distinction found in the 10th and 11th houses. No, this is pure pleasure, the sheer delight of sensuality, of being an Earth creature.

3rd House

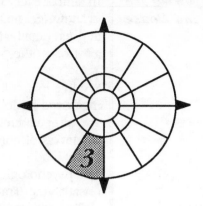

Qualities

hemisphere	*eastern*	self-directed and active
hemisphere	*lower*	subjective and personal
scope	*initial third*	self-interested or self-centered
mode	*cadent*	learning and organizing
axis	*3rd/9th*	education, exploration, and communication
planet	*Mercury*	thinking, speaking, and perceiving

Traditional Meanings

the lower mind (rational)
routine interactions with others
communication through writing and speaking
short journeys and immediate, normal activity
brothers and sisters
neighbors

Contemporary Meanings

outreach — day-to-day environment, one's relation to it; the quality and style of daily activity

concrete mind — development and use of mentality as a way of understanding the real world

curiosity — the experience of rational inquisitiveness, the desire to know

education — the orientation toward basic learning, especially through grammar and high school

communication — the experience of language as a tool; writing, and the style of speaking

The existence of an aware self is linked with 1st house experience; the 2nd reveals a relationship between the self and its identity. In the 3rd house, this experience is taken further, moving past pure self-awareness and territorial self-possession. The 1st was kinetic, the 2nd was substantial, but with the 3rd, we reach the initial mental realm—mind operating as a tool for organization and communication.

The nervous system extends beyond the physical limits of the body. It reaches out into the environment to define and categorize the infinite world of objects found there—both inanimate (things) and animate (people). The 3rd represents learning in the classical sense, and is generally agreed to focus on "concrete mentality," although that phrase is somewhat ill-chosen. Nothing in the realm of mind is actually concrete, but in the 3rd house we operate out of the rational mind, as opposed to the conceptual mentality linked with the 9th house.

This is mentality at its most structural level, providing us with building blocks, a basic grammar of experience, a way of understanding and interacting with the immediate environment just beyond ourselves. The 3rd is an area of activity, showing how we approach our ordinary, day-to-day environment. Analysis of the 1st and 3rd houses together provide an indication of normal activity levels.

Every house refers to the basic human experience of relatedness. Awareness itself is linked with relationship. Astrology is one system for exploring the interrelatedness that forms our reality, both within the self and beyond the self. However, certain houses are specified as areas of relationship more than others, since their meanings refer more directly to obvious relatedness.

The 3rd house is not about intimacy. It does have to do with recognition, but more on an "I-It" level than "I-Thou." Other people are experienced as interesting objects, stimulating basic curiosity. We want to understand how others are different from us, to find out what separates and distinguishes ourselves. However, the 3rd is crucial to the potential for intimacy, for it involves communication through language. Every species has "languages," but ours—homo sapiens—is distinguished by the evolved specialization of our brains, especially the language centers of the neo-cortex. We not only use language, we think about language, separating it from our natural behaviors, giving it a structure and evolution all its own. The 3rd house refers to the development of this uniquely human quality.

Traditional 3rd house interpretations concerning siblings, relatives, and neighbors have never seemed especially useful to me. They may be helpful in clarifying "unfinished business" when attracting new people to work through old, unresolved family issues. And the logic of their inclusion in 3rd house experience is straightforward enough, since these are relationships that are part of the immediate environment in early life, and as such they have a naturalness borne of familiarity. But their emphasis seems linked more with the Horary branch of astrology (dealing with specific questions, situations, and events) than to the psychological investigation of individual reality (which deals with issues and patterns surrounding the growth and maturation of consciousness).

So I use the 3rd house primarily as an indicator of the basic aptitude in communication —the raw ability to understand what's happening in the surrounding environment, and to interact with it successfully.

4th House

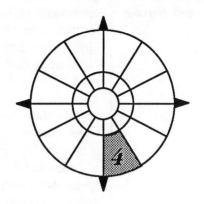

Qualities

hemisphere	*western*	other-directed and responsive
hemisphere	*lower*	subjective and personal
scope	*initial third*	self-interested or self-centered
mode	*angular*	initiating and establishing
axis	*4th/10th*	security, stability, and responsibility
planet	*Moon*	protection, nurturance, and emotions

Traditional Meanings

home and security
the family, both childhood and adult
one parent
ancestors and traditional background
conditions at the end of life

Contemporary Meanings

microcosm — the experience of being at the center of life, as the divine source of all meaning

personal security — home and family, the sense of "rootedness" in the experience of place

emotional imprints — conditions in the early childhood environment (reflected also at the end of life)

"inner-link" parent — the parental figure associated with emotions, most often the mother

private intuition — nonrational knowing about oneself; in occultism, the connection to one's guides

Exploring the 4th House

The 4th is the last of the four personal houses, so it culminates the experience of self-centeredness. But it's also the first house of the western hemisphere, implying an other-directedness in orientation. Additionally, its linkage with the Moon (and parallels to the sign Cancer) make it the first truly emotional area, linked with nurturing and need fulfillment. Finally, it's the middle point of the lower hemisphere, the section of individual space directly beneath our feet, pointing at the middle of the Earth.

What experiences in life combine self-centeredness and other-direction at the same time? Where are we concerned with others in an emotional way, but still with an orientation that is primarily self-interested and aimed at fulfillment of our own needs? We could suggest that relationships like marriage satisfy such conditions, but equal, one-to-one partnerships are more "air" (interactive) than "water" (emotional), and, ideally at least, they involve the experience of mutual agreement more than need fulfillment.

The critical factor is that the 4th house is the space directly beneath us. It represents roots or being grounded firmly in the earth. Plants need good root systems to achieve flowering. It is the fertility of the decomposed past that allows us to grow.

Family is the experience that satisfies all the conditions. The 4th involves everything surrounding our personal security, our need to nurture and be nurtured. It is our sense of home, both as a physical place, and more importantly, as an emotional safe haven.

The core imprints of early conditioning in childhood are revealed by the 4th house. Certainly there are other factors to be considered—for instance, the condition of the Moon and Saturn. But no other house can tell us so much about the unconscious but deeply personal attitudes we absorbed in infancy. No other house reveals so much about the basic attitudes we formed about security, for better or worse.

The growing momentum in family therapy, the women's movement, Alcoholics Anonymous, and other 12-step programs are now bringing to light a disturbing revelation: that more of us than anyone would have imagined come from families which are, to a greater or lesser extent, disturbed in the imprinting of their inner relations. Being emotionally limited seems the general rule rather than the exception, and many millions of us suffer from emotional disturbances which are at the root of our life problems. We may be operating from unconscious systems of belief and neural patterning that place us in extraordinary double-binds: security requires suffering, security requires pain, security requires sacrifice, security requires pretending not to need anything (including security itself), etc. Why this occurs is gradually becoming clear, but how to change it within any individual life is less certain.

The approach to 4th house attitudes is difficult to change, because the assumptions are made so early, preconsciously, and yet they exert tremendous influence over our adult decisions precisely because they form an important part of our basic "emotional set." Being in the womb, at the center, being protected, feeling safe—these are all 4th house experiences. Many of us strive mightily to change the forms of our security, especially when they are unfulfilling or painful, but fewer people succeed in altering the basic structure of their attitudes, their fundamental approaches to security.

However, careful understanding of the 4th house can be a resource for understanding how to reform our self-defeating paradoxes around the issues of home, family, and personal security. It can teach us how to subtly alter our imprints by revealing how our double binds are linked with our natural evolution, and it can suggest alternate ways of integrating those paradoxes into our lives, so we can experience a more graceful and coherent sense of belonging at the center of the universe.

5th House

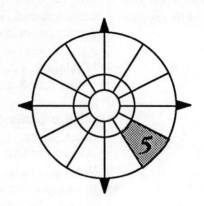

Qualities

hemisphere ....*western* ....other-directed and responsive
hemisphere ....*lower* ....subjective and personal
scope ....*middle third*..........interactive and interpersonal
mode ....*succeedent* ....reactive and definite
axis ....*5th/11th* ....behavior, creativity, and love
planet ....*Sun* ....power, purpose, and pride

Traditional Meanings

creative self-expression
pleasure
sex, romance, and love affairs
having children
sports, games, and amusements
gambling, speculation, and investments

Contemporary Meanings

conscious persona   intentional ego presentation, life-as-a-stage, personal charisma

romance, giving love   the experience of active courtship; the characteristic way love is offered

sexual performance   making love as exaltation of the ego; performing for the beloved

personal creativity   all forms of ego-centered self-expression, both artistic and otherwise

competition   the experience of risk in any contest involving personal excellence

Theoretically, at this point in the evolution of the houses, we are now conscious of ourselves. We have birthed self-awareness (1st house), grounded ourselves in our bodies (2nd house), extended our nervous systems to explore the immediate environment (3rd house), and achieved safety and a sense of our personal importance through the fulfillment of our emotional needs (4th house).

Having culminated the realm of personal growth so that we actually have a secure identity, we now move to a new process in the unfoldment of experience, to the second group of four houses, out into the social realm of interactions with relative strangers.

Most of us, of course, achieve less than a totally secure identity, but even if we did, the movement into the social realm would still be a risk. And this is what the 5th house is all about, conscious risks. We know who we are, but we begin to realize that strangers may not care, that indeed, there's no particular reason why they should. We have to create a personality that can win their attention, affection, and approval.

The 5th house is like the 1st, in that each area is concerned with the expression of personality. But they differ fundamentally in that the 1st is spontaneous, natural, and relatively automatic. The 5th is consciously chosen, created by intention, and very purposeful. It is presenting yourself as if you were an actor on stage, aware of the fact that there's an audience present. The two houses tend to blend in our overall expression of personality, but a careful observer can tell when one kicks in and the other recedes.

The ideal, of course, is to make your "act" so convincing that the audience doesn't know you're acting, and if you do it well enough, you can dissolve into the character you're portraying. It's not that you surrender your natural self, but rather that you blend your latent temperament with a more conscious persona; you heighten your effectiveness as a person, enchancing your relation to the divine by becoming a more creative force.

All forms of personal creativity or conscious risk involve the 5th house, from thinking about what you're going to say next, all the way to painting the Mona Lisa. The 5th is succeedent and below the horizon, and is therefore an area of subjective judgment, like the 2nd house. But the 5th is western, so it's other-directed. We're still subjective here (involved primarily in our own perceptions and feelings), but now we're going to make judgments about ourselves through our experience of our perception of other people's reactions to us. At first glance, that statement may seem overly complex, but the experience it describes is natural and constantly ongoing for all of us.

It is in the 5th that we suffer the first real fears of social rejection from outside. This is one reason why romance, courtship, and affairs of the heart are 5th house levels—because they involve a very real risk of rejection.

If you're standing in the courtyard at the bottom of the trellis, Spanish guitar in hand, wooing the fair damsel, hoping she will emerge on the balcony in response to your virtuoso performance, you run the risk that she may simply ignore you, or worse, that she will emerge above only to dump last night's dishwater on your head. Choose the right song, but sing it badly, and you lose. Sing beautifully, but choose the wrong song, and it's dishwater time again. You have to combine the right script with the best performance in order to win.

It's like that with all personal adventures, all personal risks, whatever the level of experience; you're laying yourself on the line—consciously, intentionally—and that's what the 5th house is about.

6th House

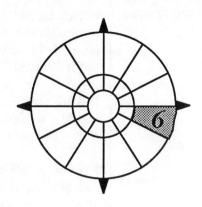

Qualities

hemisphere ....*western* ....other-directed and responsive
hemisphere ....*lower* ....subjective and personal
scope ....*middle third* ....interactive, interpersonal (one-to-one)
mode ....*cadent* ....learning and organizing
axis ....*6th/12th* ....understanding, healing, and helping
planet ....*Mercury* ....cognition, analysis, and categorization

Traditional Meanings

service
work
employees and servants
sickness
hygiene and diet
pets and small animals

Contemporary Meanings

disease and healing   bodily disease, neurosis or misunderstanding, and techniques to restore homeostasis

unequal relationships   superior/inferior, dominant/submissive, and other relationships involving unequal status

duty and subservience   dutiful helping, purification through humility, conscious subservience to another

technical mind   discrimination, organization, analysis, the mind working for personal growth

disciplined routines   efficient routines to increase productivity, the experience of regularity in lifestyle

Exploring the 6th House

The 6th house is best understood by looking at what precedes it. Having become self-aware (1st house), established personal territory (2nd house), developed means of communication (3rd house), achieved a secure identity (4th house), propelled the self into creativity and the risks of socialization (5th house), we reach a crossroads.

We may discover that we've burned the candle at both ends, in the adrenaline-charged performing of the 5th house. If we can't stem the emotional momentum, we may break down, falling victim to disease through stress, or the neuroses caused by too much, too soon. Wine, women, and song is all very well, but it doesn't make for a good daily diet. We may find that our ego has become so large that others are pushed away, so that we must somehow counter our own arrogance. All these reactions, however negative they may seem, are within the territory of 6th house experience.

The 6th is the last house of the lower hemisphere. Its cadency represents transition. In the complex evolution into social awareness, we've remained primarily self-centered even as we became sensitive to others' reactions. Now we sense a basic shift coming.

To this point, everyone in our lives has been essentially a character in our dream, mere supporting players in the movie we're writing, producing, directing, and in which we star. Now we begin to see that there could be something more. We aren't certain what it is yet, what it will look like when we get there, but we're moving inexorably toward the recognition that others have lives of their own. This is objectivity, the awareness that we are bit players in other people's movies just as they are bit players in ours.

We are about to evolve from subjectivity to objectivity. The transition requires a period of self-purification. We certify our worthiness for this elevation in stature by perfecting ourselves, eradicating any personal flaws that might carry over from subjective living.

There are many forms of purification and self-perfection, but all involve recognition of the need to find a relationship with a master, either someone in physical form, or a system of personal discipline we can live by. The chela kisses the feet of the guru in the hope that he may aspire to the Godliness he sees before him. It doesn't matter whether or not the guru is actually the Realized Being the devotee imagines; what is important is humility and the sincere wish for self-perfection through service, the willingness to shed old skins, to let accumulated toxins be washed away through loving discipline. This is the spiritual essence of 6th house experience.

More pragmatically, people want to be effective. The want to reach their goals. We can see our own waste and inefficiency, and the 6th represents the experience of gradual self-improvement to achieve measurable results.

Once again, I have to question a traditional level of meaning. I understand why "pets and small animals" are sometimes listed in textbooks as being associated with the 6th. It has to do with the symbolism involved in unequal relationships. That's clear enough. But I have questions. How is it relevant? What do you do with that in interpretation? Very few of my clients ask me about small animals, and as important as pets are to many people, I don't spend much time analyzing those relationships.

Perhaps the social movement around "animal rights" will rebirth this meaning, but that remains to be seen. My feeling is that it's an interesting item to know symbolically, but I think it's time we stopped listing it as one of the fundamental levels of the 6th house. There are enough significant experiences in the 6th that we can relegate "pets and small animals" to their appropriate stature as an interesting footnote.

7th House

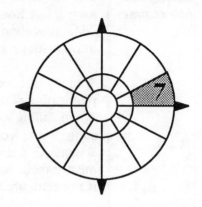

Qualities			
hemisphere	*western*	other-directed and responsive
hemisphere	*upper*	objective and collective
scope	*middle third*	interactive, interpersonal (one-to-one)
mode	*angular*	initiating and establishing
axis	*1st/7th*	action, awareness, and boundaries
planet	*Venus*	cooperation, receptivity, and harmony

Traditional Meanings

marriage and partnership
the spouse
contracts
cooperation
open enemies, open conflicts
the public

Contemporary Meanings

mirrored awareness	awareness of the self through the mirroring effect of others in relationship
equal partnerships	all one-to-one partnerships involving equals such as marriage, business partnerships, etc.
contracts, commitments	the experience of a social contract; the implications of making a promise
cooperation	negotiation, compromise, and cooperation in a purposeful relationship
partners or partnerships	qualities of the self's alter-ego, the natural partner, or the natural relationship

Exploring the 7th House

The 7th is the first house of the upper or objective hemisphere, opposite the 1st house. Both areas concern self-awareness, but the 1st works through direct radiance of personality into the environment, while the 7th operates by reflection. Self-awareness is generated through a "mirroring effect"—seeing oneself in others, recognizing and identifying with qualities in them you weren't aware of, or couldn't contact in yourself.

The 7th house is about relationships, specifically those between equals. Individuals we consider inferior are beneath consideration; we discount them out of hand. And though we may aspire to the qualities of people we perceive as superior, we don't truly identify with them. So to recognize oneself in another, there must be equality.

Traditional meanings of the 7th continue to work well for psychological astrologers. One-to-one partnerships, marriage, contracts, cooperation, and commitment require self-awareness and shared equality. However, in classical texts, these were often taken too literally. The old adage that your partner's Sun or rising sign will be the same as the sign on your 7th house cusp is predictably dogmatic and unsupported by empirical evidence. Things just ain't that simple, folks.

The fundamental problem of the 7th house is projection. If I look at you, do I truly see your existence separate from myself? Or do I create an image of you in my mind out of my own assumptions and unconscious beliefs about myself? Are you you, or are you me? And even if I know that both are probably true, how do I tell where one stops and the other begins? How do I know what to do with what I see in you? If I react strongly to certain of your qualities, then surely I must embody them somewhere within myself, or I wouldn't be so sensitized when I experience them coming from you. That's what an agreement is, whether it's conscious or unconscious. To agree is to share.

If I'm attracted to form a relationship with you, it means you have qualities I seek to integrate into my life, qualities I don't consciously experience as already within me. It's as if I can see those qualities in my life only when we're connected. The obvious challenge of intimate relationships is to recognize these qualities as having parallels within the self, to bring them out into the everyday awareness of self so their functions can be consciously expressed. But what if I don't assimilate what I see in the mirror?

What if I'm so dazzled by your wonderful qualities that I remain hypnotized, unable to see their parallels in myself? In that case, I am bound to you. If you leave, I lose the experience of a part of myself with which I'm longing to connect. Intimacy is destroyed by my constant fear of loss. Conversely, what if I'm so horrified by certain of your "negative" qualities that I can't overcome my fear of their parallel presence within my own psyche? Then I blame you for my own invisible qualities even as I continue to be caught in attraction/repulsion. This is not intimacy either, but entanglement or co-dependency. Often both ends of the spectrum occur simultaneously, manifesting as love/hate, involving issues the chart reveals to be differing sides of the same paradox. This type of relationship usually breaks, ending in bitter incompleteness.

Beyond these unfulfilling projections, there is another problem. What happens if I do assimilate? What if I gradually come to be aware of your qualities in myself? What happens when I don't unconsciously need you as a mirror anymore? Theoretically, it should be the beginning of true intimacy, for then we can really begin to share as equals, conscious of our whole selves, and joyful to be in the presence of another who embodies similar qualities. All too often, however, it signifies the end of the relationship.

These are great paradoxes of human life, and working through them is the key to all 7th house experience.

8th House

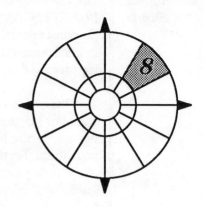

Qualities			
hemisphere	*western*	other-directed and responsive
hemisphere	*upper*	objective and collective
scope	*middle third*	interactive, interpersonal (one-to-one)
mode	*succeedent*	reactive and definite
axis	*2nd/8th*	values, judgments, and gratification
planet	*Pluto*	intensity, regeneration, and renewal

Traditional Meanings

death
inheritances and legacies
other people's resources
sex and regeneration
the occult

Contemporary Meanings

union	the experience of sharing; issues of power and trust in partnerships
transformation	the mysteries of ego-death and rebirth through intense experiences with others
sexual merging	the experience of true sexual union; tantric release
focused intuition	nonrational knowing as it operates in the specific context of one-to-one relatedness
shared assets	the concrete legacies of relationships; shared finances, possessions, or property

Arriving at the 8th house, we come again to the end of a phase. The 8th is the last of the second group of four consecutive houses, the "water" house signifying the culmination of relationships between individuals. The 7th house represented the peak of one-to-one intimate relatedness in the objective experience of contracts and commitments—the promise. But it's one thing to promise, to formalize a contractual commitment, say, "to love, honor, and cherish;" it's quite another to actually live what's been promised.

If the 7th can be considered the ceremony of marriage, the 8th house is the honeymoon and what comes afterward in the long haul of shared living. The 8th has to do with expanding beyond the former boundaries of selfhood, leaving behind the sense of separateness to merge with what is beyond the self. Specifically, it is the experience of union with others, the fulfillment of sharing in all its most profound ramifications.

Since the 8th is the succeedent house opposite the 2nd, it represents worth—value through relationships. But the Plutonian nature of the house reveals the necessity to relinquish individuality in order to gain the new value. If you want to become greater, to be more than you were, to have your perspective altered and enlarged through union and merger, something has to die. Thus, the classical 8th house connection with death.

This is an experience not of simple surrender, but of pushing outward and then inward, recreating the birth struggle. It's death and rebirth, a process achieved by going deeply into partnership and dragging out everything within the self that needs to be transformed. It does not always occur literally with another person, but there is always the aura of another's influence. When you reach the edge of the symbolical cliff of "Lover's Leap," will he or she jump with you? Or will you be overwhelmed by seduction, fooled into jumping alone, or worse, pushed off by your partner? The paradox is that you must trust, and yet you must jump alone.

The sexual connotations of the 8th house are strong. This is not the pure, self-centered sensuality of the 2nd house, nor is it the lovemaking ego-performance of the 5th. Here was see the peak of the sexual experience, the release that comes as stimulation has built to a crescendo—the temporary loss of consciousness contained in the orgasm. This linkage of sex and death is neither morbid nor facetious; it is a higher level of sexual creativity—not procreative in physically making babies, but creative in psychologically making a new seed of self. The fact that most of us remain sensitive only to the drives of sexuality doesn't necessarily mean we're missing the transformations. In the 8th house, you need not be conscious to be transformed, but you must go all the way.

The 8th is an area of mysteries. What lies just beyond the self? If I reach for it, will I die as I break free of the boundaries of my body? Will I end or go through? It is an arena for experimentation, thus its linkage with the realms of occultism and intuition.

As with the 2nd, money is relevant, but again, it tends to be overplayed. The 8th is another of the houses that falls prey to over-literal interpretations, and that simplistic bent is damaging to an understanding of its psychological relevance. The 8th is not for the faint-hearted. Its experiences require the strength of an oak and the grace of a willow, for it is about change, not merely the alterations in form that pass for it in many lives, but real, no-kidding, CHANGE—a fundamental reweaving of personhood.

Each of us gets the chance many times during our lives; not all of us take it. For those who don't learn to "die while living"—the quintessence of the 8th house—rest assured that they'll have the opportunity at the end of their lives in their final bodily experience, physical death. Only one thing is absolutely certain: nobody's getting out of here alive.

9th House

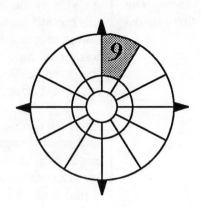

Qualities

hemisphere ....*western*.................other-directed and responsive
hemisphere ....*upper*.....................objective and collective
scope ....*last third* ....sociocultural or universal
mode ....*cadent*....................learning and organizing
axis ....*3rd/9th* ....education, exploration, and communication
planet ....*Jupiter*..................expansion, enthusiasm, and philosophy

Traditional Meanings

the higher mind
philosophy, religion, and the law
long-distance journeys

Contemporary Meanings

conceptual frameworks   organized mental frameworks as they apply to the larger social environment

cultural perspective   increased relativity in cultural knowledge; long-distance travel (either physical or mental)

higher education   all adult learning to broaden the self, including informal experience

the search for truth   the quest for generalizable truths, both in understanding and communication

ideal society   the visualization of an ideal culture, characteristics of the "perfect" world

Each group of four consecutive houses (personal, interpersonal, and collective) begins with a "fire" house—the 1st (analogous to the sign Aries), the 5th (paralleling Leo), and the 9th (similar to Sagittarius). The three spirals conform to the same element structure. However, each group begins with a house of a different modality.

The personal group begins with an angular house, the 1st, so the tone of the first four houses reflect that feeling of angularity. Personal experience has an urgent undertone; establishing a relationship to self is so essential that the push to do so is built into us. Babies and small children devour life, drinking it in as if there were no tomorrow. The second angular house, the 4th, culminates the strictly personal growth through the establishment of a secure family system as protection for the individual.

The interpersonal group starts with a succeedent house, the 5th, so the subtle tone of the second four houses reflects that modality. One-to-one relatedness is informed and structured by the search for values and systems of judgment. This experience can be a wonderful revelation as different approaches blend, or it can be nightmare as they collide. Is it any wonder that intimacy so often degenerates into power struggles?

The collective group begins with a cadent house, the 9th, so it unfolds in the poetic rhythms of cadency. To find our true place in the larger world, we must flow with the current, becoming malleable as we permit our former boundaries to be stretched (9th), restabilized (10th), reevaluated (11th), and finally dissolved (12th). No wonder the politics of social experience are chaotic, for the world is cadent while we are angular. No wonder the investigation of spiritual life is filled with paradox and wonder. We cannot establish (angular) or evaluate (succeedent) spirit; we can only receive understanding (cadent) as it descends down through the pathways of the higher chakras.

The 9th house begins the process of political understanding through the experience of an expanded mind. Its natural association with Jupiter tells us that growth, assimilation, and abstraction are components of 9th house. In the 8th, we culminated relationships with individuals. Here in the 9th, we begin relating to groups of human beings and organized understanding. We are interacting not with individuals, but with the distilled essence of what various individuals have thought. Their ideas have been codified into coherent systems of thought. Thus the 9th house meanings of philosophy, ethics, organized religion, and law.

In the opposite house, the 3rd, we built the framework for the concrete mind, which allows us to communicate basic information. In the 9th house, we're concerned with the framework itself. Mental structure and mental content become one. How many movies have been made about Hollywood? About the movie business? About making movies? Lots, and more as time goes on. This is the process of abstraction, moving from concern with concreteness to concern with process—from the literal to the symbolic— and it is a significant 9th house level.

The 9th concerns mental awareness in its largest, most far-reaching context. Curiosity extends past the immediate and the known, toward the long-range and the unknown. This is the origin of the classical 9th house meaning of "long-distance journeys."

In the sexual intimacy of the 8th house, we confronted the awesome mysteries of what lies beyond the self. Having transformed ourselves as that mystery pierced the heart, we move into the 9th house, the first conscious step on the odyssey to comprehend the meaning of mystery itself. We begin the adventure of exploring the whole cosmos. Having pierced the heart, we then free the mind.

10th House

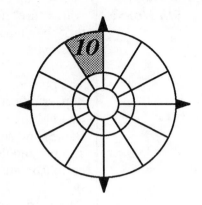

Qualities

hemisphere	*eastern*	self-directed and expressive
hemisphere	*upper*	objective and collective
scope	*last third*	sociocultural or universal
mode	*angular*	initiating and establishing
axis	*4th/10th*	security, stability, and responsibility
planet	*Saturn*	ambition, authority, and maturation

Traditional Meanings

ambition through career or profession
social status and public reputation
social contribution
one parent

Contemporary Meanings

collective responsibility the experience of responsibility that extends beyond the self; universal *dharma*

professional ambition developing and maintaining an adult niche in the world; career, social status

missions and messages that which God offers to all of humanity through any specific individual

"outer-link" parent the parental figure associate with structure, most often the father

authority the experience of wielding collective power, and the reaction to external authorities

The 10th is the angular house of the collective group, and the initial area of the eastern (self-actualizing) hemisphere. It represents the establishment of an enduring relation to the world-at-large. It involves carving out a social niche for yourself by answering the question, "What am I going to do when I grow up?" This question is relevant whether one's age is nine or ninety, for "adulthood" usually seems oddly far off, in the distance yet to come.

The Sun in any chart is the symbol for personal power, the conduit through which we are connected to Cosmic Central. This part of ourselves fuels us, providing a direction, a purpose, and a sense of meaning for the individuality. Whichever houses the Sun occupies and rules are the strongest areas of personal life-purpose.

The 10th house is the section of personal space directly overhead. It is the part of the sky where the sun reaches its highest elevation around midday. It represents the culmination of solar meaning, the apex of purpose, but since it is the center of the upper hemisphere, it does so through the collective, through the culture of which each of us is but a small part. So the 10th house reveals the experience of impersonal life-purpose.

The combination of angularity, upper and eastern hemisphere emphasis, plus the association with the planet Saturn, produce a powerful blend of personal and collective responsibility. There is self-interest here, and the awareness that you must generate something through your own efforts. Being in charge becomes an issue, taking control over one's own life and the lives of others. You are climbing the mountain, acutely aware of your stature at any given moment. Reach the summit, and you can share your vision with the world. Fulfill your responsibilities, and you'll be recognized as an authority.

The 4th house symbolized the personal security of home and family; the 10th represents the social security of knowing that you have a secure place in the culture.

The traditional meanings of the 10th house as the area of ambition, career, social status, and public reputation continue to be as relevant today as they ever were. But many traditional texts focus almost exclusively on these relatively concrete achievements. We need to be aware that the experience of the 10th goes beyond simple concerns of success at the material or social level, important though these may be. Cultural influence and fame are intoxicatingly powerful images, but we know all too well how often they backfire. Ambition can be like a drug, and drugs are not a safe path to real fulfillment.

Beyond the experience of power and ordinary success, the 10th house also has to do with success at the spiritual level—the assumption of full responsibility for oneself, the experience of truly growing up as an individual, and in so doing, coming into touch with the divinity that flows through us. The condition of the 10th shows what tasks are involved in maturation, toward what Jungians call "true individuation."

At this less tangible level, the 10th is the experience of making your full contribution to the universe and thus gaining recognition, not so much through the ordinary payoffs of respect, fame, or power, but instead through the inward, personal recognition that you are living at the highest level of your capabilities.

Success here means that you are secure in the experience of being at home on the Earth—through the conscious expression your personal divinity, and beyond those personal goals, by becoming a responsible representative for the expression of a larger divinity, that of the universe itself.

11th House

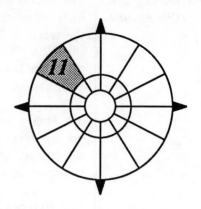

Qualities			
hemisphere	*eastern*	self-directed and expressive
hemisphere	*upper*	objective and collective
scope	*last third*	sociocultural or universal
mode	*succeedent*	reactive and definite
axis	*5th/11th*	behavior, creativity, and love
planet	*Uranus*	humanitarian, independent, and original

Traditional
Meanings

friends
social activity
groups and organizations
hopes and wishes

Contemporary
Meanings

group participation — involvement with groups, organizations, or cultural institutions

appropriate behavior — sensitivity toward "correct" behavior, as defined by group standards

friendship, social circle — the experience of identification with friends belonging to a coherent social community

shared creativity — group orientation in the creative process; allegiance to a collective goal

receiving love — being loved, specifically, the qualities of others' behavior understood as loving

The 9th house began the process of universalization with expansion into collective mental systems. The 10th followed this exploration by establishing a niche for the individual within the larger group reality. Here in the 11th house—the third of the last group of four, the final house of obvious relatedness, and the last succeedent area in the house structure—we arrive at the experience of full participation in groups. The 11th concerns the judgments we make about ourselves and our world based on our group affiliations, and the profound desire each of us has for acceptance within any group.

Thus the traditional meaning of "friends," or more specifically, the social circle of comrades and associates with whom we we bond to secure our place in the matrix of social relationships. 11th house relationships usually blend emotional attraction with the mental affinity that was begun in the 9th. Our friends tend to both reflect and shape our philosophical, moral, or ethical outlooks.

The 11th is associated with Uranus, so it blends collective participation with the element of personal will. If the 9th represented the exploration of culture, the 10th the establishment of a secure culture, then the 11th surrounds the evaluation of self-worth in cultural terms. This is the area where we are most concerned with our perceptions of how others regard us, not others as singular individuals, but as a group, as a social whole. The 11th is where the concept of "socially appropriate behavior" has its greatest weight, where manners and mores reach their most structured and powerful form.

And yet, individuality reaches its apex here. The 5th represented the culmination of the development of personal identity and the subsequent birth of a social sensibility through which the ego could express itself. The 11th represents the culmination of the striving to create a social identity and the subsequent rebirth of reawakened individuality. Heightened sensitivity to belonging automatically creates heightened sensitivity to isolation. In part it is precisely because the pressures of socialization are so strong here that we also long to identify ourselves as separate and independent. In the 11th house, we want to belong, and yet, simultaneously, we want to be truly individual.

The opposite house, the 5th, revealed the challenge of personal, ego-centered creativity. Here in the 11th we pursue the same experience in a collective way through shared or group-oriented creativity.

The 5th indicated the passionate love discovered through intense romantic involvement, so the 11th is often understood to represent the cooler, more detached care found through friendship. This is a valid approach, and often works well in interpretation. But there's another quite different way to analyze the workings of romantic love.

The 5th was the area of conscious ego expression through the dramatic rituals of courtship. In that light, the ego was center-stage, creating courtship as an actor performs to an audience. The 11th house could be considered to reverse the experience; rather than giving love as a performer or suitor, we are in the position of receiving love as an audience. And just as an audience expects a certain kind of entertainment, the 11th indicates the expectation each of us holds in regard to being loved, the characteristic ways we recognize that love is being offered by another. (Refer to **Derived House Meanings** on **pp. 58-59** at the end of this chapter for a more detailed discussion.)

This is not love in the 4th house sense of being nurtured and having our needs fulfilled, nor in the 8th house experience of emotional unions leading to psychological transformation, but love in the sense that another person values and is drawn to us for our unique blend of individuality and social attractiveness. It is the more romantic role of the beloved.

12th House

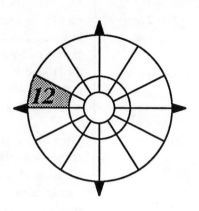

Qualities	hemisphere ....*eastern* ....self-directed and expressive
	hemisphere ....*upper*.....................objective and collective
	scope ....*last third* ....sociocultural or universal
	mode ....*cadent* ....learning and organizing
	axis ....*6th/12th* ....understanding, helping, and healing
	planet ....*Neptune*.................compassion, surrender, and imagination

Traditional Meanings

fate or karma
self-undoing or self-sacrifice
secrets and invisible enemies
isolation
hospitals, prisons, other places of confinement

Contemporary Meanings

imagination	fantasies, dreams; the intersection of the personal and the collective unconscious
unfocused intuition	nonrational knowing in its most generalized context; true mediumship
withdrawal or isolation	the experience of withdrawal from life; transparency; voluntary or enforced isolation
selfless giving	unconditional giving in response to any need; the transcendence of personal will
"past lives"	conditions prior to birth that affect the life; in occultism, the karma of alternate realities

Exploring the 12th House

In reaching the 12th house, we arrive at the end of the cycle. It's tempting to see the 12th as the "garbage house," where we dump everything we couldn't find a correlation for in any of the eleven preceding houses. And there's a certain savvy to that; if you can't find what you're looking for in the chart, if you don't understand a situation in a client's life, or if you're simply perplexed and can't figure out what the hell's going on, try checking the 12th house. You may not find the answer, but you will find what is often misunderstood, difficult to deal with rationally, or just plain incomprehensible.

The traditional meanings for the 12th house tend to promote a rather negative view: "karma" (presumably "bad karma"), forced isolation, confinement, martyrdom, confusion, deception, addiction to drugs or other escapes, even insanity. The list of horrors goes on and on. On the "hit list" in classical astrology, Saturn is the most negative planet, Scorpio the most maligned sign, and the 12th the most feared house. What do these three share in common? Nothing really, except that they all have lousy press agents. In fact, they are no more negative than any of the other planets, signs, or houses.

Since the 1st house represents dawning self-awareness, analogous to birthing the self, the 12th infers whatever comes before self-awareness, prior to birth. It's whatever is beneath or beyond ordinary levels of awareness—the womb. It can also relate to dreams or other creative visualizations, receptivity to intuitive messages and images, etc.

If the 1st is self-expression outward into the environment, then the 12th represents withdrawal from the environment—isolation from others. Yes, that can mean confinement or the feeling of imprisonment, but it can also infer voluntary withdrawal. The world is often too much with us, and we are usually too involved with it, frequently in ways that promote little fulfillment. Withdrawal can be a welcome respite. Periodically, we need to give up the struggle for control. We need to surrender, to return to the womb, to drown peacefully in the oceanic consciousness that is our source. We need to retreat.

Formal retreats, whether through vacations or more disciplined excursions such as meditation or yoga, are an important part of our remembering who we really are, and these sabbaticals have the power to refresh our relationship with everyday life. Informal, momentary retreating is also very useful. A coffee break serves to punctuate periods of effort, literally breaking up the drudgery of the workday, and daydreams have their place as a quiet alternative to brainstorming.

The 12th goes two ways: either we are in the world but not quite of it, or we are of the world but not quite in it. It's like having one foot in reality, and the other somewhere else with no name. The trick involves not being pulled apart, not getting so stuck in one that you compulsively boomerang into the other. Properly understood, the 12th is the area of positive selflessness as a relief from the effort of having a self. It is perfection through release, giving for the sheer goodness that comes from true humility. It invokes renewal of the self through the experience of letting go.

Yes, the 12th can be the garbage dump of spiritual evolution. It can represent disintegration into meaninglessness, escape into fantasy, and susceptibility to addictive illusion. But as with every symbolic factor in astrology, such vulnerability comes with the territory of being human. The challenge of the 12th house is regeneration of faith. It urges us to cleanse ourselves of all failures, all strivings, to allow everything skewed or out-of-round to return to natural balance by letting ego-separateness drain away.

In so doing, we complete ourselves. We come to accept life, and we prepare for the birth of a new cycle of self-awareness, a new round of experience through the houses.

In reading many traditional textbooks on the houses, we could easily conclude that each major experience in life is associated primarily with only a single house, since this is the usual way they are presented—the 2nd house is money; the 5th house is love affairs; the 7th is marriage; the 8th is death; etc. However, this is not how life works, and it's not how charts work either.

While it is true that each house may reasonably be considered to have dominion over specialized types of experience, the general categories of life inevitably touch on more than a single house. In reality, any experience or specific situation in life activates the symbolism of all twelve areas, and we could create interpretations that move consecutively through the houses, starting with the 1st and continuing right through the 12th.

One system for derived house meanings uses the juxtaposition of actual interpretive meanings with abstract meanings. In this system, the first house in any sequence represents the experience itself. The following house is considered the second area in the sequence, and is interpreted as the evaluation of the experience. The next house is third in the sequence, the understanding of the experience; the sixth, any misunderstandings or disharmony in the experience, the tenth, the cultural purpose of the experience, etc.

So if we're dealing with a life-situation focusing primarily on an individual's intimate partner, then the 7th house is considered to be first in the sequence. Each succeeding house is then interpreted based on its numerical position in the derived cycle.

The 8th house is the second in the sequence, representing the real value brought to the individual by the partner, at a concrete level the money gained or lost through the partnership. The 9th house (third of the 7th) is the characteristic way the partner communicates, the 10th (fourth of the 7th) is the emotional security needs of the partner, the 12th (sixth in sequence starting from the 7th) is the partner's diseases, neuroses, or misunderstandings, especially as they affect the person whose chart we're analyzing. The ultimate example of this technique, and an illustration of how absurdly solipsistic the interpretations can sometimes sound, is that the 1st house is the seventh in a sequence starting with the 7th house—the seventh of the 7th—so it represents your partner's partner—in other words, you.

Derived interpretation has far-reaching significance in determining house meanings. For instance, the 5th/11th axis symbolizes the conditions an individual will characteristically undergo around the issue of affection for others. For many astrologers, the 5th represents passionate involvement in love affairs and indicates the way the person gives and receives love in these relationships. The 11th is then considered to reveal the same giving and receiving in more detached relationships, such as friendships. It's as if we've made giving and receiving one whole experience, but divided it into two categories, hot and cool, aligning one with each house on the 5th/11th axis. And there is certainly a logic to this, since the 5th house bears tonal similarity to the passionate fire sign Leo, while the 11th aligns with the independence of the air sign Aquarius.

However, there is another way to delineate the issue of giving and receiving love, one revealed almost solely by application of the derived house approach.

If the 5th is understood to symbolize "creativity" and "conscious, active performance," then it leans more strongly toward the "giving" end of the love experience. An actor on stage is creating a performance. He offers it to his audience, quite literally giving it to them. The payoff for his efforts lies in the acceptance and admiration his audience will bestow if his performance pleases them. This is what he hopes to receive.

Certainly, the actor isn't looking for the audience to give him back the same performance he offered them. He doesn't want them to perform at all. What he wishes to receive is a completely different kind of experience than what he gives.

It's the same situation in a love affair. The lover creates a conscious, intentional performance for her beloved in courtship, but when she does that, she's not looking to receive the identical experience in return. So should we continue to interpret the 5th house as indicating both giving and receiving in love?

In the derived system, the 11th house is the fifth area in a sequence starting with the 7th house (7th/1, 8th/2, 9th/3, 10th/4, 11th/5), so it naturally should symbolize the creative performance—the courtship—of the partner. Turned around to bring it back to relevance for the self, the 11th indicates the individual's posture as an audience. It shows the most natural way for courtship to be received.

This approach increases our understanding of the complexity of giving and receiving in love. There is **active giving** (5th house), where one hopes to receive a positive response from the audience, and there is also **responsive giving** (11th house), where one is initially in the receiving mode, but responds by giving affirmation.

This method offers valuable subtlety in interpretation, and it's the way I've chosen to discuss the 5th and 11th houses in the 20 relevant delineations of **Part Two**, with the 5th house carrying the meaning of **active giving** (and **responsive receiving**), and the 11th house symbolizing **active receiving** (and **responsive giving**).

This view doesn't invalidate the traditional understanding of those two houses as indicating "emotionally involved" versus "socially detached" love. It simply adds more options to our view of any particular chart, like letting us look through different filters to discover different layers of experience. The fact that the two approaches may be paradoxical serves to remind us that astrology, like life, is composed largely of paradoxical elements. In part, it is the interweave of these paradoxes that gives human life its unique quality—both wonderful and terrible at the same time—and makes astrology such a compelling tool. By itself, it does not solve the paradoxes, but it may help to clarify them. It may even promote our ability to eventually embrace them and remove their sting.

Any in-depth understanding of the houses requires facility with the logic of derived meanings. As a fundamental study in astrological thought processes, it is positively invaluable. For instance, the 10th house represents not only the native's cultural security and collective responsibility, it also indicates the emotional needs and family background of the marriage partner (fourth area in the 7th house sequence).

This study is occasionally hilarious in light of the odd juxtapositions of meaning that can result when different house levels are connected at random. For instance, you might find a symbol in the chart that "supposedly" represents the career scandals that could result from the secret sexual adventures of your brother's wife's uncle's dog! Admittedly, it's somewhat vulnerable to that brand of late-night absurdity.

But more seriously, exploring these presumptions is often intensely thought-provoking, and it can produce wonderful revelations, revealing linkages in life we would normally overlook. It has been fully detailed in other textbooks, so I'll leave this as only a brief introduction, but it's a technique that clearly deserves the attention of any astrological student interested in fully comprehending the implications of the houses.

Using the Houses

Enough philosophy. We want to learn to use the houses in a real-life way, to describe and understand actual people through what is called "interpretation" or "delineation," and that requires a mastery of technique. The first step in the process involves defining how the planets are distributed through the twelve houses. Each major body is located at a certain point in the sphere of space surrounding the individual at birth, and we need to determine which of the twelve houses each planet occupies.

This is neither as easy nor straightforward as it may initially seem, for there are many factors that go into the determination of house positions.

First, there is the question of which house system to use, since each system uses different mathematical references to divide the circle into twelve sections, and the boundaries of the houses can vary considerably from one system to another. Mars may be placed in the 7th house in the Placidean House System, while occupying the 8th house according to Campanus or Koch. Please refer to **Chapter Five: Technical versus Human Issues** for a discussion of this question.

Once we've chosen a particular house system to use in charting, that doesn't solve all our problems in determining planetary placement. There is still the issue of cusps.

All boundaries between houses (and between signs as well) are called **cusps**, and the challenge we face in dealing with cusps is that there is little consensus among astrologers as to what constitutes the actual boundary between one house and the next. There are no lines in the sky, of course, and though mathematics may be precise, real life is not. Where exactly does one house stop and the next begin?

The diagram below is a typical graphic that would appear on the printed chart form an astrologer might use, or on a printout from many astrological computer programs. It's basically the same graphic that's repeated throughout the book:

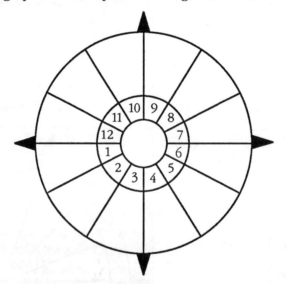

The outer circle represents the sphere of individual space. The twelve lines radiating outward from the center mark the boundaries of the twelve houses. The horizontal axis marks the beginning cusps of the 1st house, on the left or eastern edge of the horizon, and the 7th house, on the right or western edge. The vertical axis defines the cusps of the 10th house, above, and the 4th house, below. Arrows visually mark these angular areas. The other lines define the eight cusps of what are termed intermediate houses, 2nd/8th and 5th/11th (succeedent), 3rd/9th and 6th/12th (cadent).

Graphic Factors

Unlike signs of the zodiac, houses are not usually equal divisions of space/time, unless you happen to be using the Equal House System, where each house is defined as a 30° section of the whole circle. If, like the majority of astrologers, you use one of the quadrant systems, the houses often vary in the number of zodiacal degrees encompassed within their pie-shaped sections. Some houses may be 40°, others only 20°.

When the house sections and the sign sections don't coincide proportionately, one of the two levels has to be stretched and compressed to fit over the even sections of the other. You can either leave the signs in even proportion, thus graphing the houses to appear as uneven sections of space, or you can graph the houses as if they were even and alter the zodiac to fit.

In this country, most printed forms and computer chart printouts use the latter method—they make the houses look even and stretch or compress the zodiac. In many of these chart forms, the circle of the zodiac is not shown at all. Instead, the particular sign and degree of the zodiac that's aligned with each of the twelve house cusps are merely printed over the appropriate cusp. However, in the diagrams below, the signs are displayed as an outer ring so you can see the disproportionality:

Chart form with houses graphed equal, signs adjusted to fit

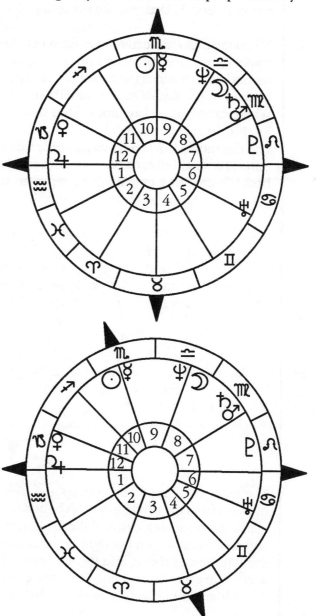

Chart form with signs graphed equal, Houses adjusted to fit

I prefer to see the charts I erect in the second form: where the belt of the zodiac is an outer circle of even proportions, each sign being equal size. Then the house cusps are drawn inside that circle radiating from the center of the chart, and they're drawn so that if they are unequal in size, they appear so. The main reason I choose this method of equal signs/unequal houses is that I go to some pains to draw in the interplanetary aspects, using different colors for the "soft" versus the "hard" angles, as well as differing thicknesses of lines to indicate the relative importance of each aspect: how close the orb is to exact, whether it's applying or separating, generational or personal, etc.

The overall aspect pattern in a natal chart is immensely revealing; it shows what amounts to a personal circuit diagram, indicating the natural "energy pathways" through which attitudes, perceptions, and emotions flow in an individual. Awareness of the aspect pattern adds extraordinary levels of precision and subtlety to the basics of planets, signs, and houses, helping the chart to truly come alive in the astrologer's mind. Since my primary attention during a session is on the person who's there as a client, I want to minimize the amount of energy I spend actually thinking about the chart. I like to be able to visually analyze the aspects and their patterns at a glance, without taking too many of my brain cells to construct the aspect circuitry in my mind. This is facilitated by using equal signs/unequal houses.

When the signs are drawn in even proportion, each aspect is a characteristic length—squares always look like 90° or one-quarter sections of the wheel, trines always 120° or one-third. Each aspect retains its natural visual integrity. If you use the other method—graphically equal houses with unequal signs—then a chart could easily have sextiles that looked like trines if the chart were sufficiently skewed in its proportions. Two squares in the same chart could be different lengths, and I don't like that idea. It disrupts the instantaneous visual comprehension of the aspect circuitry. Imagine how difficult it would be for an engineer to read the schematic diagram of an electronic circuit board if capacitors looked like resistors, or if transistors could appear to be transformers. Equal signs/unequal houses graphically standardizes all interplanetary aspects.

But finally it's a matter of personal preference. Either approach to visual charting is acceptable, and each has its champions among very good astrologers. The chart itself isn't altered in any real way; it's just the visual "look" of the chart that changes from one method to the other. In this book, we'll use equal houses/unequal signs in the graphics, because we want to focus on teaching houses rather than viewing aspects.

The Judgment of Planetary Position

To illustrate different approaches to the judgment of planetary position in the houses, let's look at a smaller segment of the whole chart, just the three sections comprising the 5th, 6th, and 7th houses:

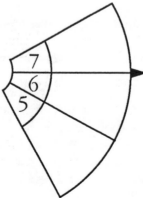

Now we've got only three houses to deal with. But are the pie-shaped sections actually the areas that correspond to those houses? Well, maybe yes, maybe no. First, let's see where the cusps are:

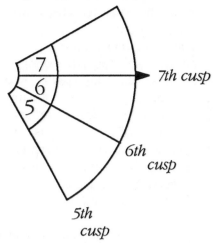

So far so good. If we placed a planet in this diagram so it would logically be considered occupying the 6th house, in which part of the diagram could it be positioned?

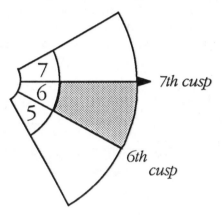

That's the **obvious** answer, right? That's how almost all computer programs locate the planets' house positions, and how many otherwise competent astrologers interpret planetary placement. If it appears to be located inside the pie-shaped section marked "6," then it's occupying the 6th house, right? Well, maybe yes, and maybe no...

The Importance of the Cusp

The problem is that in spite of the obvious indications of the chart form, in spite of the "visuals," the actual span of 6th house significance does not necessarily coincide with the cusps as they're defined and marked. I can hear some readers saying, "What? You mean the houses aren't where they appear to be? Then where are they, and why aren't they shown that way?" Unfortunately, as with so many other technical questions in astrology, the answers are not necessarily straightforward.

House cusps are not necessarily the firm boundaries they seem. They actually aren't "boundaries" at all in the classical sense, but instead represent the point of maximum emphasis for each house. In other words, the strongest point of house meaning is right at the cusp, and a planet located exactly on the cusp will express its functions through the relevant experiences of that house. So instead of seeing each house as a pie-shaped section, it might be better to think of houses as spokes radiating from a central hub.

The question still remains of how to consider the spaces between the spoke-like cusps. Where do we "draw the line" between one house and the next? And in fact, can firm distinctions be made at all, or do the houses tend to blend together, to flow from one to another between cuspal zones of strongest emphasis?

There are many differing opinions about this. Some astrologers contend that the midpoint of the space between two house cusps should be considered a relevant boundary for purposes of interpretive planetary placement. Others use a different system: if a planet is located anywhere from 5 degrees in the zodiac before a house cusp to within 5 degrees of the next cusp, it's located firmly in that particular house. Some use blended interpretations, combining the meanings of two adjacent houses, or moving back and forth in the interpretation as it suits them or seems sensible. Finally, many of us don't feel bound by any particular approach to location, preferring to let our perceptions of the person in question help us make the determination when there is a question as to which house a planet "belongs" (and there often is such a question...).

My own best opinion is as much a subjective matter as it is informed authority. The experience I've had with my own chart, with the charts of everyone I know and love, and with the charts of over 5,000 clients suggest to me that there is no single "correct" answer to the question of planetary house position. I've not found one system I could present as infallibly true or undeniably reliable. But my authorship of this textbook does allow the privilege of stating my opinion (even when I know there are other valid viewpoints), so here's what I use:

The "effective" realm of a house's interpretive significance can be considered to gradually phase in at some point prior to the cusp of the house. That much is certain. As to how far behind the cusp the house's symbolism becomes linked with a planet's function, I'd suggest as a rule of thumb that the signficance of the house begins somewhere in a zone located about one-quarter of the way back through the pie-shaped section preceding its cusp. This last quarter prior to the cusp would then be considered an area of gradually-building symbolism.

With that in mind, there are two relatively obvious conditions:

- **Placement exactly on or just after the cusp indicates that the planet is firmly wedded to the experiences of the given house.**

- **From 5° after the cusp through approximately three-quarters of the pie-shaped section that follows, a planet is still linked in meaning to the ordinary significance of the house.**

But in the last quarter prior to the next cusp, placement is largely a judgment call:

- **A planet located just before the cusp (within 5°) is best dealt with in either of two ways:**

   1) **Consider the planet in the house of the cusp it precedes;**
   2) **Interpret it as transitional, using both adjacent houses, either by moving back and forth between the delineations, or by synthetically blending the meanings of both houses.**

- **When the planet is clearly in the final quarter of visual space between one cusp and the next, but is more than 5° away from the latter cusp, it's up for grabs. It could be in either house, or both.**

The issue of planetary house placement is complicated not only by the varied opinions of astrologers concerning the meaning of cusps and the spaces between them, but is further aggravated by the fact that different house systems will pinpoint the cusps in different locations along the zodiac. (Refer to **Chapter Five: Technical versus Human Issues** for a more in-depth discussion of this problem.)

I want to reemphasize that we're dealing in very gray areas here. In spite of the wonderful research resulting from the painstaking efforts of careful statisticians such as Michel and Francoise Gauquelin (and others), astrology remains more an art than a pure statistical science. Our subject is Consciousness, especially as it pertains to individual development, and this does not lend itself well to bell curves or chi-square analyses. The clarification of anachronisms is an important dimension of modern astrology, but we need to remember the fact that "scientific" revelations can be just as seductively misleading as "archaic" traditions. As Pete Townshend said in the Who's song, *Won't Get Fooled Again*—"Out with the old boss; in with the new boss."

Our clients tell us as much about their charts as the charts do about them, and we should not underestimate the symbiotic relationship that exists between the chart and the person. When in doubt, keep in mind your best hunch about the chart, but go with what you see, or feel from the person.

What's important here is not the creation of a rigid formula, since there are far too many factors to consider for any precise technique, but rather reliance on a general rule:

**To locate the effective zone of any house,
visualize it rotated backwards roughly one-quarter
of the way into the previous house section.**

Diagrammed, the effective zone would look like this:

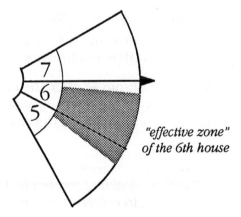

*"effective zone"
of the 6th house*

Let's look at an example containing planets. For simplicity, I've left out any listing of degrees of the zodiac for the house cusps or sign positions of the planets. Just presume that they're located in the zodiac according to the visual position. We'll deal with three houses—the 5th, 6th, and 7th—and four planets—Saturn, Venus, Mars, and the Moon.

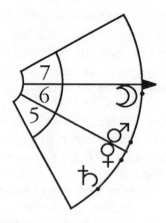

Where are the planets located? Which house does each occupy? If this were a typical computer-erected chart, the planets would be listed exactly as we see them: Saturn and Venus occupying the 5th, with Mars and the Moon in the 6th. But in all probability, that would be technically incorrect. If you had ordered computer-generated interpretive text along with the erection of your chart—what passes in astrological marketing circles as high-tech interpretations—you might be reading the wrong house interpretations for planets in your chart. Here's how I would place them:

Saturn is in the 5th house, just as it appears. Venus, however, is not. It is located just before the 6th house cusp, easily close enough to consider it in the house, though not as strong as it would be if located on the other side of the cusp. Since the planets are moving clockwise (meaning backwards) through the houses, making one complete circuit each day, Venus has already passed over the 6th house cusp and is now moving gradually toward the 5th. It's already peaked and is now beyond critical weighting.

We could give Venus transitional emphasis, considering it equally divided between 5th and 6th house themes. My suggestion is to begin by thinking of it as a 6th house planet, while remaining open to the possibility that it may operate through 5th house levels of experience also, especially if interaction with your client suggests that.

Mars, however, is definitely in the 6th, and its position just after the cusp (meaning it will pass over the cusp in the moments following birth) gives it stronger 6th house emphasis. Its relevance to 6th house issues is more critical than that of Venus.

The Moon is in the same relative position as Venus, one house further. It's interpreted in the 7th house. Once again, you might choose to subtly blend some 6th house meanings into your overall sense of the Moon's symbolic functioning.

[**NOTE:** In writing about this very important issue of house placement, I've tried to keep the discussion as simple as possible. In so doing, I've chosen to ignore certain technical considerations and specialized circumstances, which any sophisticated astrologer will no doubt understand and consider. However, even the generalized instructions I've given may overwhelm the beginner, who is already struggling to keep the basics clear and is now foundering under the weight of so many if's, and's, or but's. For those readers, let me assure you that experience will gradually burn off the fog. If (as my editor suggested) this is a bit much for you, just ignore it for the time being. However, if your interest in astrology is intense, you'll eventually need a working basis to resolve the issue of planetary placement, for it's central to the use of houses in interpretation. But take your time with it, as much as you need. Learn at your own speed.]

Unoccupied Houses

The house occupied by a given planet operates as the primary area of expression for that planet's psychological function. The various levels of experience linked with the house provide the arena for manifestation of the planetary urge.

But what of unoccupied houses, areas of experience containing no planets? Since there are only ten planets and twelve houses, there must be at least two unoccupied houses, and in most charts, given the uneven distribution of planets around the sphere of individual space, there will be more than two, occasionally as many as seven or eight.

Are these houses "empty," devoid of relevance in the person's experience of life? If the 7th house is unoccupied, does the individual have no partners? If the 2nd is empty, is there no money nor feelings of self-worth? If the 4th house has no planets, were there no parents, no family? If the 8th is empty, will there be no death? The answer in these and in all cases is **NO**, of course not. If this were how charts worked, then astrology would indeed be the foolishness many people believe it to be.

The houses symbolize the complete panorama of life experiences available to any individual. Though the areas occupied by planets do reveal a natural focus of energies into certain types of experience more than others, it's characteristic of human beings to round out their lives. Emphasis is not an absolute—it's relative, a little more here, a little less there. The notion of half a reality is foreign to human beings. Certainly there are damaged individuals who have constructed their worlds in dramatically incomplete ways, expanding some levels of experience to the total exclusion of others, but these are obviously cases where life has failed to fill the person, or vice versa.

Generally speaking, and especially in the spiritual ideal, human beings find ways to touch every major type of experience. We may not integrate every possibility, nor be expressively aware of every level of each type, but it's the biological tendency of our pattern-making nervous systems to experience life in wholes rather than pieces.

So really, there is no such thing as "empty space" in a natal chart. Every space is potentially vital and alive, waiting to be given form, to be filled with personal meaning.

Thus, astrology must incorporate systems to understand how apparently unoccupied houses are integrated into the scheme of planetary symbolism. Every space in a chart is meaningful, but a planet represents what might be thought of as "concentrated space" that has been densified and focused into a gravitational center—a microuniverse operating with relative autonomy within the all-encompassing patterns of the larger macrocosm. The zodiac is a metaphor for the macrocosm, and planets represent strong eddies within that collective flow—patterns within patterns. With the houses symbolizing the time-space matrix of an individual's personal orientation toward reality, we need to discover not merely where the eddies are located in that matrix, but also how these concentrated currents spread through the whole of an individual reality.

One way is through midpoints; another is Arabic Parts (see **Chapter Four: Other Ways to Emphasize Houses**). A third way is through the discovery of additional bodies in the solar system: asteroids, planetoids, etc. These newly-discovered bodies are increasingly being integrated into astrological symbolism. Thanks especially to feminist astrologers, we can now begin to fill the chart with many new symbols—**Chiron, Ceres, Pallas, Juno, Vesta, Eros, Psyche, Lilith, Toro, Sappho, Amor, Pandora, Icarus, Diana, Hidalgo, Urania**—the list is expanding more rapidly than we can comprehend. However, it isn't necessary to use these admittedly experimental urges to deal with "empty" houses. There are other more traditional ways, such as planetary rulership.

Rulership is one of the older and more archaic schemes still used in modern astrology. Its origins reflect a graceful symmetry that's been forced out of shape by the discoveries of the past two centuries. Originally, each planet was associated with one or two of the signs of the zodiac. The Sun was deemed the natural "ruler" of the sign Leo, which meant that the planetary function of the Sun had an unusually high degree of correspondence and similarity to the attitude represented by the sign Leo. The two were parallel in meaning, though different in application. The Moon was seen as the ruler of the adjacent sign Cancer, reflecting the same high degree of connection as Sun/Leo.

From those two fundamental associations, each planet progressively further outward in its orbit around the sun was linked with the adjacent signs on either side of Cancer/Leo. Mercury, the closest planet in orbit, was made the ruler of Gemini and Virgo, the first two signs on either side. Venus was then the ruler of next two, Taurus and Libra, Mars ruled Aries and Scorpio, Jupiter ruled of Pisces and Sagittarius, and Saturn ruled of Aquarius and Capricorn.

Astrology, like every human system, seeks to link together the symmetry of logic with the pragmatic ability to reflect reality. The concept of rulership provided a neat way to link the seven planets with the twelve signs. Mars did indeed have a striking correlation with Aries and Scorpio; Venus did indeed seem to reflect both Taurus and Libra. These associations were not merely pragmatic observations; they could also be justified on the basis of a "pure" idea.

The system of rulership survived unaltered for many centuries, promoting the Renaissance idea of nature operating through a graceful logic, in which it was humanity's unique duty to reveal that harmony through the senses and the brain.

The Emperor Has No Clothes

But this "divinely logical" human rationale was rocked by the discovery over the past two centuries of other planets and quasi-planetary bodies. We found out that in spite of the crude evidence of our senses, the solar system was not composed solely of the Earth and seven other bodies. The developing tools of astronomy helped us learn that other planets had moons of their own. We discovered the outer planets **Uranus, Neptune,** and **Pluto**. We found the asteroid belt and the four major asteroids **Ceres, Vesta, Pallas,** and **Juno**. Astronomers only recently discovered **Chiron**, a body too large to be classified as an asteroid, but too small for a typical planet.

These discoveries took the beautiful symmetry of planetary rulership and knocked it into a cocked hat. As each new discovery was made, astrologers comfortable with the old system made adjustments and compromises. Uranus was given co-rulership (with Saturn) over the sign Aquarius. Neptune was made the primary co-ruler (with Jupiter) of Pisces. Then Pluto was discovered, and astrologers began a debate concerning its co-rulership with Mars of the signs Aries and Scorpio. That debate—which planet rules which sign?—still goes on today.

As this information became available, astrologers struggled to create new rationales. Some said that since the Sun and Saturn had a natural linkage—the Sun being the inner limit of the solar system and Saturn the outer limit (at least in terms of our sensory perception)—then the trans-Saturnian planets Uranus, Neptune, and Pluto represented the beginning of a new repetition of the old order, in much the same way that octaves repeat themselves as one goes higher on the musical scale. In this scheme, the three outer planets were the "higher octave" expression of the first three inner planets. If the Sun is linked with Saturn, then Uranus is naturally linked with Mercury, Neptune with Venus, and Pluto with Mars. So Mars and Pluto should share the rulership of their respective two signs.

But if this were the case, why doesn't Uranus share the rulership of Virgo rather than Aquarius? Why doesn't Neptune share Libra rather than Pisces? And wouldn't such a scheme awkwardly require the existence of undiscovered planets to correlate with Jupiter and Saturn?

Criticisms such as these go on and on. It's no great challenge to pick apart the logic of astrologers seeking to maintain continuity between archaic understanding and current data. Astrology, like many other schemes of understanding, is an odd marriage between medieval and modern thinking. Don't look too closely or the whole system comes apart at the seams. But in some ways, this is a necessary trick of mastering human life: don't look too closely or the whole thing comes apart. It's like leprechauns dancing on the periphery of vision. Look at them directly and they vanish; look away, however, and they reappear, still dancing, still slightly out of reach.

We shouldn't be too harsh in criticizing astrology's attempts at logic, however. The history of humanity is chock full of what might be termed "divine foolishness." Some of our most precious beliefs would disintegrate before our eyes if not for the emotional force of human consensus to bind them together—faith in the dollar, belief in family, trust in government. Astrology is a system that investigates and codifies some of these collective beliefs. Its real subject is humanity, not the heavens.

So should we abandon the concept of rulership? Should we trash it with all the other anachronisms of dead cultures, discarding it like so much flotsam? Some astrologers lobby for doing just that.

But I think we should reconsider. There is still something relevant about the concept, still something useful and hopefully valid. Saturn clearly does have a connection with Capricorn (and the 10th house), and Mercury clearly does have a parallel to Gemini (and the 3rd house). The attitudes of Pisces (and the experiences of the 12th house) are obviously linked with the function of Neptune, etc. There's something here that works, something that makes sense, both intuitively and pragmatically, and making sense is a crucial part of what astrology is about, why it exists in the first place.

All logic aside, are these planetary rulerships simply the result of selective perception on the part of astrologers predisposed to see things in a certain way? Are they nothing more than self-fulfilling prophecies, unprovable, a system feeding on its own abstract presumptions? Perhaps, but I think no more here than with any other discipline. The same traps exists in other conceptual systems, from the theoretical sciences through the aesthetics of automotive design, all the way to something as mundane as plumbing. There are certain anomalies that exist when we explore a path that begins in the past and extends into the future. The pitfalls simply come with the territory.

The bottom line is this: **if it works, don't fix it**. And rulerships work. They give us a way of gleaning real information that seems relevant and valid. As we evolve a better system, we'll use it, but for the time being, this one works surprisingly well.

Here are the planet/sign rulerships I use in my own work:

Mars	**rules**	**Aries**
Venus	**rules**	**Taurus**
Mercury	**rules**	**Gemini**
Moon	**rules**	**Cancer**
Sun	**rules**	**Leo**
Mercury	**rules**	**Virgo**
Venus	**rules**	**Libra**
Pluto	**rules**	**Scorpio**
Jupiter	**rules**	**Sagittarius**
Saturn	**rules**	**Capricorn**
Uranus	**rules**	**Aquarius**
Neptune	**rules**	**Pisces**

Rulerships make possible two crucial interpretive abilities. First, they allow us to solve the puzzle of how to deal with unoccupied houses. That alone would justify their use. But second, and more important, they provide us with a method of linking the houses together into a matrix of active relationships, a multileveled tapestry of individual experience. Let's take these one at a time, and see how they work.

The Sign on the Cusp

As previously stated, there is no such thing as an empty house. It may be unoccupied by planets, but the experience signified by each house is so fundamental to human beings that it cannot possibly be omitted from life. Any one category of experience may be of greater or lesser importance in the overall scheme of a particular individual's life, but it will nonetheless be included. Therefore, we need techniques to understand how each person approaches the experience indicated by any house.

If a given house is unoccupied by planets, it's still aligned with a certain section of the zodiac. In other words, the house is linked with a sign. Generally speaking, the degree of the zodiac aligned with the cusp of the house determines the association. Using our diagram of the 5th, 6th, and 7th houses, this is how they would appear when graphed in "standard" form.

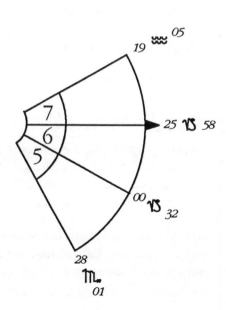

Let's assume that the three houses are all "empty," unoccupied by planets. The cusp of the 5th—strongest point of the house—is precisely aligned to the zodiac at 27° 01´ of the sign Scorpio. The 6th house cusp falls at the beginning of Capricorn, 0° 32´. The 7th house cusp is also in Capricorn, toward the end, at 25° 58´. Thus, the 5th house is aligned with Scorpio, the 6th and 7th houses with Capricorn, and somewhere in there is the "missing" sign of Sagittarius. How can we interpret the characteristic manner through which the experiences of these houses will be approached?

One method of interpreting "empty" areas is to presume that the experiences of the house reflect the values and attitudes of the sign located at the cusp. We could assume that the 7th house will tend to reflect the emotional attitudes of Capricorn—where partnerships are concerned, there is likely to be both caution and ambition, as well as a sensitivity to status. This individual would want to marry for stability or security, to a person who conforms to collective images of conservatism. There might be a tendency to form partnerships with someone who could function as a father figure, perhaps an older person (or even someone conspicuously younger—the important factor is difference in maturity). Marriage might be delayed until later in life; early marriages would tend to be unsuccessful or broken.

We could interpret the 5th house in exactly the same fashion. Here the experiences of the 5th will tend to reflect the emotional attitudes of Scorpio—personal creativity will tend to be intense, focused, magnetic, and oriented toward one-to-one relationships involving a sensitivity to power. There might be a deep compulsion toward competitive risks, an approach based on challenges and dares. And there could be something vaguely subterranean about the orientation toward intentional self-expression; the conscious persona would likely be both iron-willed and very controlled.

But there's a problem with that interpretation. It leaves out a missing factor, the sign Sagittarius. In this particular chart example, the cusp of the 5th aligns with the last 3° of Scorpio, with the 6th house cusp located at the beginning of Capricorn. The span of the 5th house is about 33°, and the entire 30° of Sagittarius are contained between the two cusps:

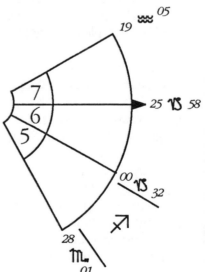

This is known as an **intercepted sign**, and if you use a quadrant house system, you'll see it often. It infers that 5th house experiences are both Scorpionic and Sagittarian. So we have to account for both attitudes regarding the experiences of the house.

There are numerous approaches to intercepted signs. Some astrologers believe that the sign on the cusp is dominant, while the intercepted sign indicates a more subtle meaning. Others contend that the cuspal sign is conscious, while the intercepted sign represents a more subconscious motif. Still other astrologers maintain that the intercepted sign represents attitudes that are psychologically confused, not well-integrated into the workings of personality, and therefore a source of difficulty. Relative weight could even depend on such subtle factors as the placement or aspects to the planetary ruler of an intercepted sign.

I recommend the first approach—cuspal dominance and intercepted subtlety. But that's affected very strongly by the exact position of the sign on the cusp. The last 2° of each sign seem to be transitional, as one sign fades and the next approaches. At approximately 28° 00′ of the sign Scorpio, we enter into the transitional area. From that point until the end of the sign, the significance of Scorpio is fading, blending with and gradually being displaced by Sagittarian orientations. At 0° 01′ of Sagittarius, all Scorpionic issues have vanished, and Sagittarian reality is completely effective.

[In fairness, I should note that there are widely divergent opinions in astrology about the cuspal zones of signs, just as there are differing opinions concerning houses. Some astrologers feel that the beginning of a sign is a transitional zone. Again, there are no lines in the sky, and everything here is open to interpretation...]

So when the cusp falls close to the end of one sign and the house also contains an intercepted sign, we need to make a judgment about the relative strengths of the two. If the cusp is at 27°, it's probable that the attitudes of the cuspal sign dominate the house, while the intercepted sign has more subtle message. If, however, the cusp falls at 29°, then the intercepted sign may actually require greater weight in the interpretation.

There are numerous other factors to take into consideration as well. If the cusp of the 4th house falls in early Scorpio, at say 2°, and the cusp of the 5th falls late in Scorpio, at 28° or 29°, then that's another factor to consider in making our judgment. In other words, if Scorpio clearly rules the 4th house, and the cusp of the 5th is well into the transitional zone, then we might consider interpreting the 4th house as Scorpionic and the 5th as completely Sagittarian in tone.

What if the only cusp in Scorpio is the 5th house cusp, located at 27°, with Sagittarius intercepted, but there are three or four planets in very early Sagittarius clearly in the strongest part of the 5th house? This kind of situation comes up with surprising regularity, and it might lead us to give most of the weight in our interpretative analysis to Sagittarian rather than Scorpionic attitudes.

Ultimately, there are no hard-and-fast rules, only general guidelines. I don't mean to hedge, and I certainly appreciate how confusing this may seem to a beginner. I could of course present my own opinions as if they were law, in the style of ancient texts, but that would hardly account for all the possibilities, and it would undoubtedly alienate many experienced professionals in the astrological community. The point is that these are difficult questions with no pat answers.

As always, there is no substitute for direct experience. Use what you've learned, and don't get stuck in the authority trap; it's alright not to be certain about something in the chart. If you're a beginner who's been roped into interpreting the chart of a friend, or even if you're a professional with decades of experience sitting with a client, go ahead and ask questions. The answers you get (and often the answers you don't get) can be very helpful in making your assessment of the ideal way the chart could operate, as well as the way the person is already operating.

Finally, if worse comes to worse, don't fry your brains trying to figure it out. The worst thing you can do is get stuck over some tiny piece of the chart. This is a disservice to you and to the person with whom you're working.

Charts are so full of information, much of which is apparent and clear, that you need to be willing to focus on what's obviously important first. Then as you develop a trusting dialogue, you can move back to the areas of doubt in your own mind, and you may well find they've been cleared by the process of interaction. Sometimes just being with a person for awhile can have a profound effect in making the chart clear to you.

So, to reiterate, one method for analyzing unoccupied houses is to determine which sign goes with the house, and to link the various levels of experience for that house with the emotional attitudes of the particular sign. This is fine as far as it goes, but it's limited in both scope and subtlety. Such a technique tends to discount the individual dynamics of a particular chart.

Happily for us, there's a better method: **the use of planetary rulers**.

Planetary Rulers in Interpretation

Let's use our diagram again, but this time we'll include the planets we were formerly using to illustrate the determination of occupied house positions. In addition, we'll list the sign position for each of the four planets:

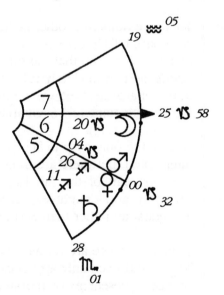

Here we see that Saturn is at 11° of Sagittarius, occupying the 5th house; Venus is at 26° of Sagittarius, occupying the 6th house; Mars is at 4° of Capricorn, very strong in the 6th, and the Moon is at 20° of Capricorn, located near the cusp of the 7th house.

These houses are no longer unoccupied; we have planets to link with each: Saturn in the 5th, Venus and Mars in the 6th, and the Moon in the 7th. But occupied or not, we can still add new dimensions to the depth of our interpretive potential by using the concept of zodiacal planetary rulers.

Look at the 7th house. Capricorn is the sign on the cusp, and therefore Capricornian attitudes shape the experiences of the 7th. But Saturn is the natural ruler of Capricorn, so we can say that although Saturn occupies the 5th house, it rules the 7th. This is technically known as accidental rulership. Because Saturn's natural association is with Capricorn, and also the experiences of the 10th house, its linkage here with the 7th house is called accidental. That's an unfortunate term, for there's nothing accidental about it. If this were your chart, you certainly wouldn't consider it an accident.

A better term would be **personal rulership**, since that's actually the distinction we're making. Saturn's position in Sagittarius is not especially personal, since everyone in your high school class also has Saturn in Sagittarius. Its house position, however, is personal to you, since that's determined by the exact moment and place of your birth. Even someone born on the same day won't necessarily have Capricorn setting on the western horizon. Thus, rulership of the 7th house by Saturn, through the intermediary of the sign Capricorn, is individual to you, as is its occupied position in the 5th.

This opens an extraordinary matrix of interpretive nuance. We now know that the Moon is in Capricorn in the 7th house, and that Saturn is in Sagittarius in the 5th house. This by itself allows a great deal of real interpreting. But we also know something else: that the 7th house and the 5th house are linked, tied together in experience through the functioning of the Sagittarian Saturn.

We see that the experiences of marriage and romance are connected, that making love is related to negotiation and compromise, that performance is linked with partnership, that financial speculations are tied to equality and commitment, and that all the different combinations of these experiences work through the functioning of Saturn: slow maturation by overcoming fears of inadequacy or rejection, terrific internal ambition, the drive to succeed by gradually desensitizing strong anxieties about failure.

Occupied versus Ruled Houses

We know that the 5th and 7th houses are Saturnian, because Saturn occupies the 5th and is the natural ruler of the sign on the cusp of the 7th. But how exactly are they connected? What is the dynamic existing between these two areas of experience? Are they equal? Is one more important than the other? Is there a cause/effect relationship?

What I want to offer here is pure, intuitive hunch. I can't in good conscience tell you that I know it because I've had so much experience, or talked to so many people about their charts, or seen it operate in my own life and the lives of those around me. What I'm going to suggest comes from a different level of my awareness.

Astrology is a reality system designed, on the one hand, to reflect and interpret human life as it already exists. It does that pretty well, all things considered. It can predict attitudes, characteristic approaches to experience, internal paradoxes and conflicts, patterns of behavior, and sometimes even literal events with an accuracy that is astonishing in the hands of someone skilled at interpretation and communication.

But explaining the way things are is not its primary application. More truly, astrology is a spiritual path, a *raja yoga*, a structural road map for any individual to follow in moving from what is—naturally, unconsciously, habitually—toward what is possible, toward what that person might become if tuned to the highest levels of his or her unique life process.

It's in that spirit that I want to offer this formula. Try it out for yourself; see if it feels right. If not, then by all means try another way. But if it works, then you have a technique for seeing and sensing your divinity that may lead you to a more fulfilled existence. This is not what you'd call an occult secret; it's just a simple technique for understanding how your life might be put together.

The occupied house represents an area of spiritual challenge in your life.

The ruled house is the area where you see the results.

In the astrological mode of perception, each of us comes to life with the same set of planetary functions. We're born at a certain moment in time and space, and based on the natal chart erected for that time/space moment, we can see that each function has its own natural set of attitudes or expectations regarding reality—that's what planets in signs tell us. We can also see that each function is linked with certain experiences in life—that's what the occupied house tells us.

What's difficult to understand about astrology is that although we begin with planets, they're a universal factor; we've all got the same basic functions as beings struggling to understand and operate our human machines. It isn't the planets themselves that are finally so important; it's the experiences we create while here on the Earth, and the way we feel and understand and process those experiences that is crucial.

We can let our experiences run our lives, dominating us even as we strive to select or create certain types over others. In that case, living is mainly unconscious, mainly automatic, mainly a function of our biology. I don't mean to denigrate that level of life. It's basic for all of us because we are animals, creatures of habit, comfort, and survival.

But we can also use the experiences we create and receive to change ourselves in special ways. There are many words to describe these special changes: conscious, awakened, grown up, truly mature, individuated, enlightened, transcended, realized. The words themselves don't do justice to our extraordinary possibilities, however rare they may seem. We can touch a little piece of the divinity that allows us to live, even while we continue to experience all the suffering and joy of human life.

Planets tell us what we've got to work with in constructing our human vehicles. Signs tell us the whole range of available human attitudes and emotional sets in perceiving how to go about interacting with Life. Aspects tell us where we came from, where we're headed, how we internally struggle and flow in expression.

But houses tell us about our lives on the Earth now. They reveal real experiences we may encounter, and those we seek to create. They talk to us about the fuel we can use to reach for our divinity, even as we strive to satisfy ordinary human hungers. The placement of planets in houses shows us where our challenges are—what experiences we have to master. Every planet occupying a house defines a level of challenge in real life—the challenge to understand what experience means, to comprehend how to approach each type of experience differently.

Life is complicated, multilayered, with all its experiences interwoven. Even in the best of times, it's difficult to tell whether or not we're really responding to the challenge well, in a way that's correct for our particular spiritual path. We are often simply too involved in our lives, too attached to see clearly. How are we to know if a given pattern of experience will lead to Heaven or to Hell?—not in the religious sense, but here and now, in real life. How are we to judge whether we're setting ourselves up for fulfillment or failure when these are so often interchangeable? What looks like victory can lead to defeat, and equally, some defeats are essential to pave the way for ultimate victory.

How often have we heard someone say, "It was the worst thing that ever happened to me, but it was the point where I realized how I needed to change, and it's lead me to the fulfillment I'm experiencing now." Given life's awesome paradoxes, given that we so frequently can't trust our immediate judgments, how do we know if we're on the right track, moving on our own path toward human fulfillment and divine revelation?

In my system, the challenges of our lives are contained within the occupied houses. You move into these realms of experience using your best wisdom—both head and heart, gut and intuition—about the planetary or psychic urges you are likely to express through specific areas. And obviously, like everyone, you hope for the best. You hope for joy and happiness and fulfillment and success and all the good things in life. But whether or not you have them, whether you are happy or sad, ecstatic or depressed, hopeful or hopeless, don't judge the validity of your living by experiences of the challenge areas.

In other words, rather than assessing your experience directly through the occupied houses, judge instead by an examination of what's happening in your ruled houses.

If you're satisfied or even moderately fulfilled in the experiences of a ruled house, then you're addressing the challenge of the occupied house well. Even when you're getting the stuffing beaten out of you in the occupied house, if you're doing OK in the ruled house, then you're moving correctly on your path. You're on the right track. Conversely, if the experience in an occupied house is all peaches and cream, but you're struggling terribly in the ruled area, then you've lost touch with yourself. Something's gone wrong. Change your approach to living in the challenge area—the occupied house.

Ruled houses are the barometer of spiritual progress in the challenge experiences indicated by occupied houses.

Is It Really So Simple?

Well, in theory it's simple. Naturally, it becomes more complicated when applied to real life. Every house is ruled by a planet, but some houses are also occupied by one or more planets. This means that every house is a result area, a barometer, but some houses are also challenge areas. It can get pretty sticky when you're trying to interpret experience, separating the challenge mode from the result mode within the same house. Doing this well requires a steadily evolving awareness of the network of different functions, attitudes, and experiences that make up your life. We have to become sensitive to our machinery without impatiently ripping it apart.

You can learn to feel the planetary principles operating within your psyche. When you experience fear, recognize it as a Saturnian function. But recognize equally that your ability to be stable and productive also come from the urging within you of what we call Saturn. When you long for pleasure or the connectedness of personal love, see Venus in operation. And learn also that when you are glutted with indolence, your inner Venus has assumed too great a measure of importance in your life. When there is a sudden upheaval, feel the Uranian connection. If something vanishes mysteriously, go to the inner level where your Neptune is functioning. And most of all, learn to feel the shining of your Sun. What does it feel like to be connected to a cosmic energy source? What does it feel like when you disconnect?

You can become sensitized to the attitudes of the signs, learning to recognize which are positive (or life-affirming) for you and which are negative (or life-destructive). Certainly the Arian attitude of ardent spontaneity is life-affirming, but keep in mind that the backside of that attitude is reckless abandon, which may be somewhat more questionable as an approach to life. Intensely focused emotions penetrating to the heart of another person is positively Scorpionic, but the backside—refusal to let go, and revenge motivation—is life-destroying. The Leonine attitude of dignity in expression is a wonderful quality each of us needs, but we have to recognize when the shadow aspect of huffy egotism and condescension have kicked in. The Piscean attitudes of abiding faith and willingness to believe can flip over into fanaticism, irrationality, and escapism. Being pragmatic and doing what is necessary are admirable Capricornic traits, but it's all too short a trip to insensitivity and brutish coldness.

You can become aware of the different levels of experience for each house, sensing the parallels and connections between the levels. Is having money really a parallel experience to feeling good about oneself (2nd house)? Are sexual union and ego-death linked (8th house)? Is it true that isolation is tied to fantasy, which is also linked to the possibility of pure intuition (12th house)? Surely disease is connected to self-discipline and purification, but might it also be influenced by humility and service (6th house)? Is travel analogous to philosophy (9th house)? Can social ideals actually run parallel to your experience of being loved (11th house)? Are cultural recognition and prestige tied to spiritual responsibility (10th house)? If you follow the path of astrology, you will have to consider these questions, and you'll to learn when you're operating exclusively out of one level of experience and should shift into another level of the same area to balance yourself and restore psychic homeostasis.

The trick here is not to analyze yourself to death, carrying around an ephemeris and thinking about the factors in your chart. Don't simply break yourself into a thousand parts and pieces—don't treat yourself like a machine. If that sorry state befalls us, as it often does with disturbing predictability, we lose our individuality, our humanity, and—ultimately—we lose our divinity, our connection to the Mystery of Life, and we are in Big Trouble, with a capital B and a capital T.

No, Life is to be lived fully, and the trick involves learning to recognize and feel these various components of personality in all their amazing interactive relatedness while still experiencing ourselves as whole, still able to feel ourselves as living, breathing creatures, both earthly animals and spiritual beings, uniquely individual but connected to others beyond ourselves in larger wholes of life. And that is one hell of a trick.

In our example, the Moon occupies the 7th, but Saturn rules the 7th while occupying the 5th. For the 7th house then, the Moon is the function associated with a spiritual challenge, while Saturn's function is linked with the results of a 5th house challenge.

The challenge is to be responsive to your own or other people's needs toward creating stable, enduring partnerships, to anchor your emotional experience in the equality you share with another. The result level of 7th house experience is to judge how well you're coping with fears of rejection around romance, sexual performance, or other conscious risks by examining how you feel about the responsible durability of your relationships.

You might be very dissatisfied with the fulfillment of your needs through partnership, and yet still be feeling fine about the responsibility aspect of those same relationships. That would indicate that you're responding well to your 5th house Saturn challenge. Conversely, you may be getting your needs met wonderfully through your partnerships, experiencing security and safety, but at the same time feeling restrained or dominated by your partner—your needs are fulfilled, but the structure is all wrong. This would indicate that you must make a conscious change in your approach to personal risk, to romance, or to sexual performance, for the result level of the 7th (structure) is being experienced negatively, indicating that you're off course in the 5th house challenge.

The challenge/result system is complicated by other factors as well.

Mutual reception is a prime example. This describes a situation in which two planets occupy houses that are ruled by each other. In my own chart, the Sun is in the 10th house in Scorpio, and it rules the 7th house, which has Leo at the cusp. Pluto occupies the 7th house in Leo, and it rules the 10th. To make matters worse, the two planets are in square to one another. This makes application of the value system more textured than usual. Ambition, career and social stature are the result experiences for the Plutonian challenge around one-to-one relationships, and yet those same partnerships are the result area for the Solar challenge of ambition and cultural stature. Every time one changes, it produces radical shifts in the other, but it's been very difficult to gracefully guide either level of my experience.

When a planet is in its natural sign, it often occupies the same house it rules. In this case, the challenge and result areas are the same. It's the one instance where you must judge your spiritual progress directly through the experience of your challenge level.

If Venus is in Libra, occupying the 3rd, with Libra on the cusp of that house, then the spiritual challenge is to experience satisfaction, receptivity, and enjoyment in the areas of communication, thinking, and concrete learning—the use of your rational mind. But since Venus not only occupies the 3rd house but also rules it, then how well you're doing with the challenge can only be judged directly through the experience itself. This creates a kind of blind spot in the psyche, a tendency toward extremes of expression. You may nearly bloat yourself with the pleasures of mentality before you realize you're abusing yourself and not responding to the spiritual challenge in a balanced way. You may equally lose track of the importance of aesthetic mental enjoyment without fully realizing that something is lacking. Anytime a planet occupies the same house it rules, there is an exaggerated sense of importance for that urge in those levels of experience. It provides a special focus, standing out in the chart, separate from the matrix of other planets and houses.

So, no, it's not that simple. But try it out with your chart or that of someone you know or love. See if it works, check out how often, and judge for yourself whether this is a good way to interpret charts.

Other Ways to Emphasize Houses

Thus far, we've focused on the emphasis of houses exclusively through their linkage with planets, either by the planet's actual placement in the house, or through the intermediary of zodiacal signs and the resulting planet/house association. These two methods of house emphasis are the bread-and-butter of interpretation, approaches used by almost every astrologer with each chart. Certainly our astrological talents can evolve, increasing in sensitivity and sophistication as we learn an increasingly broad range of techniques, but what I've discussed are the basics, the solid foundation that supports everything else.

However, there are many other ways specific houses could be emphasized in an individual's chart (and more importantly, in his or her life) than just by planetary occupation or rulership. I want to discuss three of these: **midpoints**, **Arabic Parts**, and **planetary patterns**.

Midpoints

Midpoints are a significant development of 20th-century astrology. There is, in fact, a whole school of astrology originated by the Germans Witte and Ebertin built almost entirely around midpoints and hard aspects. In this tradition, houses are often excluded entirely, although I find it difficult to believe that any professional astrologer worth his salt would omit them in any comprehensive overview.

The theory of midpoints is beautifully simple. Imagine two points, *A* and *B*, located anywhere on a circle:

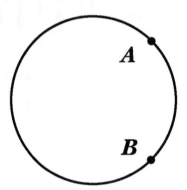

We can then draw a line through the center of the circle located an equal distance from both points, which is to say, every point on that line, no matter how far we extend it, is the same distance from either *A* or *B*. [Please bear in mind that the points could be located anywhere on the circle, and the equidistant line through the circle's center could have any "tilt." My use of a horizontal orientation is purely a matter of convenience.]

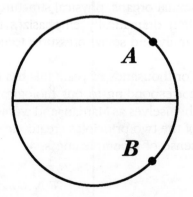

Where the line crosses the circumference of the circle, two new points are defined, which we'll name *Y* and *X:*

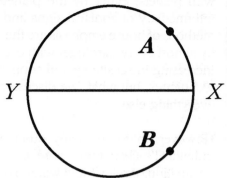

If *A* and *B* are considered not simply as two points, but instead as a relationship *(AB)*, then *X* and *Y* represent the parts of the circle where the significance of *AB* (the meaning, whatever it happens to be...) is most naturally released. The nearer of the two points *(X)* is considered the **evolutionary midpoint**—the goal, where *AB* is headed toward release. The further of the two *(Y)*, is the **devolutionary midpoint**—the source, where the meaning originates.

This modest geometrical theorem has quietly provoked a revolution in astrology, for it translates perfectly into the form of our system. If we rename points *A* and *B*, instead calling them Venus and Mars, and if we put in house cusps, then presto, we're looking at an astrological chart!

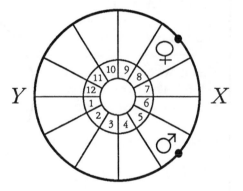

Mars/Venus:
The Midpoint
of Intimacy

Venus and Mars—considered together—form the "dyad of intimacy." As a paired set of symbols, they represent the total lover within each of us: the feminine or magnetic aspect of self, called the **anima** or **inner woman**; and the masculine or penetrating aspect of self, called the **animus** or **inner man**. Nature gives one of these qualities superficial dominance by making us genetically male or female, endowing our bodies with the sexual organs, physical structure, and hormonal chemistry of one or the other. Culture then dramatically emphasizes this one quality's psychological domination through family and social pressures to conform to one's "biological role."

For thousands of years this has meant that most of us identify with the planetary urge corresponding to our biological organs and cultural roles: men tend to experience themselves as Martian, and women as Venusian. The tendency to identify with only one of the two principles creates an intolerable imbalance within our personalities, a deep sense of incompleteness.

Since the nonemphasized planet is sublimated by repression or emotional dissociation from self-awareness, it becomes an unconscious aspect of self, rather like a shadow self lost within the psyche—misplaced but not forgotten. Men long to be connected to Venus, and women long to be connected with Mars.

Unfortunately, we've attempted to work out the balance by forcing each sex to project its own inner shadow aspect upon members of the opposite sex, seeing them as the "missing quality." At least that's how it's supposed to work heterosexually. Actually, it works precisely the same way no matter what an individual's "sexual preference" may be. If we identify with the male aspect of self, we look for another person in whom we can find evidence of our missing female aspect. If we identify with femaleness, we look for someone who embodies male qualities. To be heterosexual means simply that you look for your lost quality in someone whose physical sex is opposite your own.

But whether you are heterosexual, homosexual, bisexual, pansexual, or even asexual, it still works the same way: we seek to find someone whose image in our eyes brings us into contact with the lost half of our intimate self.

At least part of this awesome problem in human intimacy is natural. Mother Nature has seen fit to give us these polarized bodies with one or the other type of form and chemistry, so we can presume it's in the scheme of things for us to have to grapple with the feeling of incompleteness, usually by seeking union with others outside ourselves. Nature is cunning in the ways she insures the continuation of the species.

But much of the incomplete feeling and the projection of intimate roles onto others is a tyranny of culture. What nature created as a subtle paradox, civilization turned into an agonizing prison of constraint and expectation. Thankfully, we are finally beginning to break out of these prisons. Perhaps at some point we will destroy the prison itself.

This is where astrology comes into the picture, where the natal chart can often be helpful. The two midpoints of the Mars/Venus dyad show where we come from and where we're headed on the path toward restoration of our intimate wholeness.

The Mars/Venus Midpoint in Interpretation

In our example, Venus is positioned well into the 8th house, Mars far into the 5th:

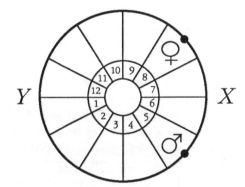

We can presume that this individual would have a pronounced sexual orientation in the approach to intimacy, since the 5th and the 8th are both sexual areas of experience. If the person were male, we could assume that he would identify with the role of the courtier, the swashbuckler, the performance artist, considering it his natural birthright to please, seduce or conquer his feminine consort (5th house Mars). He would tend to look for another person who embodied the qualities of intense receptivity, someone whose femaleness was mysterious and compelling, and perhaps slightly dangerous (as symbolized by his 8th house Venus). If the individual were female, we could assume that the situation would be reversed.

This is the "classical" approach, not only in astrological interpretation, but in life as well. Often, however, it doesn't work out. We hope to remember and complete our intimate wholeness by finding "Mr. or Ms. Right." And when we do—or think we have—we are ecstatic. Romance blossoms. Everybody gets wet.

But what happens if Mr. or Ms. Right tires of having to provide our sense of intimate wholeness? What happens if he or she leaves? Most of us go right back into a state of incompleteness again.

Ideally, each intimate relationship allows us the opportunity to gradually assimilate the qualities of our beloved so that we eventually regain our intimate integrity. Then we relate to our partner as a person, not just a psychic screen upon which to project our shadows. But there's no insurance that this will occur, and too often it doesn't.

Many people move from one intimate relationship to another, perpetually hunting for the same perfect archetype of femaleness or maleness without realizing what's going on. They become mired in the stage of fantasy projection onto others, continually picking the wrong people. Worst of all, they don't experience reunion with themselves through loving another human being.

But every natal chart offers insights into this perplexing issue through the house positions of planetary midpoints.

Mars/Venus: Evolution and Devolution

In the example, the devolutionary midpoint of the Venus/Mars dyad coincides with the Ascendant, the strongest point of the 1st house, while the evolutionary midpoint falls on the Descendant, strongest point of the 7th house. This tells us two important things.

First, the sense of being a self-aware individual, free to act spontaneously, beholden to no one, is linked with the person's evolutionary past. That's the source of wholeness. If this individual asked us how to reconcile or rediscover intimate wholeness, we could point to the Ascendant, emphasizing independent self-awareness and spontaneous activity as a key to getting in touch with the roots of intimacy.

Second, negotiation and compromise, experiences that lead to committed partnership, is linked with his or her evolutionary future. We could emphasize the importance of seeing others as equals, the necessity of establishing working relationships based on cooperation. Finally, and bottom line, we would underscore the significance of true commitment. Conscious development of 7th house qualities can help this individual shift out of the insecurity of sexual romances as a basis for intimacy, toward a restoration of intimate wholeness, health, and fulfillment.

The evolutionary midpoint would reveal the same healing quality no matter which house it happened to occupy. If in the 10th, we would presume that the development of career, social stature, and a contribution to the world through personal maturity would facilitate intimate wholeness.

If a client with Venus in the 7th and Mars in the 12th came to you to discuss painful problems in relationship—arguments, disharmony, confusion, frustrated desires—you could look at the chart, find the Venus/Mars midpoint in the 10th, and gradually shift the conversation toward a discussion of career and responsibility, helping your client see the connection between these seemingly unrelated areas of experience. That would be good astrology, and good therapy as well.

If the midpoint were in the 12th house, you could discuss the importance of conscious retreats from the hustle of everyday life. You could teach visualization techniques of creative fantasy. You could talk over the possibility of entering a service discipline, such as helping at a foster home or volunteering time at a crisis center.

No matter where the Venus/Mars midpoint fell, the house position would reveal experiences and techniques for rediscovering intimate wholeness.

There are **45 planetary pairs** (Sun/Moon, Sun/Mercury, Moon/Mercury, etc.). Certain pairs are more obviously relevant than others (Sun/Moon, Venus/Mars, Jupiter/Saturn), and each of us will be tuned more to some than to others because of our own interests and temperaments. Keep in mind that you don't have to fill the chart with midpoints to be a good astrologer, but remember equally that these midpoints can be linked with houses in a way that enhances interpretation and improves the effectiveness of your own searches for self-understanding or the counsel you provide others.

Arabic Parts

The Arabic Parts are so named because of their origins a millennia ago in the Middle East. Astrologers there devised a system for exploring the relationships of points in the natal chart based on the analog equation: *A is to B as C is to D,* or, in more traditional mathematical form: *A : B = C : D.*

Any pair of points in the horoscope can be seen as a dyadic relationship, and the arc between them in degrees measures their relatedness. In our previous example, Venus and Mars were separated by an arc of 90°, with Venus further in the zodiac than Mars. This means that their relationship is entering the First Quarter Phase. If you pick out another point in the chart, say the Ascendant, since that is so often used in the Arabic system, then you can create a correspondence with Mars. So far the analog would look like this: **Mars : Venus = Ascendant : ?**, or stated in English, **Mars is to Venus as the Ascendant is to what point in the zodiac?** The "Part" is the imaginary point that corresponds to Venus' relationship to Mars. If Venus is 90° ahead of Mars, then our Part is 90° ahead of the Ascendant. The point is conventionally given a name, usually called "The Part of **Something.**"

The best-known and most often-used of the hundreds of Arabic Parts is called "**The Part of Fortune.**" It links the Sun/Moon phase relationship in the chart with the Ascendant. The analog is: **Sun : Moon = Ascendant : Part of Fortune**. In essence, what we're doing is calculating the phase arc between the Sun and Moon, then asking, "If we moved the Sun and Moon together as a unit and placed the Sun exactly on the Ascendant, where then would the Moon be?"

Philosophically, the Soli-Lunar relationship is an important indicator of fundamental energies, with lunar emotions mediating or "softening" the power of solar life-purpose, showing how cosmological energy is likely to be played out in the earthly realm of existence. Linking the Sun with the Ascendant establishes a relationship between basic life-energy and dawning self-awareness. This shows how raw cosmic power is given a uniquely personal meaning. The Part of Fortune then represents the product of these two different relationships, symbolizing the release of the cosmic power that fuels individual purpose in the most personal and satisfying manner.

As with every symbolic level in astrology, there are many ways to use the Part of Fortune.

Aspects to natal planets reveal subtle connections to other layers of our psyches. If Venus is conjuncting the Part of Fortune, it reveals that personal love is especially important in the integration of cosmic purpose and individual fulfillment. If Jupiter opposes the Part, socialization is similarly emphasized.

The specific zodiacal degree occupied by the Part of Fortune can be interpreted through the Sabian Symbols, giving a more poetic feeling for the personal meaning of the point.

Transits or progressions over the Part could show evolutionary triggers we might otherwise miss if we used only the natal positions of planets. Every time the Part is activated in transit, it subtly activates three of the chart's most important positions—Sun, Moon, and Ascendant.

In chart comparisons, conjunctions or oppositions from planets or angles in one person's chart to the Part of Fortune in the other's can reveal subtle interpersonal sensitivities—attractions and repulsions in the inner chemistry between two people.

All these techniques can elevate a standard interpretive understanding to a new level of sophistication and comprehension. But most important for our purposes here is the house position. The house occupied by the Part of Fortune reveals specific experiences that offer a way to integrate cosmic purpose with individual fulfillment.

If the Part of Fortune is in the 10th house, you're probably dealing with someone born during the last-quarter Moon, and the life reflects a concern with movement from the personal toward the collective, often through issues of career and responsibility in group settings. If the Part is in the 4th house, it's a first-quarter Moon natally, and the individual is pushing to establish a personal center in life, often through experiences surrounding home and family.

All the Parts can be understood in this fashion, and it's an important and basic way of using the Arabic system.

Planetary Patterns

Both methods discussed so far in this section have relied upon the precise calculation of mathematical points of significance, based on relationships between significant natal pairs. However, you needn't have a fancy astrological computer program or spend hours hunched over a sheet full of scribbled calculations. Sometimes it's enough just to look at the chart—don't calculate anything, just look at it.

Look at the way the planets are grouped around the wheel. You needn't pay particular attention to the individual planets themselves. Get a feel for the Big Picture. Do the planets as a group form any recognizable patterns?

Many decades ago, Marc Edmund Jones was the originator of an interpretive technique based on seven **planetary patterns**, each of which is easily recognizable, and all of which you'll see over and over if you have access to a sufficient number of charts.

Each of the seven types corresponds to a definite psychological orientation, and in interpretation, when the pattern is distinct or emphatic, it can carry as much weight as other more obviously important symbolic factors like the Sun or Moon surrounding the formation and expression of individual personality.

Planetary patterns are defined and interpreted through the structure of the houses—hemispheres, quadrants, and the twelve separate areas of experience. They can be used wihout specific reference to particular planets or signs, although naturally any additional references will extend the interpretive scope and subtlety, since this technique, like most in astrology, is best used in combination with other indicators.

The Myth of Stereotypes

In fact, one of the main criticisms of planetary patterns is that individuals do not always obviously reflect the "personality types" of their patterns. This is often the case, but it is no less true with other astrological levels. For instance, many people do not obviously act like their Sun signs are "supposed" to. But that's a not a question of types, but rather of stereotypes. Consider nationality: are all Scandinavians blonde? are all Italians dark?

Typology on any level carries its own built-in pitfalls. It is easy to overgeneralize, and in the wrong hands, such systems can become downright vicious, fraught with the bias of "good-versus-bad" moral judgments. Negative bias becomes codified as group myth. Individuality vanishes under a haze of fearful expectations, and innocent people suffer.

This is one reason used to justify suspicion of astrology as a system, that its information is too general, too easily misunderstood, and too often misused. Just as Sicilians suffer the myth that they are all Mafiosi, people with the Sun in Scorpio suffer the myth that they are secretive and vindictive. Just as Poles are ridiculed in bad jokes, Piscean Sun people are labeled "wishy-washy," Librans are accused of "laziness," and Virgoans are branded "dull."

It's undeniable that in a system like astrology, abuse is easily possible. But this should be blamed not on the system, but instead on the immaturity and blindness of some people who happen to use it.

Human beings are not naturally one-dimensional. Good systems of typology should not be one-dimensional either. A creative astrologer realizes that our system has many facets to aid in the exploration of human potential. The line between comprehensive understanding and unnecessary complication is sometimes a fine one, but in general, the abundance of different levels in astrological typology provide an opportunity for greater comprehension.

This is part of the usefulness of learning planetary patterns. They constitute another alternative in the approach to understanding. But since it's a two-way street, we need to remember to use them in harmony with other indicators in the system. Coherent synthesis is the challenge.

The following seven pages contain a brief introduction to the seven different patterns—their names, characteristics, and psychological tones, with an example illustration for each type.

Bundle Type

The Bundle Pattern occurs when all ten planets are grouped together within one-third of the circle, with two-thirds unoccupied. Ideally, a "perfect" Bundle would contain all ten planets within one of the four quadrants, but this occurs very rarely. Hopefully, all the planets are contained within one hemisphere, leaving the opposite half "empty." [Keep in mind that "empty" is used here only as a reference to the placement of the ten major bodies. Actually, there's no such thing as "empty space" in a chart—every space is vital and alive.] When the "tilt" of the Bundle is such that there are planets in two (or even three) hemispheres, the strength is somewhat diminished.

This is the case in our example, where the bulk of planets are in the 4th quadrant (self-actualizing and social). Visually, it appears at first glance that the lower hemisphere is empty. But keep in mind that the strongest point of a house is the cusp, and it becomes clear that one planet would be interpreted as below the horizon in the 1st house.

The Bundle personality is very focused into a set range of life-experience, usually the span covered by only three or four houses. There is a narrowness here, as if the individual has constructed his or her world with a limited span of conscious awareness, expanding it so that all reality is interpreted through only certain types of experience. He or she may be astonishingly subtle or sensitive in those house areas occupied by the Bundle of planets, but simultaneously, be largely insensitive or blind to the true implications of the unoccupied sections of experience. The person is aware of the unoccupied houses, but their experiences might be somewhat flat or two-dimensional.

This person may empathize very strongly with people who share a similar focus, but be curiously aloof and distant with everyone in other situations, unconcerned and un-appreciative. This is a very special-purpose life. The individual has a high degree of intentionality (or compulsion), and the personality should radiate a recognizable intensity, almost a sense of urgency in whatever psychological features the chart reveals.

In much the same way that Sun signs are not always recognizable in the overt personality, the Bundle personality may at times mask its concentration. For instance, a Bundle in the fourth quadrant with a stellium in the 12th could correlate with a disturbing paradox: what is being focused is the experience of unfocusing. In that case, we would need to shift our semantic: the experience of unfocusing, unhinging from the ordinary self is being amplified, as if raised to a higher power.

In our example, the Bundle is focused into the 4th quadrant, so this individual is driven from within to experience life within a larger collective. The midpoint of the occupied section falls in the transitional zone between the 10th and 11th houses, so we could expect a psychological focus on career, and especially on group involvement. Most judgments will be made on the basis of group acceptance and cultural standards, and for this person, the notion that anyone could function from within a more self-contained sense of ego-values might be a difficult idea to entertain.

Bowl Type
The Bowl Pattern is similar to the Bundle, but here the geometry is more polar, since the chart is now half-and-half rather than one-third/two-thirds. In the ideal Bowl, all ten planets occupy one hemisphere, in an even distribution covering the span, with the opposite hemisphere totally unoccupied.

At least five consecutive houses must be devoid of planets for the pattern to qualify as a Bowl. This is the case in our example, since the planet at the nadir is actually in the 4th house, leaving houses 5-9 empty.

The psychological tone of the Bowl type reflects the age-old Zen riddle: Is the glass half empty or half full? The personality is not quite rounded, not complete unto itself. There's a strong awareness of self, but an equally strong sense that something may be missing. Searching for that missing something can be either a joyful quest or a frustrating need. Where the Bundle was characterized by extremely personal focus—the satisfactions of self-interest backed with the blindness of narcissism—the Bowl type is not so lodged within the self—blessed with heightened awareness, but burdened by incompleteness.

Often, the Bowl personality seeks completion by attracting people into his or her life who embody the half of experience that is more difficult to understand, and there may be a particular fascination with those individuals. There may be unconscious hesitation about moving into the empty hemisphere. On the other hand, when such movement occurs, it is exhilarating, an adventure into new territory.

Our example shows an extremely self-generating individual who presumes that you get where you're going in life through the quality of your own efforts. It's not who you know that counts, it's what you do (the 1st house is the midpoint of the occupied half).

And yet there is a curious awareness that somehow relationships are more important than he or she may fully realize, because time and again, obstacles in the path of fulfillment won't respond to simple action or pressure. In fact, they may not give way no matter how much this person pushes at them, for the obstacles will tend to emanate from the area of relationship rather than direct self-expression.

That might create a tentative decision to explore relatedness through commitment and cooperation, probably by connecting with someone who is very relationship-oriented or other-directed (since the midpoint of the empty half coincides with the Descendant, inferring that the 7th house is the critical area of experience).

The partner tends to take care of the relationship itself, whereas the Bowl person uses the energy to round out reality while pushing ahead assertively, always in the lead position, pulling the partnership along behind.

Locomotive Type

The Locomotive Pattern is so named because of its inverted similarity to the wheel on a locomotive engine, which has a weighted section on one-third of its surface. This is the reverse of the Bundle pattern; here we see a chart two-thirds full and one-third empty. The requirements for a Locomotive are that the planets should be evenly distributed through the occupied section, and there should be no less than three nor more than four consecutive unoccupied houses (more than four and the chart shifts into the Bowl pattern; less than three and the Splash type emerges…).

The Bundle was one-third full, and therefore focused. The Bowl was half full, and subsequently polarized in awareness. The Locomotive is two-thirds full, so the individual is closing in on rounded experience, squeezing the unoccupied space, moving from what he or she already understands toward what is less well known.

The pattern corresponds to competence, strategy, and a powerful psychological drive toward achievement, all of which are qualities held in high esteem in a culture such as ours that values personal ambition. On the other hand, this person may be fairly calculating about using others. Where the Bundle type is sometimes unaware of different perspectives, the Locomotive type can see other views, but may not care if they conflict with his or her strong goal-orientation. This can result in climbing the mountain over the backs of others.

Of all seven types, this is the only one that dramatically emphasizes the unoccupied houses. In fact, the nearer midpoint of the two planets at the outer edges of the occupied section is an especially sensitive point, and the unoccupied house of that midpoint reveals the "solution" to the life challenge, the bull's-eye of spiritual ambition.

In the example, the cusp of the 4th house is the life-goal. This person already understands what it means to live in the larger world of social relationships and cultural involvement. Collective responsibility and its rewards come naturally. What is desired, however, is subjective centeredness, something that can only be discovered in the realm of personal security—the family of origin with its lasting childhood imprints, or the later family created in adult life, with its experience of being both protective and protected.

There may be convolutions around personal security or the sense of belonging, although the pattern alone won't reveal the exact form. Since ambition is this individual's strong suit, he or she may work in a profession that provides products for the home or family services. Being an architect or an interior decorator may help address the issue. Even working out of the home rather than going to an office is a possible expression.

Creating a private world is the challenge, a place where the self can relax. Hopefully, this will unfold like the grain of sand in the oyster—a frustration that is gradually coated until it is finally transformed into a pearl.

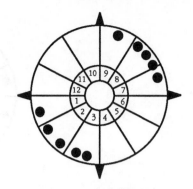

Seesaw Type

The Seesaw Pattern is characterized by two groups of planets opposite each other, with at least two empty houses on either side between the groups. If there's only one empty house on one of the sides, then the chart is probably a Locomotive, but as with all these patterns, the visual feel is as important as the technical definitions.

Ideally, the groupings contain five planets on either side, with the center of the two bundles in nearly perfect opposition, and no empty houses within the span of planets in either group. The perfect Seesaw would be contained in two opposite quadrants, although this is rare in actual practice. More often, each bundle covers two quadrants, so the two-sidedness applies to either upper/lower or eastern/western hemispheres.

The psychology of the Seesaw is much like the sign Libra, dualistic in experience, with a tendency to see two sides to every question. There is often indecision here, and a sense of vacillation between opposing modes of interpreting experience. The midpoint of each planetary group often falls within opposite houses, activating one house axis as the central core of life experience. A sense of balance is crucial.

In our example, the 2nd/8th axis is predominant, so we're dealing with an individual whose central life questions surround the creation and evaluation of personal worth. He or she vacillates between the 2nd and 8th house approaches: self-worth through personal efforts or self-containment, versus shared worth with its sensitivity to partners and an emphasis on productivity through relationship. Is this person self-centered or other-directed? Sensual or sexual in psychic orientation? The answer is all, but with a tendency to flip back and forth from one to the other on both levels.

Money could be an important concern, a kind of lowest common denominator, but the person could just as easily focus on other levels of worth: the pursuit of good feelings or positive attitudes about the self, or conversely, the struggle with shame and rejection.

The tendency here when feeling good within oneself is to expect resistance from others, or to experience the opposite, by receiving support from relationships but somehow feeling bad personally. The challenge is to harmonize each side, self and other, to balance the two experiences rather than swinging back and forth between them.

The 2nd/8th axis can be worked with more effectively if the individual activates the empty perpendicular axis, 5th/11th. The unconscious emphasis on worth with its exaggerated flip-flops can be moderated by consciously focusing on creativity in both personal and shared forms, and by intentionally seeing in every life experience the content of love given and received. The planetary rulers of the empty 5th and 11th houses can provide additional information on how to activate these new levels of awareness through the challenge of their occupied houses.

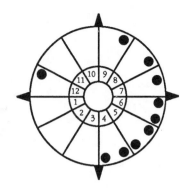

*Fanhandle
Type*

The fifth pattern goes by three names: Fanhandle, Wedge, or Funnel. It is essentially a Bowl with a single planet separated from the other nine, isolated in the otherwise empty hemisphere. In a perfect Fanhandle, the grouped planets occupy one hemisphere with the "singleton" alone at the midpoint of the other half. Ideally, there'll be an opposition between the lone planet and others near the middle of the occupied Bowl.

Psychologically, the Fanhandle type is a personality resting finally on the experiences of one house, that occupied by the singleton planet. The focus can be obviously intense, as in the Bundle, but there may equally be great subtlety of expression in the emphasized house, as if its importance were masked. Much depends on the nature of the particular planet and house being isolated. But if you observe this person over any significant period of time, you'll discover that again and again, the peak experiences of life operate through the singleton and its area, like the Plutonian process of slow-building energy moving toward critical mass, erupting finally into overt significance.

Like the Bundle and the Locomotive, the Fanhandle reveals a life constructed for a very special purpose. This person is spiritually set up to learn the multileveled nature of a specific teaching. It can be joyously enlightening or catastrophically difficult, and may well move from one to the other at various phases in the life.

In our example, the 12th house is the emphasized area. Here was have an individual for whom the ultimate mysteries of life are crucial. There is a powerful need to understand transcendence and surrender in positive ways, to master the trick of letting go without descent into meaningless realms of escapism or destructive fantasy. Separating dreams from reality is a major task, as well as finding their proper relation. One quest is to discover the way they can become mutually supportive.

The sense of subtle isolation is persistent, as if the person has one foot in reality and one foot out, straddling the worlds of manifested, Earthly life on the one hand, and pure cosmic potential on the other.

This person operates as a conduit, a secret passageway, allowing life's contents to be dissolved and returned to the cosmos, yet also infusing life with new, hitherto unknown forms of energy and meaning. Helping or healing others to achieve purification is critical, and there may be a subtle tone of sainthood or martyrdom in the personality.

Apart from the obvious relevance of the Sun, Moon, and Saturn and their respective areas, there are three houses linked together in this pattern's special purpose: the 12th, because it is the singleton; but also the house ruled by the lone planet in the 12th, as well as the house occupied by the ruler of the sign on the cusp of the 12th. Understanding the relation of these three areas of experience is an integral part of interpreting this individual's path.

Splash Type

The Splash Pattern is the first and only pattern to reveal no significant geometrical or visual emphasis. It is so named because of the even, circular "splash" that occurs when dropping an object into water. Here we see an at least relatively even distribution of planets around the heavens.

The perfect Splash chart has only one planet occupying each house, leaving two empty houses. This ideal is extremely rare, but there should be at least eight occupied houses, and the empty houses should not be consecutive, but instead separated around the wheel. Often there are many more interplanetary aspects than one usually sees in an average chart, and they form a complex network of interactions.

This individual is likely to be responsive to many different levels of life, and there may be a wide-eyed naivete, or a subtle sense of wonder inherent in the personality. Confusion can be a significant problem in this life, since the person can easily feel overwhelmed by the sheer bigness of his or her experience, and the difficulty of organizing life into sensible categories. Human beings are very selective about experiencing reality, but this person has few, if any, natural filters. As a result, universal empathy tends to develop.

The Splash personality is characterized by general receptivity to all life experience. Certainly the Sun, Moon, and Saturn can be emphasized in interpretation, along with planets that are angular or are otherwise sensitized by the aspects or rulership. But the basic planetary pattern indicates that any emphasis will be somewhat diminished. The Splash typology bathes the chart in a feeling similar to Neptune's significance as a planet, tending to blur and unfocus what might otherwise be emphasized.

What's meaningful about this pattern is its very lack of specific information. It tells you what not to look for, giving the basic instruction to interpret every chart factor within a framework of overall balance. In the same way that a good caricaturist brings out the individuality of a face on canvas by emphasizing and exaggerating the most important features, a good astrologer paints the same kind of psychological or spiritual portrait of an individual by verbally emphasizing and exaggerating the most salient characteristics of the life. However, in special cases such as this, exaggeration of any particular quality works against the wholeness of the life, as well as the accuracy of the interpretation.

Unless other groups of analytical factors give a strongly contrary impression, the message of a strong Splash chart is to keep bringing the interpretation back to center, to make sure that your view of the person is well rounded, with few if any jagged edges.

Splay Type

The last pattern is called Splay. It occurs when there is pronounced visual emphasis in the chart, when the geometry is obviously definite, but where none of the necessary requirements for the first five categories can be satisfied.

The "conditions" I'm referring to here are not only technical, but visual and emotional as well; you may look at a chart sometime and find yourself thinking, "Hmm, it could be a Bowl, but no, it's more like a Locomotive maybe, however there are are those two empty houses together so perhaps it's a Seesaw, but the groups of planets aren't opposite and there's that one almost sticking out by itself…, ah hell, I don't know what to call it."

If that's what you're thinking, then it's quite probably a Splay chart.

Put very simply, the Splay pattern is unique. It shows emphasis, has a definite shape and feel, but its geometry isn't regular, at least not along lines of the other six types.

We can't characterize the Splay temperament. You have to deal with this chart—and the person—in an individual manner, recognizing that the chart is uniquely itself. Certain houses may be emphasized in the pattern, perhaps by a stellium of three or four planets, but don't make any particular house the keynote of the interpretation.

You're on your own with a Splay chart, free to approach the interpretation through whatever your favorite factors happen to be. If analyzing the elements and modes is revealing for you, then great, go ahead and do it. If you like using midpoints, use them. There may be transits or progressions that point to certain sections of the chart being much more critical now. Naturally, the basic rules of interpretation always apply—Sun, Moon, Saturn, ruled and occupied houses, aspects from outer to inner planets, etc. And of course, you'll use all your "pet" approaches anyway, regardless of the pattern. But here you can pretty much forget about integrating the Splayness into a geometric archetype, except that of individuality. It's similar to Uranian symbolism in this regard.

If you attempt to use or explain technical terms to your clients (something I shy away from), you may choose to tell your client that the chart is Splay, and that it represents a unique construction of personal reality. You could conceivably discuss the astrological concepts of patterning in charts and weave into your discussion an appreciation for how different this irregularity is, both positively and negatively. But basically, Splay patterns don't lend themselves especially well to use as a structure around which to build an interpretive dialogue. The very oddness that defines this as a type makes it difficult to discuss, almost as if it were an anti-type.

Conclusion | In this chapter, we've seen that houses do not need to be occupied by planets to have significance in the natal chart. There are many different ways to analyze the meaning of unoccupied houses. We've discussed only a few of the most typical ways—midpoints, Arabic Parts, and planetary patterns.

Certainly planets occupying houses form the foundation of most delineation. That is the day-to-day, bread-and-butter, bottom line approach. It's what most of us tend to notice first. It's so important I've devoted 600 interpretive sections to it in **Part Two** of the book.

But whether it's occupied or not, every house has a place in the matrix of an individual's life experience, and each of the twelve houses can be related to the evolution of human selfhood.

This is true in the concrete experiences of day-to-day life with its mundane necessities and common sense requirements. And it is equally true in the more intangible strivings we all make as we stumble toward true spiritual adulthood.

Every house counts.

Technical versus Human Issues

Introduction

In this chapter, we'll discuss technical systems for deriving houses, specifically, the different methods of dividing personal space into twelve sections, and their relationship to artful interpretation. The "art" of interpretation has little connection to textbook delineations. It involves working with clients and requires many other skills and sensitivities to make astrological information come alive.

The further we go in astrology, the more confusing issues arise. As we gain sophistication, and especially as we learn to use the houses, the issue of making choices becomes more relevant in our use of the astrological method. Questions arise surrounding the many different structural techniques available.

With regard to the zodiac, we have to decide which one to use—tropical (the zodiac of seasons) or sidereal (the zodiac of constellations)? There is also the question of sign cusps and how to work with them, and the issue of rulerships. With the planets, the questions multiply: shall we use just the ten major planets, or add the ever-increasing number of smaller bodies—asteroids, planetoids, comets, etc.? With aspects, there are questions about allowable orbs, the differing effects of applying versus separating angles, and whether or not to use the minor or more esoteric aspects.

Needless to say, there are endless other issues besides these lying in wait to ambush our minds: transit timing, the various systems of symbolic progressions, harmonic analysis, the techniques of synastry, chart comparisons and composites, and on and on. It's endless, and it gets worse before it gets better.

Investigating these various techniques and the choices they offer demands at least some mastery of the technical background of astrology. Certain astrologers love the technical side of our discipline; on the other hand, many astrologers and most students hate it. But even if you can't balance your checking account, even if you use a computer service to erect charts, you still need to comprehend at least an overview of the technical levels involved in astrology. Otherwise, you'll lack true understanding of what you're looking at, and that will eventually limit your interpretive skill.

In many cases, we resolve these issues by simply going with what we originally learned or were first taught. It's human nature to lean strongly toward our initial imprints, and there's a great deal to be said for the common sense rationale of staying with what you know. It keeps things clear, and mentally it's much easier to add onto a preexisting base than to start over from scratch.

Though many astrologers continue to use the house system they were first taught, it's important to know that there are, in fact, hundreds of different house systems, each using its own mathematical and astronomical structures. Far and away the most popular house system in use today is the one called Placidus, named for the monk who invented it in the middle ages. But there's also Koch, and Campanus, and Regiomontanus, and Porphyry, and the Equal House System, and many other more obscure house structures.

The Placidean system is so popular because it was the first house system to have its mathematical tables available in published form. Prior to the printing press, anyone who wanted to practice natal astrology had to be either very well-versed in astronomical mathematics or very rich—because the tables used to erect natal charts were laboriously calculated, a task involving literally thousands of hours of work, and then they were handwritten in manuscripts that were, needless to say, nearly priceless, and far beyond the means of ordinary people.

Gutenburg's printing press made astrology available to a growing middle class. So when publishers like Raphael in England chose to use the Placidean system in the first press runs of their astrological ephemerides and tables, it created a tremendous advantage for Placidus. People practiced astrology their whole lives without knowing that other systems existed, because this was the only one they'd ever seen in printed form.

Especially in this age of computer-calculated tables, we are no longer bound by the tyranny of limited access. Some of us even have computer programs from companies like Astrolabe and Matrix Software that build numerous house systems into their programs, allowing the luxury of choice. So we need to understand the differences, if only to choose a house system we can work with comfortably on a day-to-day basis.

This is not a technically-oriented textbook, and I'm certainly no expert on the mathematics of theoretical astrology, so we're not going to drown ourselves in terms like Prime Vertical, great circles, or azimuth. If you want to learn about those factors, there are excellent books on the subject. Two such books are *The Houses* by Dona Marie Lorenz (the best source work I know on the mathematical astronomy of different house systems), or *The Astrologer's Astronomical Handbook* by Jeff Mayo (a very clear introduction into the astronomical factors used in astrology).

What I want to do instead is write as matter-of-factly as possible about the practical considerations distinguishing various house systems, and how those relate to actual interpretations. Among the major house systems in popular use today, there are two basic categories: **equal house systems** and **quadrant systems**.

Equal House Systems

The equal house systems are simple and, to some astrologers' minds, elegant. A specific factor in the chart is chosen as the zero point, and the twelve houses are marked off from that point, with each succeeding cusp 30° further in the zodiac—thus the name, equal house. Most often, the Ascendant is used as the reference cusp, but we could just as easily use the Midheaven, or any other point.

There are well known and respected astrologers who are staunch proponents of these systems of house division. However, I am not among them. To my mind, the equal house systems do not account sufficiently for the importance of personal space, since they use only a single point as the reference for individual selfhood. In so doing, they elevate the importance of the zodiac, reducing the houses to a subservient position, making them effectively no more than a sublevel of the signs.

But houses are a completely independent structure, not just a clone of the zodiac. The tropical zodiac is a measure of the Earth's motion around the sun each year, based on the ebb and flow of seasonal change; houses, however, reflect the Earth's rotation on its own axis, the diurnal motion of one 24-hour day. These are distinctly different Earth motions, and one cannot be subordinate to the other—the day is as important symbolically as the year.

Signs are collective while houses are individual. Their interweaving should reflect the coexistence of these two paradoxical factors in human life—we need to belong and feel togetherness, but we need equally to be unique and independent. Integration of personality depends to a large extent on how creatively we resolve the conflict. By subordinating houses to the zodiac, the equal house systems presume that collectivity is fundamentally more important than individuality, and I can't go along with that.

Equal house advocates will insist that this argument is merely conceptual justification, that the system works for them, that they'll continue to use it despite my sour grapes. And well they should, for "if it works, don't fix it." But every time I look at an equal house chart, I see the graphic discounting personal space, and that bothers me enough that I don't recommend the equal house systems.

There is, however, one great argument in support of equal houses. They work for the whole Earth, and the same cannot be said for the other main type of house division, quadrant systems. But more about that in the next section.

Quadrant Systems

This type of house division is based on the measurement of two axes—horizontal and vertical—and the resulting quadrants that are formed. Symbolically, it represents the cross of individuality superimposed on the sphere of universality. Every house system you're likely to encounter other than equal house is probably based on quadrants. The Ascendant and Descendant are used as the cusps of the 1st/7th axis; the Midheaven and Lower Heaven define the 10th/4th cusps.

Each popular quadrant system uses the same mathematics to derive the horizontal and vertical axes of individual space, so the angular cusps (1st/7th, 4th/10th) remain the same from one system to the next. Where they differ is in the measurement of intermediate cusps—the succeedent houses (2nd/8th, 5th/11th), and the cadent houses (3rd/9th, 6th/12th.)

If equal house systems are at least relatively straightforward, the quadrant systems can be bewilderingly complex in their celestial mechanics, in the choice or combination of specific astronomical and earthly frames of reference used to calculate the intermediate house cusps. As a result, there are many different quadrant systems, each of which has advocates among astrologers. Some, like Placidus, have existed for centuries, and others, like Koch, are relative newcomers to the lexicon of astrology.

Only a small percentage of astrologers actually understand the mathematics behind these systems, and an even smaller number comprehend their symbolic implications, which accounts for the misinformation and innuendo surrounding their differences.

The major criticism of all quadrant systems is their complete breakdown in extreme latitudes. In the far northern and southern regions near the Arctic and Antarctic Circles, including some areas in places such as Norway, Alaska, or Venezuela, the lengthening of daytime in summer and nighttime in winter are exaggerated. For instance, there are periods during winter when the sun never rises. So the Midheaven—the highest point of the sun's daily arc—is below the Ascendant. We can't erect a chart when the 10th house is under the 1st house. It's mathematically impossible; the formulas simply fail.

As far as I'm aware, there has been no acceptable solution offered by the creators of the quadrant systems. However, this flaw hasn't prevented quadrant systems from maintaining their overwhelming popularity, if for no other reason than the fact that most American astrologers meet very few people born near the polar regions. Damning as it may seem at first glance, this particular technical glitch just doesn't come up very often in real life, and is therefore relegated to cold storage in the warehouse of unresolved astrological paradoxes.

The differences between house systems are not just a mathematical or philosophical issue. The problem in natal interpretation is quite real. Since the cusps of the houses fall in different degrees of the zodiac from one system to the next, we get actual changes in the house positions of major bodies and other symbolic points. A planet seemingly located in the 8th house by one system may be clearly positioned in the 9th in another. A planet ruling the 11th in one system rules the 12th in the other.

So which is it? Which is the "correct" house position? And by extension, which is the best house system to use?

There's an adage in "New Age" astrology that differences between systems shouldn't matter, that in the hands of competent and creative astrologers, you'll get the same "accuracy" of interpretation regardless. For instance, a good siderealist is supposedly able to interpret a natal chart just as well as a good tropical astrologer, even though all the planets are displaced one sign between the two zodiacs.

So, according to the same logic, two astrologers using different house systems should be able to deliver equally artful interpretations, even though they may understand certain planets to occupy or rule conflicting houses.

That view strikes me as sheer nonsense. While it may be true that two surgeons using different techniques could perform the same operation with equal success, two astrologers using different techniques cannot. Removing a gall bladder is not like interpreting a natal chart. One is essentially a mechanical procedure, admittedly very sophisticated, but mechanical nonetheless; the other is decidedly not. As astrologers, we deal with the psyche, with the roots of personality rather than the components of the body, and that aspect of human machinery is hardly cut-and-dried—it's not even tangibly visible.

We operate not on the physical structures of the brain, but on the neurological contents, the patterns of perception and response out of which personality is created. We're concerned not with the heart as a cardiovascular pump, but with the heartfelt emotions that make life either a joy or a terror, and sometimes both simultaneously. Two astrologers using different techniques aren't performing the same surgery; they're operating on separate levels of the client's psyche, and their results are likely to be as different as their techniques.

Conflicting chart information from different house systems creates profound changes in interpretation. If one house system places the Sun in the 5th house, while another indicates it occupying the 6th, this is going to radically affect the most fundamental tonality of the whole interpretive session, since so much rides on the house position of the Sun—everything flows from the Sun's meaning and must be referenced back to it. No matter how you slice it, you can't make a 6th house Sun sound like a 5th house interpretation and get away with it.

Since it is generally agreed that Placidus is not inherently more "correct" as a house system than Koch (and vice versa), there's no simple solution for this vexing difficulty. There are, however, many ways of approaching a workable solution. They apply not only to the selection of a particular house system, but also to the more general problems of house placement, something you'll encounter no matter what system you use.

First and foremost, keep in mind that human beings are complicated animals. Our aware personalities are but a tiny piece of total consciousness, merely the tip of the iceberg, and the understanding we have of ourselves at any given time is likely to be partial.

Individual human personalities are not an amalgam of neat components. We're much more than the sum of our parts, especially when those parts are actually abstract categories imposed from outside. The astrological houses appear on a chart form to be "pie-shaped boxes," and we're naturally concerned with accurately placing the planets and signs in the boxes, but life is experienced whole, not as boxes. We need to remember that experience is a continuum, and that the houses are only a device for better understanding experience by revealing its abstract structure.

Charts are not people, and we must not relate to people as if they "were" their charts. They are not the same thing.

A natal horoscope is a schematic diagram of the vehicle through which a person is operating, rather like the car one drives. We can learn a great deal by analyzing the machinery of personality, but that does not account for the experience of the driver.

Two people with very similar charts may live them out in very different directions. Even though there are obvious parallels in their characteristic attitudes and approaches to living, and even more striking parallels in the timing of circumstantial peaks and crises of life evolution, the differences become greater as time goes on and each person "customizes" his vehicle. Biology offers us lessons of experience, but there is no telling which lessons we'll learn, nor how well we'll learn them, nor when we'll learn them. You can lead a horse to water, but you can't make him drink.

It's not enough to be expert at astrological delineation, for charts contain no consciousness—that intangible is contacted only through the living person. Being a good astrologer requires a facility for moving back and forth from the person to the chart, allowing your understanding of each to be altered by the other in a creative symbiosis.

So if you come up against an occasional chart that doesn't lend itself to even the most basic certainties in planetary categorization—you can't be sure of the house position of both the Sun and Moon, the aspects refuse to form into coherent patterns, the transits are contradictory, etc.—all is not lost. You can still be artful in your interpretation by relating first to the person, then taking those perceptions and intuitions and organizing your view of the chart around them.

People are looking for something when they seek out astrological counsel. Some know exactly what they want; others are confused, and still others are pursuing red herrings— they have an issue they're focused on, but it can be addressed only by unearthing deeper, more subterranean levels of self. Whatever the condition, your clients believe (or hope) that astrology can offer them illumination and greater peace of mind.

However, it's not the chart that helps them achieve whatever they want—it's you. While clients might think they're coming to have their chart "interpreted," they're actually coming to see you—to be with you, to interact with you, to share themselves with you. And though your reputation may be superficially based on your skill as an astrologer, what's required to make those skills shine is the sensitivity of being a good counselor, someone who knows how to interact in a way that fosters intimate openness.

Even in a chart where every placement is absolutely clear, you can still encounter the most vexing resistance from your client, because people are not as straightforward as machines. Often, an individual is neither ready nor willing to hear the truth about himself, even though he will deny this—sometimes vehemently ("thou dost protest too much, methinks...")—and insist upon your telling him exactly what you "see" in the chart. The fact that someone comes for a session does usually indicates some desire to change, but that desire may initially be motivated more by the need to anesthetize pain than by a sincere wish to understand.

One part of your job to find out what level of themselves your clients are seeking to get in touch with, and this is not always an astrological factor. While the chart is truly an amazing tool for exploring those very levels of self, there will be many times when you must discover their motivation through other means before you can use the chart to help illuminate the riddle.

Sometimes this can be as simple as a direct question to your client, e.g., "What are you looking for?" or "What are you dealing with in your life now?" But often you'll need to probe deeper to discover the real motives, since clients sometimes consciously mask their intentions, mistakenly believing that it will somehow "skew the reading" if they reveal too much.

More frequently, they mask themselves unconsciously in an inadvertent game of hide and seek. This is very human. We all struggle with self-awareness, phasing in and out of touch with ourselves, often from moment to moment. In the immortal words of the Firesign Theatre: "As far as I know, we're all Bozos on this bus."

So use everything you know to contact the person whose chart you are interpreting. Read the keys—watch the body language, notice the posture, the tension in the body. Look at your clients' eyes. Do they shine with a gleam, or is that a glint? Are they dulled over? Do the pupils occasionally dilate? Is there anyone home behind the eyes? When do your clients look at you and when do they look away? Does their eye color change as the session goes on? Does their skin flush? Listen to the semantics your clients use when speaking to you, the word choices and the sentence structures. How does their emotional inflection change as the conversation ebbs and flows?

Allow yourself to notice everything: how they're dressed, even what kind of car they drove to the session. Stay open intuitively—watch how the feeling in the room changes when certain subjects come up in conversation. And while all that's going on, keep one eye on the chart, for it can change in your vision as you get a "radar fix" on your client.

When the chart is clear, people will show you how to talk to them about it. They'll let you know in a thousand subtle ways how to discuss the information, what they can hear and what they can't, which words and concepts work for them, and which don't. But even when the chart is mud, they will help you interpret it by the totality of their being, the radiance of a thousand cues. Use all your resources; that's what you have them for.

There are people who will undoubtedly say this is cheating, asserting that it corrupts the purity of astrology as an "objective" system. Horsefeathers! There's no such thing as "objective" chart interpretation. If we tried to do that, we'd have no way of selecting between the different levels through which each chart factor can operate, no way of paring down the infinite potentials every chart contains into a coherent, human scope.

Consider the placement of even a single planet. Abstractly, it has a basic principle, but pragmatically, perhaps ten to twenty distinctly different interpretive meanings; the same is true of each sign and house. As a result, there would be over 8,000 different interpretive combinations for that planet alone (20 times 20 times 20).

Now, easily half of these make little or no logical sense. That pares it down to 4,000. Another quarter are clearly irrelevant. Great, only 2,000 left. Of those, you might be able to shave another 1,500 by sheer personal bias. That still leaves a mere 500 possible interpretations, each of which could be verbally expanded at length.

Even this considers only the sign and occupied house; add the subtlety of the ruled house, the aspects to other planets, transits, etc., and we've factored back into the infinite range again. Human brains can organize immense amounts of information, but even if we could hold every factor in our minds, we couldn't possibly discuss them all.

Functional human beings don't experience every potentiality of their lives at once, thank God. We're very selective in how we organize our consciousness. In any particular phase of our lives, at any given moment, only two or three of those 500 levels may be relevant. And more often than astrologers like to admit, the chart itself won't tell you which. It remains a diagram of infinite levels and myriad possibilities.

To understand the chart, we have to tune into the full range of potentials, allowing our brains to glow with the whole range of possibilities, but to interpret the chart in a way that has real-life relevance—and more to the point, to effectively communicate that relevance—we have to limit the possibilities.

The significance of astrology as a system lies in its ability to help us in opposite ways, by better understanding how to operate within our limits, but also by reminding us that we can expand those limits, and showing us how. Using astrology well demands an integration of both approaches—respect for **acceptance** (the perfection of love; staying within limits), and respect for **change** (the use of power; expanding beyond limits). But we can use the chart for expansion only when we have a clear sense of where the current limits are, and to see that, we have to have some feeling for the person.

This is true whether it's our own chart or someone else's. It doesn't matter how we plug in—being with the person physically, interacting verbally, feeling the emotions, or even by sheer psychic receptivity—but we have to connect with the person to use the chart productively. Otherwise, it's just head games.

One of the best techniques to use when chart positions are unclear is to simply tell the truth. This means saying what's really in your mind rather than making up something to maintain the appearance of wisdom.

Astrologers are subject to the same vulnerabilities as other professionals whose work places them in artificial positions of authority—too often, we tend to presume that we must be omniscient, that we must have an answer for every question. We are asked so many questions that it's easy to succumb to the pressure by answering as if we knew. Much of the time, regardless of the amount of information we have access to, we simply don't know the answer. In a session involving astrological interpretation, it can be immensely helpful to say, "**I don't know.**"

Certainly there's a risk involved in that honesty; some clients have the mistaken belief that everything about their lives is magically "written" in their charts. Not only that, but they believe the chart talks to you in English, rather than just sitting there on the table staring up at you, waiting for you to decipher and translate it. These individuals may have some trouble accepting that you're human.

But most of the time, admitting that you don't know the answer to a question, the solution to a situation, or even the meaning of an event increases the intimacy and trust between you and your client. And that's what this game is really all about—trust. As George Burns said, "**Acting is all sincerity; if you can fake that, you've got it made**." Well, being a good astrologer involves real sincerity. You don't even have to fake it.

Choosing a House System

Since different house systems can and often do produce contradictory information, the question arises, "How do you choose a house system for day-to-day work?"

Certainly you can go to the trouble of using four or five different systems with every chart, but this is not only time-consuming, it's also a royal pain, something to be reserved for special occasions. Even with computerized chart erection programs that offer a virtual plethora of houses systems, you've still got to go to the trouble of sorting out all the variables—which planets change houses, which signs change house cusps. Most of the time, it's just too much trouble and too many brain cells.

The route most of us take is to choose a house system and pretty much stick with it. This is hardly infallible, but it's natural. Especially for a professional astrologer or someone who works with many charts on a regular basis, changing house systems can represent a major shift in the orientation toward interpretation, a change in the levels of the psyche that are being addressed, and this is something not to be taken lightly.

I began using Equal House, but quickly switched to Placidus. That stuck for about a decade. Then I went through a period of graphing in Porphyry but also listing the cusps for Placidus, Campanus, and Regiomontanus. After two years of that, I found myself spending too much energy comparing differences and making mental compromises. It was subtly taking me away from the real interaction with my clients. So I trashed that method, adopted Koch, and have been using it ever since. However, I might go back to Placidus tomorrow...

So how do you know which one to pick? You can certainly study the theory behind various house systems to better understand the philosophical implications of their mathematical frames of reference. But I would recommend a more pragmatic approach. Erect your own chart and the charts of individuals you know intimately using numerous house systems, and compare what you know from real experience with what you interpret in differing house positions. This technique may not be "scientific," but it's probably the most grounded way to find a house system well-suited to your particular astrological bent.

Even with your own chart, it won't always work perfectly. Sometimes you'll find the different house positions of the various systems reflecting contradictions in your own experience of yourself. For example, planets might shift from the 7th house to the 8th in two different systems, or from the 2nd to the 3rd, and you could easily identify with some of the levels in both interpretations. So, as I've said in this book so often before, keep in mind that astrology is multileveled, just like your life.

When I began studying astrology, I felt certain that my Libra Moon was in the 9th house. Philosophy was almost second nature to me, and teaching felt natural. Then, as my 20's progressed into my 30's, I began to feel my Moon in an 8th house mode, since issues of intimacy and sexuality came to dominate my interior landscape. Coincidentally, I switched from Placidus, which placed my Moon in the 9th, to Koch, which indicated it in the 8th. Now, as my 30's come to a close, I seem to be leaning back toward the 9th. Insofar as I can stand back and observe my life, it's clear to me that both houses have some lunar overtones. So the question remains unresolved.

You can also use the word-of-mouth technique. Talk to other astrologers. Find out what house system they're using, and why. If you choose this method, be aware that the majority of working astrologers don't really know much about the differences between house systems, so be skeptical of the rationales you may hear. Again, misinformation runs rampant in astrology, especially where the technique of houses is concerned.

Five House Systems: A Critique

What follows is a list of five of the more popular house systems currently in vogue, with a tongue-in-cheek "psychological profile" of the personality types who tend to use each one. You might want to select a house system based on this critique. More likely, you might not. But it may give you a chuckle, and a little ammo to throw at the competition.

Equal House

Astrologers who prefer the Equal House system usually appreciate symmetry as much as they abhor complications. They can't be bothered with details, tending to be philosophers. Fond of defending their pet system by endlessly pointing out that quadrant systems break down in the extreme latitudes, they insist that Equal House is the only system that works for the whole globe, and therefore the best.

> If house systems were like automobile companies, then Equal House would be like American Motors: not ever in the lead, not even close, but hanging in there doggedly by selling jeeps: good, basic transportation that sacrifices sophisticated design for rugged durability.

Placidus

These astrologers are often dyed-in-the-wool traditionalists, but for heaven's sake don't tell them that, since astrologers like to think of themselves as a rugged individualists. They like the security of group acceptance and technical conformity, although they'll insist that the Placidean system is "time-tested," rather than merely conventional, which is closer to the truth. Almost everyone who uses Placidus started out with it—like buying the same car your parents bought when you were a kid.

> Placidus is the General Motors of houses: Chevrolet, Buick, and Pontiac all rolled into one. Always popular, with a zillion dealerships, it continues to lead in sales—year in and year out. It's still the industry standard, and parts are cheap because everybody and his brother drives one.

Campanus

Many siderealists use the Campanus system, and that alone should tell you that it's at least a little weird. This is the kind of house system you really have to fanatically believe in to use consistently, and it attracts just that kind of astrologer, someone who is proud to say he's studied houses intensively and is convinced that Campanus is right. It produces the most extreme disproportions of any of these five major systems.

> This is the DeLorean of house systems, very esoteric, somewhat elitist, and not all that accessible. Still, like a stainless steel DeLorean, you'll continue to see it driven fast by die-hard enthusiasts.

Koch

Astrologers who use the Koch system—also called the Birthplace method, for obscure reasons—tend to think of themselves as hipper than average. They're also somewhat status conscious, like astrological yuppies who like to believe they're on the cutting edge. There is probably more conflict and misinformation around the Koch system than any other, and there are relatively few people who understand its mathematical implications (although this could be said of almost any house system). In the past ten years, its popularity has grown immensely, but this is due more to imagined status than hard evidence supporting its superiority. I use it myself, but you'll have to decide whether that's a recommendation or an indictment.

> Koch is the new kid on the block, the German high-performance vehicle of houses, rather like Mercedes-Benz or BMW. It's probably not quite as wonderful as some astrologers would like to think, but it does incorporate sophisticated design and impeccable workmanship.

Porphyry

Last is the system known as Porphyry. It's not as popular as the others, in part because it has no fancy tables and requires the astrologer to calculate the intermediate house positions. Rather than basing its cusps on astronomical circles and complex formulae, Porphyry merely trisects each of the quadrants. In this, it attempts to combine the best features of the equal house and quadrant systems, since it uses unequal quadrants, but equal houses within each opposite pair of quadrants.

> Porphyry is criticized for being a cheap hybrid, like old Karmann Ghias, which were merely Volkswagen bugs hidden under Porsche-designed bodies. In fairness, it does have a certain graceful symmetry, and more than one disgruntled astrologer has adopted Porphyry after tiring of the absurdly disproportionate houses that sometimes occur in many other quadrant systems.

Conclusion | Whichever house system you select, please remember at least this one rule-of-thumb that's been mentioned previously:

There are no lines in the sky.

Human beings invented the lines you see on the chart as a way of making the heavens easier to understand and interpret. When those lines start getting in the way of our understanding, confusing rather than clarifying the process of using charts to find better solutions to life's confusion and paradox, it defeats the whole purpose of astrology.

Whatever level we deal with—technical, psychological, emotional, mental, physical, or even spiritual—it's usually safer to start with what you're sure of. Get grounded there, then gradually move into areas of uncertainty. If you have trouble with a certain house position (or any interpretive factor), file it away rather than get stuck trying to figure it out, for there are likely to be other levels of the chart that are clearer and easier to understand. It's a lot like Little Bo Peep's flock of lost sheep: Leave them alone and they'll come home, wagging their tails behind them…

In the meantime, while you're waiting for the chart to clarify in your mind, work on relating to other human beings. Practice really connecting with your client.

I've known astrologers who are absolutely brilliant at thinking about charts, but who are total morons in how they interact with clients. All their sophisticated knowledge of astrology is useless when it comes to communicating in English or demonstrating the most minimal sensitivity toward others.

I've also known astrologers whose technical comprehension was limited to little more than the basics of astrology, but who are virtually magical in using that knowledge to help others gain a truer understanding of themselves. They won't have 27 harmonic charts erected when you walk in, and they don't throw 19 systems of progressions at you, and their conversation isn't peppered with terms like Antivertex, Finger of God, dwadashamsa, or any other jargon. But they can use charts like a window to the soul, and when you leave, you really got your money's worth, because they knew how to translate their knowledge in ways relevant to your life, and they were honest and sincere in their interaction.

Finally, there is no substitute for being with a person. Astrology isn't real without it.

Part Two

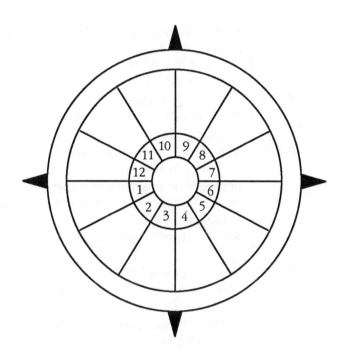

Planetary
Delineations

Introduction to Part Two

Limits of the
Interpretations

In reading any of the 600 interpretations that follow, please keep certain limitations in mind. The interpretations are often written as if they stood alone, unaffected by other planets, aspects, or other configurations in the natal chart, and beyond that, by many factors that have nothing to do with astrology, but are simply part of the complexity of being human. While I fully realize the dangers of writing the interpretations in this manner, the other approach—to disclaim every statement because of the awareness that it will be affected and altered by thousands of factors no one writing a textbook could know—well, this is simply impossible. So as an author, I'm faced with compromises, none of which are especially attractive.

I chose to write the interpretations as firmly as I could, to help students pinpoint the relevant principles and possible meanings of planetary symbolism as they relate to the houses. But I know as surely as I breathe that certain readers will misapprehend the intent of these 600 sections, or (more likely) simply ignore the admonitions in this statement of intent.

Some will dismiss the book because of its occasionally didactic tone. "Life is not this simple!" they will proclaim. And I agree, life is infinitely more complex, textured, and full of possibility than this textbook can possibly convey. Others will read the interpretations relevant to their own charts and defiantly accuse me of a lack of understanding, since those sections will inevitably vary from their real experience and knowledge of themselves. Or they will condemn astrology as a psychological discipline, judging it invalid because the interpretations don't suit their particular pattern of life-circumstances or their current understanding.

However, I will lose no sleep over these first two possibilities, because people of that bent are not likely to be reading the book in the first place. What worries me more is the likelihood that the readership will be composed largely of individuals who already "believe" in astrology. I have little trouble with skeptics; however, "true believers" cause me great anxiety, whether their fanaticism is about astrology, religion, politics, or anything else.

There will inevitably be a certain number of readers who are already convinced—or want to be convinced—that astrology can magically tell them who they are. It is for these vulnerable individuals that I have concern, the ones who who are looking for external certainty to shore up confusion or escape from pain, the people who are so eager to banish negativity and fear that they find it everywhere they look.

These particular individuals will tend to choose the invisible but insidious authority of the printed page over their own authentic experience, and they will suffer as a result, fearing that the interpretations must be gospel, or that the various pitfalls discussed are necessarily true in their lives. They'll interpret not on the basis of what's actually written, but rather by what their fears tell them.

I very nearly didn't write the book because of the certainty that misunderstanding would result. And even after I had decided to write it, I spent two years working over the form and content of these interpretations, trying to minimize the dangers. Ultimately, of course, there is no way to perfectly insure readers against the traps; you can't protect people from themselves.

But please, take this disclaimer seriously:

These interpretations DO NOT apply directly to real, living human beings.

If you learn a little about yourself in the pages that follow, that's great. If your understanding of other people is enhanced, or your appreciation of the human condition in general, so much the better. But as written, the delineations don't apply to actual people.

They cannot. They take into consideration only two factors: a planet and a house. That leaves out contradictory information from other planets in the same or other houses, the meaning of specific aspects to the planet in question, the larger issues of aspect patterns and the overall direction of the chart. These interpretations are archetypes of poetry and metaphor designed to teach astrological principles of interpretation. The principles must then be applied very carefully, and always with awareness that in astrology as in life, **everything affects everything else.**

Real Astrology versus Textbooks

The "cookbook" format leaves much to be desired. The art of interpretation is not found in books, and too often what passes for astrology is little more than formulaic, pre-packaged thinking. Take a cup of Mars, season liberally with Sagittarius, and microwave it in the 5th house for ten minutes. Presto! Instant interpretation. It's very seductive to serve up "meals" composed of such fast food. We can offer our clients a ton of the stuff, a smorgasbord of textbook delineations, like eating at an astrological automat. But if we choose that route, we end up sacrificing quality for quantity.

Did Leonardo da Vinci create the Mona Lisa with a paint-by-number kit? Did Frank Lloyd Wright create the Museum of Modern Art out of Lego's or Lincoln Logs? Hardly.

In the hands of a skilled astrological counselor, interpretation is alive, a two-way interaction. It is infinitely more personal, subtle, and powerful than anything written in this or any other textbook. Especially when using astrology as a personal discipline to understand your own life, charts are everchanging mandalas of sublime revelation.

Repetition In interpreting each planet at five different levels of experience for every house, repetition becomes an unavoidable problem. Planetary concepts only stretch so far. Even after wearing out the pages of my thesaurus, it was difficult to find fresh phrases to describe different but related levels of interpretation. Since one level's delineation can usually be applied to other levels of the same house, I tried to minimize needless repetition by using certain concepts or phrases only once.

**As a result, please read all the levels
of any planet/house combination.**

On the other hand, the repetition that does occur is integral to the book's teaching method. Part of the beauty of astrology is that you don't have to memorize an infinite number of specifics in order to master the art of interpretation. If you learn, say, ten different functions for a given planet, and you know that each house has five major levels of experience, your mind will naturally search for the most coherent ways to think about the fifty possible combinations. Not every one will make sense, but many will. The book is designed to aid that process.

Also, be sure to check the descriptions for the levels in each house. These appear on the first two pages of every chapter in **Part Two**; they explain the concepts and define the terms that are later used in the delineations.

Longer Further You'll notice that the interpretations tend to increase in length as they move further through the cycle of houses. This has meaningful implications: the houses increase in complexity as we move through them. Each house builds on the experiences of those in prior houses, integrating previous meanings while adding new layers, like the concentric rings of a tree's growth. The 1st house is no less important than the 12th, but it is more direct in its symbolic meanings, and it does indicate a more self-contained kind of experience.

A person whose planets are clustered in the earlier houses does not have a simpler life than one whose planets are distributed in the later houses. Reality is awesome for everyone. However, in the first case, the person's approach to experience may be more straightforward, or perhaps more direct than in the latter condition. The mysteries, paradoxes, and challenges of life are no easier, but they may be painted in somewhat broader strokes, and confronted more boldly. The interpretations are designed to reflect this subtle dimension.

Planets
in
the
1st House

1st House

self-expression | ***the natural, spontaneous, unconditioned projection of self outward into the environment***

Each individual has an "inner self," a basic essence that drives the outer life. This core self is indicated in astrology by the condition of the Sun: its sign, its occupied and ruled houses, and its aspects to other planets in the chart. The inner self fuels the basic life direction. But this essential self is often not visible through the overt expression of what in common language is called "personality." It exists within, not entirely separate from overt personality, but frequently not revealed by it.

There are some individuals for whom essence and outer personality are virtually the same (those people born just before dawn), and all of us occasionally reveal our inner selves in situations of heightened importance or great stress, but generally, the medium of our apparent personalities is not the same as the essence of our inner selves.

The 1st house describes the experience of personality radiance, the natural way of projecting oneself into the world. It's not conditioned or "conscious;" rather, it is thoroughly spontaneous. It's also pure activity; when we respond, we're linked less with the 1st house and more with the planetary symbolism of the Moon.

The condition of the 1st reveals what type of active radiance we tend to project as a visible personality—mental or emotional, cautious or optimistic, earthy or ethereal.

natural persona | ***the characteristic face shown to the world; the "name-tag"***

At a convention or any such gathering among relative strangers, we're usually given a name-tag to wear. This tag identifies us to others; it gives them a way to relate to us comfortably, facilitating interaction, in spite of the fact that they don't really know anything about us or our lives.

Each of us needs a way to "introduce ourselves to others," to define ourselves to our environments. This natural introduction or "face" encourages contact with those in the outside world, but it also accomplishes a subtler task—it guards the integrity of our inner identity, allowing us to stay whole within ourselves.

We are all incredibly receptive to other people, much more so than is readily apparent, so much so that we need clear, sound boundaries to prevent caving in to the opinions and desires of others, losing ourselves in the wish for acceptance. The 1st house symbolizes that boundary by the natural creation of a working persona.

Such a persona is indeed a mask, but that need not imply falseness nor artificiality. Instead, it is a symbolic set of natural characteristics that reveal who we are while safeguarding the integrity of our deeper self.

The condition of the 1st house indicates the characteristics of the natural "name-tag" worn most the time, to allow interaction while protecting the inner self. The 1st also indicates the relative importance of this "surface identity" and the special talents or difficulties any individual experiences in "naming" the self for others.

self-awareness | ***awareness of the existence of an "I," generated through activity***

Curiously, most of us spend much of our time unaware of the real existence of an inner self. We exist day by day, growing, moving, eating, sleeping, working, and interacting, yet we are often asleep to our core reality. The 1st house represents the experience of radiating a persona into the world, and through that process, becoming aware of the inner self. The natural mask not only defines us for others, but it awakens us to ourselves. This is the most crucial function of the 1st, to provide a spark to inner self-awareness. It is the birthing point of the personality's relationship to the core self, just as dawn is the birthing point of the day.

Through action, through the radiance of a persona into the world, we create the potential for awareness of our deeper, more inward selves; the condition of the 1st reveals the natural form of expression an individual uses to generate this self-awareness.

boundaries | ***the bridge between inner and outer realities; the lens through which we focus***

Each of us forms an image in our brains of the world outside, and yet the world is also actually there, objectively real. We "live" in the image environment we've created, processing and evaluating our experience from within. But we also simultaneously move through the objective world, the shared reality in which we are all truly together.

To live well, to grow and mature as individuals, and eventually to reach toward the spiritual heights of enlightenment, we must establish a successful working relationship between the real world and the "image world" we construct to shelter and house our essences. The 1st house is the interface, the bridge that allows negotiation and cross-talk between our conception of the environment, and the actual environment itself. Clearly, the nature of the bridge affects the substance of our interactions, just as the materials and design of an actual bridge affect the kind of traffic it transports. The 1st house can also be thought of as the "lens" our essences look through, the periscope we use to see what's happening on surface of life.

The condition of the 1st indicates the kinds of interactions we naturally encourage. It also shows the relative importance of our bridge, and its natural qualities.

vitality | ***overall personal energy as it pertains to general health***

Classically, the 1st is considered an area of health. It doesn't indicate the presence or absence of disease in the medical sense, but rather it defines the type of vitality an individual characteristically radiates in living. A person could conceivably be disease-free, yet not very vital, and another could struggle with illness constantly, but possess great vitality. This vigor cannot prevent disease or systemic breakdown, but it is a conspicuous factor in healing, by providing stamina to weather life's many difficulties.

In league with the condition of the Sun and Moon, and the 6th and 12th houses, the 1st reveals the "constitution" of the individual, the type of energies available to grow, maintain, or heal the self through release.

Sun/1st

self-expression

The placement of the Sun in the 1st house indicates that your life-purpose centers around spontaneous self-expression. Everything else is secondary to self-discovery. You are not necessarily selfish, although that **pitfall** exists, but you are a self-motivated and self-generating individual. What you express is certainly meaningful, for it conditions the feedback you get from others and from the environment. But expression itself is the single most crucial factor. Inhibit or block expression, and you cut yourself off from life-energy. The **challenge** is to radiate outward, letting yourself flow into behavior. Fill your spirit with vibrant life.

natural persona

Ordinarily, the 1st house masks the inner essence. In your life, however, we see your essence projected directly through spontaneous outer personality. When the ascending and Sun signs are the same, there is a basic naiveté toward life, expressed along lines of the zodiacal sign. However, much depends on whether the Sun's support planets, Mercury and Venus, are located in the 12th, 1st, or 2nd. When the ascending and Sun signs are different, personality still retains the "what-you-see-is-what-you-get" tonality, but there is greater complexity in self-expression. However, any conflicts are open for all to see. The **pitfall** lies in assuming that others are put together in the same way, and can be understood directly through their actions. This is definitely not the case—most people are constructed differently than you. The **challenge** is to be yourself.

Your name-tag says, **"I am exactly who you see,"** and you believe that, even though finally it can hardly be true.

self-awareness

You are constantly "birthing" self-awareness through activity, and when that activity stops, your awareness subtly begins to fade. The sign placement of the Sun determines what "activity" is. For fire signs like Aries or Sagittarius, it often implies literal physical movement—you have to do something. For water signs like Cancer or Pisces, activity may mean simply emotional radiance—the expression of feeling. Your **challenge** is to awaken the awareness that you exist as a separate individual. You live for the here and now experience of discovering yourself, over and over and over...

boundaries

What is usually a means to an end is for you an end in itself. The Sun represents the inner essence, and ordinarily we create a bridge to connect with the outer world. For you, the bridge is the same as the essence. The "lens" and the essence looking through it are identical. Any self-expression not true to your core self damages the lens, making real interaction impossible, and purely egoistic excess blurs the distinction between the self's inner world and the outer environment, causing social blindness, flawed perceptions, and the recurring experience of rejection. The **challenge** is to express yourself fully while recognizing that others have the same rights of self-expression.

vitality

The condition of the Sun by sign and aspect is crucial to understanding your health, but in general you are vital and strong, with the ability to recover from otherwise devastating setbacks, both psychologically and medically. You are pushing into life, determined to "get born," willing to thrust through any and all obstacles, including the personal vulnerability to disease or breakdown. Your strength is not "conscious," but instead reflects a fundamental will to survive at a very basic level.

Moon/1st

self-expression

Here we have a paradox: when the Moon is in the 1st house, the natural and "active" projection of self is inverted, so self-expression becomes "re-active" or, more properly, responsive. Your natural personality radiance is emotional, sensitive, maternal, and subject to the ebb and flow of moodiness. Needs are immediately projected from the surface, visible for others to see. When your needs are not met, there may be explosive tantrums, defensive shutdown, or collapse into hysteria, all major **pitfalls.** In general, however, this placement correlates with a "softness" of personality. You are protective toward those you love or feel drawn to, with urgent sensitivity to those individuals' needs, and you're subtly defensive toward strangers, who may seem alien or threatening. The **challenge** is to make sure you're safe, then open up.

natural persona

Your natural face is soft and maternal, almost "moist," either sympathetic or needy, and sometimes both. This is especially true when the Moon occupies an expressive or emotional sign; it is less true when the Moon's placement is in a sign like Capricorn. There the moist quality may be replaced by a solid wall of seeming passivity.

Your name-tag says, **"I am responsive. Tell me what you need and I will provide it for you, for needs are the most important thing in the world."**

self-awareness

Spontaneous projection of emotional receptivity births awareness of the central, core self. Radiating yourself outward as either "mother" or "child"—defending, protecting, feeding, needing, clinging—reveals to you whatever your inner nature actually is. Awareness ebbs and flows in tandem with feelings. Once you're in touch with your needs and have discovered your inner self in any momentary setting, then come through your persona and act on what you've realized. Responsiveness to the outside world makes you aware of what you truly are, and what you truly want to do.

boundaries

You buffer the tension between internal and external realities by being sympathetic to the needs of others. Insensitivity or lack of emotional expression disconnects the two different realities, creating a numbing alienation from self, while compulsive mothering or unconscious neediness destroys the distinction between the two, causing a sense of perpetual hunger and emptiness. The **challenge,** however, is to nourish yourself and your environment without creating dependencies. The positive result is contentment.

vitality

Vitality is directly linked to emotional well-being. Proper diet and emotional comforts maintain your life force, although there may be heightened sensitivity to fluids, as well as vulnerability in the digestive or reproductive systems. You must learn the meaning of action in order to balance your tendency toward reaction. The force of habit has a profound effect on your stamina, either protecting and maintaining it, or disrupting and draining it. To heal yourself, discover what your habits are and reroute the imprints. Your relationship with your own mother is one of the most important of these factors, whether the connection is current and ongoing, or merely the result of childhood experience long buried within.

Mercury/1st

self-expression

Mercury in the 1st reveals that your spontaneous personality is nervous, mental, quick to perceive, and just as quick to change direction. There is a certain "short-term" orientation; the mental focus is immediate, but your attention span is short. You love solving riddles and are fascinated by any activity that propels your mind into immediate action. As with every Mercury interpretation, this can be altered significantly by its sign position and interplanetary aspects, and even more importantly by the placement and condition of the Sun. It is also affected strongly by environmental factors like education, family, and sociocultural background. Those considerations aside, however, the basic indication of the house placement alone suggests that you have a loquacious, verbal type of persona, one which is quick and clever.

natural persona

Mercury indicates a mental face, with an emphasis on rationality and cognition. How talkative you are depends on other considerations, but your persona certainly indicates an interest in communication. The mask is nervous and quick, as likely to question others as to reveal anything about the self.

Your name-tag says, **"I am curious, interested in your mind, mobile in my focus, and objective in my perceptions."**

self-awareness

Activation of the thinking, perceiving, and communicating functions of the nervous system promote awareness of your true inner self. The more you think, the more you awaken to yourself. It's not at all necessary that your thoughts be about yourself; in fact, the more they remain objective perceptions of the world around you, the more self-awareness results. Curiosity about the world and everything in it wakes you up.

boundaries

The bridge between inner and outer realities is associative, rational, and nervous, with mental interplay providing the connection. Expression without thought or communication without content can send the two environments spinning around one another in a meaningless whirlwind, while too much nervous energy or strictly impersonal calculation alienates them, destroying the linkage. The **challenge** is to analyze and communicate with both environments without falling into cold, mechanical rationality.

vitality

Clear perceptions and logical thinking provide support for your essential vitality, but vulnerability to nervous disorders may exist. You live in your mind, but you must learn to trust your body. Observe yourself; learn as much as you can about the physical and mental disciplines that keep you vital.

Venus/1st

self-expression

As with the Moon, Venus in the 1st house presents a picture of "active receptivity." Grace, beauty, aesthetics, and a basic appreciation for social interaction shape your spontaneous radiance of self. There is "femaleness" here, a wish to project yourself as womanly. This by no means indicates a tendency toward the effeminate, but rather it infers the promise of true receptivity. As with all astrological interpretations, however, whether or not that promise is fulfilled, as well as how it is fulfilled, depend upon a myriad of other factors. The **pitfall** lies in overeager surrender to outer stimulus; not taking a stand may result in your having no position at all, except that defined by others. The **challenge** is to be definite about who you are while remaining cooperative about interacting with others.

natural persona

The face shown to the world is pliant and focused on the imagery surrounding love and sharing. There is the promise of acceptance, the lure of romance.

Your name-tag says, **"I will love you if you allow, but more important, I will let you love me if you wish, for I am the personification of beauty and grace."**

self-awareness

You can naturally plug into your inner self whenever you project personal love, interpersonal harmony, or aesthetic beauty. The more lovingly you behave, the more consciousness you gain. The better you manage social harmony, the more self-aware you become. And finally, the more beautifully you project yourself, the more you find awareness of your true inner nature, whatever that may be.

boundaries

Social poise, harmony, and the projection of physical grace allow maximum interaction between your inner and outer environments. Disagreement, conflict, or chaos in expression close the lens and alienate the environments, as does excess aggression or unconscious anger. On the other hand, too much romance, seductive receptivity, or purely sensory pleasure merges the two worlds in false union, provoking a surprising and abrupt end to relatedness. The **challenge** is to provide clear, warm receptivity without falling "in love with love."

vitality

At every level of living, harmony supports your life force. Excess love of sensual pleasures, oversensitivity to conflict, and a distaste for hard work reduce the efficiency of your long-term well-being. You need to learn the value of exercise and sustained effort, not with grave discipline, but as part of bringing everything into proper balance, for balance is the key concept in maintaining your smooth vitality. Remember: moderation in all things.

Mars/1st

self-expression

With Mars in the 1st, there is an urgency to the spontaneous expression of personality. You have a cutting edge, a sharp thrust to the radiance of self, and this thrust is natural rather than intentional. Desire is paramount, even when it is not fully conscious. You "come on" strong, and your personality has a voracious feel, a natural hunger. The **pitfall** involves confronting life too combatively, while the **challenge** is to act as spontaneously and directly as you can.

natural persona

The natural face you show the world is pointed, focused on the next crisis just around the corner. You tend to be assertive, razor-sharp, and sometimes downright pushy, although you rarely see it that way. You lead with the cutting edge of personal desire.

Your name-tag, almost more challenge than statement, says simply, **"HOT."**

self-awareness

"Maleness" is the key to dawning self-awareness. The more spontaneously assertive you are, the more natural radiance is formed around the desire, and the greater will be the awareness of your central, core self. You must reach out of yourself, beyond yourself, in order to become aware of yourself. When you want something, you open the doorway to your inner self. When you go after it, you become who you really are.

boundaries

Competition, confrontation, and direct urgency of self-expression function as the bridge between inner and outer realities. Nonaction or passivity damages the bridge between the two environments, but heated aggression or brash pushiness provoke misinterpretation and embarrassing errors of judgment as the "arrow and the bull's-eye" forfeit their mutual perspectives. The **challenge** is to spontaneously fire yourself outward, but without overkill. Remember: your high energy is a bridge with which to connect, not a missile used to destroy. If you forget this, others may launch their missiles in response.

vitality

Your vitality is naturally high and your recuperative powers excellent in any crisis, but there may be susceptibility to fevers and an exaggerated tendency toward sudden injuries, such as cuts, abrasions, or broken bones that could require surgery. There's a marked tendency here to "lead with the head," and you may eventually have the facial scars to prove it. The main culprit is stress and the artificial but intense feeling of crisis it provokes. You must learn techniques of relaxation, but this does not mean inactivity. Rather, it infers relaxed action. Be sure to give yourself enough physical outlets for the high energy of your personality.

Jupiter/1st

self-expression

With Jupiter in the 1st house there is wide scope, a sense of bigness to the natural expression of personality. You are gregarious and generous in spontaneous expression, holding back little and amplifying most everything. The breadth can be profound or simply extravagant, and there is a tendency toward the **pitfall** of exaggeration. You're very social in your orientation, passing up few opportunities to express yourself in group situations. It's as if you feel more comfortable when there is a group audience; it draws out the natural buoyancy of your expression. Often, you'll find yourself projecting a positive self-image toward others even when your inner world is depressed or you're feeling pessimistic. The **challenge** is to let your personality maintain optimism.

natural persona

Easy expression characterizes Jupiter in the 1st. The face here is intelligent, positive, and generally winning, although excessive posturing and calculated opportunism can sometimes cloud the image.

Your name-tag says, **"I am social and friendly, open and honest, and very wise. Trust and believe me, even if I exaggerate my own self-importance."**

self-awareness

You become aware of your inner self by radiating generosity, social conscience, and a positive, philosophical worldview. You are most aware of yourself in social or group settings, but even when you're alone, you often "pretend" to be in the presence of others. It's as if you're preparing behind the scenes, practicing your lines, for this process births your self-awareness. Similarly, you're likely to spend much time examining social issues, and when you embrace a broadly philosophical perspective, self-awareness grows. It's not necessary that you work at wisdom; simply let it happen.

boundaries

Enthusiasm and an easy, flowing feel for social process keep your internal and external worlds linked. Inhibition, restraint, or pessimism split the worlds apart, but inflated ego and careless exaggeration confound the clarity between the two, resulting in wasted opportunities and unfulfilled promise. Others tend to trust you; do not break that trust. The **challenge** is to radiate buoyancy and a visionary social awareness without pretense. Let your perspectives grow naturally; don't push them to distortion.

vitality

With Jupiter, the 1st house indications around vitality are generally positive, with a large and resurgent life force, but there is a marked leaning toward excessive pleasures and a specific tendency toward obesity, with vulnerability in the bodily regulators of growth. The liver is an especially important and sensitive organ. As with Venus, you must learn moderation in all things, but what is most necessary is a sense of broad stimulation; too much of any one thing can blow you out.

Saturn/1st

self-expression

Saturn in the 1st house indicates natural restraint and concentrated self-expression. Conservatism, caution, and pragmatism condition the spontaneous radiance into something more measured. What is inferred is more important than what is expressed, and the tone of persona is often critical. Beware of the **pitfalls** of cynicism or harshness toward others. You may feel an intangible sense of stage fright, an awkwardness as you prepare to express yourself. It's often difficult to get your hands around your personality, as if you can't quite lift it. There is a weight, a burden of responsibility existing right at the surface of the self, like a boulder blocking the mouth of a cave. The **challenge** is to let time alleviate such feeling of heaviness, replacing them with solid maturity.

natural persona

Your natural face is smooth and solid, often silent, and "cool to the touch"—a sculpture of stone.

Your name-tag says, **"I am a rock of responsibility and strength. Do not think you can budge me, but know that I have wisdom borne of great endurance locked within. I will offer it slowly, carefully, and only if I trust that I have your respect."**

self-awareness

Restraint, conservatism, solidly pragmatic responsibility, and respect for authority reveal to you the existence and the meaning of your fundamental inner self. This is a paradoxical placement: the less you radiate, the more self-aware you become. Keep your self-expression spare and ascetic; pack a lot of substance into a little expression. Be patient in letting your personality fill up before radiating it outward into the environment, and you'll maximize the awareness you gain of your true inner self.

boundaries

You buffer your inner and outer environments with a solid wall of caution and self-control. Unconsidered actions or emotional risks based solely on faith or hope detach the two different environments wrenchingly, but self-denial or fear of authority fuse them agonizingly, resulting in paranoia and imprisonment of the self. The **challenge** is to keep your essence well-defined, self-contained, and grounded in real life, without slipping into pessimism, alienation, or self-punishment. Remind yourself often that you are in this world, but not of it. Your inner and outer realities are designed to be separate but connected, and if you keep them that way, you'll grow into glowing maturity.

vitality

Health considerations are especially sensitive with Saturn in the 1st, for your natural vitality is likely to be somewhat restrained. Minor ailments may abound, such as colds or other infections, but your worst enemy is psychological depression and a marked tendency toward hypochondria. Part of what life demands from you is learning to flow more comfortably, to accept yourself as you are, rather than as you think you should be. A well-paced sense of discipline is also a necessity, for your vitality is released in a measured flow rather than all at once.

Uranus/1st

self-expression

Uranus in the 1st house reveals you to be radical in natural expression, revolutionary in radiance. Your personality can alternate quickly between quiet calm and nervous electricity. There is willfulness in great measure, triggered at any time by the semiconscious need for total freedom. And there is almost certain eccentricity of expression, an idiosyncratic feeling that will be noticed by others more than by the self. Even the calm is pregnant, charged, waiting for the right moment to pop open like a jack-in-the-box. The **pitfall** is needless iconoclasm, while the **challenge** is to be truly unique.

natural persona

The face you show is unpredictable, marked by sudden and occasionally extreme shifts. Nervous energy shapes your persona, even though it may not always appear as an active presence. It is a symbolic mask of paradox and distance, conveying the sense of standing apart, of being a cool, dispassionate observer.

Your name-tag is a neon sign that changes messages drastically at the most unexpected times, but the basic message is, **"I am an unusual individual."**

self-awareness

Your central self can be awakened when the radiance of personality is uniquely individual, unpredictable, and crisp. Awareness occurs in bursts. When you are quiet and calm, as you are much of the time, you are merely observing, "on hold," waiting for the trigger. When you are ordinary, you vanish. It is only when you suddenly explode into extraordinary aliveness that you become truly conscious of yourself. You must carry a strong sense of independence in order to know who you really are.

boundaries

You don't so much build bridges as leap back and forth between your inner reality and the outer world. Consistency or passive obedience disrupt the contact, but disruptive behavior for its own sake defeats the necessary distinction between the two different worlds. In the first case you are ignored, not taken seriously, and in the second you are ostracized, ridden out of town on a rail. Your **challenge** is to inject into the world new and freer forms of selfhood without provoking blind, knee-jerk opposition.

vitality

Uranus in the 1st indicates the possibility of sudden or radical shifts in both health and vitality. The placement is especially prone to nervous disorders, and like Mercury and Mars, there is a likelihood of higher-than-normal susceptibility to stress, since your personality is especially high-strung. You need to learn to roll with the life's punches, taking as well as you give. In a crisis, marshal your energies and detach from the situation, to observe—separate from your body, separate from the world.

Neptune/1st

self-expression

With Neptune in the 1st house, the spontaneous personality is dreamy and perhaps mystical. There is some of the "soft" receptivity of Venus, but it is much more other-worldly, as if somehow you sense a different world than the rest of us. You are not likely to radiate with precision, and indeed, you may suffer the **pitfall** of confusion about how to express yourself when exactitude is necessary. However, in those situations where definiteness is not required, your personality glows with an almost magical understanding, far beyond what is ordinary or rational. You may feel that you don't quite "fit" in your personality, as if you're wearing someone else's clothes. On the other hand, you pretend wonderfully, and the **challenge** is to elevate a strong imagination into profound empathy for others.

natural persona

Of the ten planetary symbols, Neptune is the most characteristically "masked." It is like looking at a picture taken with extremely soft focus; the edges are blurred, and the picture is more impressionistic than expressionistic.

Your name-tag says, **"I am sensitive, soft, transparent, clairvoyant, slightly confused, emotionally vulnerable, and very receptive."**

self-awareness

Compassion, sensitivity, and a soft or dreamy expression of personality fosters awareness of your true inner nature. Your method of becoming conscious is a mystery of inversion: the less you act like yourself, the more you become conscious that you exist. The more you transcend yourself, let go of yourself, float beyond yourself, the more you suddenly discover who you are. When you allow yourself to merge back into the overall Oneness of Life, then you awaken into your individual selfhood. It can be perplexing, but it needn't be. Just remember that finding yourself requires that you surrender yourself—not to us, but to something larger than any of us. Whenever you lose your inner self, let go, and it will return.

boundaries

Natural sympathy for others, universality of love, and a soft fantasy focus in the spontaneous personality correctly link internal and external realities. Lack of faith in the cosmos breaks the link, alienating you from your true self, but self-deception, escapism, or fanaticism muddy the two different realities, resulting in martyrdom or disintegration of meaning. The **challenge** is to reunite yourself with all that exists, but to do so without drowning your own individuality.

vitality

Receptivity and merging are so pronounced that infection and addiction become significant concerns, as do all forms of psychosomatic illness. Be careful with drugs. You need to learn to use intuitive imagery in a disciplined way, both to promote well-being and to literally transcend the specter of disease. Disintegration and reintegration are key processes, and you can promote reintegration by graceful transcendence of any psychological negativity or physical malfunction. Disease is released rather than conquered. Love yourself back to health. Physical vitality is not your strength; faith is.

Pluto/1st

self-expression

With Pluto in the 1st, there is a deep intensity of self-expression. It's as if the power of the unconscious exists for all to see right at the surface of self, and that power has great impact. People tend to immediately like or dislike you, sometimes in spite of themselves. In some instances others both like and dislike you simultaneously, experiencing attraction and repulsion together. This is because your natural radiance demands psychological confrontation between yourself and others, even though that demand is largely unintentional. Your projected energy is mysterious, promising more than is shown, with a hint of danger. Curiously, you are often blind to the compelling nature of your own personality, and you wonder why others respond to you as they do.

natural persona

Your natural face is difficult to read, but impossible to ignore. Something dark and brooding is present, indefinable, unseen, but strongly felt.

Your name-tag says, **"I am not what I seem; I am more and less than you realize."**

self-awareness

Quiet intensity of expression and powerful release of subconscious energies furthers inner self-awareness. You have deep emotions waiting under the surface, and when they are released, you become more conscious of your existence. While they are "cooking," however, you tend to be a blank page in your inner awareness, just being, without knowing anything about your current state. When these intense feelings come out of the oven to erupt through your external personality, they create a sense of self so heightened that the awareness stays with you long after the eruption has subsided. You then operate on the memory of self until the next eruption. It's like drilling for oil. You'll strike a geyser only rarely, but when you do, it will fuel all your efforts to come through the many dry wells you may drill before hitting the next strike.

boundaries

The magnetism of powerful and purposeful emotions provide contact between your inner reality and the outer world. Superficiality, blockage, or "frozen" expression destroys the lens, but all forms of subterranean manipulation—such as emotional dominance—bind the two worlds together in chaotic compulsivity and the experience of silent terror. The **challenge** is hunt for a way to fuse your inner and outer environments without obliterating either in the process.

vitality

You have truly remarkable powers of recuperation, although psychological disorders are more crucial than physical ones. You are subject to all manner of intense and compulsive habits, but the will to live is symbolized more strongly here than with any other planet. You absolutely must learn to temper the tendency to burn out your body through love of intense excess. If you must "rev" on something, let yourself rev on your own positive vitality. Feedback techniques are immensely powerful here, so remind yourself often that Life wants to come through you. Should negativity still exist, then exorcise it in a cleansing purge. "If thine eye offends thee, pluck it out." Remember, however, that such extreme techniques are to be used only when all other avenues have been exhausted.

Planets
in
the
2nd House

2nd House

self-worth

***psychological judgment of the self by the self
(involving basic feelings of liking or disliking)***

If the 1st house represents spontaneous action creating initial self-awareness, then the 2nd house represents the reaction to what was projected. It is an area of evaluation of whatever was created or discovered about the self through expression. Thus, the 2nd reveals the characteristic way an individual judges him or herself.

This evaluation of worth is characteristically a gut process, rather than a rational experience, for what is paramount in the 2nd are the broad categories of goodness versus badness at the psychological level. What is the worth of your self-awareness? Do you like being yourself? If not, what must you create to establish healthier self-worth?

The condition of the 2nd house indicates the importance of self-worth in the overall scheme of an individual's life-path, and it reveals the characteristic issues forming the basis for validating or invalidating the essential self.

possession

ownership, personal possessions, property; the sense of "mine"

The 2nd house is the domain of ownership. It represents making concrete the kinetic activity and awareness generated in the 1st, focusing the awareness into a sense of identity. And with identity comes the consciousness that there is a difference between self and not-self, as well as the knowledge that on the Earth, the self is made manifest and tangible according to what it has.

For instance, we are not our bodies, but we do own our bodies, and that sense of possession is basic. To some extent, each of us identifies with what we possess. Rich or poor, covetous or unconcerned, we tend to invest our inner emotions into tangible objects that remind us of ourselves. The physical possessions we acquire through our own efforts represent in a very real way the products of our labors. "Mine" is important because we are animals, and territory is still linked with power and survival.

So the condition of the 2nd house reveals the characteristic attitudes and orientations we exhibit around the issues of personal ownership, possessions, and real property.

money

the experience of personal wealth; money, especially as it's used

With the development of culture, the territoriality of mere possessions has been superceded by another form of personal asset: money. The 2nd house concerns money, both as a raw resource and a highly abstract symbol—raw since money is the lowest common denominator of cultural worth, the "bottom line;" but highly abstract in that money has no innate, real value of its own. In fact, in this modern age of telecommunications, money often has no existence at all except as digits in a computer chip.

Its importance as an indicator of personal worth cannot be overlooked, although the almost exclusive monetary emphasis in many traditional 2nd house interpretations is clearly a misrepresentation of the true meaning of the house.

Still, the 2nd does indeed indicate the characteristic importance of and the attitudes surrounding money earned as a product of one's own labors, as well as the characteristic way such money may be spent.

self-exertion — *the experience of effort, and the style of actual work*

Every individual has a natural orientation toward the act of energetic work—the actual experience of exerting effort. We enjoy certain kinds of effort, and we select those if at all possible over other activities that may be objectively neutral, but are for us psychologically difficult or awkward, as if we couldn't fit ourselves into the labors. These feelings of attraction and repulsion toward effort can be subtle and intangible, or intensely gripping.

Some people work intensely, with great concentration; others work slowly and rhythmically. Some people are very physical in their exertion; others more mental or emotional in their approach. The variations are infinite, but we can reveal certain general tendencies from the natal planetary positions.

The condition of the 2nd house reveals the most characteristic modes of an individual's basic exertion, the orientation toward effort in general, the value placed on efforts, and finally, the satisfaction required from the work itself.

Later, other houses will build on this basic emotional orientation through the more complex processes of task orientation, with its emphasis on duty and shared productivity (6th), and career development, with its implications of stature and responsibility (10th).

sensuality — *pure, self-centered, self-involved physicality, and the general capacity for pleasure*

The 2nd house is the first of three principal areas of "sexuality" (the others are the 5th house and the 8th house), the initial experience of sexuality through the pleasure of sensual awareness. When a baby suckles at the breast of its mother, it is receiving more than sustenance. There is also pure, self-centered pleasure. The infant is not a "lover," not concerned with the mother's pleasure in the exchange. On the contrary, the child simply soaks up what is provided, feeling the sensations in rhythmic suckling.

This area is particularly fertile when assessing the psychological health of any individual, for paradoxes, inhibitions, excesses, or other problems in self-indulgence show up here, linked with the condition surrounding basic psychological self-worth.

Each of us has this experience of self-involved sensuality, the delight in pure sensation, the joy of earthly pleasures, and the condition of the 2nd reveals natural ways this is approached, felt, and understood, as well as the innate capacity for such experience.

Sun/2nd

self-worth

The Sun in the 2nd house shows an essential life-purpose centered around the issue of self-judgment. Psychological self-worth conditions the direction and fulfillment of your life as a whole. Everything else in your life will ultimately come back to this, and the value of any experience can be measured directly from within your personal feelings about the goodness that results—out of you, for you, through you. If you don't believe in yourself, you get nowhere in a hurry. So accept yourself first, no matter what happens, then strive to make that acceptance manifest through you.

possession

We also see the fundamental importance of personal identity through ownership. The core purpose of your life can be understood through the experience of personal ownership—what is "mine?" The particular kind of ownership most natural for you is indicated by other factors, such as the natal sign and interplanetary aspects of the Sun. Envy is a **pitfall,** but your ambition to be more by having more is a road that leads to fulfillment. Recognition of self-importance is the **challenge** to be achieved, while exclusion of or insensitivity toward others is the trap to be avoided.

money

Acquiring wealth is a central issue around which your life unfolds. Is there ever enough money? Can you have too much for your own good? Does money really indicate your true value as a human being? You have come to the earth to learn the meaning of "earnings;" possessions or money are valuable to life fulfillment only to the extent that they are earned, and can thus be considered truly a product of personal labors. The **pitfall** involves judging everything on a purely monetary basis. The **challenge** is to base your self-worth on the quality of work done to earn the money, not on the money itself, and then to enjoy the profits by reinvesting them back into yourself.

self-exertion

The core of the self should be involved in any personal effort. Spare nothing, and be clear; either work with your whole self, or relax with your whole self. Work is the essence of self-generation, and productivity is the proof of personal value. As with all house levels where the Sun is involved, the Sun's sign and interplanetary aspects are of particular importance in assessing the style of personal labors. The **pitfalls** are contradictory. You may undermine your efforts by believing on the one hand that they are undeserving, and on the other, that you deserve more for your work than market value. The **challenge** is to feel your bodily nature fully. The sweat of your labors is the tangible expression of your spiritual goodness.

sensuality

The pleasure principle is crucial. You're learning about the physicality of temporal existence, and a significant part of being physical is the sensation of pleasure. Touch is a uniquely personal experience, and you live from touch more than others, for it connects you with cosmic energy sources, tapping into the juice needed to operate your human machinery. Your life-purpose involves experiencing personal love for your own body, and your **challenge** is to make every physical event reveal its positive sensations. Squeeze every drop of pleasure out of the world.

Moon/2nd

self-worth

With the Moon in the 2nd, the psychological evaluation of self-worth is linked with the ability to emotionally respond to needs. If you protect yourself (and others) in a sensitive way, you'll feel good about yourself. However, even in the best living, the Moon is connected to the ebb and flow of the temperament. There will be fluctuations, mood shifts from good to bad feeling, and back again. These are cyclic and should be understood as temporary. Flow through the changes. Also, when personal needs for comfort or security go unfulfilled, good feelings invariably decay. The **challenge** is to provide yourself with what you need, not as others define it, but as you feel it.

possession

The experience of "mine" is tied to personal security more strongly here than with any other planet. There is an attitude of sentimentality attached to possessions, and the older they are, the more attachment is likely to be felt. On the other hand, the sense of "mine" tends to wax and wane—when needs are strong or go unmet, possessiveness is heightened; when needs are fulfilled, however, the grip of ownership fades quickly. Thus, possessions tend to come and go with momentary tides of feeling. Don't get stuck demanding a particular type of possession; try one thing, and if it's unsatisfying, move to another form. The **pitfall** is unconscious possessiveness, while the **challenge** is to recognize ownership as a tangible way of grounding the emotions.

money

Money is a primary source of security, an issue of regular daily concern. To feel comfortable, you need to know that you have enough. The **pitfall** is a feeling of constant "hunger" no matter how much money is stockpiled. Fortunes tend to fluctuate, and your anxiety level mirrors the monetary ups and downs. Don't just sit around and worry— you'll make yourself crazy. Channel your concern into pragmatic, disciplined efforts to acquire the wealth you need. The **challenge** is to protect your personal security by conservation of your finances. Save, but do not scrimp, and when you spend, get your money's worth in full emotional satisfaction.

self-exertion

Work is strongly influenced by changing moods. As with the Sun, there is considerable immersion, but here it is not the center of the consciousness that is immersed, but instead the level of personality we might term "habitual" or "automatic." You need to exert yourself physically in order to remain centered in the flow of day-to-day well-being. The **pitfall** involves inconstancy; working only when you feel like it. The **challenge** is to moderate effort in tune with the ebb and flow of inner feelings.

sensuality

You need sensory pleasure to feel nourished, to maintain regular emotional balance. The pleasures of physical movement, of muscles and skin, trigger interpersonal warmth and sensitivity, producing a maternal consciousness. Conversely, feelings are palpable sensations, linked strongly with the body. Whenever you feel responsive, it's natural to want the pleasure of touch. You need sensory stimulation, for it's a kind of food, and will satisfy many hungers. The **challenge** is to fulfill basic needs through adequate sensation, to see the necessity of physical pleasure in life, and to luxuriate in the comfort it provides.

Mercury/2nd

self-worth

Mercury in the 2nd house reveals that self-judgments are based on mentality. There is a certain self-absorption in the mind, as the issues of personal "goodness or badness" are debated within. The **challenge** is to make judgments about yourself from the sound and rational base of accurate and objective self-perception. Clear knowledge of yourself, however painful it may occasionally seem, can only help you.

possession

You organize ownership rationally, and the very nature of your possessions reflects a mental orientation. Tools of communication or objects that can be used to further general relatedness are attractive possessions. As with the Moon, there is constant movement within the realm of ownership, but the reasons here are tied not to feelings, but instead to curiosity. Possessions, especially new ones, alleviate boredom. When an object has lost its mental fascination for you, when it no longer stimulates the mind, it has no further value. The **challenge** is to use possession to fulfill the constant demands of your nervous system for fresh stimulation.

money

Your thoughts and communication often center around the issue of monetary resources, both in terms of acquisition and use. As with the Moon, fortunes may fluctuate, but the emphasis here is entirely mental rather than emotional. Money is appropriately used to provide mental stimulus, to further your education, or to promote communication, the sense of connectedness to a network of ideas. The **challenge** is to see the acquisition and use of money as an endless game, a stimulant toward developing rational faculties of clear perception and organization.

self-exertion

The main method of exerting effort is mental rather than physical, working through the nervous system. You prefer to analyze tasks rather than use sheer muscle power to accomplish them. Thinking and communicating are the most natural work orientation, although physical movement is necessary to provide a sense of satisfaction. Boring repetition deadens your motivation. The **challenge** is to divide any job into a series of smaller tasks, turning your attention from one to the other in sequence until the job is finished, thus keeping interest high and turning work into play.

sensuality

There is a quickening of sensation, an increased sensitivity in the nervous system to the pleasures of touch. You have much curiosity about physical sensation, a basic interest in figuring out the correlations between bodily experience and emotional reaction. This is not an inordinately sensual placement, for Mercury is essentially a neutral planet, indicating more a detached interest than any definite feelings of liking or disliking. Conversely, Mercury's placement in the 2nd shows that thinking and communicating are almost sensory experiences; physical pleasure is experienced from the stroking of mental stimulus. The **challenge** is to see mentality as an expression of personal enjoyment, to understand that the brain is the most sensual organ of the body.

Venus/2nd

self-worth

In the 2nd house, Venus indicates that personal value is assessed through the success or failure of personal love. The experience of beauty or pleasure makes you feel good, especially as those qualities can be directly related to the self. The prima donna syndrome is a **pitfall** to be avoided, for the **challenge** is to understand that personal worth is your birthright only when you allow feelings of true generosity, receptivity, and sincere caring to flow through you.

possession

Venus tends toward pronounced physicality when occupying the 2nd. Beautiful or expensive possessions are considered proof of your personal beauty, and ownership in general must enhance your sense of aesthetic grace. You want to be surrounded by loveliness—objects d'art, so to speak. The **pitfall** lies in confusing objects of beauty with the beauty contained within yourself, feeling that the objects themselves are the beauty. The **challenge** is to see possessions as a symbolic but concrete extension of your inner grace, to make tangible the personal beauty of the soul.

money

Money is also a symbol of pleasure or beauty. Financial resources are seen as a road to aesthetic fulfillment or interpersonal sharing, and frequently money is linked with the fundamental ability to feel and express personal love—you could conceivably marry to secure wealth. With this placement, money can indeed buy happiness, and the **challenge** is to focus on that positive aspect, for the **pitfall** is to assume the opposite, that not enough money produces unhappiness.

self-exertion

The style of exerting effort is primarily smooth. You are more dancer than worker, more aesthete than athlete. Tasks that involve the creation of beauty or harmony are attractive. Hard manual labor is usually rejected. However, you are a very consistent, steady worker once in the flow of effort. Work is better shared than alone. The **challenge** is to put into effect the "Tom Sawyer stratagem," to make even difficult work look so enjoyable that others want to share in it, for the endeavors of social process are preferable to the effort of manual labor.

sensuality

Physical pleasure for its own sake reaches an unequalled peak here. Pure enjoyment is paramount, for touch is a form of appreciation, and bodies, especially your own, are a living source of aesthetic satisfaction. Sensation is luxurious, a song of harmony, and physical stimulation is a delight. The emotional experience of love merges with physicality, and you use touch both to express love that already exists and to encourage love that could blossom. The **pitfall** is excessive self-involvement, a tendency to drown in personal pleasure, forgetting the relatedness that is the truest source of interpersonal love. The **challenge** is to manifest love as physically as possible, to feel the natural receptivity of the body, and to enjoy touch in a way that beautifies the essence of self.

Mars/2nd

self-worth

With Mars in the 2nd house, self-judgment is both a desire and a struggle. You must assert yourself to gain personal value. You must push for it, and often fight for it. There can be inner arguments, pitched battles surrounding the issue. Inverted anger directed at yourself is the **pitfall,** and the **challenge** is to aggressively destroy negative feelings you may discover yourself to believe, to consume them in the flame of desire for good feeling and the kinetic movement of productive action.

possession

You exert considerable energy around the issue of ownership. There are territorial battles; you must fight for what belongs to you. Conquest is emphasized in the desire to prove your mettle through territorial expansion. The focus is usually on acquisition rather than preservation or maintenance. The **challenge** is to keep moving forward, moving through possessions, not looking back, and to regard the issue of ownership as a field of honor.

money

Both the acquisition and the use of monetary resources are experienced as issues of considerable heat within your personality. At times this is felt and expressed as passionate interest, at other times as angry aggression. Money is often a battleground for proving the courage and assertiveness of the self. There is great desire for personal resources and the power they provide, for wealth is symbolic of victory, and it is occasionally used as a weapon in the struggle for personal success, although its primary use is acceleration—to enable you to move with speed. The **challenge** is to compete with full power, but by the rules. Be sure that competition is primarily with yourself rather than against others.

self-exertion

You are like a racehorse that loves to run. Long, complicated work rituals are not your forte; you are more sprinter than long-distance runner. The natural orientation is to race flat-out for a clearly visible finish line. Nor are you a craftsman, for precision, polishing, and detail work are uninteresting. Mistakes are inevitable, and often overlooked, necessitating that some jobs be done over. Physical effort with a strong emotional component is ideal for this placement, and there is a strong crisis orientation, a "rising to the occasion." Don't go around obstacles; push through them instead, tackling each problem one at a time. The **challenge** is to keep your motivation high, and confront problems directly.

sensuality

Sensation and desire come together. There is not nearly the emphasis on pleasure that Venus experiences, but instead a passionate fire aroused through touch. This fire builds from a spark into a flame, and can explode into a conflagration of activity and kinetic urgency. Similarly, desire and emotional heat are experienced more in the body than in the psyche, for physicality is the natural area of aggression. The **pitfall** is that such explosive energies can sometimes be disrespectful to your body when touch is made into a field of combat rather than a source of pleasure. The **challenge** is to use sensuality in an assertive way, as the cutting edge of the psyche, but to remember also that full sexuality involves a great deal more than simple physicality. It can begin with the body, but it must end with the soul.

Jupiter/2nd

self-worth

With Jupiter in the 2nd, self-judgment is linked to optimism and social advantage. Optimism enhances positive feelings about yourself. The more opportunities for social expression are recognized and acted upon, the better you feel about your life. However, exaggerated feelings of personal worth lead to disappointment, for the **challenge** is not simply to feel good, but to convert the ease of social relating into real and grounded benefits. Lady luck is often with you, but do not depend on her presence.

possession

Ownership becomes an area of opportunity. There is bounty here, but it's hardly the result of "good luck." It comes from well-developed intuition and a equally well-developed social network. The key is to take advantage of social opportunities for the acquisition of possessions, and be generous with personal property. Don't hold on, don't cling selfishly, for the **challenge** is to understand the fundamental truth of the old phrase, "Easy come, easy go."

money

Acquisition of money is associated with a positive attitude and the broad development of social skills. These qualities should be used freely and without restraint to further social position, to enhance the sense of opportunity for expression into cultural realms of collective involvement and sharing. The **pitfall** is waste of personal resources by resting too heavily on your laurels or counting on luck to provide a continuing flow of money. The **challenge** is to build an increasingly broad networking base through continual reinvestment of resources back into the social world.

self-exertion

With Jupiter, as with Mercury, there is a mental orientation to the effort of working. But the mentality is different in that it is essentially conceptual rather than analytical; an overview of productivity is more important than the solution of specific problems. As with Venus, there is a tendency to take the path of least resistance in accomplishing tasks. This placement is well-suited to a networking orientation, for the bent toward work is essentially social in motivation, and you excel at motivating, organizing, or supervising others. The **challenge** is to flow around obstacles like water. Don't let yourself be dammed up or bogged down, for the psychological sense of free movement is crucial. Whistle while you work.

sensuality

Your experience of sensuality is full and flowing. Touch is seen as a way of connecting with others, and the pleasure that results is palpable proof of social participation in a shared reality. There is an ease in physicality, a sense of comfort or naturalness with your body. This may lead to a love of athleticism, the sheer joy of movement. It also inclines, as does Venus or the Moon, to a love of good food as purely sensual pleasure, but there is an increased appreciation of the social ritual of gourmet eating or the cultural history of food. Every opportunity for physical stimulus is enjoyed, since there is little in the way of moral restraint, but this can lead to the **pitfalls** of excess and an exaggerated tendency to use your body to take advantage of others. The **challenge** is to fully recognize the opportunities for self-expression that touch can provide, but to do so in a way that ennobles the self.

Saturn/2nd

self-worth

Saturn in the 2nd house indicates that good feelings about yourself are necessarily restrained, in order that they may be concentrated and correctly developed over time. You may feel inadequate as an individual, somehow innately flawed, but your work is to build a solid foundation for good feeling. The **challenge** is to patiently learn the discipline of suspending harsh judgments about yourself, and to move toward positiveness in small steps, sustained efforts that persevere throughout the entire life.

possession

Ownership is a very serious question, a problem often linked with feelings of shame or unworthiness. You tend to resent the difficulty in acquiring and holding possessions or property. Keep the focus of your efforts on permanence and quality; transient possessions or shabby goods are not worth having. The **challenge** is to realize that ownership is not a given; in your life it must be earned and attentively maintained through careful and enduring effort. Build your estate slowly.

money

You must be disciplined, pragmatic, and patient with regard to money. The issue is not necessarily lack of money, although may seem the case, but rather the serious responsibilities you must shoulder, however much wealth is produced. Do not spend foolishly, but once the decision is made to buy something, remember to enjoy it. Don't go for the quick buck or the big score—follow through with plans. Sustained application and cautious strategies are the key, with an emphasis on blue chip investments that will be permanent, stable, and solid. Money cannot buy happiness, but disciplined effort can promote eventual fulfillment. Concentrate on the process, the means rather than the end. The **challenge** is to recognize and deal with the belief that money is more important than it really is, so maintain perspective. Manage your attitudes as well as your dollars.

self-exertion

You are generally a tireless worker, well-suited for efforts requiring strength, stamina, and perfection. You have the ability to grind away like the mills of God, eventually reducing even the most Herculean mountain to rubble through sustained and disciplined effort. There is often the presence of an inner "supervisor" whose only job is to push the "worker" toward greater productivity. Your attitude is "pay now, fly later," but too often you pay full price without ever taking the vacation. Duty is formidable and ever-present, and you risk the **pitfall** of blowout through discouragement. The **challenge** is to work slowly, recognizing progress, and to reward yourself for effort. Quality is important, but putting in your time also counts for something.

sensuality

You are so sensitive to physical stimulus that it often results in sensory overload and a blunting of pleasure. You could alternate between denial of the body and an inordinate lust for pure physical sensation. In both cases, you risk being trapped in the **pitfall** of diminished appreciation. The **challenge** is to understand that your body is indeed a temple, and to honor the temple through a gradual evolution of mastery and worship, proceeding one step at a time to slowly increase the density of pleasure and the enjoyment of touch. Chew the world slowly, not so much because it's good for you as because it enhances the taste of reality.

Uranus/2nd

self-worth

With Uranus in the 2nd, self-judgment is based on the uniqueness or independence you generate in living. To feel good about yourself, you must psychologically separate from the cultural imprints or family background and be able to see yourself as free. There can be radical changes in self-worth, sudden and unpredictable upsets in personal judgment, and just as sudden revivals of good feeling. The **challenge** is to be an original, to have a humanitarian focus, and to be beholden to no one.

possession

You like unusual or unique objects, and are attracted to anything that demonstrates genius of design or originality in execution. There is a solid but dramatically changeable philosophy of personal ownership, and you may have times of great or sudden bounty in acquisition followed by periods of surrender, loss, or severe asceticism. The **challenge** is to choose possessions that mirror your uniqueness, yet to allow upheavals of property to awaken in you a greater awareness of independence from the physical world. You're not what you own; you are the attitudes you hold about ownership.

money

Fortunes can be won with electrifying suddenness, but lost just as quickly. Money is often earned by unusual means—sometimes outside the boundaries of cultural acceptability or law. You're a potential genius for finding money in what appear to others barren environments, a "divining rod" for producing income in the worst of circumstances. Generally, the earning and spending of money are divided into separate phases; money is obtained during periods of willful discipline, followed by times of indulgent expenditure. Your monetary sense is marked by radical philosophical views: the "self-made" conservative relishing every advantage, the warm humanitarian eager to share personal resources, the "Robin Hood" social crusader seeking political and economic fairness in the collective. The **challenge** is to accept money as a symbol of change in your life, important only insofar as it enhances your personal independence.

self-exertion

Uranus indicates unusual work methods. Never one to read instructions or follow accepted procedures, you prefer to figure things out on your own. You like to accomplish tasks without interference from others, and even when cooperation is appropriate or necessary, a strong sense of self-will prevails. You have an electric awareness of the tasks at hand, yet there are frequent and sudden shifts from one task to another, seemingly without rhyme or reason. But others should not be fooled; you follow an inner and wholly self-generated scheme of accomplishment. The **challenge** is to merge genius with effort, and to do so in a way that does not alienate others, but instead awakens them to new and more productive methods.

sensuality

Your sensuality is normally characterized by a calm, self-contained physicality, but it belies explosive kinetic and nervous activity. You can trigger into the pleasures of touch at a moment's notice. The neural receptors are especially alert here, but not in an ordinary form of sensuality. It's almost as if consciousness leaps into and out of your body in a totally unpredictable manner, directed by sources in the self other than the conscious will. The **challenge** is to use pleasure consciously to awaken yourself, and once awake, to remain alert to your true individuality.

Neptune/2nd

self-worth

Self-judgment is linked to feelings of compassion or universal love. If you understand and accept others as individuals, if the goodness of life in general is affirmed with faith and humor, love for self follows. The **pitfalls** involve confusion and mistrust of yourself, not being able to define what your innate value is, resulting in a tendency to devalue yourself and allow others unfair advantage. The **challenge** is to renew personal faith by letting it be absorbed constantly from the environment. Receive the love that God offers you through all of us; take it in with true humility, of course, but do take it in.

possession

Neptune indicates sentimental feelings associated with personal possessions. Like Venus, there is a love of beautiful objects, but the emphasis here is on form rather than on substance. What is important is access and use, not ownership *per se,* for you have neither the temperament nor the interest to maintain, protect, or preserve what is owned. You've come to the earth not to acquire and hold, but to inspire and share, to feel more in harmony with the universe, more compassionate, and less isolated. The **challenge** is to make the real value of your possessions spiritual rather than physical.

money

Money is seen as infinite and omnipresent, but intangible. The presence may be an illusion or a fantasy, and it's difficult to focus your resources into a concretely usable form. At times, there is confusion, deception, and seductiveness surrounding the issue, for you are vulnerable to the glamor of wealth. Money is used primarily to further your personal dreams, for ideal rather than pragmatic purposes. This placement works best in a receptive mode, when resources are allowed to come to you almost magically, and the **challenge** is to have faith that gains and losses are essentially meaningless, to maintain good humor and strong faith that in spite of the ebb and flow of personal fortunes, the universe will dependably provide for you.

self-exertion

You work as if entranced. There is an intuitive merging with the task at hand, a sense of oneness between subject and object, so that the "doer" vanishes, resulting in the Zen-like experience of simple doing without any doer present. This absorption into the process of working can be uplifting, cleansing, and purifying for you, but it can also be draining if approached without sufficient lightness of spirit. Because you may not appreciate hard work for its own merit, you create a sense of flow or rhythm in the movement of physical labor. The **challenge** is to envision the ideal end product of your effort, then to observe reality-in-the-becoming manifest out of your graceful effort.

sensuality

You have an ineffable, liquid, almost mystical appreciation for the body and its senses. At times, touch can be a source of unspeakable awe, so much so that you won't be able to distinguish the physical boundaries between yourself and others. Pleasure is the same as merging, with the body a conduit back to God. However, physicality can be a leaden weight, a heavy and unwanted burden that no glut of pleasure can alleviate. In those moments, your body seems proof of the fragmented nature of human living, an alienation from the divinity of spirit. The **challenge** is to compassionately accept the paradoxical nature of physical sensation, to transcend addiction to pleasure, yet to rejoice in the magic and renewed oneness such pleasures can often provide.

Pluto/2nd

self-worth

Your potential for self-worth is tremendous, but the personality is too small to encompass such vast feeling, so it's developed beneath the conscious awareness. You may lose a sense of yourself for extended periods, allowing others to dominate or use you in the process, only to burst into the full bloom of self-worth after a long process of inner change. The **challenge** is to allow this transformation to occur in its own way, in its own time. During dry spells you may have to pretend that you're valuable, based on memory alone, but do it, even if it feels like merely going through the motions.

possession

Acquisitiveness can sink to the depths of childish selfishness, but it can also rise to the heights of devoted stewardship. The most desirable possessions are those which connote either psychological mastery or cultural power. Quality is a very definite factor—possessions must be the best available. Bounty and scarcity alternate as the natural outcome of your psychological feelings of worth, but amplified almost to exaggeration as they densify into the physical. Possessions must be acquired, maintained, renewed, or even destroyed as changes in subconscious self-worth demand. The **challenge** is to see in ownership a perfect mirror of inner feeling, and to keep the two in synch, one reflecting the other.

money

Money is connected to expansion into a larger worldview, and your ego sometimes has difficulty seeing the whole picture. Personal wealth and cultural power are linked. Negatively, money can be used solely to promote your ego-power in manipulating others. Positively, it can be a source of spiritual rejuvenation, allowing release into a fuller sense of being. Capital is often used either to promote or prevent real maturity— does money belong to you, or do you "belong" to it? The **challenge** is to become a "money magnet," but to do so without obsession.

self-exertion

You have great emotional concentration in the effort of working, with a single-minded sense of purpose once a task is locked into your sights. However, to you it may be no more than ordinary effort, for it emanates directly from subconscious power bases, bypassing your awareness entirely. You're sensitive to hierarchies of authority, tending toward extremes. You may command absolutely, imposing your own ideas about productivity, or you might submit completely, carrying out instructions with blind obedience. Don't hesitate to stop work that feels unproductive, and equally, go ahead with projects even if their value is uncertain. The **challenge** is to release your true power through work, by directing your endeavors toward cooperative social effort.

sensuality

Your capacity for sensual enjoyment is enormous, but it has to "cook" beneath the surface for long periods before being sumptuously served up to the consciousness. When it does, you gorge, as if the long fast must be made up for in a single meal of release and satiation. Like Saturn, Pluto shows a tendency toward periodic overload of the senses, but with Saturn there are built-in fuses to prevent the pleasure circuits from frying. Pluto's circuits have no such fuses, and the emotional heat of enjoyment can be so intense that it melts your personality. The **challenge** is to let the flood of pleasure wash through you, cleansing, rejuvenating, resulting in release of old feeling-imprints.

Planets
in
the
3rd House

3rd House

***day-to-day environment, one's relation to it;
the quality and style of daily activity***

In human development, birth marks the beginnings of spontaneous self-expression (1st house), followed by identification with the mother and the beginnings of self-conscious separation, the possession of an "I" distinct from the environment (2nd house). Then the nervous system reaches a point of growth where the child turns toward exploration. Having a sense of "me" or "mine," he becomes fascinated with what is "not-me," and the increasing coordination of motor skills is fueled by insatiable curiosity.

The 3rd house represents the child exploring the immediate surroundings, tasting everything that is not-self, engaging in a self-teaching process of categorizing the diverse elements all around. At the adult level, this phase loses some of its fascination and calms into a general pattern of interaction with the environment at hand.

The condition of the 3rd house shows how a person characteristically approaches, experiences, and interacts with the daily environment. Some people are direct, focused, or purposeful, burrowing laserlike through their daily schedule, while others are scattered, lighter in their "touch," attention darting from one stimulus to the next like a water strider hunting for food on the "skin" of a pond's surface. Some of us need more daily activity than others, more contact with the environment, more brief connections in encounter, and the 3rd indicates not only the relative importance of such nervously kinetic activity, but also what types of stimulus a person naturally seeks.

***development and use of mentality as a way
of understanding the real world***

Children are amazing in their capacity to enfold and assimilate experience whole, yet they can be almost comic in the limitations of their conceptual frameworks. They must be able to recognize a tree as a concrete object before they can begin to understand the metaphor of "tree-ness," the qualities that make a tree what it is, qualities that can be applied to other life-forms beside trees.

The 3rd house is the first of the four cadent houses (the others are the 6th, 9th and 12th). All cadent houses are concerned with mentality, both in its development and use. The 3rd is the initial experience of relationship between "I" and "it," the province of the concrete mind. This is the area of basic learning, of quicksilver attention, of the will toward exploration that characterized 19th-century science with its penchant for understanding life by mechanically breaking it into component parts.

The rational, pragmatic, left-brain type of mentality is emphasized here, and the 3rd house shows how that level of mind develops and is used.

[**NOTE:** Neither this nor any other level of the 3rd house denotes "intelligence," *per se,* as it is measured in socially-based evaluations such as IQ tests. Astrology does not reveal how completely an individual will develop his or her potential in this or other areas, nor does it suggest that one person is innately smarter than another. It does, however, indicate the type of intellect and the forms of expression that can naturally develop.]

curiosity

the experience of rational inquisitiveness, the desire to know

Mental development is not solely an issue of rational exercise. For basic learning to occur, there must be fundamental interest in the immediate environment. Mental ability is in some ways a function of mental inquisitiveness.

All four cadent houses share, to some extent, this quality of curiosity, though each has its own specialized arena. The 3rd house is the most general, concrete, and immediate. The 6th moves on to an interest in how things work, still tangible, but systematic. The 9th reaches toward mental abstractions and far away places, and the 12th culminates the journey by unhinging curiosity from the world altogether, moving into fascination with the mysteries of cosmos, both micro- and macro-.

The condition of the 3rd house reveals the importance and tone of basic curiosity for each individual, as well as its relevance to the development of rational intelligence.

*basic
education*

the orientation toward basic learning, especially through grammar and high school

Our ability to interact well with our environment is dependent not only on the proper development of the nervous system, but more specifically on how well we learn to communicate. Thus, all formal and informal education is a 3rd house experience, especially the formative education our society provides and requires.

The 3rd shows what experience we're likely to encounter or create in relation to basic education. It also reveals attitudes toward learning we tend to carry with us later in life.

communication

language as a tool; writing, and the style of speaking

Finally, the 3rd house shows how one communicates, especially in the areas of speaking and writing. The nervous system, in its penchant for naming and categorizing the diverse elements in the external world, involves a basic understanding of language: nouns, verbs, adjectives, adverbs, subjects, predicates, etc. This is not an area of interest in the philosophy of semantics, for such pure conceptualizing is linked with the opposite house, the 9th. Here in the 3rd one masters the mechanics of language, building a vocabulary by the most basic, rote learning.

Literally, the style of communication is indicated here. For instance, the tone of voice can often be predicted—mellifluous or strident, slow or rushing, etc. But beyond the manner of expression, the 3rd house reveals the attitudes surrounding verbal or written communication. Is there precision in the choice of words? Does emotional mood affect what is said and how it is communicated? Exactly how much? Are the words an accurate reflection of the person's inner truth? Analysis of the 3rd can often provide the answers.

The condition of the 3rd does not dependably reveal the level of one's skills, but it does show the importance of communication through words in any overall assessment of personality, as well as the characteristic way speaking or writing is approached.

Sun/3rd

outreach

With the Sun in the 3rd house, you are fascinated with the stimulus provided by any natural or human environment. Quality is less important than quantity, content less important than form, for in your life it is the sheer kineticism of activity at the surface that provides the essential energy for all other life processes. Depth has less meaning than breadth. Additionally, simple day-to-day activity is crucial. Where there is no kinetic movement, there is no vitality. The central **challenge** of your life is to discover the infinite variety of that which is not-self, to fuel yourself from that diversity, and to move energetically through the environment.

concrete mind

This level is the core of 3rd house meaning, and with the Sun it indicates that the essence of your life-purpose is in the evolution of concrete mentality. The development and use of rational intelligence become paramount. Pride is directly tied to the development and expression of your intellect, as is its negative shadow, shame. The view that all experiences in life should be seen as learning experiences is in some ways true for us all, but it is specifically true for 3rd house Sun individuals. For you, learning is at the center of all things, and logic, rationality, and categorization are all ways life-energy is absorbed and transformed for personal use.

curiosity

Curiosity may or may not be a strong trait in your apparent personality. You could conceivably seem calm and self-absorbed. What is overtly visible to us depends upon many other factors. But however you appear, you're likely to experience curiosity as a fundamental source of motivation. It gets you up, gets you going, and even when life is too much, as it sometimes can be, curiosity will renew you, lifting your spirits.

basic education

Basic education is central to the fulfillment of your life. It is not simply one of a number of equally important phases of growth, but rather it is the touchstone from which everything else will later blossom. If the experience of primary education is a positive one, then the child's life unfolds with vibrancy. On the other hand, if the experience is stultifying, much of what comes later will be a struggle. In either case, the emphasis usually returns to the fundamental concepts of basic education: reading, writing, and speaking. A significant part of life's essence is education, and with this placement especially, learning is built on the cornerstone of communication.

communication

You depend more than others on the ability to communicate with words, since development and use of the nervous system's rational capabilities are so strongly indicated as a key to life-purpose. You want to shine through your words. As usual with the Sun, the sign and aspects reveal the tonal quality of communication and speech patterns. But whatever the sign, whatever the interplanetary connections, the issue of communication is central. Anything that can't be understood through thinking or speaking has lowered value in the evolution of self. Communication is a battery charge, filling the tank of life-energy.

Moon/3rd

outreach

A 3rd house Moon indicates that you need motion and movement on a daily basis more strongly than other types. Curiosity is linked to emotional temperament, and since the Moon is strongly people-oriented, there is usually a desire to interact with others at the level of feelings rather than facts or figures. Interestingly, your maternal instincts are often directed at relative strangers as much or more than at intimate family. It's almost as if the very sense of family becomes a function of the immediate environment. Thus, when people enter into your world, they are first approached with caution, but are soon welcomed with open arms. However, as they become less a source of curiosity and more three-dimensionally human, your interest may fade. So this placement embodies an odd blend of depth and superficiality. The **challenge** is to fulfill your needs for diverse stimulation while also providing interactive stability.

concrete mind

You have a sense of cunning, a kind of "feeling" basis for mentality, rather than the cold logic of sheer rationality itself. Needs are conditioned by the influx of information, and conversely, perceptions are heavily influenced by emotional needs, which can be wonderful or terrible, depending on the situation. The **pitfalls** surround misinformation or misunderstanding through substitution of feelings for logic, while the **challenge** is to combine emotions and mentality into a mutually supportive and seamless whole.

curiosity

There is a hunger to know, to understand, and you "eat" information. Depending very much on your particular temperament, this can lead to profound temporary satisfaction, or it can produce an invisible "mental indigestion," which will register in uncomfortable feelings. Curiosity waxes and wanes accordingly. When the need to know goes unsatisfied, your security dissolves, so do everything you can to find out what interests you. However, deeper insecurity can produce a condition where nothing will satisfy your need to know, in which case you must look within for the knowledge. Distinguishing between these two conditions is a real **challenge.**

basic education

Early education is conditioned very much by the maternal figures through whom the child forms imprints. The mother's bent shines through in the child's attitudes toward school and learning. There is a real appetite for knowledge, and when this appetite goes unfulfilled, the relationship to the real world is gradually damaged, first through frustration, then through disinterest. The **challenge** is to learn something new every day, and this is no less authentic than any physical need such as hunger or sleep.

communication

Speech and emotion flow together into a seamless whole, with each influencing the other. The voice is often pleasing in tone, soothing to the ear. Emotional defensiveness can be heard as well as felt. Both thinking and speaking reflect the emotion of the moment; the mind is often the servant of the temperament, directed according to the current status of your feelings. In addition, what is said feeds back to and influences the emotions. The only surprise here is that both speaker and listener are often fooled into believing that what's being offered is "objective" data. If others want clear communication with you, be sure they understand your underlying emotional state before they interpret what's being said.

Mercury/3rd

outreach

Mercury in the 3rd reveals an overriding interest in the experience of environmental stimulus. You often dart from issue to issue, fueled by a nervous system that is almost insatiable in its drive to discover and taste new levels of the environment. Activity here is both mental and physical, with the emphasis on investigation and perception. You're usually on the go, seeking new and better sources of interest. While every house placement of Mercury is active, linking it with the 3rd creates a situation where boredom is anathema and downright deadening to the spirit. The **challenge** is to develop the quickness and facility of your mind through a perpetually active life.

concrete mind

Your mentality is agile, quick, and very well-suited to the manipulation of data. You can be computerlike in your approach to thought, juggling huge amounts of information in a perpetually ongoing search-and-sort operation aimed at the creation of new insights. Pure rationality is emphasized and must be maintained for clarity. The **pitfall** is loss of overall meaning in the endless pursuit of new data, and the **challenge** is to experience an ever-changing kaleidoscope of information relationships.

curiosity

As an insatiably curious person, the process of mentality is more pronounced than the pursuit of any particular information. Knowing is not an end *per se,* but rather a continuing means of stroking your nervous system. The **pitfall** surrounds not focusing long enough to ever really learn anything, creating a perpetual state of nervous aggravation, an "itch you can't scratch." The **challenge** is to enjoy the desire to know rather than the knowing itself.

basic education

The child with this placement often has a natural facility for learning. Communication skills can develop earlier than usual, although interest must be kept high through a diversity of stimuli. All the skills of understanding language can be successfully emphasized. Later in life, there will likely be a wide-reaching interests—"jack of all trades, master of none," for there is at least a little to be learned in everything.

communication

Mercury is usually presumed to indicate an individual who is very talkative, even verbose. This may or may not be the case, for with Mercury, as with all other planets, the sign position and interplanetary associations can substantially modify the symbolic patterns. What is safe to say, however, is that you are usually processing information. When it is expressed, what is most important is the information itself, not stylistic concerns such as tone of voice. In communicating with you, others should listen carefully to the words themselves. They hold the key.

Venus/3rd

outreach

This is a somewhat paradoxical placement, for although Venus shows what is loved or appreciated, and thus indicates an appreciation for movement, in the 3rd house Venus is sometimes drawn more toward the mental or emotional realms of experience. The appropriate image here is one of dance, of flowing movement within and through an environment. Daily activity and the immediate environment must reflect beauty and harmony to be satisfying for you. The **challenge** is to represent grace in motion, to develop an aesthetic appreciation of the kinetic relationships that form and flow through any environment.

concrete mind

You derive immense pleasure from the workings of mind. There is an almost geometrical aesthetic in mentality, an appreciation of the music of thought processes with their individual fact melodies and overriding chord patterns. Thinking becomes here more artistry than reason, more warm sensuality than cold logic. The **pitfall** can appear through an unwillingness to acknowledge any information that is perceived as ugly, confusing the content of mentality with its form, while the **challenge** is first to experience and then to express the natural beauty of logical associations, to enhance appreciation and the joy of mind itself.

curiosity

You are not so much curious as you are appreciative. Additionally, things do not interest you nearly so much as people, so you tend toward interview rather than inquiry. You may be less interested in a person's essence than you are fascinated by all the details of their living, the infinity of small facts that contribute to an overall impression of personality. In this regard, you may occasionally succumb to the **pitfalls** of superficiality or gossip, but the **challenge** is to develop your ability to pinpoint the heart of a person by composing these individually unimportant factors into a relevant matrix.

basic education

Although arts are more pronounced than sciences with Venus, the general sense of learning as an enjoyable activity is paramount. The sheer pleasure of education can be emphasized so the child regards learning with positive feelings of anticipation. Later, this person will love to be in the flow of new information, especially when the information comes from someone seen as intelligent. A good teacher is very similar to a good lover, and romance blossoms around the exchange of information.

communication

Unless there are other planetary positions or modifying aspects to the contrary, you probably have a very pleasing, even beautiful speaking voice, and a charming manner of presentation. There is smoothness, a rounded and soothing quality to the words, sometimes extending into the word choice itself. You love beauty in conversation, and strive to reach the ideal of a perfect aesthetic in speech and writing. The content is not nearly so important as the form to you, and because tact is of such fundamental importance, we can extend the statement to say that truth is not nearly so important as interpersonal harmony.

Mars/3rd

Mars in the 3rd house indicates that the focus of assertive energies is directed into daily activity through the immediate environment. You "shoot" yourself into the world. Depending on the sign quality of Mars, this can be reflected in a pointed, almost laser-like approach, somewhat on the order of a "self-arrow," or it can be more spread, more shotgun-like, a splay pattern of "self-pellets" covering a broad range of activity. Regardless of the bore and the gauge, Mars here indicates an urgency toward real action, revealing a person who must push into external surroundings. A self-starter, you are almost always busy, relentlessly confronting some obstacle or problem in the environment. Objectives are usually short-term, and results must be immediate. The **challenge** here is to keep emotionally steady in personal centeredness, to regulate the energies of desire so they're competitive but fair and even-tempered. Master the physical release of aggression; conquer the environment, but do not destroy it, and remember that people are more than objects in a force field.

concrete mind

You are a mental warrior, passionately involved in the mission to seek out and capture the essence of information. The mind becomes keen, even combative in the desire to prove points by cutting through irrelevance to the very heart of the matter, and vanquishing opponents by the superior use of mental weapons—the "sword" of acute perception and the "shield" of logic. Sometimes, however, the game of mental victory becomes more important than life or truth, and the **pitfall** of mental vanity can lead to dishonor: bending the facts to support your own bias. The **challenge** is to use reason as a surgical instrument cutting away facades of deception to reveal deeper truths, and finally, the wisdom hidden within.

curiosity

Curiosity here is razor-sharp, a siren sounding a red alert that mobilizes the entire being. It is a very basic itch, and you're not likely to hesitate in scratching it. The relation between subject and object is interesting: initially, it is what catches your attention that galvanizes you, but once aware of your desire, it becomes the drive to know that's your focus of attention. The object changes from a curiosity into a target.

basic education

Physical skills often develop early, and all games and sports are excellent vehicles for learning. Getting along with others is not likely to be one of the easier aspects of this placement, however, for aggression and territoriality are quite strong in ordinary socialization. Early education tend to be an arena of conflict, but curiously, this is often quite positive, for it can lead later in life to an incisive and inquiring mentality.

communication

The speaking voice is direct, urgent, and often sharp. Speed and power rather than beauty and form are the emphasized qualities. The words themselves as well as the style of delivery are chosen for maximum impact, and they often seem to explode out to the listener. You make your points with certainty, leaving no margin for doubt or interpretation. Confrontation replaces tact, and volume replaces grace, for mental competition is the keynote, mental victory the ambition. Others should not engage you in conversation unless they are prepared for at least subtle combat.

Jupiter/3rd

outreach

In the 3rd, Jupiter reveals that stimulus and movement are both natural and easy to assimilate. You lean strongly toward social environments and collective or group involvement. You take great joy in revving your nervous system, and equal joy in exploring any environment fully. Acceleration of perception, so urgent with Mars, is here so natural as to be almost unnoticed. Where Mars is like the sports car with a tight suspension and a definite feel for the road, Jupiter is more like the basic luxury liner plushmobile, equally fast but more buffered, with a cushier ride. As a result, speed often goes unnoticed and details are easily missed. The **challenge** here is to see everything, to digest the whole without missing the parts.

concrete mind

Your rational mind is buoyant and expansive. It weaves together individual strands of information into a new and more encompassing whole. So marked is this emphasis on pattern-making that it sometimes becomes more important than the particular components of information. Rules of logic can be slighted, sometimes even totally ignored, in the rush toward a single encompassing overview. Thus the **pitfall** lies in seeing a forest where there is only a stand of trees. The **challenge** is to allow your mind to construct coherent wholes from the cornucopia of available data, but to insure that logic dictates this wholism rather than the wish for simplistic insights.

curiosity

Your curiosity takes the form of wanting to know everything. What's lovely about this is that any particular thing you become interested in will spin off into many different directions, since each answer spawns new questions. What's not so wonderful is that you may forget to understand what you're exploring. The **challenge** is to give your inquiries an open, public platform, so that others can share the discoveries.

basic education

Socialization is the most important product of early education. The child has the temperament necessary to learn to deal successfully with others in group situations. If this is encouraged, the child can become quite adept in expressing a natural sense of goodwill, and thus be more readily accepted into the world of social relationships. Later in life there may be an easy facility with learning, a confidence and aplomb around the mastery of concrete mentality, or, less positively, a tendency to speak too freely without regard for the social consequences.

communication

You often speak in generalities, in classes or principles rather than specifics. There is the natural amplitude of Mars without the cutting edge, for while the volume is often high, the effect is cushioned rather than pointed. A born politician, you can talk your way out of any situation, and you may on occasion need to do just that. The truth is important, but you understand very well that truth can be delivered in many diverse forms, and you will eventually try them all.

Saturn/3rd

You have a natural eye toward detail, and a particular focus on the structural qualities of any environment. Regulations are an issue of great sensitivity, and you tend to be largely obedient to environmental limitations on your freedom of movement even while you are also frustrated by them. The **pitfall** involves being too active. Overstimulation blows out your nervous system, causing at least temporary shutdown. So the **challenge** is to focus your intense nervous interest upon only a small number of activities, and to move on them or with them slowly, completing each step before the next step is taken.

concrete mind

You have a special sensitivity to the rules of mentality, often accompanied by the disturbing feeling that formal procedures should be followed to the letter. You work ceaselessly to improve the structure of mental machinery, slowly and painstakingly going over the logic again and again to "debug" the program. The **pitfalls** lie in being so duty-bound that all the fun goes out of mentality. If that occurs, you can become cold and self-loathing, either rejecting rationality altogether or becoming ambitiously cynical, shooting down others' flights of mental fancy. The **challenge** is to let your mental skills age and mature like fine wine, until what began as uncertainty and fear blossoms into a marvelously grounded sensibility, a pragmatism that is unassumingly matter-of-fact, yet so strong it cannot be shaken.

curiosity

You are more ambitious to know than curious in the usual sense. This is quite fine, and well-suited to your temperament as long as the impulses to know are rewarded with a real experience of satisfaction at the end of the quest. Sometimes, however, you regard your own curiosity as if it were homework assigned by an invisible and strict teacher, so realize this for the **pitfall** it is. Instead, tune in to the **challenge** of curiosity, that of providing you with a structure to better secure your world through understanding.

basic education

Gentle but firm authority and consistent structure are key concepts. If the child's experience of rules, regulations, and hierarchies of power are benign, skills will develop slowly but steadily. Learning can become a life-long ambition, a gradual quest for greater fulfillment. Otherwise, early schooling may later be regarded as a time of trial and trauma. The issue of basic intelligence is serious. It moves along a scale with resistance at one end, marked by fears of mental inadequacy ("I'm not smart, and I can't learn."); and ambition to prove the mind at the other end, marked by determination to master the quest for knowledge ("I can eventually learn everything I want to know.").

communication

You tend to be economical and pragmatic in speech. Less is more here, and you prefer to think things through before opening your mouth. When you do choose to speak, others should listen carefully to the words, for they will be few and prudently chosen. The style of speech with this placement is terse, sometimes slow or heavy, rarely revealing your true inner character. Your speaking voice is a mask, a very important one, but a mask nonetheless. If others seek to understand and communicate with you, they should not listen for emotional clues; none are likely to be forthcoming. They must concentrate instead on the structure and content of what you're actually saying.

Uranus/3rd

outreach

Uranus in the 3rd indicates that the natural experience of environment is electric, somewhat chaotic, constantly changing, and an everlasting source of fascination. Interaction with the immediate world is definite, challenging, and marked by a strong tendency toward willful but erratic movement. You can go from quiet and passive to frenetically active in the blinking of an eye, but when questioned about the abruptness of changes in activity, you shrug and say it seemed perfectly ordinary. No stimulus is too extreme, no activity too bizarre for at least passing experimentation, and the **pitfall** lies in the old adage, "curiosity killed the cat." Fortunately, you do seem to possess nine lives. The **challenge** is to have provocative effect on the immediate world around you, and on others within that world, but to do so without alienating their goodwill.

concrete mind

Uranus reveals rationality to be an avenue of creative expression, scientific experimentation, and personal freedom. If Mars is the "mental warrior," then Uranus is the "mental commando," existing beyond logic's ordinary laws, a raider who strikes like lightning, out of the blue. And yet much of the time you seem mentally quiet, observing almost passively. But the storm of thinking is quietly brewing. The **pitfall** is mental iconoclasm, rebellion for its own sake. The **challenge** is enlightenment, the sudden insight, the light bulb over the head, the *"Eureka!"* of genius that transcends personal ego.

curiosity

As with Mercury, there is constant curiosity here, but unlike Saturn, complete fearlessness. As with Mars, there is a sense of challenge, but it is not usually competitive, not aimed at others. Rather, the competition is with Life itself. Can She be persuaded to divulge Her secrets? You're not curious about everything. In fact, your interest is usually marked by a quality of cool observation. But every now and then something will flash before your mind, and you will have to satisfy the urgent wish to know at any cost. You are thinking in both conditions, but calmly in the first, and electrically in the second.

basic education

Here a child can experience the first real excitement with the thrill of learning, the delightful shock of discovery. Somewhat paradoxically, The child also undergoes the first revolutionary impulses, the initial experience of defiant self-will. Primary schooling may later be regarded as having encouraged self-reliance and independence, but it may equally be seen as the initial experience of ostracism and not fitting in. The adult with this placement often has strong intellectual self-confidence, ranging from willful contrariety on the negative side, to brilliant insight on the positive.

communication

There is something unusual or idiosyncratic about your speech patterns. It may be in the voice quality itself, such as a slight lisp, or it may be an odd pronunciation of certain letters or diphthongs. In any case, it is not necessarily unpleasant. Rather, it is seen as a charming affectation, and becomes irrevocably associated with the uniqueness of your personality. Others aren't quite certain what to expect from you verbally. Just when they think they've got you pegged, you'll surprise them with some statement from left field, or a perverse twist in your style of delivery.

Neptune/3rd

outreach

In the 3rd house, Neptune reveals that environmental boundaries are almost impossible to define. There is no clear distinction between the edge of the self and the edge of the outer environment, and you float dreamily through your worlds, absorbing stimulus rather than seeking it. There is an oceanic feeling, as if you were a fish swimming through the sea. Movement is poetic and graceful. Kinetic energy levels are linked to the natural or social energy contained in any immediate environment, and you reflect movement, as in a dance where someone else is leading. The **pitfall** here, as with Jupiter but profoundly more pronounced, is in not paying attention, missing crucial elements such as traffic signals and cliff drop-offs. The **challenge** is to extend yourself into the environment, to become as one with the world.

concrete mind

The processes of mentality are a pathway back to the mystical center of the universe. With Mercury, the machinery of mental process is emphasized: facts, figures, subtle differences in flavor. Here, however, the machinery is often completely ignored. With Jupiter, leaps are made toward an increasingly wholistic synthesis. Here, however, the leap has already been made to ultimate wholeness. It is not an act of philosophical optimism, but instead a condition of faith, a state of grace. With Venus, mind is an avenue to pleasure. Here, however, it is a source of mystical awe. By its nature, logic requires separation: this is distinct from that. The **challenge** of a 3rd house Neptune is to stay tuned to the ultimate goal of mind: the awareness that All is One. The **pitfalls** to be avoided include allowing faith to become gullibility, grace to become laziness, and idealism to become self-deceit.

curiosity

Curiosity takes the form of wonderment. Life is so much, so altogether amazing, that it's almost overwhelming. It can be "awe-full." There is an old Hindu myth describing the universe, which says that life is like an infinite number of diamonds strung together in a webbing that goes on forever. Each diamond has an infinite number of facets, and every other diamond is reflected off each crystalline surface. For you, curiosity about anything leads you back to everything.

basic education

Learning can provide the child with vistas far beyond physical limits. Adventurous fantasy may become part of the educational imprint. But there may also be great confusion as former limits evaporate. Early religious education can have a pronounced effect on personality integration, for better or worse. An adult with this placement often has a fascination with the mystical implications of learning.

communication

Judging from Neptune's symbolism alone, your speaking voice is a marvel of delicacy. There is translucence, gentleness, and a marvelous sense of subtlety—you soothe, inspire or deceive. Neptune is more conducive to poetry or singing than to speaking or writing, and of all ten planetary types, you are the most difficult to decipher. This goes beyond the emotionality of the Moon, beyond the social tact of Venus, all the way to a realm where what is said is more intuition than concrete meaning, more vibration than physical sound. Seduction is at its height here, for both listener and speaker.

Pluto/3rd

outreach

Pluto in the 3rd house shows that your subconscious speaks to you through the immediate surroundings. It's like an Easter egg hunt, or a search for buried treasure. What makes stimulus and movement in the real world a positive or negative experience is the presence or absence of a "psychic map" of the environment. Activity for its own sake is meaningless; what matters instead is the ability to see signals and signposts at critical points. The **pitfall** is that you may be blind to your own need for exploration, for digging up valuable but hidden treasures existing all around, often right under your nose. The **challenge** is to keep activity deeply purposeful, and to remember that reality is often quite different from appearance.

concrete mind

The intricacies of rationality are compelling. Though your mentality may work toward the surface slowly, like magma rising within a volcano, the process is inexorable, for you are sensitized to the power that comes through knowledge. If the power can be harnessed, it can work wonders, both for yourself and those around you. The **pitfall** is being asleep to the intensity of your own mind, while the **challenge** is to gain control over these resources by studying the rules of logic.

curiosity

For you, curiosity is a probing tool, an auger bit cutting through the surface to reach into the hidden inner workings of life. Never content with appearances, you want to see the wiring within the walls, the plumbing beneath the floors. At times you are likely to be bored stiff by otherwise interesting puzzles, and you won't hesitate to brush them aside in the quest for what you believe lies underneath or beyond. Inquisitiveness is mentally intense, but sometimes emotionally blind. The **pitfall** is symbolic vivisection, while the **challenge** is respect for life's mysterious wholeness.

basic education

Here a child encounters the first experiences with something larger and more powerful than the self. It may be the authority of teachers; it may be the sudden onset of group and peer pressures; it may be the astonishment of learning itself. But in any case, the life can be dramatically affected by these early years in one of two directions: either open or closed psychologically. Basic education repeats itself over and over in the adult life. Fundamental learning is the key.

communication

Your speech is a direct outlet from the deepest realms of inner feeling, realms often unknown to your awareness. The key image here is invisibility. Words and feelings bubble away together far below the surface, gradually producing an amalgam that is neither fish nor fowl. There may be long periods of inarticulate silence, followed by eruptions of profound expression. In the insights, though, there exists an irresistible power. Your insights about the people in your world may be communicated more didactically than you intend, so be prepared for strong reactions to your words, since they often cut to the bone. Others should not expect self-revelation from you, but if it comes, it will be direct, blunt, and total.

Planets in the 4th House

4th House

microcosm | *the experience of being at the center of life, as the divine source of all meaning*

The 4th house is the section of personal space directly underfoot. Point straight down, and you are pointing into the 4th. But since the earth is a sphere, if everyone on the Earth pointed straight down, we would all aim at the same place, a single infinitesimal point in the center of the Earth.

The 4th represents the "microcosm," the sense of being at the center of life. It's the experience where each one of us is God, where everyone and everything around us is secondary to our own importance, as if we had somehow created them as characters in our own dream. It is the "inner sanctum" of personhood, the most personal and private space in one's life.

The condition of the 4th house reveals the characteristic way each of us approaches this private and subjective sense of being the most important spirit in the universe.

personal security | *home and family, the sense of "rootedness" in the experience of place*

The 4th house represents the roots of self, the hereditary background. Each family lineage is, in essence, a tiny civilization, a "country" unto itself, separated from other families by the concrete fact of bloodlines. So the 4th could be considered "small world culture" (as opposed to the 10th, which we will later see symbolizes "big world culture"). Each of us adopts this microculture, or more precisely, we absorb it in our infancies, and we form our most basic sense of social structure and personal security from these imprints, however contradictory they may be. More true love and more heartrending pain has occurred in the name of family than in any other shared human experience.

How do you approach the issue of personal security? What is the scope of "home," the type of family you seek to create, again and again? What are the paradoxes you struggle with in seeking to root your life in a self-centeredness that includes selected others?

The relative importance of and characteristic attitudes toward one's home and family are revealed by the condition of the 4th house.

emotional imprints | *conditions of the early childhood environment (reflected also at the end of life)*

Viewed from a metaphysical perspective, we come into the world as fully-formed entities. Each spirit has its own unique heritage of experience and paradox, with specific intentions to learn, create, share and contribute. But at birth, all knowing is crushed out of awareness, buried in the unconscious storehouse of images and archetypes.

Cut adrift, awash in a sea of dizzying amnesia, we compromise between spiritual intentions and the biological requirements of earthly life by reconstructing ourselves in a way that translates into the codes of information used by the synaptic neuro-transmitters of our nervous system. This is done by absorbing emotional information from the environment, especially the attitudes and behaviors of our parents, in an incredibly accelerated education. No wonder babies sleep eighteen hours a day; they're exhausted from the sheer effort of learning, of laying a foundation for the life to come.

These imprints often manifest again at the end of life, as the nervous system folds back upon itself, a dragon eating its own tail. Actual death is within the province of the 8th house, not relevant here, but the 4th reveals the experiences in life just after birth and before death, at the interfaces—the boundaries between cosmic and human awareness.

The 4th shows the nature of what was learned in our earliest emotional conditioning, the first "facts" we constructed about ourselves and the world. The condition of the house reveals the importance of these initial imprints, the characteristic way we selectively absorbed the emotional information out of which personality emerged.

"inner-link" parent

the parental figure more associated with emotional attitudes, most often the mother

Human parenting is historically marked by a division of protective labor—one parent provides emotional nourishment, while the other defends the family unit from the dangers of the world at large. Since the 4th house symbolizes the earliest personal worldview, one that is created and absorbed during infancy and childhood, it is usually the nurturing parent who has greater initial impact. In most cultures, this is the mother.

However, with the radical changes in role expectations occurring today, these pat divisions may no longer apply. Thus, the 4th house is termed the area of the "inner-link" parent. In real life, parents are often experienced in imprint as a single operating unit, a "set" of parents, but usually one parent is more associated with the 4th house (while the other tends to be more associated with the opposite house, the 10th).

Do planetary indications here represent an individual's selective perception, or do they indeed correlate with objective traits existing in the parent? The former is certainly true, and the latter may also be. In any case, the planetary associations of the 4th house reveal the developmental emphasis of the maternal or inner-link parent, as well as certain special qualities interpreted by the individual as coming from that parent.

private intuition

nonrational knowing about oneself; in occultism, the connection to one's personal guides

There are three levels of intuitive experience. They are personal (4th), interpersonal (8th), and collective (12th). Personal intuition is the experience of focusing on the inner self. It is essentially private in that the information revealed through such intuitive experience is received directly through the self, about the self, and for the self.

Metaphysically, these ultrapersonal experiences can be considered an interaction between the conscious human ego and more intangible levels of being, perhaps of one's own spirit, often called "the Higher Self." In occultism, they are often seen as separate entities not existing in our physical realm, called "guides," living spirits who work with the human being to foster growth and further right development.

In any case, whether considered in esoteric or purely pragmatic ways, the condition of the 4th house reveals the characteristic way the conscious "I" connects to the deeper, more inward Self in an attempt to better define personal needs.

Sun/4th

microcosm

A 4th house Sun indicates that you have come to the Earth to realize that you are ultimately the center of all things in life. This is the essence of the life-purpose, to experience fulfilled self-centeredness in as personal a way as possible. You're decidedly modest where overt expression is concerned, as the 4th is not only conservative, but private, and the Sun's placement here shows that you plug into life-energy by maintaining essential privacy, as a way of guarding your importance. The **challenge** is to protect your sense of divine centeredness without denying others their own subjective experience of Godliness.

personal security

Home, family, and the traditional values that form our cultural sense of personal security are at your core. Your life goal is to achieve and maintain security, to define what family means, and to experience the fulfillment of total safety for yourself and complete acceptance by those you emotionally value. At any given moment, you may or may not feel secure, but you inevitably return to the search for the perfect nest. The sign and aspects of the Sun reveal the type of family security most suited to your particular evolutionary dance. In a crisis, you will sacrifice everything else to protect your family.

emotional imprints

Emotional imprints and the conditioning of early life form the center from which everything grows. Though the matrix of family systems is important to each of us, regardless of the Sun's placement, for you it is the hub of existence. You experienced an early sense of self-importance in your family system, but curiously, what was even more critical was your reception by the world outside your family. This was likely either a triumph of confirmation or a trauma of contradiction. Insofar as the imprints were positive, your life unfolds in a kind of perpetual, happy sentimentality, and where they were negative, your life becomes a long and painful ambition to dig up, reveal, and free yourself through understanding and acceptance.

"inner-link" parent

One or both of your parents had extraordinary importance in your development, even more than we would normally expect. You were very attached to nourishment, since you needed more emotional warmth than other individuals. This attachment occurs whether your experience was positive or negative. Whether the inner-link was your mother or your father, you tend to "maternalize" the memories. What you learned from and about your own parents has direct and powerful relevance to the way you understand the central role of parenting as an adult, since your life-purpose revolves around the issues of protection and security. It is often helpful with this placement to unearth your parents' backgrounds, to separate myth from fact, for your **challenge** is to amplify what was best about them while improving on their flaws.

private intuition

Private intuition is a natural method of rejuvenation, something too important to be overlooked or taken for granted. The radar of inner guidance is often more compelling than the rationales of ordinary life. You seek to contact the deepest, most personal inner sanctum of selfhood. Every time you truly feel your inner self, life-energy rushes into your whole being. It is a "coming home" to oneself, a life built around private answers to the question, "What do I need to feel whole, safe, and secure?"

Moon/4th

microcosm

In the 4th, the Moon reveals that your inner sanctum is truly emotional in nature. Security, self-protection, and privacy are key issues. The ebb and flow of daily emotional needs and their fulfillment is more important for you than for others. Maternal imprints form the walls here, both for better and for worse. The **pitfall** lies in overly defensive emotions, feeling too insecure to risk fulfillment with others; the **challenge** is to provide yourself and all your loved ones with a firm, enduring emotional groundwork.

personal security

The nesting instinct is strong, deep, and permanent. Giving security to family and taking security from family become fused into the same emotions, the same actions. Your safety cannot be distinguished from the safety of your loved ones. The pull of the past is persistent, and the imprints are both conservative and traditional. The **pitfall** lies in the risk of giving up too much of your life to achieve and maintain security that may be illusory, or at best, temporary. The **challenge** is to learn that taking care of yourself begins within, since control of the environment is an ineffective way to make yourself feel safe. Instead, regulating personal emotions and understanding your early relationship to your mother aids fulfillment.

emotional imprints

Early conditioning was a river of wet and warm emotions coursing through an otherwise forbidding landscape. Imprints were absorbed largely through feeling-empathy. You felt it necessary to become a nurturer yourself, for someone around you seemed to need protection, so you learned to take care of yourself by taking care of others. Early habits die hard; they cling long after they have outlived their usefulness. Nourishment and protection form the core of these imprints.

"inner-link" parent

The mother is ultimately important with the Moon in the 4th. She was very likely the most dominant influence in your life. It's almost as if there had been a direct transfer of instinct between mother and child, for you are polarized not only to your mother's perceived traits, but also her role in the family. Although the Moon's house associations always have basic relevance in the life-structure, this one in particular is immensely potent in what it reveals about personality. We cannot predict the actual relationship with the mother; that depends on factors that go far beyond simple planet/house connection, but what we can assert is that her role as a symbol in your psyche extends far beyond normal expectations.

private intuition

Private intuition ebbs and flows on a daily basis, sometimes profoundly strong, other times conspicuous by its absence. Don't lose contact with the emotional self within, for your inner guides are guardians, the source of your protection from harm. Curiously for a placement indicating such strong self-absorption, there is often an inversion: you interpret what you intuitively receive not in terms of your own life, but rather as instructions surrounding protection or nourishment of others, especially those you love. This is because your sense of self does not end at the physical boundaries of the body; your psychological territory extends outward to embrace all those with whom you have emotional attachments. In a very real sense, you consider them part of you.

Mercury/4th

microcosm

With Mercury in the 4th, thoughts, ideas, and all forms of communication are linked with the most personal levels of self. You spend much time thinking about yourself and those you love. What is known is often kept secret, and though it's certainly natural that you be conservative with your information, this can occasionally work to your disadvantage. The **challenge** is to realize that your thoughts are private rather than secret, and to learn to share these private thoughts selectively, joyfully, with those you most trust.

personal security

Home is correctly a place of mental stimulation, a movable feast of ideas and physical change. Mobility is essential, for boredom and stultification lie in wait, ready to pounce whenever stagnation overcomes vibrancy, so you may want to think of yourself as having a "mobile home." Mercury is naturally subordinate to the Sun, and the actual tendency toward frequent relocation is subject to the Sun's condition, as well as that of the chart in general. However, no matter what is revealed by the rest of the chart, ties of communication are always important: conversational, by telephone, or written. These are the tools with which you build a sense of permanent security. The **pitfall** lies in uprooting yourself or being uprooted too often, and the **challenge** is to keep extending your security, moving and changing with the times as growth requires.

emotional imprints

Your imprints were basically derived from observed behavior and mental instructions. What you saw and heard were powerful motivators of future behavior, for imitative modeling is the rule here: "monkey see, monkey do." Your intelligence was emphasized, either positively or negatively. In and of itself, however, Mercury is the least important of the ten planets in revealing the imprint structure.

"inner-link" parent

Though Mercury's placement acts mainly as a modifier of the Sun's more primary impact, its placement here indicates that your mother had greater than ordinary importance as a teacher. Her imprint effect involved structuring your nervous system and mental machinery during infancy. Especially with the Sun in the 3rd or 5th houses, she may have vacillated a great deal about her maternal role, possibly preferring the cool dryness of mental contact rather than the warm wetness of the emotional.

private intuition

Rational processes are the natural key to private intuitions. You must figure things out with this placement, and much time is spent "in conversation" with the inner self, getting a handle on situations, problems, or choices. Answers may not be straightforward, but questions abound in an ongoing Socratic dialogue: you ask questions, and your guides respond by posing other questions. Even when they give you direct answers, it will stimulate you to further questions. They are more than willing to engage you in conversation, but be sure to keep the channels open, since they depend on your call. Reach out and touch someone, even if the being in question may not have a body.

Venus/4th

microcosm

Venus in the 4th indicates that personal love is ultimately very personal indeed. Love constitutes the essence of your private self. Your most personal levels of experience center around comfort, pleasure, and aesthetic appreciation. The **pitfalls** lie in seeming closed or self-centered emotionally, while the **challenge** is to safeguard your feelings of care by expressing them warmly to the people who are loved, in exquisite private moments of tangible sharing.

personal security

Your home is a place of beauty. No expense is spared to make your domain comfortable and aesthetically charming. Style is important, and the emphasis moves from the surface inward: if your surroundings are effectively restful, then surely your relationships will become peaceful also. The **pitfall** is that you often rely too heavily on the home for pleasurable experience, gradually withdrawing into a narrow and constricted sense of family. The **challenge** is to make your home a haven for sharing with all loved ones.

emotional imprints

Your imprints originated largely from pleasure/pain impulses. That which represented love or pleasure was absorbed; that which represented discomfort or denial was avoided. Like the Moon, but less intensely, Venus indicates that maternal or feminine influences formed the major imprints. Harmony or its absence were important conditioning factors. You felt yourself to be an object of beauty within your family, and you learned very early that you would be judged on the basis of certain feminine qualities in your expression, qualities such as receptivity and the willingness to maintain peace and promote harmony in social situations.

"inner-link" parent

Your mother was a model for beauty and pleasure, the person who taught you what being a woman meant. This could have been positive, or negative, or more likely, a blend of both. Later in life, you'll tend use that inner model in any situation involving your private life, such as the style of your home or the way you approach love. This doesn't necessarily mean that as an adult you'll be "just like her," although that's possible. It means that you'll either strive to create your style from her modeling, or strive to avoid what she symbolized for you. Alternately, you could use the same approach in finding a person with whom to form family, either looking for someone like her or opposite from her.

private intuition

Private intuition occupies the realm of "good feelings." Inner guides are experienced not so much as effective, real-life advisors, since they are not likely to give information. Instead, messages from the Higher Self function to remind you of the beauty of life. They perform the function of relief, offering a respite from the trials and tribulations of pragmatic, external living. Your guides bring you loveliness. They open your eyes, pointing the way toward truer beauty, renewing your sense of lovingness, revitalizing the appreciation of both your own life and life around you.

Mars/4th

microcosm

With Mars in the 4th, your inner sanctum is constructed around the imagery and feeling of desire. What you want becomes almost sacredly personal. Your inner focus is honed to a razor's edge. But you may experience caution around overtly going after what you want. The **pitfall** involves this tendency to postpone action and thus inadvertently delay fulfillment; too often, you want to be sure you're safe before you act. The **challenge** is to express desire with all the depth it deserves.

personal security

Security is much desired, but difficult to achieve, in large part because you are by nature polarized toward those closest to you. You want so much with them and from them that ordinary fulfillment is sometimes not enough. You tend to be extremely sentimental and protective, but remember that even softness can be smothering. As an adult, you're concerned with the scars of the past. You want to clear the air with your family, to get one clean shot at making your points, so you can finally connect with them on your own terms. The **pitfalls** are continual restlessness and a lack of true relaxation, while the **challenge** is to learn the difference between passion and aggression.

emotional imprints

Your imprints were probably more event-oriented than would be the case with most of the other planets. Peak experiences were more significant than subtler conditioning, and the classical assumptions of childhood trauma, especially separations, have greater relevance if they occurred. The sheer weight of territoriality was a profound influence: fighting for what was "mine." You felt you were being judged according to male standards: desire, assertiveness, and willful action.

"inner-link" parent

Here we see a contradiction, a masculine symbol in the mother's area. It can indicate a number of distinctly different possibilities. If your mother was feminine on the surface, you still felt her masculinity assert itself often. She might have been a woman of high energies, the natural ruler of the roost, someone who could easily have moved her talents into the external world of cultural power. On the other hand, your father may have taken over some of the classical duties of motherhood. Or you could have imprinted on the urgency of your relationship for him, with desire spilling over into interaction. This placement sometimes indicates long-standing disagreement or bitterness with parents, often resulting from a conflict in the parent-child roles. However, even when that is the case, there is a sense of strength that pervades the imprints.

private intuition

Your relationship to inner guidance moves through heated and volatile exchanges. You go within to energize yourself, to charge your batteries, to light the flames of desire. Again and again, you momentarily withdraw from the world during times of difficulty, only to emerge soon after with an entirely new direction or fresh approach, almost like a slingshot. Your guides remind you of what you truly want. They are not, however, always friendly. Often they confront you, pushing you to get it up once more, to live your life adventurously and with real passion.

Jupiter/4th

microcosm

With Jupiter in the 4th house, observation, learning, and wisdom form the core of the private self. Your inner sanctum is buoyantly social and interested in the world. Opportunities for growth and interaction are sacred to your inward self, and the **pitfall** lies in not taking advantage of your natural optimism. The **challenge** is to allow others into the your private space of self, for you are more secure in social settings.

personal security

You must understand the philosophy of your family, the assumptions and ideals that shaped the family system. Security itself is of relatively small importance, while appropriate behavior looms large as an issue. The family is a team, and each person in the family is a player with a definite role. Understanding the roles learned in childhood has a definite value, for team spirit is too often a cover for deeper and more Machiavellian power relationships. The **challenge** is to be free enough to make full and respectful use of the opportunities you are heir to.

emotional imprints

Your early childhood experiences were bountiful. This can be literal, indicating a large family, but more often it reveals tone rather than size, indicating a family system full of cultural stimulation: open discussions of philosophy, current events, art, politics—the free flow of ideas. Sometimes the effect is more psychological, showing that your family was proud of its presumed social distinctions, its lineage, or its educational achievements. You may have felt motivated to great achievements, or burdened by expectations that were too high for your capabilities. In any case, your imprints surround the issue of "royal status," the sense of belonging to a special group of people chosen for higher position in the social strata.

"inner-link" parent

Jupiter in particular tends to emphasize the family unit as a whole, rather than singling out one parent as the major inward imprint. There is an emphasis on mentality in your relationship to your parents, a tendency for one or both of them to have seemed impressively wise. This could have been seen as sincere, embodying maturity and optimism, or as insincere, full of bluster and bombast. In either case, the **challenge** is to use the imprints to motivate development of broad-based understanding.

private intuition

This is the "Guru on the Mountaintop." The inner guides are felt to be a "higher" or more evolved dimension of self than the ordinary ego consciousness. They are seen as wise and beneficent, and their advice is usually not pragmatic in nature, but more Zen in tone, resulting in the "aha's" of reflective realization. They smile reassuringly and offer puzzles for your consciousness to solve. Their methods usually involve paradigm shifts—using paradoxes to promote changes in perspective rather than solutions to problems. They can be gentle pranksters. Sometimes their jokes will make you smile during dark hours. Your guides like you; laugh with them.

Saturn/4th

microcosm

In the 4th house, Saturn reveals the seriousness of self-importance. Privacy is a difficult issue. At times it seems forced rather than chosen, more solitary confinement than secure space, as if you cannot really connect with others. However, at other moments, privacy feels denied by circumstantial responsibilities, and you must steal your aloneness, protecting it jealously. The **pitfalls** revolve around fear that you may never achieve truly balanced self-centeredness. How can you be the center of everything, yet remain humble? The **challenge** is to realize that your personal identity is inviolable, a source of strength buried deeply within the self, like the roots of a giant oak.

personal security

Security is linked with responsibility, especially the feeling that you must carry on some fundamental family tradition, whatever the cost. You probably believe it would be selfish to do otherwise, even when what you must carry is a difficult burden. You may have trouble realizing the weight of these traditions, bearing them dutifully rather than examining them directly. This is part of your basic conservatism, a special sensitivity toward solid, dependable structures. Though you are cautious, you work like "the little piggy who built his house out of bricks" to establish a home and family of permanent value. While we all deal with the **pitfalls** of shame in our families, you in particular must devote enduring efforts toward overcoming any crippling effects from shame-based experience. The **challenge** is to honor the past without sacrificing yourself.

emotional imprints

Your family was highly structured, marked on the one hand by solid respect for authority, and on the other by a sense of brittle rigidity. Identifying your role in the family was difficult. You may have felt unimportant, unwanted, or unloved, or conversely, you may have felt far too important, like a bird in a gilded cage. In either case, alienation is a real, if sometimes unconscious presence. It's lonely both at the bottom and at the top. But you learned how to satisfy your desires and avoid getting caught with your hand in the cookie jar. Whatever you couldn't have, couldn't do, couldn't be is what you most remember and work to achieve.

"inner-link" parent

What can we make of the father's symbol in the mother's place? It may indeed be that the father is the inner-link parent in this situation, but more likely, it indicates that the mother took over the father's role. She came to represent authority and external structuring power for you as a child. This placement often corresponds with a "missing" father, someone not necessarily physically absent, but psychologically neutralized in one way or another.

private intuition

Can you trust yourself? You want aid from your guides, but may be afraid to seek it out for fear you may be unworthy of your own best counsel. The key is self-respect developed over a long period of growth, self-respect that can mature into trust—truly believing in yourself. Honor the justice of your inner guides; they may at times seem stern, cold, even unfeeling, but finally they are on your side, helping you to become strong, capable, and grown-up. Real, honest adulthood is very difficult for all of us. Your guides want to see you achieve that rare state.

Uranus/4th

microcosm

Your private self is eccentric, probably very different in tone and spirit from the self shown to the world. There is freedom in your inner sanctum, freedom from the restrictions of social rules and cultural appropriateness. The **pitfall** surrounds hiding your individuality too well, so that no one ever sees it. The **challenge** is to drink deeply from the well of personal freedom and uniqueness. More than with any other 4th house planetary association, Uranus indicates a heightened possibility of feeling like a stranger in a strange land. All human beings occasionally experience alienation. But for most, that feeling is negative and quickly shaken off, like a bad cold. For you, it's more than psychological, more than merely metaphorical, Being an alien is something you hold onto privately. Whether you feel privileged or cursed, it remains a treasured secret.

personal security

Family is a continual source of revolution. You feel it your task to upset the applecart, to be the reformer of the family, and you will tend to live out that role through phases alternating between exuberantly positive individuality and staunchly defiant outrage. Abnormality is emphasized in all aspects of home and family, and instability is actually more comfortable than permanence. The **pitfall** involves a rejection of real security through ego eccentricities, while the **challenge** is to awaken yourself to the miracle of true interdependence, and to realize that change is the only constant.

emotional imprints

Here, as with Mars, events condition the imprint system, but whatever shocks you suffered as a child—loss, separation, sudden change—tended to produce not heat or conflict, but withdrawal to a safer world inside yourself. So you learned to rely on yourself very early, and those imprints toward separateness or independence remain strong throughout the entire life. You also may have felt (or been made to feel) that you were different from the rest of your family, either "special" or "a black sheep."

"inner-link" parent

Your mother's brilliant eccentricity is emphasized in your imprints of her. However traditional her values may have seemed, there was something very willful—even perhaps defiant—that stood out in your early understanding of her. She may have seemed unstable, or she might have ruled the household with an iron hand. Even if she was a quiet, calm person, you would have been impressed by her strong sense of self-possession. The precise effect cannot be determined from the house placement alone, but what is certain is that her imprint is emphatic and in some way unusual.

private intuition

Contact with inward guidance is sporadic. Your guides are powerful but unpredictable, remaining silent and invisible for awhile, then bursting suddenly onto the scene. There is sometimes the sensation that they are in control—"don't call us, we'll call you"—although that is, of course, an illusion. More likely, they regard you with detached friendship, a kind of "cool warmth," and they simply check in when they're in the neighborhood. More than any other planet, this one corresponds to the epiphany of revelation: moments of blinding mental "light" suddenly explode into the consciousness, revealing not only what you didn't see, but what no one has ever seen before: your own uniqueness, your own special truth.

Neptune/4th

microcosm

Neptune in the 4th reveals that your inner sanctum contains no personal self. Instead, the space usually reserved for privacy is utilized to release you from the pressures of individual living. It is a space of universality, a return home to the essence of all things as One Together. The **pitfall** lies in a tendency to escape into emotional formlessness, to mistake ego inflation for cosmic reunion. The **challenge** is to allow everything to penetrate you without ever losing the ability to function well in real life.

personal security

Personal security has no pragmatic meaning. You are fascinated by a sense of family that extends far beyond the limited scope of biological bloodlines. Family is universal, and home is anywhere. The **pitfall** is that openness, translucidity, and idealism may so completely evaporate boundaries that you lose all sense of meaning, disintegrating into a state of permanent insecurity. The **challenge** is to realize that all men are indeed brothers, both within and beyond the flesh.

emotional imprints

Your early conditioning was full of idealism, fantasy, and often illusion, perhaps even lies. Dreams formed the basis of the imprint system, weaving an invisible pattern in your habits. Somewhere in your imprints may be the dark shadow of victim consciousness or drug problems, but even these can be turned toward the positive if you are willing to connect with a universal vision of life. Don't look toward an event-oriented background; what actually happened was of far less importance than what occurred in your fantasies. The sense of selfless spiritual purpose was important from the start, and may have manifested itself in religious training or attitudes.

"inner-link" parent

There are echoes of both sainthood or martyrdom in your maternal impressions. Your mother may have been seen as a woman of delicacy and compassion, yet she might just as easily have been perceived as foolish dreamer or unwitting victim. In either case, she promoted in your early development a strongly intuitive orientation. Later in adulthood, you could easily be telepathic or psychic without ever thinking about it, since it would seem second nature to you. The **pitfall** you have with your mother surrounds boundaries. It's difficult for you to tell the difference between what's hers and what's yours. The **challenge** is to embrace her spirit without succumbing to her melodrama.

private intuition

Inner guidance is an evanescent presence, floating just beyond the periphery of vision. It is like an echo, a constant "AUM," often felt but seldom seen. Private intuitions are not truly private here; information about life is absorbed from every sector of the environment—within the self, from the world around you, and directly from others. The information may be about anyone, for anyone, not solely your personal self. It is all experienced as relevant, and with this placement we see the first developments of universal channelship. You are a conduit, a conveyor, a conductor of information you may not fully understand. Hold the information until life asks you for it, and then give it purely. For you, intuition bleeds into every thought, every feeling, every activity.

Pluto/4th

microcosm

Your inner sanctum is a dark and mysterious place. It may be foreboding or comforting, but in either case it involves contact with the unknown. Your private self is an enigma existing in a region of psychological turbulence, an oven of transformation rather than a secure haven. The **pitfall** is the possibility that your conscious self will be devoured by this unknown space, while the **challenge** is to use the inner sanctum as a caterpillar uses its chrysalis: to promote fundamental changes of consciousness.

personal security

Personal security emanates from deep within the self. Home as a physical place has no natural meaning, but home as a psychological construct is all-encompassing. You are often blind to your own complexity around family issues, protesting that you need no security even as you dig deeper and deeper to find a safe place. The family is an event of confrontation with great power, the power of the unconscious, and the **pitfall** lies in being consumed or dominated by this power. The **challenge** is to rebirth a more loving and self-respectful form of family security, one without the compulsive need to control others or subjugate the self.

emotional imprints

Your imprints are of a most profound nature. There was no distinguishing between events and emotions, for everything blended together in a deep, pressurized chamber, locked within the self below the level of awareness. Though you may have always possessed an almost absolute sense of belonging in your family, it's more likely that you didn't know why you were there, what your function was, or how you were linked to your family members. No other planet indicates so strong a need to unearth one's early imprints. This is the stuff of classical psychotherapy, where culminating realizations achieved after great effort and long periods of time can completely transform your understanding of your background.

"inner-link" parent

Pluto indicates even more deeply than Mars the presence of power conflicts existing between mother and child. These may form an unshakeable inner bond, but curiously, the depth of the connection is often unseen or denied. It's possible that you felt dominated or driven by the powerful love of a mother who sought fulfillment through you, but any resentments that may exist are often buried beneath a sugar coating of feigned love and respect. Even in the best childhood, there is here a presence, a compulsion surrounding the care. If you eventually reach the bottom of your feelings about her (and hers for you), you will discover profound evidence of the sacred relationship of all mothers to all children.

private intuition

There is a source of infinite power and knowledge buried somewhere within you, existing like a secret weapon to be used only in times of profound significance or great peril. The catch is that it's ordinarily invisible to the conscious mind: you must hunt for it until it decides to be found; you chase it until it catches you. The function of private intuitions here is to destroy outmoded life games, to utterly change your emotional perspective from the inside out. Access to your guides is allowed rarely, but when it happens, you'll know. They are like psychic surgeons with very sharp scalpels, and they don't mess around with superficialities. Instead, they cut right to the heart of the matter.

Planets in the 5th House

5th House

intentional ego presentation, life as a stage, personal charisma

Following the establishment of true, inner self-centeredness, resulting in the security of home and family, the achievement of a completely personal sphere (4th house), we begin turning our attention to the larger world beyond. Having experienced acceptance, we become aware of its opposite: the risk of rejection. We conquer this fear through the development of social skills involving the use of a conscious persona.

The 1st house represented the natural and spontaneous expression of self; the 5th house represents conscious and intentional presentation through a fully formed ego. The 1st embodied the experience of kinetic radiance, the discovery of self-awareness by action into the environment; the 5th symbolizes the next stage in self-expression, the creation of a conscious image to be formally presented to the world.

"All the world's a stage, and all the people players." The 5th house is the level of experience where we possess a heightened awareness of life's theatrical reality. Everyone is the star of his or her own "movie." We're "onstage" whenever we relate to someone else, giving a performance in the character of our own carefully chosen roles. And like the Hollywood stars of the 1940's, Jimmy Stewart, John Wayne, Bogart, Tracy and Hepburn, we tend to identify ourselves as singularly unique, regardless of the different roles we're called on to portray. Everyone else is seen as audience or critic, and we seek to entertain them, to win them over, to convince them of the creativity of our characterization.

The 5th reveals the experience of performing, and the condition of the house reveals the natural "script" used in the development of this conscious image, the psychological elements we'll draw upon to create our character.

the experience of active courtship; the characteristic way love is offered

The 5th house and its opposite, the 11th, form the axis of romantic love. In the 5th, we are the lover; in the 11th, the beloved. 5th house experience is that of active, conscious courtship. As with all 5th house levels, the sense of romantic courtship requires a bravura performance, stimulated by the continually challenging awareness that we may be rejected by the object of our affections. We stand in the courtyard at the bottom of the trellis, Spanish guitar in hand, singing love songs in the hope that the fair one will emerge on the balcony, smile, and toss us the rose symbolic of receptivity to our seduction. The experience of giving love consciously, opening the heart in spite of the risk of rejection, is the essence of personal creativity.

The condition of the 5th shows the elements of character involved in our identity as lovers, and it also shows what we feel to be our most consciously loving qualities, as well as how we offer love to others.

sexual
performance

making love as an exaltation of the ego; performing for the beloved

The 5th house is the second of the three sexual areas, the first being the 2nd house (pure, self-involved sensuality), and the third being the 8th house (the union of two becoming one). Here in the 5th, the emphasis is on making love to another. Essentially emotional, the act is similar to theatre, with the individual performing the role of lover, seeking through the conscious ego to please the beloved, and affirm the social ability of the self. This is the area of giving pleasure; in the experience of the partner's satisfaction, the self gains confidence in its own talents.

The proof we need here is physical, not abstract, and since the most tangible proof of personal fertility is the experience of making babies, having children becomes a 5th house experience, especially the first pregnancy.

The condition of the 5th reveals the characteristic way we approach lovemaking, the emotional style we use to stimulate our beloved, and the predicaments or paradoxes we're likely to encounter in the self-absorbed but other-directed expression of sexuality.

personal
creativity

all forms of ego-centered self-expression, both artistic and otherwise

All forms of personal creativity are 5th house levels. These impulses emanate from deep within the self, often from beyond the self, but here they are given original form through the medium of the conscious ego.

This is the area of traditional artistry: painting, sculpting, acting, and all artistic forms that glorify the creativity of the individual. But it also indicates the more general tone of creativity in less formally structured ways through ingenious presentation to others in day-to-day life.

The condition of the 5th indicates the characteristic importance for any individual of personally creative endeavors and the creative process in general, as well as the tone with which such processes will naturally resonate through the personality.

competition

the experience of risk in any contest involving personal excellence

The 5th is also an area of competition, embodying the sense of personal challenge, the intentional testing of the ego in contests of skill. This includes traditional sports, especially one-on-one sports such as tennis or boxing, where the individual stands alone, risking failure in the attempt to prove himself the superior performer. Even gambling applies here, not simply the Las Vegas variety, but all speculative investments, such as the stock market, real estate ventures, or drilling for oil. These are as much sport as business, since the ego is on the line in competition with others.

The condition of the 5th reveals both the characteristic importance of and the natural approach to any competition involving personal ego-risk.

Sun/5th

conscious persona

With the Sun in the 5th house you are truly the "star" of your own life-movie. Persona, and the paradox of controlled yet spontaneous behavior that accompanies it, is crucial. You have come to the Earth to develop more awareness of the self's radiant power, and to use that power as an actor would, fueling a consciously chosen ego-role. Every time you see your name in lights on the marquee, every time you occupy centerstage successfully, you absorb basic life-energy, which is then transformed for use in other areas of the psyche. The **pitfall** involves becoming so self-centered, so enamored of your ego presentation that others are alienated. Pomposity is not becoming to your essential dignity. The **challenge** is to develop a consciously powerful personal charisma that retains its sensitivity both to the audience and to other performers.

romance, giving love

Life is a continual romantic adventure. You are the courtier who loves nothing better than the pursuit of a possible beloved. The very center of your life-purpose lies in loving, in the risks, the excitement, the sheer thrill of personal impact through the game of courtship. The aspect of performance in loving is part of your core, one way life-energy is absorbed from the cosmos. If you stop the creative flow of the risk to love for a short time, energy intake is reduced sharply, allowing any backlog to radiate outward, thus reestablishing homeostasis. But if the risk to love is curtailed for any prolonged period, your life-energy can be endangered. Love alone is not enough; you must have powerful impact on others for love to be fulfilled. First generate charisma; then learn to use it well.

sexual performance

Sexual performance is an important part of your life-purpose. You are charged by the impetus toward being "the world's greatest lover." Directing energy into another person, having the thrill of seeing, sensing, and feeling the result of that psychic—and physical—penetration is an experience that goes right to your core. Naturally, the Sun's sign and interplanetary aspects strongly highlight your natural approach to lovemaking, but with any condition, what's important is the concrete experience of self-validation through the successful expression of sexual ardor. You love the idea of having children. However, whether you love the sustained effort of raising them is another matter entirely.

personal creativity

You are creative by nature, and it is a significant part of what you intend to develop and express in this life. You may choose an obviously artistic path, but it is more likely that you will choose your niche in the world based on other considerations, then attempt to use that niche as the outlet and arena for your creative impulses. Whether or not your creativity ever fully fleshes itself out, and whether or not it is considered successful, depends on a myriad of factors beyond the condition of the Sun, factors that go beyond even the symbolic indications of astrology in general, qualities such as "heart," depth of character, and especially, flexibility in the face of criticism.

competition

Life is a gamble, a game to be won or lost, and no one appreciates this more than you. Every time a risk is chosen, every time competition is accepted, life-energy flows into you. The very essence of your life involves the paradoxical dance between confidence and risk. Winning or losing is not the crucial issue. The **challenge** is to play the game fully, with all the consciousness you can muster. Go for the gusto.

Moon/5th

conscious persona

The 5th house is an area of active radiance and conscious behavior—life as a stage with the ego as star. The Moon is a psychological function of responsive caretaking and habit-oriented behaviors. How can you be the star in what is—by definition—a supporting role? How can you be conscious and unconscious at the same time? You often adopt a role coming from childhood imprints, especially those surrounding protection. The **pitfall** is overly self-centered nurturing—seeing others as needy when in reality it is you who has the need—the need to give, to feel necessary and important. The **challenge** is to make these emotions as conscious as possible, and to respond in a way that offers others what they truly require. Give boldly, but only when it is requested.

romance, giving love

You're drawn to courtship like a moth to a flame. It is one of the basic necessities of life, like food and shelter. Love is more automatic than conscious, more a product of habit than an intentional pattern of action. Even desire is to some extent automatic. Characteristically, your romances are based on security—yours, your beloved's, or more likely, both. If there's one **pitfall** to watch out for, it's the syndrome mentioned above: fostering neediness to create an artificial sense of dependency on your strong, capable shoulders. The **challenge** is to nourish your beloved, but to do so in a way that promotes healthy, independent adulthood.

sexual performance

This is the placement of "mother-as-lover" (or vice versa), and it carries with it all the complications implied in such a melding of roles. Sexual activity is seen as food to quell inward hungers. But since your sexuality is responsive in nature, you often have to manipulate your beloved to initiate the contact. The sexual tone is emotional, lodged more in feelings than physicality, and you are rarely happier than when sexuality is ongoing. You judge your performance by how "full" your partner feels. Literal fertility is more emphasized here than in other placements. The **challenge** is to respond in appropriate sexual ways, without creating the **pitfalls** of codependency, and to fulfill your personal needs for security through warm and moist sexual expression.

personal creativity

Creativity is second nature to you. However, it does tend to be somewhat more synthetic than original, in that it emerges out of the stockpile of everything you've ever absorbed. This is not to suggest that there is anything invalid about what you create, but rather to emphasize that the act is aided by processes occurring beneath the level of your conscious awareness. If you have children, much of your creativity will likely be directed toward their upbringing, and while this may be somewhat more emphasized if you are a woman and a mother, it is still a strong likelihood even if you are male.

competition

You need to be competitive, and yet the whole notion of risk is antithetical to the Moon's basic function of security and self-protection. Paradoxically, you can only protect yourself by continuing to risk your ego. The Moon shows how a person stays fluid and well-fed, and here that method involves stepping beyond the ordinary boundaries of self, out into the world, onto fields of battle or play. However, your caretaking can both obscure and complicate the natural competitiveness of the placement. As a result, you often support others by challenging them, and this may or may not succeed.

Mercury/5th

conscious persona

Mercury in the 5th house reveals you to be a performer of the mind, someone capable of mental pyrotechnics or verbal gymnastics. You imagine every communication to be delivered to an audience, as in a speech or press conference, and you have a heightened awareness that words are the most creative part of your act. The **pitfalls** are mental vanity and pedantic overkill, while the **challenge** is to develop a charismatic and conscious sense of mind and its presentation.

romance, giving love

Where love is concerned, you are a poet, a magician of words. Courtship exists between the minds, and what is said is of much greater importance than what is done. There is acceleration in the urgency of loving, as the nervous system galvanizes instantly to the clarion call of romance. On levels other than mental, however, love is cooled, and that is a consistent **pitfall.** Stimulus and imagery are the keys here; flirtation in the mind becomes an art. The **challenge,** of course, is to reach deeply into the thoughts of your beloved, penetrating both your thoughts about her, and her thoughts about everything. To win the heart, you must fascinate the mind.

sexual performance

The act of making love is something you think about—before, during, and after. Technique is critical, and your mind works overtime to develop scenarios for successful sexual performance. Communication is as important as touch, often more so, because for you, making love is like "dancing in the mind." There is usually a quicksilver attitude here, an air of slight detachment from the act itself, almost as if you were a photographer recording the experience. And like a photographer, there is a sense of rushing to the next image, capturing the perfect pose one moment, then moving on. Mercury does not savor, but rather forms a rapidly moving collection of images, so the **pitfall** is subtle voyeurism. The **challenge** is first to satisfy the hunger of your nervous system for the stimulation of beautiful images, then to convey that beauty back to your beloved.

personal creativity

Your mind is involved in any creative endeavors. However, Mercury's placement here indicates little about the use of your full intelligence. Instead, the focus is on quickness of perception, facility with words, and wit. The sign placement and aspects are of special significance in determining your motivation and style. For example, you could be light and playful, producing enjoyment as your main creative products, or you could be serious and intense, working on creative projects that require intricate schedules and strategies. The **challenge** is to create new ways to communicate emotional realities.

competition

Competition is exciting to your nervous system. You are stimulated by mental competition, enjoying the gymnastics of mental skill. You risk much more verbally than any other way, often through intricate games of logic and strategy. The **pitfall** lies in "talking the talk" without really being able to "walk the walk;" you sound like you're a confident and willing risker when you may only be playing a game of words. The **challenge** is not to conquer others with a show of brilliance, but to fully engage them so the games can continue.

Venus/5th

conscious persona

In the 5th house, Venus indicates a life role formed around images of personal beauty and grace. You want to be seen as loving. Psychologically, you're more a dancer or model than an actor. The conscious ego presentation is socially tactful, with an emphasis on magnetic receptivity. The **pitfall** surrounds confusion between subject and object, between entertaining and being entertained, while the **challenge** is to make your personal beauty shine forth for all to see and enjoy.

romance, giving love

You tend to fall in love with love. This is the ingenue placement, and as with the other receptive planets, the Moon and Neptune, there is an inversion of ordinary 5th house modes. You give love by receiving it. Put another way, you characteristically attract others through the presentation of personal "loveliness"—the method is magnetic and receptive rather than assertive. Seduction and insincerity become possible **pitfalls,** along with confusion between giving and receiving affection. The **challenge** is to love with great poise, as well as beauty, to turn the risk of courtship into a smooth dance where the beloved feels charmed rather than pushed. The importance of beautiful images reaches a peak with Venus.

sexual performance

Lovemaking is an aesthetic art, a display of grace and beauty. The "woman" energy is strong within you, regardless of biology, and centripetal charisma is your natural form of self-expression—drawing the beloved further and further into the current of your personal beauty. As with the Moon, this placement indicates an active expression of self that is reactive in form, but unlike the Moon, there is receptivity here rather than responsiveness. You receive so graciously that others are charmed. Sometimes you succumb to the **pitfall** of vanity—"mirror, mirror, on the wall..."—but Venus is so smooth that even this indignity rarely provokes protest from your lovers, at least not at first. Your **challenge** is to become beauty personified in the act of lovemaking, to bring heaven to earth.

personal creativity

Artistic creativity is emphasized, of course, but in a way that blends in rather than standing out. You have a broad appreciation of aesthetics, and often your body and personality are the canvasses upon which you paint your loveliest pictures. The **pitfall** lies in becoming narcissistically sensitized to your own ego, falling in love with your image in the mirror. The **challenge** is to make every creative process seem a natural extension of self, and to make your gracious acceptance of applause truly sincere.

competition

By its nature, Venus wants to minimize any discord, so competition is not attractive to you, except insofar as you compete around beauty. The ordinary connotation is altered; here it becomes the ability to achieve harmonious interaction in the face of conflict. You'll "fight" inside to maintain balanced self-presentation in a social setting. It's not "winning over others," but rather "winning them over" to your side—winning their affection, friendship, and affirmation. The **pitfall** involves shrinking from any competition, while the **challenge** is to make every risk seem a flowing, effortless dance.

Mars/5th

conscious persona

Mars in the 5th reveals that your conscious persona is spontaneous, direct, and very male in tone. Self-projection is autonomous and assertive, so much so that impact on others (the audience) can often become the main motivation. You're like a heat-seeking missile, hurling yourself onstage into the limelight. Desires for personal recognition and an ability to improvise in an immediate crisis are hallmarks. Your ego loves rising to the occasion. The **pitfall** involves overbearing penetration, while the **challenge** is to develop a razor-sharp, hawklike focus for brilliant activity.

romance, giving love

You live on the passionate side of romance. There is tremendous urgency, a sense of conscious desire. That sense is competitive, almost challenging, just short of aggressive. You are the arrow streaking toward the bull's eye. The performance of love in courtship is more direct here than with any other placement, more physical, more immediate, and hair-triggered. You often won't take "no" for an answer, and that is a serious **pitfall.** You can be fooled into believing receptivity exists, where, in truth, it may not, but your special **challenge** is to create successful romance out of the sheer adrenaline of personal fire. Desire is everything.

sexual performance

Mars is the complement to Venus, and in the 5th, provides the male aspect of sexuality. This "maleness" in sexual expression is appropriate regardless of your biological sex. It indicates a pressing drive in lovemaking, a sense of the warrior plunging into the breach, charging up the mountain. To say that this placement indicates a passionate nature is to revel in understatement. Sex is expressed in the most physical terms possible as bodies are made molten by the heat. The **pitfall** involves losing yourself too quickly in the push toward fulfillment and release, while the **challenge** is reveal the desire inherent in a given relationship, allowing it to emerge fully.

personal creativity

Creativity is not merely an event for you. Rather, it is the cutting edge of your aliveness. When you create, you do more than simply express yourself. You birth yourself in each creative event. As a result, your ego is much more involved in creativity, and you are more vulnerable to the onus of failure. Happily though, even when you are crushed by rejection, you come back as soon as a new adventure is envisioned. The **challenge** is to use creativity for self-renewal.

competition

You are a fierce competitor and an honorable adversary. This placement indicates adolescent bravado, where all challenges—"cross that line if you dare"—are both personal and territorial. You love to hurl yourself into new arenas, for every time a risk is undertaken, you can prove not only your mastery, but more primally, the validity of your very existence. A gamble is often an irresistible lure, like a red flag waved in front of a bull. Just prior to action, however, you may experience overpowering fear. The military metaphor works especially well here: they don't give medals for accomplishing what's easy; they give medals for courage—action in the presence of fear. The higher the mountain, the more you want to climb it.

Jupiter/5th

conscious persona

In the 5th house, Jupiter reveals that you seek to project an aura of buoyant generosity, easygoing optimism, social aplomb, and most of all, naturally wise intelligence. As with Mercury, mentality is important, but here it is less precise, less verbal, and more generalized, with the emphasis on an image of understanding. As with Venus, there is social grace and natural tact, but less peaceful, more enthusiastically expressive. You have a strong sense of appropriate social behavior and a love for grand social rituals. The **pitfall** is overconfidence—not studying your lines well enough, counting too often on talent to pull you through. The **challenge** is to take full advantage of the effortless charisma that seems your birthright.

romance, giving love

The rituals of courtship are smoother for you than for others. There is a reduced sense of risk involved, as if you had unshakeable inner confidence. There is also extravagance in loving, a sense of abundance, a cornucopia of romantic conceptions. Love is a plurality, a "we" experience. The **pitfall** involves the difference between performance and reality; while love is easy in its outward flow, sometimes your promises exceed what you deliver. The **challenge** is to let love expand from within yourself to blossom in the outer world of personal relationships.

sexual performance

Making love is a natural unimpeded act of self-expression, an opportunity for the self to flow outward. Movement is exhilarating, something you look forward to and savor in all its kinetic and physical sensations. You tend to be slightly indiscriminate in your choice of partners, for you experience more sheer joy in courtship's active culmination than concern over your beloved's reaction. The **pitfall** of such easygoing attitudes involve the possibility of taking too much for granted in the way of assumed acceptance, while the **challenge** is to take full advantage of every opportunity to express your sexual creativity, to joyfully perform.

personal creativity

Jupiter is the symbol for expansion, and here it implies an increased scope of expression, making every creative action larger and more dramatic. You are not very likely to be satisfied with one or two creative outlets. The ability to synthesize old forms into original ones is so broad that you will probably dabble in many different arenas, pulling this from one and that from another, sometimes creating an entirely new category of artistry. The **pitfall** is needless extravagance, while the **challenge** is purposeful drama.

competition

You are a natural team player all the way, one who can integrate completely into a group setting, yet become captain as a result. There is appreciation of any aesthetic forms that have social currency, but you are more commentator than participant in the art world. A deep sense of your natural good luck pervades this placement. You are confident of victory, and this belief is often accurate due to subtly intuitive factors—being in the right place at the right time—but it can also be your downfall when luck is counted on too often without corresponding effort and attention to detail. The **challenge** is to use your natural talents to win graciously, portraying for others how much fun the gambles of life can be, and in that process, enhancing your self-recognition and social acceptance.

Saturn/5th

conscious persona

You are very sensitized to the imperative of conscious persona. Sensitivity is so high, however, that stage fright is a continual **pitfall**. You want to conquer fear of criticism by an audience you imagine to be reserved and judgmental, if not downright antagonistic. Early in life, your "acting style" tends to be blunt and too loud, but later the persona can evolve toward greater subtlety, becoming conservative and low-key, with a calm sense of authority. Less is more; calculated reserve is often interpreted by others as quiet depth. The **challenge** is to turn vulnerabilities into strengths by slow movement from walk-ons and character parts, finally achieving durable stardom. Study your lines diligently, and know that you're safe behind the solidity of your character.

romance, giving love

The risks of courtship are very serious business. You want romance almost desperately, but rejection anxieties are strong and persistent. You imagine every possible form of rejection in advance of any activity, so as not to be surprised by its pain. This technique rarely succeeds, of course, since romance can hardly get off the ground in the presence of such pessimism. On the other hand, you may blind yourself to the very real risks of loving and hurl yourself at the beloved with such blunt force that you alienate her, causing the very rejection you most fear. To succeed at love, move cautiously, keeping your feet on the ground. The **challenge** is to realize that patience and maturity bring romantic success. Gentle persistence furthers.

sexual performance

You feel the burden of "carrying the whole show" during lovemaking. Heightened awareness of risk and the onus of failure is accompanied by deep ambition to overcome your fears and prove yourself finally as a brilliant lover. Too much failure or prolonged frustration can cause you to reject yourself, others, or both. Curiously, however, immediate sexual success produces precisely the same results. A slow, middle road is demanded. Sexual performance is understood in its most physical dimensions, and lovemaking is thick, sometimes too much for your partner's enjoyment. The **pitfalls** are impatience and frustration, and the **challenge** is to develop sexual confidence and expertise through gentle caution, to take raw drive and refine it into a polished product.

personal creativity

Whenever possible, make your creativity physical. Saturn is the symbol for grounded earth reality, for the understanding of matter, so your natural arena is that of solid structures. Mentality may certainly be involved, and emotions are a natural part of creativity, but the emphasis here is on structures. This can be literal, as in sculpting or architecture, or it may take a different tack, such as organizing resources, bringing together the necessary ingredients for an end product. The **challenge** is to make your work creative, and equally, to make creativity your work.

competition

You are competitive, but you may believe yourself to be unlucky, so you must conquer chance itself. You feel ashamed of your fear, so you risk everything. Avoid the contradictory **pitfalls** of total refusal to take a chance, alternating with foolhardy gambles on long shots. The **challenge** is to appreciate every small victory on the road to confidence in your skills. Banish your worry that the rules of any game single you out for disadvantage; learn the rules inside out, and don't bet when the odds are against you. Security and success are achieved only through measured risks.

Uranus/5th

conscious persona

Eccentricity is the key to conscious persona. You like to surprise and even shock the audience by nonconformity to expectations. One moment there is passivity, an almost pregnant calm in your conscious expression, the next moment there is an explosion of energy, a whirlwind of electricity as you grab centerstage. For you, charisma involves the unexpected demonstration of an unyielding will, combined with a revolutionary sensibility. The **pitfall** is an almost perverse disregard for the sensitivity of audience, while the **challenge** is to demonstrate your ability to perform any number of unusual roles in the most unlikely of situations.

romance, giving love

You're truly individualistic in courtship. Often you radiate detached self-possession, almost passive self-containment, and others see you as disinterested in the risks and rewards of love. But at some point you inevitably trigger into turbulent romantic feeling. The rules of ordinary social process are hurled out the window; love here is not a ritual, it's a hurricane fueled by the ego. Your focus on the beloved becomes a laser beam of mental and emotional obsession. The **pitfalls** lie in inconsistency and rigid frenzy toward fulfillment: "give or else." Keep in mind that love can't survive if you willfully demand your own freedom while denying that same freedom to others. The **challenge** is let the shock effect of romance change your direction by cracking old expectations.

sexual performance

Your attitudes and approaches toward lovemaking are revolutionary, experimental, and impossible to predict logically. There is extremism here. Detachment and involvement flip back and forth, often mutually exclusive. A willfulness that transcends conscious personality can kick in, propelling you either toward or away from the beloved. Sexual style varies from situation to situation, and from moment to moment. But there is an ever-present sensitivity to the electric shock of change, coupled with a need to be seen as absolutely unique, unlike any other. The **pitfall** involves a perplexing cycle of insatiable demand alternating with defiant refusal, and the **challenge** is to allow shared sexuality to be a vehicle of transformation, the awakening to a self beyond the ordinary.

personal creativity

You have a strong desire, almost a compulsion, to break the rules, to leap beyond your own limitations in a single sweeping act of creativity and mental brilliance. And often you are spectacularly effective. Never one to sing the same song twice, you hurtle toward new creative frontiers, hardly glancing back. The **pitfall** involves mistaking the ego for the self, while the **challenge** is to fill whatever you create with true originality.

competition

You're not especially competitive, although you can demonstrate an iron determination to win when sufficiently aroused. Luck plays no part here, nor does caution; it is sheer will that dominates. The abandon that so often comes back to haunt the Saturnian personality only enhances the reputation of the Uranian: "I don't care what they say about me as long as they spell my name right." The **pitfalls** lie in unpredictability—where risk is concerned, nothing can be foreseen. The **challenge** is to learn that radical gambles are a natural part of your growth process. Success or failure matters little. New awareness is the payoff.

Neptune/5th

conscious persona

Your 5th house Neptune indicates a conscious persona marked by an otherworldly, almost mystical presence. The image of self that's created can be magical in its delicacy and compassionate in its soft receptivity. You are no egomaniac, for you're more interested in feeling of togetherness, of oneness between performer and audience. However, there can be "star" quality here, for an intangibly poetic sense of charisma overcomes many other shortcomings, such as a lack of clear strength in character. Your characterization may be solid and grounded, but the mask itself gives the impression of being almost translucent. The **pitfall** lies in deception—for the audience and also yourself—while the **challenge** is to develop a character of universal empathy, one with whom every member of the audience can identify.

romance, giving love

If Mars is the romantic warrior, Mercury the romantic poet, Venus the romantic beauty, then Neptune represents the romantic mystic. You have a transcendent, almost religious sense of courtship. A sublime holiness permeates love. You aren't especially physical where love is concerned, operating instead from Olympian heights of spiritual aspiration. There are **pitfalls,** however. Universal and personal love are confused, and too often, romance involves suffering and sacrifice—somebody gets hurt. You're such a sucker for "true love" that you'll lie to yourself and others to have the experience. The **challenge** is to successfully merge your transcendent longing for spiritual Oneness with the more pragmatic demands of earthly living.

sexual performance

For you, the sexual act is an interlude of release from worldly cares, more fantasy than reality, more emotional than physical, a dreamlike blend of Hollywood and Heaven. The mundane aspect of sex is smooth and silky, a liquid dance of empathy with your partner, as if your body were melting into the body of your beloved. The **pitfall** lies in passivity or self-absorption; your boundaries dissolve too easily and you float off to La-La Land, leaving your partner behind to do all the work. The **challenge** is to let lovemaking provide you with a pathway back to Cosmic Central. Sex should be more inspiration than perspiration; christen yourself in its cool waters—just don't drown.

personal creativity

Creativity tends to be spiritual rather than material, intangible rather than concrete. Whatever actual directions you choose for your creative drives, the process of creation will likely be slightly mysterious, more a drawing down of sublime energies than any literal push to birth something new. You are the master of the divining rod, the rain-maker, the medium in trance who connects to another world. You can also be an illusionist, a prestidigitator, a con man. Just be sure you know the difference.

competition

Neptune's symbolism is antithetical to the raw energies of competition. Your skills are based on subtlety. Something in you senses the most natural action to take in any game. But when you win, your ego steps aside. No credit is needed, no applause sought, no winnings pocketed. The concept of rules is only barely understood, however. You may cheat without knowing it, or with a naive assumption that it's part of the fun. But that **pitfall** can only lead to the eventual public ruin of your good reputation. The **challenge** is to develop a perfect instinct for the game of life, to play gently and lovingly, without violating anyone, including yourself.

Pluto/5th

conscious persona

With Pluto in the 5th, normal conscious persona with its heightened appreciation for an audience is unconscious with no audience-awareness. This is Method acting at its apex; you don't "perform" a role, you "become" the role, totally immersing yourself into it. You don't so much take on a character as become your natural self at a much more intense level than usual. Every trait is intensified and concentrated, so that the self pours out onto the stage with profound impact. Curiously, the audience assumes that you're acting, but you won't be. The "act" here is a direct reflection of what's going on in your subconscious. The **pitfall** is complete loss of personal ego control, while the **challenge** is to transform both yourself and the audience with ego power, but to do so in ways that respect everyone's dignity.

romance, giving love

You're motivated toward courtship from deep within the emotional caverns of the subconscious realm. Romance is a compulsive eruption of the need to love so totally that self and beloved fuse, forged into a new metal by the heat of passion. For you, it hardly matters how this is accomplished, and the main **pitfall** lies in misuse of power through dominance or submission. Total romantic love pulls you up by the roots, and the experience can be excruciating. Love and hate often intertwine. Your **challenge** is to allow love to arise in its own time and place, then to banish all emotions of negativity, imbalance or hatred, purging them in love's fire. Do not attempt to transform love. Rather, let love transform you.

sexual performance

The physical act of making love is paradoxical. At times it's like kissing your sister. You wonder where the passion went. But look out. It can also be ravenous, insatiable, a tidal wave of feelings erupting from God-knows-where. At either level, it is more compulsive than conscious. You could veer between charismatic impact and cruel insensitivity. Sexual success comes from the power of your emotional radiance, not from the skills of technique. The **pitfall** surrounds emotional blindness, while the **challenge** is to provoke fundamental change. But if transformation occurs only within the beloved, it has failed; you must also be receptive to the "death and rebirth" inherent in your intense sexuality. Otherwise, it's simply unconscious lust for power and control.

personal creativity

Despite your magnificent potential, you may at times fail to live up to your billing. This is due to the largely unconscious nature of the creative drive. At times you may not feel it at all, thinking yourself barren; at other times you may be compulsively driven by the urge to create. The **pitfall** is extreme reactions: you could agonize over occasional blockage, or you might equally blot out every other consideration when the flow moves through your ego. The **challenge** is to create something that touches everyone.

competition

You are more competitive than you may realize. You hurdle headlong into personal risk, or you sit glumly on the sidelines, not understanding the game. There are no rules here, no road maps. Instead, you surprise even yourself by rising to the occasion, bursting open to reveal uncharted depth, ingenuity, and sheer, competitive fire. Hold back nothing in those exquisite moments when you really go for it. The **challenge** is to let your brilliance come forth in its own time, its own way, without your ego pretending it is in control. Create something out of nothing, and share the credit with the Gods.

Planets in the 6th House

6th House

disease and healing

bodily disease, neurosis or misunderstanding, and concrete techniques to restore homeostasis

Each individual has characteristic weak spots in the body or the mind, "Achille's heel" points of special vulnerability where breakdowns are more likely to occur. This is disease in its most systematic aspects, as congenital, developmental, or chronic disorders, often stress-related.

Healing involves numerous steps. The first is recognition: to become sensitive to physical and psychological functioning. Next comes analysis: rational investigation into the causes and effects of malfunction, to understand the correlations surrounding disease. The third step is loving discipline. This is the most difficult part of healing, for the combination of love with discipline is rare. Love too often infers indulgence, while discipline too frequently means harsh restriction. Loving discipline is the trick of the 6th, and its condition shows the life-dance we create around the mastery of such magic.

The 6th house reveals the nature of these malfunctions, showing their characteristic importance in an individual life. It also points the way to heal them, to bring the body/mind back into homeostasis. An emphasized 6th indicates that disease and healing are experiences of more than average importance for an individual, not merely an unfortunate coincidence, but part of why the life exists, and essential to its fulfillment.

unequal relationships

superior/inferior, dominant/submissive, and other relationships involving unequal status between individuals

The 6th is an area of relatedness. It bridges two types of relationships: the challenging, creative ego encounters that characterized 5th house experience, and the commitments between equals that will emerge later in the 7th. The 6th, however, concerns unequal, hierarchical relationships especially those that provide a teaching or purify the ego.

All social groups form status hierarchies. Certain roles are afforded more stature and respect based on power or achievement. Other roles are identified as subordinate positions, almost apprenticeships. These unequal relationships can be formally legitimate, as in the situation of an employer/employee interaction where the employer is "superior" by definition, or they can be tacitly agreed, as in the case of marriage partners who are supposedly equal but in real life may relate with an unconscious presumption of dominance and submission.

But even beyond these postures, inequality is the general rule rather than the exception. In any given moment or situation, most interactions between individuals contain an element of inequality—superior versus inferior. One person is seen as more expert, more powerful, more charismatic, or more valuable, while the other is seen as less. In all such interactions, the superior tends to dominate, while the inferior submits.

An emphasized 6th house indicates heightened awareness toward differences of status in interaction, with a pronounced tendency to take the inferior role. The condition of the house shows the characteristic approach to relationships requiring exaggerated deference, from either the superior or the inferior posture.

duty and service | ***dutiful helping, purification through humility, conscious subservience to another***

In every ritual rite of passage from one station in life to another, higher station, the last phase prior to the ritual itself is a time of purification. The body, mind, and spirit must be cleansed in an act of humility to prove worthiness for the new status to come. This can be as simple as a boy scout helping an old lady cross the street, or as complicated as a secretary, nurse, or personal valet, whose lifelong career involves service. Every profession, no matter how lofty the stature, requires a service. So we include the doctor, the lawyer, and the Indian chief.

Humility through service often involves a Jungian concept, "the wounded healer." A wounded healer suffers from an important problem or disorder. All attempts to heal directly have failed. Expertise has been achieved, yet almost perversely, healing does not occur. Only by helping others can release be achieved. The old saying: "those who cannot do, teach," implies that if we simply lived the essence of what we knew, we wouldn't need to teach it to others. But this is too harsh a judgment. Helping, serving, and teaching are crucial steps in self-perfection at whatever level we exist: even the guru sometimes washes the feet of the disciples.

The condition of the 6th house indicates an individual's personal orientation toward self-purification through conscious, humble service to others, and it also shows the characteristic methods used to promote such healing or helping.

technical mind | ***discrimination, organization, analysis; the mind working for growth***

The 3rd house was the first cadent or predominantly mental area. There the emphasis was on basic learning, categorization, or "naming." These explorations are motivated by simple curiosity, like a child who is fascinated by a ticking clock with its gears and springs, and disassembles it, only to be left with a set of unrelated parts and no "clock."

The 6th is the next mental level, the development of technical skill, where one learns to reassemble the clock by carefully studying how each part fits together with the next. It is still linear, rational thinking, but it represents organization into a working system, the ability to see differences in function, to understand sequences of assembly.

The condition of the 6th indicates the approach to and importance of such painstaking mentality, especially as it is applies to an understanding of personal circumstances.

discipline and routines | ***efficient routines to increase productivity; regularity in lifestyle***

The 6th concerns not only mental discipline, but the more generalized experience of routine in one's day-to-day lifestyle. Each person has a particular approach to regularity, an individual orientation to the necessity of disciplined habits. This is the concept of efficiency as it relates to overall productivity.

The 6th house reveals the relevance of life routines for any individual, as well as the characteristic approach to efficient productivity.

Sun/6th

disease and healing

Disease and the careful restoration of health are at the center of life-purpose. You've come to the Earth to explore and correct anything that prevents fulfillment in wholeness, both for yourself and others. Even when you are healthy, disease is still a presence in your life; it will touch you in some significant way. Often this takes form through a professional interest in health and healing. Pride and dignity are usually involved in any significant disorders. The **pitfall** is succumbing—quite literally, surrendering to diseases of the body or neurotic attitudes. The **challenge** is to reenergize through a persistent focus on wellness, to learn and practice a wide range of healing techniques.

unequal relationships

You have great sensitivity to the protocol surrounding exchanges between persons of unequal stature. Fulfillment depends upon how well you conduct yourself when relating to superiors or inferiors. The **pitfall** is confusion about authority. When we defer to a judge, policeman, counselor, lawyer, or doctor, even a priest, we do so out of respect for the position, not the human being. A person's inherent quality is not necessarily reflected in the social role he or she portrays. Your **challenge** is to treat each person in a manner appropriate to the cultural role, while striving to honor the essential equality of our spiritual dances. Curiously, you have a much easier time when in the inferior position; it's the superior role that gives you fits.

duty and service

Being helpful is nothing short of essential; if you don't demonstrate a sincere interest in aiding others, you unplug from the source of cosmic energy that fuels your being. But that likelihood is remote, and passes quickly if it happens, for you can feel your life-energy begin to ebb. Of greater danger is the possibility that you feel too flawed to be helpful to others. It's crucial to proud of the services you offer. The worst **pitfall** lies in exaggerated subservience—false humility that's actually self-denigration masquerading as devotion. True humility needs to be focused in service, in the action of helping. Remember, however, that compensation or payment is also crucial to your life-purpose. Receiving gratitude is as important a **challenge** as offering competent aid.

technical mind

One aspect of your life-purpose is to develop analysis into an artful lifestyle. When you use your mind to organize and understand sequences of events or logical processes, you plug into a source of universal energy and your fuel tanks begin to fill. As discrimination develops into careful reasoning, you draw purer energy. Let your mind move toward significance, even when it begins with trivia. The **challenge** is to observe and interact with anything that catches your interest, to learn how it works, and to empathically understand why it exists, what function it fulfills in the larger scheme of things.

discipline and routines

The experience of regularity is essential for you. A life without discipline is no life at all. You are on the Earth to understand efficiency, to promote steady productivity in your pragmatic and spiritual goals. The actual regularity of your living depends on other factors, such as the Sun's sign and aspects, but remember that you can enhance your access to life-energy through consistency. The **pitfall** is losing the forest for the trees, while the **challenge** is to organize the layers of self into shining effectiveness.

Moon/6th

disease and healing

Disease is often linked with feelings, habits, and needs. The gastrointestinal system is especially vulnerable, so diet has primary relevance. The most significant disorders revolve around chronic problems resulting from long-standing habits. Any neuroses surround security and issues involving the family, the origins of which may possibly be traced to a difficult childhood relationship with your mother. You didn't feel safe to express needs with her, and as a result, have grown up mistrusting others, while remaining needy inside. The **pitfall** lies in rejection of your "inner child," which creates hidden hysteria and secret compulsions. The **challenge** is to learn appropriate fulfillment of your needs. Healing involves the simplicity of taking good care of yourself.

unequal relationships

All unequal relationships reflect the basic mother/child scenario. When you perceive yourself in an inferior posture, you amplify what you felt as a small child. If you were frightened, you could be terrified. If you were resistant, you could be defiant. If you were angry, you could be rageful. When in the superior position, you tend to parody your mother. If she was supportive, you'll tend toward caretaking. If she was overly protective, you may be smothering. If she had difficulty providing emotional support, you might refuse to give any, abandoning those around you when they're needy. The **pitfall** is remaining stuck in these memories forever, while the **challenge** is to grow through them. Become a mature adult by learning to recognize your inner child, and then invite that child to come home to you.

duty and service

Helping is compulsive, something you don't actually choose, but simply do because it feels so natural. You seek out individuals who seem insecure or uncomfortable, and in supporting them, feel more secure and comfortable inside yourself. The **pitfall** rests with your tendency to "help" others whether or not they wish it, like the boy scout so eager to get his merit badge that he pulls the old lady across the street even though she doesn't want to go. The **challenge** is to perfect yourself by serving the real needs of others through the emotional support you provide.

technical mind

Thinking is akin to eating a full meal. You have a personal need to dissect the world around you, to reassemble it, to pay attention to details. You want to understand how everything works, but only insofar as it has personal relevance to your own emotional life. The **pitfall** is being drawn off course by feelings that resonate through and around you, like a scientist studying trees in autumn only to be overwhelmed by the beauty of the multicolored leaves. The **challenge** is to blend insight and warm feeling. Thinking should be moist rather than dry.

discipline and routines

Your entire system is sensitive to regularity. Once you form habits in your daily routine, they become part of the hierarchy of needs, and any disruption in the pattern has immediate emotional effects. Any time you need good feelings, it's helpful to immerse yourself in the measured pace of real work, the rhythm of a task with a definite goal. The **pitfall** involves imprisonment into random or self-defeating habits, while the **challenge** is to provide yourself with a steady flow of positive, productive routines.

Mercury/6th

disease and healing

You are physically vulnerable to what are classically termed "nervous disorders." The term "misunderstanding" acquires greater relevance, since errors in perception or thinking are responsible for behavior patterns that lead to physical breakdown or malfunction. Sometimes this is caused by the brain machinery itself; sometimes it's more the human operator than the machine. The **pitfall** lies in seeing every imperfection, thus becoming negative or pessimistic. The **challenge** is to collect and analyze data about any situation (including care of oneself) with an eye toward objectivity, and an inner attitude focused on restoration and maintenance of wholeness. Disease is a breakdown of organization, and healing suggests renewed clarity—making the right connections.

unequal relationships

The emphasis on inequality in relationship is less important than with other planets. The tonal quality shifts away from general relatedness, toward the specific area of communication. You are more aware of differences in intelligence and education. The **pitfall** involves putting yourself down because others seem smarter or more eloquent. The **challenge** is to use your mind to observe the status and power distinctions that occur in all social relating.

duty and service

Service is linked with rational intelligence or communication. Figuring out logical puzzles, solving problems, deciphering situations; these are all natural. You apply your mind to external situations, typically those involving both people and "machinery." Quotation marks are necessary because the machines you so love to take apart and put back together may be literal—metal, plastic, screws and bolts—but also metaphorical—the mechanics of human social interaction, for instance. In either case, you constantly look for flaws, broken pieces, and malfunctioning units. The **challenge** is to heal your own mind by using it to help others solve problems. While this provides clarity and an understanding of how things work, it can also become compulsive. Remember: if it's not broken, don't fix it. Don't even take it apart. If it is broken, study the basic design, discover how it works, and restore its functioning by repair.

technical mind

You're possessed with a drive toward organization, an undying curiosity about the workings of things. There is detachment here, and neutrality, an almost computer-like sensibility. You process large amounts of information, constructing complex sequences of understanding, in part because you enjoy the endless feedback loop of mental stimulation. Your analyses branch out, to follow multiple lines of reasoning simultaneously. The **pitfall** involves your tendency to postpone final conclusions, instead being constantly in process with calculations. The **challenge** is to make your investigations pragmatically productive, to experience the satisfaction of problem-solving through clear analysis and critical understanding.

discipline and routines

Regularity is not as important as variety. You need an active routine, one which satisfies your need for the daily stimulation of numerous tasks. Productivity *per se* is not as critical as the process of having problems to address, puzzles to solve. As with all Mercury levels, the placement of the Sun can significantly modify the way you approach your lifestyle. The **challenge** is to keep busy, with one eye on the eventual goal.

Venus/6th

disease and healing

Disease is associated with physical or psychological pleasures. Too much gratification can be every bit as harmful as too little. As with the Moon and Jupiter, diet has high significance, for there is a tendency toward intemperance in the pursuit of "sweetness," a longing for substances that may be too rich for the body to absorb. You have anxiety about personal beauty, leading to unfavorable comparisons with others. Personal love may be psychologically misunderstood or misdirected. Your **challenge** is to recognize both the ineffable and tangible beauty you possess, to experience pleasure directly, rather than always reaching outside yourself for beauty or pleasure. Disease is often the result of failed or incomplete love, and healing is a restoration of personal grace.

unequal relationships

You have a pronounced sensitivity to the social graces. You love the rituals of formal supplication, the courtship of authority, and the privileges of position. In spite of outward appearance, you like the submissive role in love relationships, for you're enamored with the subtlety of quiet magnetism. The **pitfall** lies in confusing love and power. The **challenge** is to experience the attraction that all human beings feel for all other human beings, and to see that relationships can be loving only when you infuse your affections with dignity and self-respect.

duty and service

Loving and healing are almost identical, which is to say, the urge to create personal love is very similar to the urge to help others have more harmonious lives. So strong is this merging of "love" and "therapy" that you may focus all your romantic energy on damaged individuals. This **pitfall** could be given many names: Stray Dog Syndrome, Wounded Bird Theory, Florence Nightingale Effect. Whatever we choose to call it, you must be certain of two things: first, that your receptivity is not directed toward individuals who cannot return love in at least relatively healthy ways, and second, that you are not making your beloved sick in order to validate your healing powers. The **challenge** is to heal yourself through the conscious gift to others of grace, harmony, and pleasure. Remember: for love to flower, you need good seeds and good soil.

technical mind

Mental analysis is linked with personal care. This has, naturally enough, a "cooling" effect on romance. But the mind is warmly appreciative of logical beauty. Mental discipline is not a forced purgatory, but a fine garden lovingly tended. You relish digging into any situation with your mental spade. Clearing the dense underbrush and fostering a sense of productive order makes you glow with satisfaction. However, keep in mind that relationships have their own indefatigable eccentricities; too much organization— too much taming—can kill the intangible beauty of sharing. The **challenge** is to enjoy the quest for mental perfection, and to appreciate emotions even as you analyze them.

discipline and routines

You appreciate regularity in your lifestyle, enjoying the pleasant experience of organized habits. Routines may be oriented toward ordinary goals, but here there is an added social dimension: you need interpersonal contact in your routines to feel the full benefits, for people are more important to you than products. Work and aesthetics are linked; you want to fill your day with work aimed toward the creation of beauty.

Mars/6th

disease and healing

Disease is linked with the sharp edges of reality. Fevers, rashes, cuts, and other sudden or dramatic conditions are more likely here, and the relation of infection to deeper disorders is more pronounced than with other planets. Excess or misdirected heat are relevant **pitfalls.** Psychologically, desire and maleness are possible areas of misunderstanding or oversensitivity. This is true with both your own desires and those expressed by others. The particular pattern of vulnerability depends on other factors in Mars' condition (sign placement, aspects, and the overall planetary pattern), but we can presume that you'll struggle with "wanting." The **challenge** is to cleanse the pathways of desire. Both the causes of and treatments for disease involve vital self-expression.

unequal relationships

You fight over inequality and struggle with others over authority. Otherwise normal exchanges can result in affront to personal dignity. This occurs in both directions: in your feelings or in the feelings of others who are relating to you. It's as if there's a chip on your shoulder where power is concerned, a built-in red flag waving in front of a bull. Your **challenge** is to learn to judge which rituals of submission are appropriate and which represent abuses. Opposing abuse is imperative. However, to fight simply because two individuals are not equal is a waste of precious life-energy.

duty and service

There is an urgency to helping others. It has the feel of surgery: you want to penetrate and cut away obstructions with the sharp edge of your own desire. You're compelled to seek out blockage or resistance, to break through those walls, however hard you have to push. However, keep in mind that others are people, not problems to be solved, not walls to be smashed. You'll want to perform miracles; don't bite off more than you can chew. Service is a basic desire, so you'd be well-advised to consider a helping profession as a full-time career. This enables you to spread your heat over many interactions with numerous individuals, allowing you to hone your scalpel into a fine tool, while insuring that you don't overwhelm any single individual by too many repeated "operations."

technical mind

Thinking is passionate and direct. The speed of your mind is impressive; you learn voraciously if you can get a foothold in basic understanding of an issue or idea or process. But be aware that the very desire that drives you mentally can also trip you up. You push so hard to reach the end of a logical sequence that you're prone to error, sometimes glossing over an important step. Remember, the program won't run unless every bug is isolated and replaced by the correct instruction. Your mind is best suited to basic and direct problem-solving; it's where you shine. If the situation is too inverted or laced with complexity, frustration may override desire, and you'll lose interest before a solution is found. The **challenge** is to keep your mind focused in the present.

discipline and routines

Routines are often experienced as a contining series of confrontations. You stay with one issue until it is solved or exhausted, then turn your attention to the next urgency. With Mars, lifestyle is not so much regular as it is imperative. You could be downright irregular, always backed up, having more to accomplish than you can possibly achieve, but as long as your days are full and your ratio of victories high enough, you're happy.

Jupiter/6th

disease and healing

Disease is induced by physical or psychological excess. There is a tendency to attempt too much in a given time period, both in overt behavior and more subtly in mental attitude. You assume that no amount of stimulation is ever too much, that the self can and will "digest" any amount of experience. Do not expand too fast or your system could blow out and collapse, forcing you back inside yourself. The result is breakdown through exhaustion. Your liver is an especially vulnerable organ. The **challenge** is to discover and correct misunderstandings in the regulation of personal experience. Relax back into the self, gradually exhaling your excesses.

unequal relationships

You are not especially sensitive to unequal status relationships; instead, there is a comfortable awareness of the pragmatic necessity for inequality, an acceptance of the natural social order. With this acceptance comes an attitude of opportunism, gliding through the levels, riding on teflon surfaces of good manners and easy likability. If you feel resentment toward superiors, you rarely show it. If you feel condescension toward inferiors, you mask it, although not as well as in the reverse situation. The **pitfall** involves unconscious abuse of privilege through feigned sincerity. Don't take advantage of your position too often. Remain humble and friendly, and make sure your sincerity is authentic. The **challenge** is to use hierarchies of power for the greater good—for yourself, certainly, but for others as well.

duty and service

Helping is natural, a source of social pride. You offer to share the bounty of your life, however great or small it may be. The more you share what you've amassed, the greater is your future reward. Your particular method of helping is to remind us that God is on our side, that within ourselves are all the tools needed to create a whole and happy life. At times you may not even believe this yourself, but if you counter the pessimism around you with positive attitudes, then you'll return to an optimistic and confident state. In reminding us, you remind yourself. The **pitfalls** lie in empty promises and dashed hopes. Be certain that your message of good faith has some basis in pragmatic fact, for there is little in life more discouraging than being told that things will get better, only to have them grow worse. The **challenge** is to tell the truth in the best possible way.

technical mind

Mental discipline is "a natural addiction." The feedback loops of nervous stimulation and mental activity dovetail in perpetual rhythm. Left on your own, there's little to stem the flow of increasing self-absorption with mental stimuli. Even in a social situation, once you've begun revving on logical processes, only dramatically negative feedback from others brings you back to reality. Free association is entertaining, but not necessarily productive. Lack of precision is a major **pitfall.** The **challenge** is to observe how people behave socially, and to organize observations into a coherent body of information.

discipline and routines

You can embrace regular routines, a solid nine-to-five life, or an independent flow with no schedule at all. It's all the same to you as long as the tasks you're addressing plug you into the larger worlds of social activity. Your work is not so much based on literal tasks, although these will naturally be part of your day, but more on issues in the realm of culture. As much as possible, let others take care of the details.

Saturn/6th

disease and healing

You have tremendous sensitivity toward wellness, an almost hypnotic focus on the discipline necessary to restore health—for good reason, since this placement is often linked with serious illness or disability. You must learn to treat yourself gently, working patiently at healing your body and psyche. Stay within the boundaries of accepted medical practice, and work with respected healers of acknowledged excellence. Choose long-term strategies; do not go for quick cures or magical recoveries, for your disorders are chronic, both in attitude and in the corresponding bodily malfunctions. In regard to loving discipline, work on being loving to yourself much more than disciplined. The latter comes easily; the former is the **challenge.**

unequal relationships

Your conservatism is strong, and you believe in dominance hierarchies. You just hate being at the bottom. When in an inferior position, you feel compelled to obey superiors perfectly, and this fawning toward authority is an invitation to be abused or taken for granted. You chafe in secret resentment. In the superior position, you expect obedience, and may be in for a shock when others perceive you as cold or insensitive. The **challenge** is to get the chip off your shoulder, to replace humiliation with humility. Study the difference between deference and obsequiousness; understand that true respect for authority enhances dignity. When it's your turn to command, do so with firm, even-tempered fairness. Only a slave leads or follows blindly.

duty and service

You would rather not have to serve at all, but you do, and very dutifully. Helping involves being with others in the most difficult or frightening parts of their lives, the parts they deny, are overwhelmed by, or refuse to work on. Such a talent can be a tremendous burden. But persevere in perfecting your talent by learning to offer gentle assistance, proving your dedication and patience, and you'll be affirmed. Remember that respect is a prerequisite for love. If you become skillful in serving others, you gradually see your strength, feel your patience, and rejuvenate your self-respect.

technical mind

You put tremendous pressure on yourself to get your facts straight, and to analyze them perfectly. The tendency to be overly harsh on your mental abilities is fueled by intense ambition and fear of inadequacy. Your mind is a valuable instrument, a diamond in the rough, and to produce the finished gem, it must be cut with care and polished with love. Recognize errors of judgment and forgive yourself for them, or severe accusation will follow. Understand that you can learn from mistakes if you give yourself half a chance. Your **challenge** is to defeat gravity, transforming anxiety into calm confidence, gradually honing your mind into a smoothly working machine. Make it a trusted ally that gives you a dependable anchor in this world.

discipline and routines

You want a life that embodies the essence of structured existence. Regular routines are very important, and disruptions in plans can be unsettling. Discipline, task-orientation, and productive problem-solving are part of your foundation. Make sure it is solid. You may have to exert more effort than some people to achieve the same ends, but don't worry. You're built for hard work, designed to take on the tough jobs, and your maturity is enhanced every time you finish a task well.

Uranus/6th

disease and healing

Health is subject to unpredictable changes. Your nervous system is high-strung and particularly vulnerable. Stress-related neurological disorders can provoke unusual symptoms, which often respond well to radical or experimental treatments. Difficulties with independence or integrity are precursors to disease; imprisonment makes you sick. The **challenge** is to roll with the punches. Disease is a message provoking you to wake up, a "shock" from the system indicating that your lifestyle must change immediately.

unequal relationships

You're a natural reformer with a sharp eye for abuses of power, seeking out situations of social disequilibrium to provoke change. From the inferior position, your impulse toward upheaval begins quietly. Then suddenly, in an unlikely moment, you reveal yourself to be Robin Hood, defender of the meek, tweaking the nose of the Sheriff of Nottingham. You'd like to exist outside all power hierarchies, since your motivation is toward complete independence. The **pitfall** involves abuse of fairness. If you insist on provoking revolution as the underdog, realize that you're fair game for similar treatment in the superior position. The **challenge** is to destroy unhealthy dominance anywhere you find it. If you have a choice, be Thomas Jefferson rather than Thomas Paine.

duty and service

You take particular delight in helping, for service is the way you stand out from the crowd. In attitude, you're a loner; ordinary cultural rules of conduct are discarded in favor of a more private code. Provocative mental insight is your method. You take risks with those you serve; you want impact. You shake up people's nervous systems, challenging old emotional assumptions with new mental perspectives. The **pitfall** surrounds humility versus ego. One moment you seek only a unique solution to another's problems; the next moment you're commanding all the energy in a surge of fervent but insensitive soapbox philosophy. The **challenge** involves mastering the art of the "quiet revolution" and the use of "invisible electricity."

technical mind

Uranian mentality includes the brilliant impulses of inspired geniuses, as well as the erratic aberrations of unbalanced crackpots. What distinguishes the two? The genius solves problems by thinking about them in new ways. She looks with fresh eyes, questioning everything. Often, she sees the solution in a spark of inspiration before she knows the means. The crackpot uses the same procedures. But the genius works backward, filling in the holes, painstakingly bridging the old to the new, whereas the crackpot offers no help to those of us he has "left behind." So we disregard the crackpot while embracing the genius. Your mind pulls you away from ordinary linear rationality, to inspired bursts of new vision. Your **challenge** is to add the discipline necessary to bridge the gap, and be revered as a genius rather than denigrated as a crackpot.

discipline and routines

Regularity is antithetical to your lifestyle. There are routines, to be sure, but they are markedly erratic, distinguished by their unpredictability. You have an iron will when it comes to tasks, and you can work with astonishing discipline, but only when you choose the issue. Your skills become specialties, and your specialties then branch off to form their own peculiar patterns of expertise, sometimes seemingly unrelated to one another. Your **challenge** is to weave these disparate elements into a unique coherence.

Neptune/6th

disease and healing

Disease is a mystery. Dreams have profound effects on wellness, both in causing and treating disease. Vague fears and dimly realized phantoms damage health. Recovery involves positive visualization and right attitude. You lean strongly toward occultism or metaphysics to understand illness. Symptoms are often red herrings, so to find a cure, look beyond the obvious to reach the symbolic and subtly emotional roots of disease. The **challenge** is to understand yourself not as a machine with parts and pieces, but to see that mind and body are one complete, living whole, not subject to mechanical analysis or textbook diagnosis. Disease is not conquered; it is transcended.

unequal relationships

You assume that everything is as it should be, that if someone is your superior, they ought to be, and conversely, if someone is your inferior, then that too is cosmically correct. You believe in natural order, the divine right of kings. This is often positive, but there are **pitfalls.** You place too much trust in both superiors and inferiors, assuming they will accept their roles gracefully. This can bring disappointment and suffering. Certainly the general leads his troops into battle, but he must inspire them to follow. The **challenge** is to feel the pain of each role: oppression is painful, but oh, it's lonely at the top. Identify with everyone in the hierarchy, and forgive any real or imagined sins.

duty and service

Service to others is a full-blown spiritual mission: "it is better to give than to receive." But in spite of such lofty sentiments, you should not be selfless in your gifts. You need something in return. You want to feel further down the road to enlightenment, closer to Home, to the loving arms of the Creator. The problem is tangibility. How do you tell if others are helped or hindered by your efforts? How can you know if you're achieving true humility or only a facade of gentle giving? The **pitfall** involves deception, more often of yourself than others. Your sincerity is likely to be tested. The **challenge** is to relinquish the things of this world lightly, and to help others master the same grace.

technical mind

The whole of any system is greater than the sum of the parts. But your mind is hardly concerned with the parts at all. You "think" in a dreamy way more suited to feeling-perception. Your mentality is more art than science, more intuition than logic, more metaphysical than technical. To the extent that poetic imagery can be effective in solving a given problem, your methods are valid. However, choose your applications carefully, for such methods can get you into scandalous trouble where you'll be branded a charlatan. Your **challenge** is to use the meditative approach in as realistic a way as possible, allowing your breadth of vision to uplift others. But don't let your dreams fog your vision. You must see exactly what is, yet still be able to accept and deal with what we call the "real" world, however unreal it may seem.

discipline and routines

Routines of work are songs you sing to yourself, biofeedback lullabies. Others sometimes marvel at the seeming effortlessness of your discipline, praising you for the inexhaustible grace you display. At other times, you appear to be sitting down on the job, not working at all, but instead, just cruising. Crisis is not your strong suit; you prefer to smooth out the peaks and valleys, to make tasks as regular as possible. Fascinated with miracles, you want the results of your labors to be nothing less than magical.

Pluto/6th

disease and healing

Disease results from blocked life-force. Disorders arise from the unconscious, propelled outward into the body by the need for psychic purging. Healing involves understanding the compulsive nature of control and possession. In attempting to control what cannot be controlled, or possess what cannot be possessed, you can become convoluted by obsession, cut off from change. Emotions turn toxic, poisoning your system, and they overflow into the body as illness. The **challenge** is first to discover which attachments you need to release, then to visualize letting go of the emotions. Health is restored by uprooting old feelings and transplanting ourselves into new emotional soil.

unequal relationships

You may willingly work under superiors with a total commitment that reflects deep fidelity. But you may also subtly undermine their authority. This can provoke enmity and mistrust, resulting in pitched battles with very powerful enemies. In the superior position, you can be either charismatic, winning fanatical loyalty from followers, or despotic, forcing obedience through fear. A serious **pitfall** is that you may fail to see any of this, since your motives are often hidden even from yourself. The **challenge** is to unearth and obliterate all abuses of power by distinguishing true from false authority.

duty and service

Service runs in cycles. Every so often, you have the flash of realization. You become a divining rod, plunging your message into heart after heart, reaching others with the intensity of your own awakening. But over time, passion fades back into the unconscious. Eventually your message becomes mechanical, mere repetition of a once vibrant truth, now no more than a cliché. The plateau lasts until a new cycle bursts. The **pitfall** lies in endless reruns of realizing and forgetting without integrating any wisdom. Your **challenge** is to remember what you went through, what you learned. With each new cycle, bring all your previous lessons of humility, so that you offer not mere passion, but deeper truth. Build each service plateau on higher ground, reaching toward heaven.

technical mind

Your mind veers. At times, you probe beyond appearances, revealing the hidden linkages that unify life. Other times, you're ineffective, almost blind to what's occurring. This comes from the paradox of seeing the whole or seeing the parts. When the paradigms are in conflict, your perception falters. When they merge, your analysis becomes so deep and accurate that others marvel at your vision. The **challenge** is to let these moments of superclarity change your life. But do not curse the darkness, for it is the fertile womb out of which such amazing mentality is born. When the mind is gestating, allow it come to term. Let the birth of intelligence be natural.

discipline and routines

In systems biology, ecosystems develop naturally, growing through the matrix of relationships between various species. Following a period of stability, the system reaches a point of critical mass. Suddenly everything breaks down into chaos. The system dissolves. But almost magically, it reforms at a higher level of complexity. The routines of your lifestyle are parallel. Discipline and productivity grow in purposeful stability. Then everything changes at once. Habits disintegrate, becoming meaningless. Productivity stops. Then directions shift, and gradually you emerge at a higher level. The **challenge** is let both stability and chaos have their phases in the spiral of your efforts.

Planets
in
the
7th House

7th House

awareness of the self through the mirroring effect of relationship

Having reached with the 7th house the halfway point in the cyclic unfoldment of human experience, we see in operation the principle of complementary polarity. The 1st and 7th houses are directly opposite, marking the eastern and western limits of the horizon, so they are linked through polarity, tied together in basic meaning.

In astrology, the horizon represents the experience of self-awareness, the reference by which we orient ourselves spatially. The eastern horizon is the point of daybreak, the dawning of the Sun, so the 1st house is associated with self-awareness—recognition of personhood through the radiance of self into the environment. The western horizon is the point of sunset, and thus the 7th house symbolizes the complementary experience—self-awareness not through active radiance, but instead via reflected image. This involves recognizing or "realizing" the self through other people with whom one interacts. In the 7th house, at the level of self-awareness, "it's all done with mirrors."

The condition of the 7th reveals the characteristic way a person "bounces off others" to discover more about the self. What you may think you're experiencing is someone else, but what you'll really be experiencing is yourself.

equal
partnerships

one-to-one partnerships involving equals: marriage, business partners, etc.

The 7th is an area of relationship, but there are many kinds of relationships described by different houses. Those symbolized by the 7th are relationships between individuals defined as equal—in essence, partnerships between peers. The partners may not and probably cannot be "perfectly" equal; at any given moment, in any particular context, one is likely to be more or less powerful, loving, wealthy, or conscious than the other. But those momentary shifts in balance are of no concern here; the crucial factor is that each individual see the self and the partner as equals, for the 7th represents the recognition of true, shared mutuality.

The condition of the 7th reveals the psychological qualities an individual must work through to achieve reciprocity in relationships. The phrase "work through" refers to the characteristic approach in establishing connection, but it also reveals the struggle surrounding obstacles encountered when relating to potential partners.

contracts,
commitments

social contracts between individuals;
commitment: the implications of making a promise

In sequence, the 7th is the first house of the upper, visible, or "objective" hemisphere, and it represents the beginning of "collective" or "cultural" experience. Therefore, it is necessary that 7th house relationships go beyond simple recognition of equality by the participants. The partnership must be confirmed within the milieu of society, and this is achieved by the process of willing, contractual obligation—a promise or commitment. All 7th house experience is, by definition, public and open to the world at large.

In commitments such as marriage, business partnership, or other contracts, the rituals of bonding require a witness for validity, to assure public knowledge that the individuals involved have agreed to be partners. This is the essence of the marriage ceremony.

The condition of the 7th house shows how an individual characteristically enters into contractual, committed relationships. It reveals the nature of the contract, as well as individual qualities that will be brought into full public view via the relationship.

cooperation

negotiation, compromise, and cooperation in relationship

Cooperation is one hallmark of 7th house experience, meaning literally "to operate with," but to achieve true cooperation, each individual in a relationship needs to learn, understand, and demonstrate the skills of successful negotiation that lead to creative compromise. The willingness to be cooperative is the motivation for these two more primary procedures, and mastery of give-and-take allows the fulfilled experience of truly flowing cooperation.

The condition of the 7th shows what attitudes and functions tend to shape an individual's experience in the dynamic interactions that are necessary to create a sense of positive coexistence with others, especially intimate partners.

natural partner or partnership

natural qualities of the self's alter ego through the partner or the partnership

Part of the confusion surrounding the 7th house involves isolating the level of experience. Its symbolic identification with relationships, contracts, and committed partnerships between equals is unquestioned. But the differing and interwoven levels of intimate relationship have long been a vexing problem for astrologers.

First, the 7th represents qualities expressed **by the individual** through partnership. At this level, there is no reference to the actual partner in the relationship, only to the psychological attitudes of the individual whose chart is being considered.

Beyond this, the 7th symbolizes the beginning of objectivity, and it can also indicate actual traits of the "natural" partner, the "alter ego" of modern psychology. Here the house speaks to characteristics not of the native, but **of the person with whom the relationship is formed.** We assume that the person chosen either has characteristics described by other's 7th, or will tend to develop them as a result of the relationship.

Finally, the 7th also indicates the tonal quality **of the relationship itself,** as opposed to traits embodied by either individual. At this last level, it is the invisible "entity" of the relationship, the "personality" of the partnership which is revealed by the 7th house.

Each of the variations are possible, and a combination of all three is probable. The multi-leveled nature of the 7th house is precisely what makes astrological interpretation such a subtle art, for in astrology as in life, human relatedness is anything but simple.

Sun/7th

mirrored awareness

In the 7th house, the Sun indicates that you've come to the Earth to discover yourself through the contact you make with other human beings. This mirroring is crucial, for it's the way you plug into Cosmic Central. Every time you relate to someone, every time you even consider relating, you energize yourself. The **pitfall** lies in believing that the other person is the energy source. The **challenge** is to maintain the self-awareness you create through relationship, so that your awareness continues even when relatedness isn't present. In that way, each new encounter, whether with the same or a different person, builds on a previous foundation, the comprehension of who you truly are.

equal partnerships

The fact that you tap into power through relationships doesn't mean you need to be with a partner twenty-four hours a day. In fact, it is essential that once you have established a significant relationship, you then use the energy it generates to further your own singular pursuits. Thus, the **pitfall** is the tendency to become overly dependent on your partners, to feel incomplete without them, and as a result, to diminish your sense of self. The **challenge** is to create relationships that are mutually supportive to the unique life-paths of both partners. Do not become One with another, but instead stay in the dynamic, unresolved polarity of two-ness.

contracts, commitments

Commitment is life-affirming; noncommitment is life-denying. Honoring promises furthers life-purpose; breaking promises damages it. That much is simple. What is not so simple are the intricacies of distinguishing a good commitment from a bad one. Relationships manifest the extraordinary paradoxes between self-centeredness and other-directedness, between the experience of being alone and being together, and it is easy to lose our bearings. Partnership is a two-way street, involving mutuality by two individuals, yet each of us alone must decide for ourselves what we want and are willing to promise. Do not commit to someone else, for that surrenders your essence. Instead, commit to the willingness to share yourself with another.

cooperation

If, for any reason, you experience confrontation rather than negotiation, defiance rather than compromise, or opposition rather than cooperation, your life-purpose falters. The more you are able to see and understand the other's point of view—without giving up your own—the more vital your life becomes. Back away from relatedness when compromise is temporarily impossible. See the ebb and flow as natural, not as winning or losing. Anything can be negotiated between partners if there is sufficient time, interest, and good faith. So look for partners who will negotiate with you, partners who understand that compromise does not—and should not—require winners and losers.

natural partner or partnership

Your **natural partner** embodies essential power and visible dignity. This person's life-purpose should affect you deeply; you feel yourself responding, moved by the sense of meaning in your partner's journey. Your mate must have with a stronger-than-average will, a central core with real power. There's a radiance that others besides you can see.

A **natural partnership** stimulates your pride, not the false glory of ego-centered vanity, but the pride that results from recognition of your essential wholeness, and from the increasing ability to express yourself in open and fulfilling ways. It should clarify your life, and though it cannot hold the limelight—that is for the self alone—it must occupy a position near center-stage in your existence. **The image is dawn, with the sun breaking through the clouds, rising to warm the earth and evaporate the mists.**

Moon/7th

mirrored awareness

In the 7th house, the Moon reveals that relationships are the vehicle to awareness of your needs. They are not an end in themselves, but the means. If you succumb to the **pitfall** of believing that others are the actual source of your fulfillment, then you remain a child, seeking out only partners who reflect the real or idealized qualities of your mother. Your **challenge** is to let the awareness that comes through relatedness awaken sensitivity to your needs, so you can then fulfill them for yourself. Whenever you lose touch, move back into relatedness for more stimulation. Alone and together ebb and flow. Discover what you need with us, through us, then take care of yourself.

equal partnerships

Unlike the Sun's meaning in the 7th, where simple existence of a relationship is often enough to fuel the self, the Moon's significance is radically different. Mere existence is not enough; here there must be regular and frequent contact with the partner, a kind of "checking in" to reestablish the feeling of secure togetherness. The **pitfall** involves creating dependencies in partnership. Too much regularity or predictability may seem wonderful, but it is also a very addictive "emotional drug." The **challenge** is to create working partnerships that are both stable in structure and flowing in content. Self-protection is always a double-edged sword; keep your sword with you, but be awake—don't cut yourself with it.

contracts, commitments

Your commitments are not mental experiences, not reasonable, well thought-out decisions. This is not to say that you misunderstand commitment or enter into relationships out of faulty motives. Rather, it indicates that the natural reasons for commitment are emotional, based on deep feeling. Commitments change over time as your needs for security, certainty, and support grow toward maturity. If your needs are not being met, then by all means change your commitments by altering their level or their form, but remember also that a promise is not something to be taken lightly.

cooperation

What passes for cooperation is often compliance or caretaking. You are so hungry for shared experience that you sometimes are too willing to give in. This is compliance, and in the extreme, leads to a total collapse of sharing as you gradually retreat into a defensive shell. Taking care of your partner—or vice versa—can be natural and loving, but it can also be habitual and deeply unconscious. True cooperation is the experience of willingly mutual support based on good-faith negotiations, with each person taking care of him or herself. The fact that a healthy relationship helps fulfill your most basic emotional wishes and makes you feel good is reason enough to learn to cooperate well.

natural partner or partnership

Your **natural partner** is a very emotional person, perhaps even moody. He or she gladly responds to your true needs, and expects you to do the same, but does not prey upon you by fostering dependency in either direction. Your mate willingly shows you his or her innermost softness, even if it is shown to no one else.

A **natural partnership** has an emotional immediacy, a here-and-now presence. The relationship reveals something universal about emotion. Though you must guard against the tendency to become overly dependent upon the partnership for safety and support, the relationship teaches you a great deal about the validity of those needs, and the importance of creating a vehicle for their fulfillment. **The image is a clear stream, surrounded by woods of lush, dense foliage.**

Mercury/7th

mirrored awareness

Mercury in the 7th shows the relatedness to be the "start-up motor" for personal thinking. You are not self-generating in mental activity. Instead, it is through connection with others that you become stimulated to use your intelligence, to develop rationales for solving your own puzzles. Naturally, you will be attracted to people you see as intelligent or clear thinkers. The **pitfall** lies in a kind of inadvertent plagiarism. Don't adopt another person's mode of thought, no matter how brilliant it may seem. Rise to the **challenge** of using the mental stimulation that arises through relationship to develop thought-forms you can truly call your own.

equal partnerships

Your curiosity is a great asset for connecting with others, and you spend a lot of time thinking about relationships. The **pitfall,** curiously enough, centers around difficulties in communication. There is a tendency for you to be too passive in your efforts to reach your partner. You tend to wait, thinking all the while, but stewing, hoping that your partner will initiate communication. If you want your relationships to live vibrantly, to be interesting and exciting, you have to be willing to stimulate them, not simply wait for them to stimulate you. The **challenge** involves studying one-to-one relationships. Observe every relationship in your own life and in the lives of those around you. Learn how they work, why some succeed and others fail. Become an expert.

contracts, commitments

Commitments are formed only after exhaustive analysis. You look at every possibility, examining the relationship from every angle before making a firm commitment to it. And even then it continues to change. You love the nuts and bolts of designing contracts; structures of agreement are fascinating for you. And though it may seem paradoxical, disagreement is equally fascinating, at least in the sense of nervous stimulation. The **pitfall** is that information is endless; you can't possibly know all the factors. The **challenge** is to allow yourself analysis first, but then to comprehend the importance of decision. Each phase of the process is necessary. One without the other is not only unproductive, but boring, a cause of broken commitments and ruined relationships.

cooperation

You are compelled not so much by cooperation as by ongoing negotiations. You are not always cooperative, but you're more than willing to discuss the possibility, sometimes endlessly. You're stimulated by differences more than by togetherness. The **pitfall** is remaining in a never-ending series of negotiations, setting up the rules, defining the exceptions, tallying what's already been decided, etc., without ever cooperating productively. You're susceptible to logical argument, however, and can be convinced by a silver tongue, so remember the **challenge** of coming back to yourself, or you discover yourself creating something with which you don't even agree.

natural partner or partnership

Your **natural partner** has active, visible intelligence, a person who is curious, stimulating, and communicative. Your mate must be of high intelligence, at least in your eyes, and must be interested in a broad range of human events and experiences.

A **natural partnership** has a mobile, quicksilver nature. It should be free-ranging in association, with many outside friends and much socializing, and it must be a source of mental stimulation, opening your mind to new and exciting fields of inquiry of which you were formerly unaware. **The image is a fast car weaving through the back streets and wide boulevards of a crowded city.**

Venus/7th

mirrored awareness

With Venus in the 7th house, you don't see your beauty and grace directly. Rather, you experience these through relatedness. When you encounter someone who functions as a lovely mirror, you experience your own inner femaleness through the interaction. The **pitfalls** here are two-fold. First, it's very easy to grow weary in external pursuit of a qualities that are actually inside yourself. You may become frustrated in the search for just the right mirror. Second, you may believe that the beauty and harmony actually come from the other person. This leads to a feeling of barrenness within yourself, as well as making you cling to false images of beauty world around you. Your **challenge** is to assimilate the sense of beauty you discover through relatedness into your own awareness of yourself, so that even when you are alone, separated from others, you still experience the loveliness that is rightfully and naturally yours.

equal partnerships

You want your partnerships to be like a dance, with each partner smiling, dressed handsomely, gracefully augmenting each other by moving in perfect unison—like Ginger Rogers and Fred Astaire. This is heaven. But you're so focused on harmony that you often ignore the very serious work that comes with partnerships. Individual differences are bound to cause conflict, and you hate conflict. You are sometimes too willing to internalize conflicts, to "eat them yourself," and this can go on only for so long before the **pitfall** occurs: you succumb to the lure of superficiality. The **challenge** is not only to have beautiful partnerships, but also to maintain real equanimity with your partners. Minimize unnecessary conflict, but be willing to work through it when it arises.

contracts, commitments

Commitment is not your strong suit. Interacting is such a pure pleasure that you ignore ethical considerations in favor of sensory ones. You are keenly aware of socialization, however, so contracts assume more and more importance as your life goes on. The **pitfall** involves confusion between your own wish to make a commitment, and your desire to know that your partner wants you. The more interested someone is in you, the more seductive that interest becomes, and you so love flattery that you may talk yourself into something you don't really want. The **challenge** is to commit yourself to sincerity and gentle honesty.

cooperation

Cooperation and compromise are more natural for Venus than for any other planet. When you're with another, the experience of shared togetherness is deeply satisfying. Compromise is easy because it lets you exhibit your gracious nature. The **pitfall,** however, is negotiation. With other people's disagreements, you can stand back, isolated from the conflict, a model of balanced fairness. But in your own relationships, it's another story. Your **challenge** is to learn detachment and strength in interaction, so negotiation becomes a vehicle for restoring harmony.

natural partner or partnership

Your **natural partner** is feminine, a person whose aesthetic beauty is visible to everyone. Your mate should be calmly romantic, attuned to the delicacy of love, and he or she has a silky temper, a warm heart, and a glowing, seamless personality.

A **natural partnership** has intangible sweetness, a gentle sense of proportion, and an appreciation for the exquisite beauty of life. Even when you and your partner are in disagreement or conflict, the relationship itself still encourages a sense of balance. It should be attractive to others as well, inviting them in. **The image is a heartfelt valentine, brimming with warm sentiments.**

Mars/7th

mirrored awareness

Others may seek you out as an attractive object of desire. You might find yourself "courted" or praised, and you could develop high confidence and charisma as a result. However, it can also seem that people are overly combative with you, that they are often overly aggressive or sometimes downright disagreeable with you. But look within yourself and you'll discover some of that same energy. Find out what it's about. Don't let it lurk beneath your awareness. Mirroring is also positive. The **challenge** is to discover your own natural sharpness through relating, and then to use it to cut away any obstacles to the fulfillment of your natural desires.

equal partnerships

Your partnerships need to be energetic and focused with a clear sense of purpose. Although you are capable of sustaining long-term relationships, the emphasis is on the immediate crisis, the momentary confrontation, today's problem rather than yesterday's or tomorrow's. Equality is a struggle. You may feel that your partner is trying to conquer you, but you're just as likely to use the same strategy. In either direction, a win/lose battleground is really no partnership at all. Avoid both surrender and victory, for it is imperative that humiliation and revenge be kept out of your relationships. You are likely to be oversensitive to your partner's desires, so keep the focus on your own male qualities. Assert yourself with the intention of reaching rather than conquering your partner. Penetrate the partner's heart with your sincere desire.

contracts, commitments

When you find a relationship you want, you immediately commit yourself to having it. It's not thought-out or chosen after considered contemplation. You jump right in, urgent, propelled by desire. The only commitment you know how to make is total—forever. What gives this the flavor of paradox, however, is the fact that Mars doesn't measure forever in terms of literal time. Rather, "forever" means until the desire no longer exists. One **pitfall** involves seeing your partner as an object rather than as a person, a screen upon which you project desires. The **challenge** is to learn to make promises rather than commitments, for they are more suited to your warrior nature's appreciation of honor.

cooperation

This is a paradoxical placement for Mars. The ordinary expectations would be that you are unwilling to cooperate with others. But characteristically, the reverse occurs. You are so willing, so eager to compromise that you give your power away, blunting the sharp edge of your own desires, so to speak. Also, as stated above, you tend to be drawn to very assertive, even aggressive partners. Remember, it is not your job to give others what they want, but rather to use your natural sensitivity to their desires to get in touch with your own. The **challenge** is to overcome all obstacles to shared fulfillment, so you can reach full expression with your partner.

natural partner or partnership

Your **natural partner** is a person whose masculine nature has impact on you, who knows what he or she wants and goes for it without hesitation. This partner must not be too subtle, for that would dilute the desired effect of direct and spontaneous contact, and the more physical your partner is in approaching reality, the more you appreciate your mate. You want someone powerful, but more importantly, ardent and passionate.

A **natural partnership** for you stimulates your contact with the energies of desire. It need not be overtly sexual, but there must be an animal quality present in the sharing. If it's not compelling, it's not real. **The image is a wild stallion racing with the wind.**

Jupiter/7th

mirrored awareness

Rather than looking directly into yourself, you gain the knowledge you seek through relatedness. It is the source of wisdom, since each encounter offers unique perspectives. The **pitfall** is that you may be so oriented toward relating as a "learning experience" that you forget to truly interact with your partners. As with Venus, your tendency is to skim along the surface, often barely penetrating the emotional depths below. This can rob you of the greatest insights relationships offer. If you don't penetrate the other, you don't reveal yourself. Relatedness itself provides the opportunity, but the person with whom you are relating is sacred, not merely to be taken for granted. The **challenge** is to take full advantage of the bounty waiting for you.

equal partnerships

Relationships are like wildflowers, beautiful and free, to be enjoyed but not possessed. You flow into partnerships easily, encountering little resistance, and it's natural for you to regard others as equals. Unlike Mars, relationships are not a battleground, but a chance to learn about the human condition. The **pitfall** involves your tendency to be loyal but very freedom-loving, so that your fidelity is truthful in principle more than in fact. The **challenge** is to experience as much as you can in each partnership you create, to drink fully from the cup of sharing, becoming wise in the ways of humanity.

contracts, commitments

You are fascinated by contracts, eager to discover the ethical principles that govern their success or failure. Your own commitments in partnership are a laboratory for experimentation with ideal principles. This abstract interest is so high that you commit yourself on many levels and in many relationships, often simultaneously. Your sense of opportunism is so strong, however, that while you recognize the importance of commitments, you may fail to see the necessity of fulfilling them. Partnerships for you are more in the mind than in the heart, so remember that others of a less philosophical bent may be seduced by your enthusiasm. The **challenge** is to balance commitment and freedom, in order that you fulfill your spirit as well as your mind.

cooperation

Cooperation is easy for you, a path of least resistance. Your natural optimism makes negotiations flow smoothly. However, there are potential **pitfalls.** You are sometimes so bluntly honest that you offend others without realizing why. It may not occur to you that they could be vulnerable or sensitive. You are also very proud, and may respond to ego wounds with misplaced haughtiness. Maintaining a sense of humility is crucial if your relationships are to remain bountiful and happy. The **challenge** is to develop your natural love for socialization into tactful statesmanship. Protection of the emotions is as necessary as enthusiasm of the spirit.

natural partner or partnership

Your **natural partner** is a person whose nature is generous and noble, whose actions are optimistic and spontaneous. Your mate is a very social person, one who loves the expansive sense of relatedness with many different individuals. There is a persistent wanderlust to see the world, and he or she wants to share that experience with you.

A **natural partnership** is one that broadens your horizons and opens you to the bounty of life. It contains open and joyful exploration, and you feel enriched by its effect. It has lightness and buoyancy, a sense of flying rather than staying firmly on the ground. You feel the intangible presence of something wise and good, and it makes you feel more care for all of humanity. **The image is a hot air balloon, floating majestically in clear skies high above the earth, from which the horizon extends forever.**

Saturn/7th

mirrored awareness

With Saturn in the 7th, it's difficult to understand that the image you see in others is truly a reflection of yourself, for it often appears fearsome and threatening, either demanding or rejecting, and thus it's easier to convince yourself that the other person is emanating these qualities. The major **pitfall** here is denial, the tendency to want to look away, to avoid real relatedness, since what you may see is so fearful. The **challenge** is to give yourself time to gradually overcome the intense fear of knowing yourself, so that you can eventually discover authentic self-acceptance.

equal partnerships

Your relationships with peers have been conditioned by the anxiety that others don't want to know you as you really are. You feared rejection from your father or other authority figures, and learned to protect yourself from it. Even in adulthood, you continue seeking to prove your acceptability to authorities, so you often choose partners who are significantly older or younger, if not in age, then in some less tangible way. The **pitfall** involves pushing yourself so hard you simply blow out, collapsing in reaction into almost calculated insensitivity or irresponsibility toward your partners. The **challenge** is to respect your limits, growing through your fears. Discover that you have nothing to prove to yourself or us.

contracts, commitments

Your anxiety over relationships is never more obvious than with regard to commitment. What if you choose the wrong person? Will you be humiliated if you're not perfect in your performance of the contract? Will the Gods set you up for failure no matter how hard you try? Fear may become self-fulfilling prophecy: you could refuse to make any promises, resulting in painful isolation; or you might close your eyes and plunge into total commitment, hoping that everything will magically turn out alright—inevitably resulting in ruined relationships. The **challenge** is to learn responsibility slowly by moving through stages of commitment. If you get in over your head, pull back to a lower level. Commitment is not birthed whole; it is built one brick at a time, just like maturity.

cooperation

You want cooperation deeply, but you fear being abused, and worse, you worry that you actually deserve mistreatment for unknown flaws of character. Why would others want to cooperate with you, especially the powerful father figures to whom you are attracted? There are two **pitfalls:** first, you may bend so far in accommodation that you harm yourself; or second, you may so fear rejection that you refuse to negotiate with a coldly defensive posture. Remember that just because your partner wins, you don't have to lose. The **challenge** is to learn that you can be in unresolved negotiations safely. You're correct to be cautious in negotiations, but your ambition to achieve full cooperation won't go away; you just have to work at it.

natural partner or partnership

Your **natural partner** is one whose maturity and common sense are palpable, a person of achievement and steady endurance. Your natural mate has considerable dignity and psychological strength, with notable restraint that's backed by a clear understanding of responsibility. You must respect your mate in ways that enhance your self-respect.

A **natural partnership** for you feels very old, rocklike and solid. You needn't be totally secure, but you must feel awe and reverence at a physical level. This relationship challenges you to conquer your fears, but slowly enough that you're not overwhelmed. It helps you feel more adult. **The image is a mountain of granite.**

Uranus/7th

mirrored awareness

Uranus in the 7th house indicates that your reflection in others electrifies or awakens you. The experience can be both enlivening and upsetting, and encompasses both in the long run. One-to-one relatedness is where you discover your true uniqueness, that which separates you from the crowd and defines you as a special being. The **pitfall** lies in defiant refusal to look at what needs to change within you. The **challenge** is to see yourself with fresh eyes, letting old masks fall away.

equal partnerships

You are likely to jump into—and out of—partnerships, for not only is their appearance an unexpected surprise, but their disappearance can be equally sudden. The function of personal relationships in your life is to disturb ordinary unconsciousness. If you're "sleeping" lightly, then their appearance is a delight. If you're stuck in habit, or using unconsciousness as an escape from your life, they may well jolt you like an electric cattle prod. If you want relationships to last, you'll need to come and go often. The willingness to establish instant connection, to break that connection when necessary, and then re-establish it later is a hallmark of maturity. Do not cling, nor allow others to cling to you. The **challenge** is to let go of expectations and live in the here and now.

contracts, commitments

Commitment is hardly the tenor of this placement. Instead, you leap into contracts—and later break them, often on very short notice. The polarity is sufficiently extreme that when you're in one state, you can't conceive of ever being in the other. Commitment touches directly on the issue of personal freedom, especially in the arena of spiritual growth. Ordinary commitments too often limit our freedom, and you are very aware of these limitations, determined not to be bound by them. Your **challenge** is to find a better way, to experience the linking of your higher will with the mundane experience of making a promise. That's no easy task to master, but even the contradictions can teach you about the extraordinary freedom that come from true commitment.

cooperation

When you flow calmly, you are a joy to be with, since your boundaries are so clear, and yet your natural willingness and interest in interaction causes others to feel completely safe with you. When resistant, however, there is no one more rigid and defiant. In those moments, you would cut off your nose to spite your own face rather than engage in a substantive cooperation. What makes this placement fascinating is the switch from one posture to the other. It can take even you very much by surprise. Your **challenge** is to flow with the changes. When you are uncooperative, go away—you need separateness and a sense of freedom. When you again feel cooperative, return to sharing.

natural partner or partnership

Your **natural partner** is different from other people you've met in your life, an individual who stands apart in your mind, distinguished by independence and a distinctly revolutionary bent, a crusader for change. His or her personality should also be more than a little unpredictable, keeping you on your toes.

A **natural partnership** awakens you to new possibilities within yourself, and leads to uncharted territory. Your partnership causes you to want to throw off the shackles of false security, to reach for true freedom through the discoveries sharing can provide. **The image is an electrical generator.**

Neptune/7th

mirrored awareness

With Neptune in the 7th house, you experience the mirroring effect of relationship as a fantastic dream world, either euphoric or nightmarish. In either event, the reflected self you see through others is larger than life, often in soft focus, and usually in Technicolor. It's not necessarily your personal self you experience, but something on a quite grander scale. At best, you see your true divinity, and with it a wonderful renewal of faith in the goodness of all things. The **pitfall** lies in romanticizing trivial contacts, falling in love with glamorized images. This leads to inevitable disillusionment when the rose-colored glasses finally give way to the cold light of reality. The **challenge** is to discover your best self without illusion or self-deception.

equal partnerships

You are what is sometimes called an "incurable romantic," seeing the highest potential in others. But do you consider a person's actual level of maturity or evolution before entering the relationship? Often not. Taken to the extreme, such an approach casts you in one of numerous roles: guru, savior, martyr, victim. At best, you blend reality and fantasy in very gentle and positive ways. The **challenge** is to honor the idealized images while still seeing your partners objectively. Your intimate relationships can be the cruellest of illusions, full of lies and deceit, and yet they can also be the living fulfillment of your highest dreams, touched by God.

contracts, commitments

You float into and out of commitment, often without realizing it. The **pitfalls** are numerous—being more committed than you know, or more committed than your partner; being uncommitted but projecting the illusion of commitment, or believing yourself to be in a committed relationship when no such state of mutuality exists. Floating on wishes works for only so long; occasionally you must focus on hard facts. However, your idealistic approach can sometimes heal wounds of cynicism or mistrust. You move through periods of crisis and change with grace, which can be a great benefit in a long-term relationship of many phases. The **challenge** is to flow with what your heart tells you while still keeping your eyes open.

cooperation

You must understand the difference between cooperation and compliance. Compliance essentially means obedience or acquiescence—surrendering the self in martyrdom. Also, examine your belief that words are the same as deeds. You are so interested in flowing into oneness that you tend to be a sucker for golden tongues. Wait until behavior confirms the truth of the words: the proof is in the pudding. Cooperation literally means, "to operate with." It requires two whole beings, not one symbiotic being formed out of two partial people. The **challenge** is to learn the true meaning of compassion, to be in sympathy with your partners even as you maintain your own integrity.

natural partner or partnership

Your **natural partner** is one whose softness is tangible, a person of great compassion, a dreamer whose ideals are at the forefront of his or her personality. Your mate may be romantic in the personal sense, or in a more collective or spiritual way. He or she has a tenderness that extends far beyond relatedness with you alone.

A **natural partnership** for you is one that ennobles your highest sentiments, making you feel that you are experiencing something truly magical. The presence of God is almost tangible, something you know is there but cannot see, something you come to trust and believe in. Your faith in the goodness of humanity is enhanced. **The image is the ocean at calm, as smooth as glass, stretching to blue infinity.**

Pluto/7th

mirrored awareness

Rather than proceeding directly into your unconscious to unearth the buried contents of your past, you are guided there by interaction with others. You may meet someone and instantly feel your deepest self revealed, or you may not recognize yourself in the other for a long time. The **pitfall** is denial that what you see in others is a mirror of your unconscious. You are subject to a wide range of false beliefs, from the "positive" feeling that it is your partner who embodies the wonderful qualities you see, to the other extreme of convincing yourself that your partner is the source of all conflict or pain, and blaming him or her for every difficulty. The **challenge** is to be willing to see yourself in others, and out of that willingness, to let yourself change.

equal partnerships

You need to understand your impact on others, especially intimates. You are a powerhouse of often turbulent emotions, and it is in relatedness that these emotions are drawn up from their underground storehouses. You rise to the heights and depths of passion. The **pitfalls** involve control, the tendency to dominate your partnerships, or, by reflection, to be dominated by them. Partnerships represent psychological peaks in growth, high- and sometimes low-water marks in your emotional life. They are watersheds of personal development. Some of your relationships die absolutely; some live on through various stages of personal growth. The **challenge** is to honor the best ones, and hope that they evolve with you in your new directions.

contracts, commitments

Commitment is a gut issue. You are either in or you are out; there is no middle ground. An imbalance of commitment between you and your partner is a serious issue, and a major **pitfall** is the tendency of one to demand unreasonable proof of commitment from the other. The **challenge** is to recognize that commitment is a vehicle for the deepest possible change. Do not enter into any relationship that doesn't offer strong magnetism, and equally, once in, go all the way through. Every commitment is a promise to grow, to leave behind the old and welcome the new in yourself.

cooperation

You have a deep-seated need to cooperate, but it can be fraught with difficulty. Focus on your deepest intentions. What is it you really want from your partner? Have you examined what he or she touches in you? Are you aware how the relationship triggers your compulsions? Are you willing to experience your own demons? If so, then work hard at cooperation, knowing it will bring up your own dark world. If not, back away to examine your willingness. Do not fight what are essentially battles with yourself on ground of another's choosing. Your **challenge** is to learn that it is your responsibility, not your partner's, to exorcise your demons. Doing so frees you from inner bondage.

natural partner or partnership

Your **natural partner** is one whose emotional intensity shines forth like a beacon in a storm, a person who understands the floods of feeling necessary to periodically cleanse the landscape of personal growth. This individual has a profound effect on you, functioning as a divining rod for both the best wishes and worst terrors in human sharing, the dark side as well as the light.

A **natural partnership** for you is one that impels the essence of your self-understanding to change. There is a profound, radiant intensity, even when you and your partner are engaged in the most mundane experiences. The relationship forces you to examine your compulsions, and in release, to cleanse and renew yourself. **The image is a smoking volcano, quiet but active, cool at the surface, but molten at the core.**

Planets in the 8th House

8th House

union
the experience of sharing; issues of power and trust in partnerships

The 7th house established the concepts of agreement and equality in relationship. The 8th house converts these into reality. It represents consummation of whatever was promised, just as the honeymoon represents consummation of the marriage ceremony.

Trust and faith in one's partner become central here. Without trust, there can be no true sharing, and certainly no authentic union. Without faith, there can be no openness, no receptivity. Give-and-take too frequently becomes a skirmish conducted from behind defensive trenches. However, where trust and faith exist, magic can occur.

The 2nd house represented self-worth. The 8th house symbolizes the opposite process, shared or relationship-oriented worth. This involves evaluating oneself indirectly, through sharing. This can mean literally the partner's judgment; more likely, it is a self-imposed judgment based on perceptions of the partner's reactions.

The condition of the 8th shows the characteristic importance of and sensitivity to shared values, and the way union is approached and experienced through relationship.

transformation
the mysteries of ego death/rebirth, through experiences with others

To grow toward union, certain dimensions of private living must be surrendered. Sometimes the change is only superficial, while at other times it's more fundamental. On rare occasions, the pressure to grow results in a total transformation of self.

In any case, something about the self must die. Thus, the 8th house represents "death experiences" whenever one surrenders to a larger reality beyond the personal self. In traditional astrology, this is often understood as literal, physical death, but of greater relevance is the experience of "ego death," followed by rebirth into expanded selfhood.

The condition of the 8th shows not only the attitudes surrounding the experience of death/rebirth, but also the characteristic approach one takes in creating such transformative experiences with and through others.

sexual merging
the experience of true sexual union; tantric release

The 8th is the last of the three "sexual" houses. The first was the 2nd house with its emphasis on pure sensuality, the joy of self-absorbed pleasure. The second was the 5th, where courtship culminated in the performance of making love. Both those houses are under the horizon, so they are subjective or personal realms of experience.

The 8th is a western house, so it is relationship-oriented, but it's above the horizon, so it symbolizes the objective implications of sexual experience. The 2nd is the trigger of pleasure, the 5th the building momentum of risk and excitement, and the 8th the culmination of sharing, through consummation, the transformative release of orgasm. Certainly orgasm can occur in 2nd or 5th house terms (in the 2nd, for pure pleasure; in the 5th, for the culmination of a virtuoso performance), but the higher possibilities of orgasm are contained in the 8th.

Beyond bodily affirmation, beyond successful courtship, beyond even the magic of biological procreation, there exist higher realms, however intangible they may be. To open to the possibility, the ego must temporarily die, so death/rebirth is actually built into the structure of the nervous system. The purpose is to leave behind the old limits, beliefs, or values, to shed worn-out skins, to transcend the self in a moment of union with the unimaginable beyond (symbolized by the Godliness that manifests through the intimacy between lovers).

The condition of the 8th house reveals the path characteristically taken by any individual surrounding these intangible, occult, or spiritual possibilities.

focused intuition

nonrational knowing as it operates through one-to-one relatedness

The 8th is the second of three "intuitive" houses (the others being the 4th and 12th). Here the emphasis is on "emotional radar" directed outward from the self, focused on specific individuals other than the self.

Logically, intuition of this type works best when the relationship between seer and object is already clearly established beforehand. But real life does not evolve sequentially. It is eminently possible for such focused intuition to be "received" about someone one hardly knows, someone with whom there is no "contract," no "commitment," and only the merest intangible hint of true relatedness. In occult terms, we could say that anyone about whom you register such strong impressions is a person with whom you've already established a relationship in some dimension other than that of ordinary life.

The condition of the 8th shows the natural style and importance such relationship-oriented intuitions have in an individual's life.

shared assets

the concrete legacies of relationships;
shared finances, possessions, or property

All partnerships have resources, and by definition, they are shared. Land, property, and possessions are all 8th house levels when associated with a relationship. Thus, any inheritance or endowment received through family or marriage is an 8th house concern.

In addition, money itself is a symbol of shared worth, for the monetary system is a way of formalizing and simplifying barter in commerce along rules established by collective society. The 8th represents all money made through partnership, whereas the 2nd symbolized money made purely by the labors of the self. Most income involves consideration of both houses, since all business requires both a buyer and a seller.

One system for using the two houses suggests that the 8th be seen as the source of the money—where it comes from; while the 2nd is the use of the money—how it is spent. But keep in mind that these are interpretive theories, not hard-and-fast rules.

The condition of the 8th house reveals the characteristic attitudes an individual expresses around the issue of tangible shared assets, as well as relevant strategies surrounding such resources.

Sun/8th

union

An 8th house Sun indicates that the question of personal worth through partnership is central. The experience of being with someone—not just interacting with the person, but truly merging—is an experience so important that everything else pales in comparison. You plug into life-energy through trusting relationships. Faith in your partner parallels belief in yourself; choose the wrong partners and you short-circuit your growth. The "right" partner will work with you to achieve a state of union. The surrender is not to each other, but to something mutual, and more profound than either ego. You'll know you're on the right track when togetherness is accompanied by the feeling that you are more and more your true self. The **challenge** is to be productively connected—not dependent, yet not separate, linked in trust while still honoring your own path.

transformation

Approach transformation with your whole self. It's not a process you can flirt with, for when you undertake this path, the essence of your life-direction changes. It's like a solar eclipse. The lights of your universe temporarily go out—not something to be undertaken lightly. If you can't die well, you can't live well. You didn't come to the Earth to live one life; you came to live many, in sequence, each built from the ashes of the one preceding, and all within a single lifetime, within a single body. An ordinary life is not for you, so don't try to create one—it can result only in the suffocation of being buried alive. You need to live in the flow of the extraordinary. Forget normalcy; go for the gusto.

sexual merging

The psychological release of sexual union is central. Orgasm opens the door to the cosmos, especially that achieved by a steady increase in emotional and physical stimulation, one where you momentarily lose track of who is penetrating whom, where maleness and femaleness lose their distinctions, where lover and beloved merge together into a different sort of creature, something more than human. It's a release that may be fueled by biology, but is consummated in spirit. Needless to say, this is most effective when your heart opens, when you are with a partner you truly love. During sex, focus on the center of your being, and flood yourself with warm, inner light.

focused intuition

Intuition brings out your divinity. The tools exist innately within yourself; they merely need to be brought into play. You can see into anyone you're willing to focus on, for your radar is strong. The **pitfall** is your tendency to be overwhelmed by what you pick up. You may have difficulty distinguishing between your subtle perceptions of others and your own experience, and this can be confusing. The **challenge** is to act on what you sense, without concern for its origin. Check out your hunches. Push for full clarity. The benefits will be heartwarming.

shared assets

One level of your life-purpose involves the management, responsibilities, and benefits of money, property and possessions. There is no clear way to tell from the Sun's placement alone what your monetary circumstances are, nor what your characteristic reaction will be; the sign and interplanetary aspects must be considered for that. What we can know is that your circumstances and reactions directly influence essential fulfillment. You may have power you apparently didn't ask for, or you may lack power you desperately want, but in either case, the power of shared resources will eventually be yours. The **pitfall** is failing to see how many people you affect. The **challenge** is to own this power fully. Use it consciously, however you choose to "spend" it.

Moon/8th

union

In the 8th house, the Moon reveals a hunger for intimacy. This need is basic, and not the same as contractual obligation. Rather, it skips over the issue of agreement, beyond commitment, and moves into another realm. The sharing is based on the emotional discovery of sympathy and closeness. One **pitfall** is becoming too dependent on your partners for providing this feeling, expecting them to empathize without you having to reveal anything. The **challenge** is to move toward interactions that fulfill your emotional need for temporary but regular union, while moving away from those interactions that are blocked or too effortful. Warmth and emotional softness are the keys; if they're present in the sharing, you're taking good care of yourself.

transformation

The Moon represents the emotional need for security and safety, but by definition, ego-death feels dangerous even in the safest of circumstances. For you, safety is found in intimate danger. Others feel this danger, sensing the intensity of your feelings. You're perfectly suited to the miraculous in human feeling. You don't have to do anything to be sensitive to it; you're tuned to it naturally, by unconscious radar. Promote a little ego release every day, rather than let your emotions build up to explosive concentration. Your **challenge** is to create stability through the rhythm of regular and ongoing change.

sexual merging

Your deep sexual drive is temperamental, an automatic way of maintaining homeostasis. You need a profound sense of emotional enfoldment, more than simple closeness or intimacy. You need a safe release, for it's in the release of orgasm that you begin to relax and let down your defenses. You can live with partnerships having little or no external security, but when it comes to sexual union, there must be safety. The **pitfall** involves your tendency to develop an emotional dependency on your lover. You look to him or her to provide the vehicle for release, so guard against the habit of clinging to your lover as a child clings to its mother. Conversely, do not foster dependency in your lover. Let needs be fulfilled, but use no hooks. The **challenge** is to fully experience the broad range of emotions that flow through sexuality, to nurture relaxing mutuality.

focused intuition

Intuition is automatic, omnipresent, and impossible to ignore. You have a heightened experience of others' feelings, especially when you're emotionally involved. People become more aware of their own needs when they're around you, and this is good. But when you're close to others, or wish to be, your own needs may overwhelm you, or their needs can become dominant in your emotional experience. The **pitfalls** involve succumbing to these various levels of need, and in so doing, losing touch with the clear messages of your intuition. The **challenge** is to protect your integrity even as you are bombarded with emotions.

shared assets

You depend on the benefits of partnerships or family legacies, working overtime to protect these resources. It's not that you feel the responsibility too seriously, but rather that you identify yourself so strongly with your relationships that you take on the role of nurturer. You may support a partner at some point in life, and if done with respect and trust, this can be a most fulfilling experience. Get a partner who is trustworthy with money; suspicion here can make you crazy. The **pitfall** surrounds insecurity based on the lack of resources or money. If you focus on what you don't have, you'll emphasize your neediness to such an extent that you'll be miserable. The **challenge** is to fill your life with the tangible evidence of shared goodness.

Mercury/8th

union

The more you communicate, the more you are on-track in your intimacy. Interactions need not be based on total agreement, however. While conflict in sharing is antithetical to many 8th house planets, here it promotes a sense of stimulation. As long as disagreements are purely mental, and not emotional, greater intimacy can result. But don't rely so much on ideas that you disregard the being-to-being connection. Also, be aware of your tendency to talk about closeness without ever surrendering into a truly united state. The **challenge** is to use the connection of your mind with another person's as a kind of "radar fix" to show you the path toward real merging of your spirits.

transformation

Your thoughts lead you to the edge of what your personality can conceive, and though this may seem perverse—having a mind that leads you beyond yourself—it's actually the most natural thing in the world for you. Develop a scientist's eye; investigate all the transformations going on in the world of your relatedness. Ask people about the significance of their changes; learn their languages, and consider yourself in the same terms. Keep in mind that it's not enough to simply think about transformation. You need to put what you learn back into your life, to shift gears from being the scientist to become the guinea pig. After all, you are your own best experiment. The initial **challenge** is easy: to learn with your rational mind the syntax of transformation. The real trick lies in your mind's ability to teach your heart.

sexual merging

Physically, your nervous system is sensitized to sexual intimacy. It intertwines with that of your lover. Stimulation truly resides in the vast network of neurological sensors that finally coalesce in the brain. Talk is often more sexual than touch, for you wish to merge with your beloved's mind. You're quite changeable in activity and response, and while this can be delightful in a lover, it can also prevent the steady buildup of intensity necessary for release. Sexual feelings may occur quite suddenly, even in inappropriate settings. Equally, you may think of a joke just after the experience of culmination, and, needless to say, this tends to disrupt the mood. Fulfill your curiosity about going over Niagara Falls in a barrel—your mind is the barrel, sexual power is the Falls.

focused intuition

You are not so much a highly intuitive person as you are someone who is very interested in intuitive experience. Intuition is an invisible and largely indefinable process, and though you have the tools to be psychically sensitive, you don't easily relax into full trust of your powers. You stand back, wanting to check it out, to confirm it rationally and objectively. The **pitfall** is merely discussing the possibilities rather than really using your intuition. The **challenge** is to tune your nervous system so you hear others thinking, or at least discern the pattern of their thoughts, if not the actual words themselves.

shared assets

Your mind engages in perpetual bookkeeping, moving your resources around, reshuffling your worth. This can be energizing, a fully natural experience, in which case you enjoy the changes, or it can be enervating for your nervous system, in which case you gradually exhaust yourself with imaginary crises. The question here isn't how much you have, but what you do with what you have. Keep the money in motion—whether it is your own or money you manage for others. Recognize that the significant time you spend thinking about resources is perfectly alright, for money and possessions are essentially a game to be played for your stimulation. Winning or losing is not the **challenge;** playing the game is.

Venus/8th

union

You enjoy being close to another. You appreciate the experience of surrendering to love. But first make sure that love is indeed present before you surrender, and second, be certain that the other person is also in the flow of the same love. Do not seduce another into union; this leads to the **pitfalls** of inevitable betrayal and loss of harmony. Instead, take advantage of every good feeling to promote shared intimacy. The **challenge** is to understand that even personal love is a presence between two individuals, something that does not originate in their separate lives, but is instead created out of the harmony that arises from togetherness.

transformation

Venus loves ritual in all forms, even the extreme rituals of ego-transcendence. The possibility of rebirth offers its own aesthetic, so you willingly participate. You're receptive to psychological change, since you embrace more than you currently embody. The **pitfall** surrounds the belief that you'll be able to keep all your existing value systems after you've changed. It's as if you look forward to a future self that is the same as your present self, only better able to enjoy the fruits of life. Though this can work to your benefit in some ways, it's still a carrot-and-donkey approach to growth. The **challenge** is to understand that ego-death means completely giving up old ways of understanding pleasure in favor of new values, and, happily, new pleasures.

sexual merging

The chemistry of sexual union is a powerful aphrodisiac, a perfume of lovely and delicate scent, a very magical potion. For you, it's the icing on the cake of life. Feminine qualities are emphasized here: enfolding, softening, receiving. Whether you are male or female, it's your beauty that draws others toward union with you. You know how to offer yourself to your beloved in total openness, but there are **pitfalls.** You can also be seductive, presenting an alluring mask of receptivity to entrap those you wish to snare. You can even seduce yourself into believing you're open when you're not. Remember that sexual vanity is your enemy, not your ally. The **challenge** is to understand that the aesthetic and physical pleasures of union are truly worthwhile when they occur with the right person, at the right time, in the right setting. Under those conditions, the joy of full release invites self-renewal.

focused intuition

Your intuitive capabilities have a special purpose, to tap into the vibration of personal love. You also appreciate psychic sensitivity in others. Finding it in someone fills you with pleasure, making your inner world resonate more harmoniously. The **pitfall** involves using these sensitivities in a purely self-serving manner, rather than with mutuality, to benefit both yourself and others. The **challenge** is to open yourself to the invisible worlds that exist all around us, worlds of ineffable beauty.

shared assets

It may be that you stand to inherit money, or marry someone wealthy. In any case, the struggle for money is something you may not understand. Even if you don't have money, you imagine yourself deserving of it, since you feel it to be the birthright of your superior station. Whether you're correct or deluded, it's a consideration in all your decisions. The **pitfall** lies in this attitude of complacent superiority, the tendency to overlook real suffering and deprivation in the world. Nonchalance could inspire enmity in others. The **challenge** is to use all resources to further expression of love and beauty. This may be limited to family or friends, but it should keep expanding until you've filled the world with love. You can be the shepherd of the open heart, whether or not you have a dime.

Mars/8th

union

You sense the value that resides in your beloved. It fills you with desire, and you are eager to push through the outer personality to reach the treasures stored in the queen's chamber of the inner pyramid. But you often ignore your partner's boundaries. In fact, the higher the boundaries, the more you may try storming them. This is a deadly **pitfall,** for the treasures of union are gained only when both individuals feel safe to surrender. If you insist on smashing people's walls, they will simply fortify their defenses against you. The result is constant warfare, argument rather than intimacy. Recognize the impact of your male force, the power of your thrust. Let the warmth of your desire arouse the other's receptivity. The **challenge** is to be ardent rather than combative, and thus gain entry to the inner sanctum.

transformation

You can be a consummate spiritual warrior, a crusading knight who walks out alone to confront the dragon of ego-death. The **pitfalls** involve the convoluted meanings of victory and defeat. If you slay the dragon, but your ego survives, you've suffered a spiritual defeat. The question to be asked is this: what is the dragon? You're a heat-seeking missile looking for an external target. But often, the only heat is coming from you. As in Pogo's famous remark, "We have met the enemy, and they is us." Transformation comes not from conquest, but from interpenetration. The **challenge** is to keep it simple, to go after what you want, and to know that desire itself will change in the process.

sexual merging

You are charged with sexual passion. The wish for union glows constantly in the lower chakras. When aroused, desire burns white-hot. You often blot out every other consideration. This can express itself as "going for the goal line" of orgasm without sufficient concern for sharing, but it may also mean obsession with closeness. In either case, the **pitfall** lies in assuming that the obstacles to union reside somehow outside yourself, in your beloved. That leads to explosive conflagrations around the issue of sex. Remember that it is self-defeating to turn your lover into your enemy. The **challenge** is to learn correct penetration. Passion and heat are your arrows; desire is your bow.

focused intuition

Never one to wait, you thrust yourself out of your body, pushing for intuitive contact with others. Anyone you desire becomes a target for the sharp edge of your radar. The **pitfall** involves trespassing. People's inner thoughts, feelings, and desires are often dangerous, often not an accurate reflection of their truest selves, and thus necessarily private. Learn to intuitively enter only those chambers that are open or unlocked. When you push toward someone's inner sanctum, you could tumble instead into the cesspool of their darker selves, and what you find there may not be pleasant. The **challenge** is to hone your psychic sensitivities to a razor's edge. Use these tools as a surgeon might, to cut away blockage, or as a lover would, to fill the beloved with goodness.

shared assets

You are sensitive to money and probably want more than you have. Rather than building your fortune through simple and direct effort, you're drawn toward those who already have money, or obviously desire wealth. But be careful: money, property, and possessions can easily become heated topics, both in your family, and later in your social or romantic relationships. Play down the conflicts, or you may destroy the love that exists. The **challenge** is to work with others to create shared goals your partnerships can achieve, and to extend your mutual fires into a single flame of togetherness.

Jupiter/8th

union

With Jupiter in the 8th house, you have many opportunities to experience the personal value that results from shared contact. You can achieve union with almost anyone, since you're so open to the possibility. Though the experiences may often be ephemeral, they are valid nonetheless, and you should allow yourself the luxury of absorbing personal worth from every interaction. The **pitfall** involves failure to develop deeper intimacy with one person. The **challenge** is to recognize that the world is your oyster.

transformation

You look forward to growth and change with an enthusiasm unmatched by any of the other 8th house planetary types. There is a **pitfall,** however. You tend toward the simplistic view that more is better. Since you are not basically possessive, you don't consider the necessity of surrendering anything. Since you're not "attached," why should you have to give anything up? Ah, there's the rub. What you must give up is your pride. That's what ego death means for you: surrendering excessive pride. The **challenge** is to choose true humility over false pride, rather than maintaining your ego behind a falsely humble mask.

sexual merging

The release of sexual union seems the most natural thing in the world. It is something you flow into effortlessly, because your sensitivities to the goodness of sexual sharing are sound and well-developed. Every sexual experience should take you further. If it doesn't, you grow bored with your lover, becoming a disinterested observer, and you soon move on to greener pastures. The **pitfalls** are twofold. First, you may have expectations surrounding sex that are too high for your partners to reach, and they may recoil. Second, your desire for freedom is strong, and you may disengage from your lovers following intense closeness. Do not pull back too far, for you'll sacrifice the transformative effects. The **challenge** is to let the experience of merging teach you real wisdom. Unless there are indications to the contrary, you're likely to regard the intimacy of sex with both healthy curiosity and pleasant wonder.

focused intuition

Intuition expands in all directions at once. You scan the airwaves for anything of interest; your psychic sensitivities range far beyond the narrow boundaries of what you pick up from another individual. You may be fascinated with the notion of messages coming from beyond the human realm, but you should distinguish between true messages and occult nonsense. The **pitfall** lies in waste of your resources through overreliance on intuition to provide the "right" decisions. Do not overlook the importance of concrete effort in achieving your goals; depending solely on your hunches may let you down in a crucial situation. The **challenge** is to use your intuitive sensitivities to discover your higher self reflected in others, connecting with your true wisdom.

shared assets

Your basic attitude about wealth is opportunistic. If you want money, you can't know too many people nor have too many friends. The **pitfall** lies in overlooking certain opportunities because they involve too much work. Why put out effort when relating is so much more fun? Keep in mind that opportune schemes are not the same as enduring wealth. The **challenge** is to develop a truly philanthropic attitude around your wealth networking. The world is indeed your oyster, but remember to replant the beds after each harvest. Such tithing insures the preservation of your good fortune and the world's.

Saturn/8th

union | Saturn in the 8th indicates a strong sense of responsibility surrounding intimacy. This can indicate a working dedication to achieve lasting intimacy. But it may also reveal anxieties. You could fear being held responsible for every failure in sharing, not only blame for the shortcomings of your partnerships, but for any problems your partners have in their personalities. You may mistrust others' motives, believing that they will reject you once they're close enough to expose your flaws. These worries are not groundless—it's necessary to approach with caution. Make a long-term commitment to union, and move one step at a time. Even when you feel the onrush of intimacy, remind yourself to slow down. The **pitfall** is wanting from others what you have not given yourself. The **challenge** is careful selection of partners followed by persevering effort.

transformation | Temper your sensitivity to others' reactions, your fears that you will be criticized or humiliated for not changing fast or well enough. You know very well not only what must change, but how those changes must be expressed. Do not adhere to schedules or rules imposed from outside; forcing change out of fear of rejection achieves nothing. At the same time, do not refuse to work on changing simply because others seem to be pushing you. The **challenge** is to take responsibility for where you are, not where you feel you should be. Do so calmly, without protest, while you continue gaining strength through measured steps forward. Your fears of ego death have only the power you give them, so celebrate even tiny victories over inertia. Most of all, be gentle and forgiving with yourself. You can change; time is on your side.

sexual merging | You want sex to be tangible, not ethereal, but this focus is so demanding that you may overwhelm your own capacity for the experience. You fear that if you truly let go, you will obliterate yourself, so you hold back. The closer you come, the more your own gravity holds you down. Sometimes you can't achieve release, and you regard this as a personal failure. It's not. It's the result of pushing too hard, of carrying too much seriousness. You regard your beloved's desires toward you with suspicion. This is protection against your rejection anxieties. The **challenge** is to patiently develop sexual relaxation. Remember, the trek up the mountain is long, to be achieved slowly. Only then will you appreciate the view from the summit.

focused intuition | You feel it's not enough to merely have intuition; you often demand perfect knowing. This is too much to expect. Also, you fear the repercussions of intuition, believing that others will kill the messenger. Finally, you fear that you may actually be crazy, that intuition is not real, and that you are succumbing to a form of self-delusion. Each **pitfall** warrants real concern, but none is true. Your **challenge** is to work persistently to develop your intuitive faculties, constantly checking and double-checking the accuracy of your perceptions, and slowly developing faith that invisible worlds do indeed exist, and can be of great pragmatic value.

shared assets | Money means responsibility, whether there is too little or too much. There is often delay or disappointment—your reward for patience is not as high as you hoped it would be. Happily, Saturn improves with age, like fine wine, and maturity can bring great common sense. But this is achieved only if you carefully manage the resources available through relationships. Easy money is counterfeit for you, and you must reject it. The **challenge** is to be like the little piggy who built his house out of bricks.

Uranus/8th

union

Intimate sharing is a peak experience. Much time is spent observing union rather than participating in it, staunchly maintaining detachment. In this state, your personal worth is not open to alteration through interaction with others. Then, suddenly, a spark of sharing explodes you like a rocket off the launch pad, blasting toward the heavens of union. The **pitfall** involves mutual exclusivity, the tendency when operating from either frame of mind to deny the possibility of the other. The **challenge** is to respond to intimacy whenever your life hardens into stagnant habits, knowing full well that such revolutionary unions are not likely to be permanent, but honoring them just the same.

transformation

One moment you're the person you know, and the next moment you're a stranger to yourself, an alien from another world. These changes are rarely permanent. Rather, they represent the experience of a self still in-the-becoming, a preview of who you may eventually become. What characterizes both states is the willingness to stand alone, unaffected by the pulls of ordinary human relating. The **challenge** involves clarity in seeing what is ultimately real, shucking illusions like shedding old skins. Remember these special phases, and use them as a compass to guide yourself toward maturity.

sexual merging

Why do you explode into sexual ecstasy one moment, yet remain coolly aloof another? Most of the time you don't know why. But the issues revolve around your individuality and the use of your will. When you operate from ordinary will, you may staunchly refuse to be sexually involved. It's only when you become receptive to a purer consciousness within yourself that you receive the full benefits of tantric power. However rare it may be, sexual union is a sudden awakening of your sensitivity. In release, you gain a renewed sense of your specialness, and a humbling appreciation of the power that surrounds us in the universe. Your **challenge** is to accept this power when you connect with it, to honor yourself, your partner, and the universe itself for the gift of sexual magic.

focused intuition

You are alternately fascinated and bored by intuitive realities. At times, you are the real item: a bona fide magician. At other times, you're a cipher, denying that you could ever perform feats of occult magic. You don't wish to be a trained seal, going into your act on command, and this includes even your own command. Intuition happens on its own, shocking you and others with its unpredictable urgency. You are so humanitarian in your psychic focus that you more often receive insight about strangers than about those closest to you. Somehow, distance increases sensitivity. One **pitfall** lies in your not gaining personal advantage from the occasional flashes of intuitive brilliance. The **challenge** is to give whatever you get, to allow your intuition to go where it wants to go, rather than trying to develop or force it into any disciplined application.

shared assets

There is unpredictability around money and possessions, especially as they pertain to your relationships. You can win and lose fortunes, often overnight, so expect the unexpected. It's best if you make your money in nonstandard ways, for it is outside the ordinary that your talents will lie. Lowered attachment to money and possessions liberates you from fear. The **pitfall** is excessive willfulness—bending under pressure is not one of your strong suits, and you can be incredibly stubborn when pushed, although you are also graciously flexible when you feel free to be so. Finally, you tend to play the game of money by your own rules, and though this can be an asset, it can get you into trouble. The **challenge** is to understand what is gained or lost.

Neptune/8th

union

With Neptune in the 8th house, intimacy is a direct road to Cosmic Central. You exist in perpetual readiness for it, just this side of melting, needing only the slightest contact to open your heart-of-hearts. But beware of the **pitfalls.** Your boundaries are not solid; at times they hardly exist at all, and you abandon yourself through union. True intimacy is circular—it always brings you back to yourself. If you use it as an escape, there is no self to return to, and chaos or disillusionment follow. Don't be seduced by your own fantasies of instant merging, however easy it may seem. Your **challenge** is to continually reaffirm the true spirituality of interpersonal union. Invite and recognize the presence of God through human closeness, even when cynics deny that it occurs.

transformation

You're drawn to the idea of transcendence. You want to leave the ground behind, to soar in spiritual bliss. But you overlook reality. Ecstatic visions alternate with nightmares. Which is real and which is the dream? Exaggerating every aspect of personal growth, you create imaginary transformations to solve imaginary problems. So remember that real growth is within life, not beyond it. It unfolds out of responsibility. The **challenge** is to change your understanding of spirituality itself. Bring holiness down to common sense, day-to-day living. You're a natural minister, but your greatest teaching comes from acceptance of your life and the lives of everyone around you.

sexual merging

Sexual union with a lover is easy, magical, and sublimely seductive. Since your orientation is more emotional than physical, the emphasis here is on the intensity of feeling that builds through intercourse. You envelop yourself with your lover's desire, wishing to dissolve yourself in the bliss. However, you sometimes use shared sexuality as a drug, to escape real life. The thudding reentry of gravity that inevitably occurs when romantic illusion fades is not only disappointing, but painful. Don't go so high that you leave your partner behind. By all means let your emotions soar, but do not leave the ground. Instead, fertilize it by an infusion of spirit. Your **challenge** is to elevate earth to the heavens, to release the holiness contained within matter, and make it glow.

focused intuition

The invisible flows of intuition are truly oceanic. In fact, you must consciously limit the psychic information you receive. Otherwise, you'll be swamped in an avalanche of images and feelings that have no clear source. Separate real messages from "pink noise." You must develop clarity and the ability to interpret what you receive. Is there a difference between personal fantasies—hopes, dreams, fears, anxieties—and the feelings that seem to emanate from others? Are they real, or simply the mirror of your own unconscious? Since boundaries are your issue, the **challenge** is to remain open while perfecting the ability to discern between yourself and others.

shared assets

You believe that money is an infinite cornucopia, with you on the receiving end, God's agent for distributing it, usually to save the world. Your motives are simultaneously pure and corrupt, for though you wish to see the resources that come from family or other relationships used for good causes, you still expect some of the frosting for yourself. The idea that you may have to work for money is antithetical, since you believe it should come solely on the basis of your good heart. When you love, you are generous to a fault, and you must monitor the use of money as a seduction to gain approval. The **challenge** is to share what you have with others while maintaining faith that the universe will provide for you.

Pluto/8th

union
You are completely resistant to closeness with some people, but with others the sensitivity is overpoweringly strong, almost an obsession. This cuts both ways; others often react to you in the same all-or-nothing manner. You're fascinated by the sheer power of intimacy, although you often mistake the origin, believing it to emanate from the other person. It doesn't. It arises out of the sharing, fueled by something mysterious within you. A major **pitfall** involves trying to control this unconscious power, which usually results in disaster. The **challenge** is to be receptive to unconscious sources. The power will still be present, but no one will be on top, no one on the bottom. Then the whole becomes greater than the sum of the parts, and the mystery is revealed.

transformation
You both love and fear the intensity of sharing, since you're fascinated with life's mysterious edges. When you finally tumble over, your personality may very literally change. Old habits, old ways of thinking and feeling vanish so completely you'll have difficulty imagining that they ever could have existed. But don't forget what you once were. Real transformation requires the increased perspective of relativity, not simply a wholesale change from one extreme to another. The **challenge** is to accept change without resistance. Transformation has its own peculiar physics, different from those of ordinary living. Allow ego death to come for you in its own time and its own way.

sexual merging
Sex may be curiously ordinary most of the time, in spite of your obsession with it. You could suffer through long dry spells as you subconsciously prepare for the sea change of primal release. But once you move into the rhythmic intensity of sex, you open volcanically. When you find a relationship with the right chemistry, there is no turning back. You can only submit your will to something more profound, respecting the power that obliterates your past and opens a new sense of self. The **pitfall,** as usual, surrounds control. Do not restrain yourself nor dominate your lover. The **challenge** is to trust that when you are finally sucked through the black hole of sexual union, you will emerge renewed, as a butterfly emerges out of its chrysalis.

focused intuition
Invisible data is continually absorbed into your unconscious. It exists in cold storage, like icebergs, nine-tenths beneath the surface. Then, at some point, a particular experience of sharing releases all the information at once. You enter into a period of almost unbelievable sensitivity, with enough power and impact to blow lives apart— sometimes others' and sometimes your own. The **pitfall** is blind resistance to the deeper flows of intuition, causing eventual earthquakes. The **challenge** is to allow your understanding of the universe to change as you give out what pours through you.

shared assets
You are subject to extremes of attitude and behavior when money is combined with partnership. You could be an absolute gold digger, deaf to any considerations other than what you can squeeze from a relationship. But you could just as easily be selfless, providing others with support beyond their wildest dreams. It is not the particular manifestation that matters, but the compulsive drive for recognition and wealth. Examine these drives, or they may run your life and ruin your relationships. This is the **pitfall.** The **challenge** is to learn to transmute lead to gold, to understand alchemical processes, both at monetary and psychological levels. Learn how to convert that which has no value into that which is ultimately valuable, and in so doing, change yourself into something purer and more exquisite.

Planets
in
the
9th House

9th House

organized mental frameworks as they apply to the social environment

The concrete mentality of the 3rd house dealt with the relation of specific objects to the self, attempting to organize the immediate environment in personal terms. The 9th house is concerned with the relation of classes of objects to the collective, attempting to organize the abstract environment in ways that increase the sensibility of the larger world. It is the pursuit of pure ideas about the world—how it works, how it can work, and how it might ideally work if we better understood its underlying principles.

The 9th is the first truly cultural house. Here we seek to discover the concerns that link human beings together. It's an intellectual realm, where collective agreement is investigated. It involves all abstract systems such as philosophy, ethics, religion, law, etc.

This is the mind at work as a conscious instrument, entering fully into its own natural realm, creating patterns of understanding, as opposed to accumulating information. It is the pursuit of wisdom at the collective level. The 9th is essentially a laboratory of the mind, one with unceasing questions but no final answers.

In a comparison with government, the 11th house could be considered analogous to the legislative branch, representing Congress, with group debate toward the proposal and formalization of codes for social interaction; the 10th house would be the executive branch, representing the President, with responsibility for regulation and enforcement of codified laws; finally, the 9th house is similar to the judicial branch, representing the Supreme Court, with the power of interpretation and review of laws through the application of generalized principles.

The planetary condition of the 9th reveals the characteristic importance of conceptual mentality, the way it develops, the misunderstandings or oversimplifications likely to be suffered, and the particular intellectual genius inherent in the individual.

**increased relativity in cultural knowledge;
long-distance travel (either physical or mental)**

The 9th house indicates both the extent and the nature of interest any individual feels for other human beings, not personally, but impersonally. This involves cultural perspective, the driving curiosity to see what is over the next hill, motivated by a desire to learn the myriad ways groups create and maintain themselves. How do groups form? What are their beliefs, laws, expectations, and social ethics? And how will the increased perspective gained reflect upon one's own group identity and background?

The 9th is the area of long-distance journeys in both the literal and the metaphorical senses, for a person may discover the expansiveness of new cultural learning either by travelling physically to far-off places, or simply by gathering the many information resources that are making the world an ever-smaller planet.

The condition of the 9th reveals an individual's characteristic orientation toward such mental or physical explorations in pursuit of greater understanding.

**higher
education**

all adult learning to broaden the self, including informal experience

The 3rd house described the experience of primary and secondary education, the basic learning required to function in the real world. That education was predominantly concrete and oriented toward the development of fundamental skills. It was also essentially rote memorization to insure survival and facilitate effective interaction with the immediate environment.

The 9th house carries education to the next level, that of college and beyond. But it is not limited only to formalized education, and should not be considered solely in terms of concrete learning in the educational hierarchy. The 9th concerns the individual's attitudes, desires, and capacities concerning broader conceptual understanding, and this can occur in any setting, at any age.

In broader terms then, the 9th house reveals for an individual the importance and the tone of what is coming to be termed "lifelong learning," the the wish to encompass more mature understanding of oneself, society in general, and the world in which we all live.

**the search
for truth**

the quest for generalizable truths, both in understanding and communication

Getting to the truth of any matter, at least at the level of mind, is a very tricky experience. It may involve wading through many diverse and paradoxical perceptions, and yet it can be as simple as seeing your hand before your face. But even with the formidable difficulties involved in acquiring the mental clarity that leads to an understanding of what is true, that process is likely to be much easier than effectively communicating those truths to others.

The condition of the 9th house reveals an individual's characteristic orientations toward the pursuit of truth, the process of acquiring the knowledge of what is true in the final analysis of his or her life-experience, and it also reveals the attitudes that assist or block communication of the truth to other searching minds.

**ideal
society**

the visualization of an ideal culture; characteristics of a "perfect" world

Many of us long for an ideal world, one existing in our minds rather than in reality. Every person's ideal world is based on a set of "laws," all of which start with the phrase, "people should..." People should love one another, people should not carry guns, people should respect the property of others, people should drive energy-efficient cars, etc.

There's a song from a Broadway musical called, "If I Ruled the World," and this song represents the culmination of 9th house experience, the formulated result of the philosophical relativity and the search for general truths contained in the other levels. This could be felt as an ideal, a kind of poetic vision, or as a more rigid belief, what might be termed "enlightened fascism."

The condition of the 9th house reveals the ideal or perfect world each of us would like to see, if only we had the power to create it, and were free to do so.

Sun/9th

conceptual frameworks

If the Sun is linked with the 9th house, the essence of life-purpose involves opening the mind to new realms. You've come to the Earth to pursue fresh mental perspectives, to develop, explore, and find a philosophy of life. Whenever you open mentally, you plug into the cosmos. By living at the highest ethical level you can achieve, you expand the life-energy available to you. It isn't sufficient that you adopt an existing philosophy; you must synthesize all you learn into an original understanding, a personal philosophy, one that you can live by. The **pitfalls** lie in having your head so completely in the clouds of abstraction that you lose touch with the grounded reality of living on the Earth. Understanding the secrets of the universe has little point if you can't remember your zip code. The **challenge** is to merge the delight of pure thought with the discipline of a moral life, and to convey this wisdom wherever it can uplift others' spirits.

cultural perspective

Reading about faraway places, thinking about them, and travelling to explore them are a natural way of life for you. The sense of exploration is fundamental, whether physical, mental, emotional, or spiritual. The more you can learn about other cultures, especially by direct experience, the more you fulfill your central life-purpose. You are more yourself when you're on the go, moving through foreign territory. This includes not only far-off locales, but the infinite varieties of experience right in your own backyard. Your **challenge** is to assimilate the broadest views of humanity, to act as a networker of the one human world.

higher education

You keep yourself charged by the stimulation of learning. Whether or not your early education reflected this basic enthusiasm, there is little question that you will develop into a perpetual student as your life goes on. Especially as an adult, you are an eager student of the more conceptual fields of study. While you are certainly permitted to undertake these studies on your own, there's a great deal to be said for using the formal structures of cultural education, since credentialing is a relevant concern. Learn everything you can, then teach by example.

the search for truth

Here, more than with the other 9th house planetary placements, there is little distinction between profound and pragmatic truths. What is important is the absence of untruth. And there are two kinds of untruths. The first is active lying, which is to say, believing or communicating something which is objectively false. That experience is clearly negative for you. It disconnects you from your divinity. But equally important is the experience of passive lying, either by withholding truth when it is known, or by substituting a lesser truth for the one in question. These diminish your essence—a very serious **pitfall.** It is of paramount importance that you search for the highest truths you can discover, and communicate the highest truth you know relative to any circumstance. It's not necessary that you be able to express it perfectly, nor that others totally comprehend. But it is your **challenge** to strive for honesty, integrity, and illumination. **Truth is life.**

ideal society

Your perfect society would be Olympian in scope. Humans would become like the Gods of ancient myths, with honor and wisdom sparking an unceasing flow of creativity. The consensus of opinion on any subject would reflect your own most basic beliefs. **As Ruler of the World, you would be authoritative but generous, powerful yet benevolent, noble and dignified but always accessible to your loyal subjects.**

Moon/9th

conceptual frameworks

In the 9th, the Moon reveals that you nurture yourself mentally. The higher mind is emotionally satisfying, and you need to move into those airy realms of pure thought in order to feel safe and certain, every single day of your life. Your interest in thinking is automatic and habitual, although your thoughts are not. You also nurture others by providing the same mental food for them, offering the comfort of wisdom. This is one of your strongest traits, though it can also be a **pitfall.** People don't always appreciate mental generalizations when they're needy, no matter how true nor optimistic the message may be. Your **challenge** is to learn about the protection of maternal images, including the Earth herself. Feed yourself from her wisdom.

cultural perspective

Security comes from making the unknown known. You need to travel to fulfill an inner longing, to scratch an emotional itch. You may explore vicariously, by education rather than by direct experience. But even so, you still feel pressure to literally see what's over the next hill, to protect yourself by enlarging the vistas of your experience. What you most enjoy are sentimental memories of your travels, like creating a living museum. The **challenge** is to bring everything back home, to make the world familiar.

higher education

Your education is stimulated by the movement of temperamental emotional tides. You phase in and out of higher education, putting it aside whenever your emotional life is stable, picking it up whenever there is an emotional crisis. Each period of your life brings new emotional challenges, causing you to look more deeply into systems you already understand and use, but also to reach out for new ways of seeing clearly. Of the two approaches, you are more comfortable with expanding previous knowledge, but keep in mind that there are times in life when we must make a significant shift into new understanding. Remember that however insecure it may feel to embark on an alien path, this is sometimes the most productive course.

the search for truth

Where truth is concerned, the world will provide you with the questions. You provide the answers. This is not as immense a task as it seems, for there is no requirement to have easy or simple answers, nor are you expected to know every answer. It is perfectly alright to admit that you don't know. What is crucial, however, is that you be willing to let the truth come through you, even if you can't see its source. Your truth changes from moment to moment, from setting to setting, so flow with the changes to stay in the middle of the current. Don't rationally figure out what's true—feel it. Avoid the **pitfall** of telling others what they want to hear. It's more nurturing to respond authentically. Emotional integrity is the **challenge,** both in understanding and communication. Enhance your own certainty by blending objective honesty with emotional sensitivity. **Truth is security.**

ideal society

You believe society would be a better place if it were safer for all of us to open our emotions, to express our needs more honestly. There would be no hunger, neither physical nor emotional. Pure mentality would be relegated to a back seat, used only as a tool for better communication of feeling. You idealize a more secure culture where family values are sacred, but not limited to mere biological relatedness. You want the world to become one huge family, where the predominant concern is for children, either literal young ones, or the child within each of us. **As Ruler of the World, you would be warmly maternal, firm in discipline, but willing to take us back into the fold.**

Mercury/9th

conceptual frameworks

With Mercury in the 9th house, you collect abstract systems like some people collect stamps, creating a network that links all systems together. You love nothing better than a good old, down-home philosophical discussion, preferably a debate. It won't matter what position you're defending, as long as the conversation stays lively. The **pitfalls** are numerous. Your mind is incredibly quick, but not always logical, and you leap to broad conclusions, often from a skimpy base of experiential knowledge. You'd like to know everything, but failing that, you settle for infinite variations on a particular theme. You have an answer for every occasion. A virtual master of rationalization, you can whip up a philosophy on the spur of the moment to satisfy the demands of convenience. Your **challenge** is to become a true librarian of philosophy.

cultural perspective

You can never learn too much, see too much, travel too far. Everything you've experienced is connected to everything else, making your mind a central switchboard. You love long-distance contact; often even the telephone will suffice. All media are interesting to you: magazines, travel brochures, foreign films, anything to feed the mind's curiosity. You're interested in Brain Earth, in feeling that your nervous system is well-connected to a network that extends over the globe. You regard strangers as potential friends, new outposts in your network. You want to be expanded, spread out, everywhere at once and nowhere in particular.

higher education

You aren't likely to pursue a single path of knowledge; yours is not a path of expertise in one specific field. Much more likely is an interest in diverse areas of education, taking a little from this, a little from that, more a survey than a study in depth. This broadly-based education is modified by the placement of the Sun in the natal chart. If it is in the 10th house, there may be greater specialization, or at least aiming your educational pursuits toward a more singular area, funneling knowledge into career. If the Sun occupies the 9th, you tend toward greater breadth in your mental interests. In the 8th, it can go either way, depending on other factors. The **challenge** is to remember that dialogue is more important than pure study. Learning is most alive in interaction and two-way communication, a vital exchange of inspiration and stimulus.

the search for truth

You're fascinated by the infinite forms of truth. It's natural to explore all the forks in the river, knowing that each will eventually reach the sea. You hold information in your mind's eye, turning it, squeezing and stretching to see it change shape, cutting it into a thousand pieces, looking for distinctions, contradictions, and paradoxes. You don't arrive at a final product, a finished truth. Instead, you stay in the laboratory—testing, refining, experimenting. It's more natural for you to talk about the quest for truth than to tell it directly. Your **challenge** is to communicate the structures through which we approach wisdom. **Truth is an endless source of curiosity, a study in relativity.**

ideal society

You idealize a society where people are taught to express their thoughts more effectively. Depending on Mercury's sign and the Sun's condition, you believe either in total access to information or solid control of information, with the former more probable than the latter. However, in either case, free movement from place to place would always be permitted. The perfect society would be in a state of constant change. **As Ruler of the World, you would be the ultimate nexus of information, connected to everything, yet constantly mobile, exploring your Kingdom.**

Venus/9th

conceptual frameworks

In the 9th, Venus reveals the pleasures of mentality. You love philosophy and formal concepts. You love knowing what the rules are, and searching for more aesthetic ways of understanding. Not necessarily a great intellect yourself, you are drawn to the charismatic personalities of great thinkers. You love to be in the flow of mentality, to have it wash over you like a cascading waterfall. This is not the love of conversation, nor mere mental cleverness; you quickly tire of those. No, this is the love of ideas, of understanding based on sweeping patterns of creative thought. The **pitfall** lies in the difference between simply learning philosophy, and the more disciplined effort of living a truly ethical life. The **challenge** is to fill your world with aesthetic ideas, to make it sing with the beauty of an expanded mind, and to share those pleasures with everyone.

cultural perspective

The immediate environment is less attractive than what exists over the horizon. Travel is a luxury, a lovely adventure. Being relationship-oriented, you cultivate personal relationships with individuals from different cultural backgrounds than your own. This may mean that you are drawn to foreigners in a literal sense. It may also be that you're attracted to people with enlarged and perhaps exotic perspectives on human experience. The **pitfall** involves becoming so enamored with your longing for travel and increased cultural perspective that you overlook the satisfactions existing in ordinary surroundings. Keep in mind that love, happiness, and enjoyment are ubiquitous and can be discovered everywhere on the Earth, not just over the next hill. Your **challenge** is to promote the appreciation of the world and all its diverse cultures.

higher education

Higher education is a continuing source of pleasure. You're very receptive to learning, and little in your world brings greater satisfaction than the flow of knowledge. With Mercury, active dialogue is necessary. However, you are much more comfortable when in the receiving position. It's not so much that you wish to be wise, but instead that you truly love surrounding yourself with ideas. Thus, you could be quite happy sitting at home reading a book on art or philosophy, and you're even happier attending a lecture, being in the actual living presence of a master. There is no innate sense of inferiority, however, just a love of the pure, unmitigated luxury of education.

the search for truth

For you, truth must not be ugly. A good-looking lie is more attractive than a homely truth. You want to warm it, to polish it until it shines, to bring out the beauty inherent in any truth. The **challenge** is to reveal the aesthetic goodness in what is true, to show yourself and us the way to appreciate the truth. Telling the truth must reflect this task. Communicate with grace, and you move toward greater harmony with nature and the universe. **Truth is beauty; truth is love.**

ideal society

You believe that love should fill the world, that people should be nicer to one another. In your perfect society, failure to love would be a cardinal sin. It would be a romantic culture, in soft-focus and pastel colors. You believe in art and high style. The world would be filled with lovely objects and beautiful people; ugliness would be impossible to conceive. There would be no upsets, no crises, no embarrassing social scenes. Everyone would display graceful manners and seemly behavior. **As Ruler of the World, you would be the paragon of Love and Beauty, the High Priestess of Romance, the symbol of Happiness, Receptivity, and Fertility.**

Mars/9th

conceptual frameworks

In the 9th, Mars indicates a passionate interest in mental conquest—thinking makes you hot. You want to demonstrate the nobility of your mind. Every time you encounter a new question, you must discover an answer to move forward. At first, your attitude is mere bravado, and you can be slain by any trick question. As you gain experience, however, your confidence builds. You master the game of knowledge, learning to vanquish silly questions and confront more profoundly challenging ones. The **pitfall** is argument for its own sake. The **challenge** involves thinking clearly and logically, pushing through the often veiled and convoluted patterns of religion, philosophy, or morality. Simple and direct, that is your path.

cultural perspective

Eager for adventure, you want to satisfy your wanderlust by conquering foreign territory, and are willing to drop everything and go at a moment's notice. As you move through a strange cultural setting, adrenaline surges through your system. Too much stimulation causes paranoia; you may at times feel like Custer, surrounded by hostile Indians. If that **pitfall** occurs, look for points of familiar human contact in your alien environment, for this can soothe the savage beast within. The **challenge** is to push beyond your cultural boundaries. Literal travel is more important than vicarious travel in the mind, so get up and get out as much as you can. You're happier with the rough-and-tumble of a Conastoga covered wagon than the comfort of a plush, touristy Winnebago. Live by your wits and make your adventures legend.

higher education

The cutting edge of your life is the desire to know more, to see further. It's as if the lead dog on your sled has an incredible urge to chase rabbits into the forest. What you already know soon loses its luster, so study what is most vital to you. Traditional institutions are suitable arenas, for credentials are your medals. Once you set your sights on a certain type of knowledge, don't stop until you've mastered the subject, at least in basic terms. But at times the very urgency of your direct approach prevents you from appreciating the subtleties of a conceptual system. This naiveté spurs you to greater efforts to scale the educational heights.

the search for truth

Getting to the truth is no problem. If there's a wall, you knock it down. Never one for subtlety, you ignore the convolutions, exceptions, and paradoxes, searching for basic truth. You like seeing the mind in simple terms of truth and lies. This is fine as long as the situation is clear-cut. But human interaction does not always reflect such archetypes, and you need to understand that your truth may indeed coexist with that of others. So before you batter your opponents into the ground, a serious **pitfall,** remember to ask yourself if there is a larger truth than you knew. Look before you leap, and don't shoot before you see the whites of their eyes—they may be friends rather than foes. The real **challenge** is to eradicate the hidden darkness within yourself. Fight for truth, but remember that warfare is not a philosophy, only an extreme means of establishing peace. **Truth is a sword and a shield.**

ideal society

You idealize the clarity and simplicity of archetypal morality, where good and evil are clearly defined, where everyone knows the score, and the strongest buck leads the herd. You'd create a world where sexuality could be more openly expressed, one where desire would be acknowledged as the highest of emotions, the purest of drives. **As Ruler of the World, you would be a proud samurai: strong, fierce, and noble.**

Jupiter/9th

conceptual frameworks

With Jupiter in the 9th, you teach and learn with equal enthusiasm, often combining the two in animated dialogue. You regard others' thoughts as resources to be mined, since you understand that everyone has something worth knowing. You're progressive but traditional, and not above falling into an occasional cliché. Philosophy, ethics, religion, or law are synthesized in an endless search for the perfect generalization. You throw new ideas into your mental soup-pot to see what new flavors emerge. Unfortunately, some people don't appreciate their hard-won knowledge being treated like fodder for your mental cuisinart, and you may offend others on occasion. You can be a master chef of the mind, but appreciate the dish each individual offers before scurrying off to hold court in your own kitchen. Guard against pomposity, and avoid the **pitfalls** of righteousness or mental superiority. The **challenge** is to humbly acknowledge that wisdom comes from living well rather than knowing everything.

cultural perspective

Travel in any form is a delight. You take advantage of every opportunity to increase perspective. You want to see the development of the world written in the history of its places, and you have a tremendous feeling for the effect of group-consciousness on any particular place. It delights you to discover the universal mark of culture existing in even the most remote human outposts. You're most at home when you're learning, and you learn more effectively when you're on the go, exploring the world.

higher education

You see guiding principles in every event, every experience. Thus, the whole world is your classroom, whether in school or out. As a result, all education is simply a stimulus to the productivity of your fertile mind. You may be a farmer or a professor, but beneath your outer role, you are a true intellectual at heart, a natural philosopher, and your education will continue no matter where you are, no matter what you're doing. It is your greatest joy, your most natural means of self-expression, so indulge yourself. Take advantage of every opportunity to learn.

the search for truth

You love to speculate on the truth, to philosophize your brains out, to build layer upon layer of hypothetical conjecture, and to leap from minimal data to the largest possible generalizations. In fact, what you really love are generalizations themselves. You're great at communicating. The question is, do you understand what you communicate? Don't be seduced by the **pitfall** of glib wisdom. The fact that you may be able to convince others is no guarantee of true maturity. A golden tongue is not the same as a golden mind or heart. You have a gift here. Don't abuse it. Don't stop with the obvious; the **challenge** is subtle refinement. **Truth is the end product of evolution.**

ideal society

Everything would be permitted in your ideal society, with nothing forbidden, except, of course, pessimism. Everyone would be positive, and interested in sharing their optimism with others, who would be completely receptive. Business and politics would abide by a sense of honesty and fair play. Petty concerns would drop away in the realization of larger implications. Everyone would respect the ideologies of others without conflict. **As Ruler of the World, you would be Plato's philosopher/king, conferring wisdom borne of perfect vision.**

Saturn/9th

**conceptual
frameworks**

The need for a coherent and comprehensive philosophy motivates you throughout your life. But it's hard work. Subtle anxieties about your intelligence may cause you to try too hard, or become too blunt in your approach to living. Mental exhaustion can occur, almost like a muscle cramp. That creates a reaction toward the opposite direction of moral shutdown. Don't focus on proving your intellect; rather, let it mature at its own pace. Allow yourself the safety of a conservative philosophy, but don't become a walled fortress of rigid beliefs. Keep learning. Move steadily toward understanding, and your mind will eventually become your most prized possession, your proudest achievement.

**cultural
perspective**

Your drive to discover the world is countered by equally strong caution. Achieving relativity is full of **pitfalls,** for every cultural imprint from childhood on has immense weight in your personality. If you grew up eating hamburgers, then you believe that hamburgers are what people should eat, and the strangeness of exotic cuisines will bring up the rigidity of your imprints. Should you insult your hostess by not eating the raw fish she has so carefully prepared, or should you simply grin and bear it? To grow, you have to expand your cultural perspectives, not only in the mind, but through your entire personality. The **challenge** is to keep at it; it's worth the effort.

**higher
education**

The ambition in Saturn's symbolism implies that you're aimed at higher education with a strong sense of purpose and drive. This can be a positive indication of great persistence and willingness to study, or a negative indication that you don't really want to be educated, but merely seen as an intellectually successful. You approach education pragmatically, which has benefit insofar as it encourages discovery of real-life applications for abstract knowledge, but is harmful if it results in overly materialistic belief systems. Saturn's sensitivity to authority implies that you want your efforts to result in cultural credentialing. This is positive when you use your position with maturity, as a springboard to encourage wider explorations, but negative if you become close-minded, rejecting experience outside consensual reality.

**the search
for truth**

You're a graduate of the school of hard knocks where truth is concerned. Direct experience is the best teacher, for while it may lead you astray from time to time, it is still the only trustworthy source of revelation. Early in your life, the truth you embrace tends to be rough and unpolished, and later you may regret some of your assumptions. However, the older you become, the more your experience builds, eventually proving an inexhaustible source of wisdom. It takes courage for you to tell the truth, the whole truth, and nothing but the truth. You want to hedge, to invoke external authorities as proof. But be courageous, for lies are harmful. Don't guess; it's better to say nothing. **Truth is distilled essence of grounded experience.**

**ideal
society**

Your ideal society would emphasize responsibility, integrity, and order. Each person would set an example for everyone else by standing up straight no matter what burdens there were to bear. In your ideal world, there would be strict discipline and adherence to accepted law, based not on fear of punishment, but rather on the sincere belief that this is necessary if we are to hold civilization together. Formal rituals would play a large part in the socialization process, for stability is high on your list of ideals. **As Ruler of the World, you would be the ultimate authority: responsible, firm but fair, never taking advantage of your exalted position.**

Uranus/9th

conceptual frameworks

In the 9th, Uranus indicates that the higher mind is a rollercoaster of stimulation. There is a desire to go past the acceptable, to see what lies beyond in forbidden realms of thinking. At times you become a philosophical or religious revolutionary, going after accepted beliefs with a vengeance, stopping at nothing to upset the status quo. Rarely one to mince words, you may lambast others with your opinions, and you're as likely to provoke opposition as win support. Remember, devastating social criticism is easy. Aim for something higher, for true reform. The **challenge** is to let your mind move as it wishes, to allow it to show you previously undiscovered channels to brilliance. If you live your own philosophy, you'll promote a wider revolution than by storming the walls of traditional power centers.

cultural perspective

When you travel far from home, or at least away from normal surroundings, the unexpected can and often does happen. Journeys can be pleasurable, awakening new perspectives that cause your understanding to leap beyond former boundaries. Or they can be unsettling, rattling your cage in chaotic or upsetting ways. When you want to shake up your life, leave home, and you invite radical influences into your consciousness. You may find yourself alone on your travels, even when you start out in tandem with others. This is natural, for exploring the world is a basic way to get in touch with your individuality. Use trips or relocations to establish a new sense of yourself.

higher education

Of all the 9th house planetary types, you are the least suited to classical routes of higher education. You could be found in a classroom, but there will be something unusual about the situation. Learning is not likely to be consistent. There are periods of lying fallow, simply moving with the general tide of life. But then an experience galvanizes your consciousness, and you catapult into intensive study. It may seem totally irrelevant to others, but your mind is charged by a wave of illumination. No one questions your basic intelligence, but you often engender opposition with an iconoclastic disregard for traditional wisdom. Damn the torpedoes! Full speed ahead.

the search for truth

Truths emerge not from prolonged or careful study, but as wild-cards, sudden bursts of enlightenment. Being hardheaded, you are unlikely to be interested in others' truths, and yet you insist on communicating your own discoveries. Telling the truth is something you relish. You love the element of surprise, and your communication is often outlandish. But keep in mind that shock effect is not always the best method for transmitting the truth. Remember to be gentle, and you're more likely to be considered a wise genius than a cantankerous fool. **Truth is an awakening into freedom.**

ideal society

Your perfect society would have few if any restraints on expression. No structured society for you; the less government the better. All men would be brothers (and women sisters), but each person would have ample opportunities to develop his or her particular genius. Respect for personal liberty would extend to peaceful resolution of conflict, probably by separating the combatants. There might be a revolutionary sensibility: out with the old, in with the new. **As Ruler of the World, you would be a benevolent despot. You would abolish every institution and finally abdicate the throne, and no one would know if you were serious or joking.**

Neptune/9th

conceptual frameworks

With Neptune, you are more open to the inspiration of the higher mind than any of the other 9th house planetary types. There is awareness of sweeping thought-patterns, the sensation of universal Intelligence communicating through subtle feelings and fleeting images. This can be confusing, since it becomes more difficult to express what you're thinking. At times, you experience awe-inspiring realizations in the mind. In spite of your yearning to understand, don't try to figure out a perfect moral path. Allow everything to coexist, reminding yourself that, eventually, different approaches lead people to the same end, that of infinite compassion, and an understanding that transcends thoughts and systems. Remember that your intelligence is inspirational; what you say is not as important as the grace with which you convey your ideas.

cultural perspective

You wish to find a common language, to discover what unifies cultures and people. When you travel, look for evidence of your psychic background. If you find it, relax—you're home. If you don't, relax—surrender and embrace the newness. If you can't beat 'em, join 'em. Journeys may involve what some call "astral travel," out-of-body experience. One **pitfall** is being a stranger in a strange land. Remember that ultimate Oneness means just what it says: ultimate, beyond all forms of ordinary living. Your **challenge** is to promote the universality of human experience, to remind us that we are together rather than alone. Carry that faith at all times, even in dark moments.

higher education

Education is absorbed rather than pursued. It's beyond conscious control, like floating down a river on a raft. At times the current is slow, the river expansive, and you bask in the sensation of floating on the water. At other times, the river narrows into turbulence, and you shoot the rapids of mentality, hanging on for dear life, fearing you may drown. Or you drift out of the river and into the ocean of ultimate mind, far from the concrete stability of the shore, with no bearings and no rudder. Once the journey is begun, it unfolds according to momentum all its own. When you open to higher knowledge, be gentle toward yourself and humble toward the universe. Compassion, acceptance, and wonder are hallmarks of a true education.

the search for truth

Truth has an intangible, almost mystical quality. It is not factual, nor does it stand out in bold relief when held up against the mundane in life. Instead, it is woven invisibly into everything, part of the tapestry of existence, commonplace yet extraordinary. Glimpsed out of the corner of your mind's eye, truth dances on the periphery of vision. It's better felt than known, for that which can be explained can be explained away. Communicating the truth requires grace and humor. There is the problem of translation into words; feeling is one thing, talking is something else. The best advice is to keep your words as simple as possible. This reduces the chance of your being misunderstood, since explanation promotes confusion. **Truth is ideal, transcendent, and infinite.**

ideal society

Your ideal society would be a place where faith ruled supreme, where every dream became reality. We wouldn't need to communicate verbally in your perfect world, for each person would know the thoughts and feelings of everyone else. We would be of a single mind, a single heart. Compassion would underlie every human interaction. Miracles would abound. **As Ruler of the World, you would be King of Kings, the Host of Hosts, radiantly humble and absolutely forgiving. Your message: universal love for all beings, and surrender to the divine mystery of life.**

Pluto/9th

conceptual frameworks

Your higher mind undergoes periodic purges. At certain points in life, you discover a new philosophy, and it hits with unbelievable conviction. All previous ethical understanding is swept away, obliterated by the new clarity. Your entire approach to living changes overnight as the new allegiance galvanizes your mind. Then you stabilize until the next mental housecleaning. Each plateau of mind has immense power. It can be a surgical scalpel, cutting to the essence of life, or it can be a weapon, bludgeoning others into submission. The **challenge** is to choose the former and avoid the latter.

cultural perspective

Where cultural diversity is concerned, you're either open or closed. You can be incredibly presumptuous in believing that your particular experience of the world is natural for everyone. In that state, you can't see any further than your own nose. During these periods, travel is irrelevant; your personality remains unaltered. At other times, your subconscious mind is sufficiently "cooked" to release its contents into awareness. Then travel can have a profound effect as you open. You become insatiably curious about alternate ways of living, and your pursuit of change through cultural relativity becomes a whirlwind of insights.

higher education

Education is used as a tool to support intense emotional beliefs. You look for principles to justify your passions. Whatever you're currently studying becomes the whole of your understanding, as if nothing you ever knew before had any relevance. Although it's natural that your quest for understanding will necessitate abandonment of some old ways of thinking, be very careful about what you destroy. The **challenge** is to promote enlarged awareness, not just to trade one inflexible orientation for another equally fanatical philosophy.

the search for truth

Revelation is profound for you, since, unlike some people, you change your life to fit what you understand as true. But truth is not simple; it hides between the lines. So be careful. Lies often masquerade as truth, like wolves in sheep's clothing. Be honest, but do not bludgeon people with your truth—they may hit back with truth of their own. Let others find their own paths. Relativity is what you must develop, the ability to integrate new truth into your life without completely forgetting everything you've unearthed in the past. Remember that all great truths can and do coexist, and don't use the truth destructively. It may come back to haunt you later. **Truth is powerful and dangerous, awesome and ultimate.**

ideal society

You would certainly change society, giving it more power, until it surged with volcanic intensity, pregnant with possibility. Wherever outmoded social structures inhibited growth, they would be destroyed. Emotional power would rule—pure, pulsing, primal energy. For others, it might end up being heaven or hell, Utopia or 1984. **As Ruler of the World, you would be an absolute authority. Your word would be law, but everyone would agree with you anyway, so there would be no need for dissent.**

Planets
in
the
10th House

10th House

collective
responsibility

the experience of responsibility that extends beyond the self; universal dharma

The 10th house is the section of individual space directly overhead—straight up. If everyone on the Earth pointed straight up at the same time, our direction would be outward, into the vast universe around us. Thus, the 10th represents our position within the framework of a larger world, the macrocosm, and our relation to it.

This is the Sun's position at noon, when there are no shadows. It symbolizes perfect objectivity, maximum clarity. The 10th is the experience of *dharma,* the Buddhist concept of right action—willingness to consider the implications of personal choice in light of the greater good. It is not an area of sacrifice, but rather of getting the most spiritual mileage out of personal choices, so the "goodness" produced goes beyond personal boundaries, into the realm of full, collective sharing. Each of us has a station on the "assembly line" of the cosmic factory; fulfillment of our individual responsibilities enhances the universe's ultimate product—consciousness.

The condition of the 10th indicates the importance of participation in the larger world beyond the self, and it shows qualities of special relevance to full spiritual maturity.

professional
ambition

developing and maintaining an adult niche in the world; career, social status

"What am I going to do when I grow up?" is a relevant question in every human life at any age, whether nine or ninety. It is always an evolving inquiry, one never answered absolutely. Some people act as if they have the final answer, but life has a way of surprising us just when we think everything is set. So the quest to discover our "true" vocation continues as we grow through successes and failures.

The 10th reveals our public identity, as opposed to the private identity indicated by the opposite 4th house. It can be thought of as "social security," one's niche in society, and it correlates with the ambition for success, the drive for cultural excellence, and the push toward recognition. The payoff here is not monetary—that's a function of the 2nd and 8th houses. Instead, the rewards are the satisfaction of achievement, permission to wield power in the culture, and respect from one's peers.

The condition of the 10th house reveals the characteristic qualities that fuel ambition, as well as any predicaments woven into the professional drive for success.

missions
and messages

that which God offers to all of humanity through a specific individual

There are many possible "scripts" for interpreting the structure of life. One scenario, relevant to the 10th house, revolves around the assumption that each spirit selects a human life according to its particular evolutionary needs, in cooperation with the requirements of the Earth. We choose our parents, they don't choose us. We design these lives, maximizing the opportunities to learn, create, or share certain experiences.

In this poetic vision, our lives are not borrowed, stolen, or foisted on us through some monstrous accident of random coincidence. We own these lives, and we pay for them. There are many levels of payment; that of the 10th house involves agreeing to "bring in" something God wishes to make available to humanity. Unlike individual intentions, which succeed or fail according to free will, our cosmic "mission" is predestined.

This is the most fateful part of our lives. Whatever God wishes will come through us, whether or not we integrate it into our personal lives. Ideally, it helps us achieve individual fulfillment. But even in those sad cases where fulfillment for the personality falls by the wayside, aborted in failure, or degenerated through suffering, God's message still comes through, loud and clear.

The condition of the 10th house shows the mission we accepted, the message we agreed to convey to the world.

"outer-link" parent

the parental figure associated with structure, most often the father

The 4th house symbolized the nurturing or "inner-link" parent, most often the mother, whose imprint helps form personal identity and inner feeling. The 10th house symbolizes the structuring or "outer-link" parent, usually the father, whose imprint is more powerful in defining for the infant the nature of the world beyond the self.

Typically, mothers are experienced by their children as magical, soft, and protective. But fathers are experienced as mysterious, hard, and detached. They vanish into the world; they are somehow one with it rather than one with the child, and this creates both curiosity (what does my father know that I don't?) and anxiety (since father is alien and separate, how can I be safe with him?). So we seek to love, cherish, and hold our mothers, but we attempt to seduce, decipher, and discover our fathers. It is a flirtation with danger, with external power. In striving to understand our fathers, we create a sensitivity in ourselves to external authority, discipline, and the ways of the world.

The condition of the 10th shows the importance of the outer-link parent in our development, no matter who portrays the role—the father, the mother, or other adults outside the home.

authority

the experience of wielding collective power; reaction to external authorities

Authority is persuasive force, the power to command. It can operate on every level of expression—physical, emotional, mental, and spiritual. It may be bluntly dominant, calmly efficient, or reverently inspirational. Our experience of authority begins in infancy with total dependence on the biological parents, but our relationship with such compelling power continues throughout life. Initially, we're on the receiving end only, disciplined or limited by external figures. But we quickly develop a style of personal authority to be used on others in any interaction requiring leadership or control.

The condition of the 10th house reveals our adult relation to authority, both in reaction to that coming from others outside ourselves, and in our own natural ways of radiating strength and certainty into the world.

Sun/10th

collective responsibility

Your life-energy comes from the awareness of collective culture, life in the visible world. There's "guru consciousness" operating here. It may be profound and powerful, or subtle and almost unfelt, but others recognize the potent divinity that flows through you. Your task is to make expression of that energy as complete and correct as you can, for you are on the Earth for a purpose larger than personal fulfillment. Every time you're responsible, every time you succeed in right action, you absorb life-energy. In order to live, you must address your place in the world. The **challenge** is to carve out a niche where you make as significant a contribution as your potential allows.

professional ambition

Depending on other factors in the chart, you may be conservative, a three-piece suit-and-tie person, formal and cautious, or you might be quite the opposite, someone who rises out of the crowd to assert his own opinion. In any event, you're sensitive to the issue of cultural power, and are drawn to acquire as much as you can, whether you earn it, inherit it, borrow it, or steal it. Your life-machinery gets basic energy from career considerations, and whenever you need to energize yourself, juicing your profession is a natural way to do it. The Sun is too broad to indicate specific career choices. It does showsthat whatever you do for a living must have core importance in your life, that you must do it with great dignity, and that you want impact on the world. Your **challenge** is to achieve broad social respect. Remember—be authoritative, not authoritarian.

missions and messages

Your personal purpose and your mission are the same, although you may not experience them as the same. There is often conflict between living for yourself, and consecration to a larger purpose. You are certainly self-involved, and you may have at least a slight God complex. It's not that you see yourself as more important than others, but you are very egocentric in expression of your message. You are the message. In observing your life, we're reminded how important it is to maintain our dignity, and we remember the relevance of personal integrity. The Sun's sign and aspects reveal the tone of what's coming through you, so look to those factors to fine-tune your message.

"outer-link" parent

In either obvious or subtle ways, your father embodied strength, and you've assimilated many of his attitudes and traits. His importance in your life cannot be underestimated. If he was clearly present during your childhood, then his imprint is profound and enduring. The similarities between you grow as you age. If he was physically or psychologically absent, you'll flounder until a surrogate authority figure can be found, someone who takes the missing father's role, or until you take it for yourself.

authority

Authority may be your great strength or your Achille's heel. It all depends on your maturity, on how well you've reconciled the paradoxes surrounding pride. If your inner growth has gone well, you may be a model of responsible power. On the other hand, you could be ambivalent in your behavior, opposing any external authority wielded over you by others while commanding total authority in your own dealings with others. This **pitfall** is the "pot calling the kettle black," and results in others eventually opposing or undermining your power. The **challenge** is to understand the gentle strength of true fathering, to develop and release the authority that resides within you, in a way that is honorable, respectful to others and yourself.

Moon/10th

collective responsibility

Maternal energy is quite powerful in your personality, although you may not always recognize it in operation, since it's so natural for you to express. Taking care of others is a deep imprint, a responsibility you took on early, usually in reaction to your mother. In moderation, she may have been a constant presence, an unflagging model of dignified, receptive strength. In the extremes, she might have been strong and overly protective, or she could have been missing, weak, or inadequate to your needs. In any condition, you learned that it was your job to take care of others. Your protection is not limited to those in your personal life; it goes much further. It is a need to be responsive to the troubles of the world. You draw out the child within everyone, and this can be heartwarming or tragic, depending on how you do it. Your **challenge** is to be responsive and nurturing in ways that foster strength, and to do so spontaneously, without conscious effort.

professional ambition

Your orientation toward social status will typically be somewhat conservative, since safety is very important here. And you may be subject to worry or greater than ordinary day-to-day concern with keeping your career world in smooth running order, since regular maintenance is at the heart of this placement. As for the actual profession you might choose, it's more natural to provide a service than to produce a product, since you're more oriented toward people than toward things. You could succeed in any profession where protection, survival, or the fulfillment of personal needs are involved. Ambition is linked with personal security.

missions and messages

The combination of vulnerable softness under a strong, defensive surface is so radiant in your personality that others receive a universal message. Your personal emotions are sometimes downplayed to near invisibility, but your continual concern for the care of others' feelings is very visible. Our awareness of the basic human need for protection is stimulated when we're in your presence. We learn about mothering from you, either how to do it well, or how not to do it. In either case, your mission is to show us the meaning, process, and effects of maternal influence, the power of early imprints, and the importance of security, for better or worse.

"outer-link" parent

The classical parental roles may have been reversed in your family. It's likely that your mother played the dominant role in your external conditioning, in the imprint of beliefs about the outside world. It's possible that your father was a feminine figure, more of a warm nurturer than a firm structuring force, but this is somewhat less likely than the first condition. The reversal itself does not present any particular problems, although it does tend to unify what are ordinarily differentiated roles of fathering and mothering.

authority

You believe that the correct role of authority is to protect, to make secure, and to provide strength in emergencies. Your own need to be in an authoritative position is strong but not totally conscious. In fact, you may experience conflict when you have to make a conscious choice about authority or power, since you're more comfortable just responding instinctively to what you see as others' needs.

Mercury/10th

collective responsibility

You may or may not be responsible, since you're changeable in your nervous orientations, but you're certainly aware of the issue. In every situation, no matter how mundane, you see the spiritual handwriting on the wall, the signature of larger purpose, and you try to figure out all the factors that must be taken into consideration. The **pitfall,** of course, involves spending so much time and energy in any situation calculating the greatest good for the greatest number, that you inadvertently forget to act. Remember, you only need so much information before you take a stand. Your **challenge** is to talk to everyone about responsibility. You needn't push people, but you have a flair for delegation, for discerning each person's perfect niche in any situation. In many ways, it's your role to help others define what their responsibilities are.

professional ambition

You think about your career constantly. However, you're often sufficiently caught up in the short-run factors involved in career that you may overlook longer-term concerns. So in spite of your strategizing, your career moves of its own accord. You may have more than one career simultaneously, or a single career that requires knowledge from many diverse areas. In any case, the basis of your social status is mental. Any profession requires mastery of a specialized language, but your style tends to focus on the importance of information management. In a basic way, communication is your product, and translation is your service.

missions and messages

Your thought processes are especially visible to others. When you speak or write, we are reminded of the importance of communication in human life. Your perceptions are often not your own, but come from a universal well, and what you see, we all need to understand. So give voice to whatever wishes to come through your mind—give it the best voice you know how. Learn to express your thoughts, and your message will have positive effect on your life.

"outer-link" parent

It's not that you necessarily think just like your father, but there is definitely a connection between your mind and his. What he did was stimulating to the development of your own thought-patterns. Certainly this occurs with everyone, but in your case the effect is significantly more sweeping. Your father was on the go much of the time, moving from the home out into the world and back again. Where did he go? What did he do when he was gone? What he thought about was fascinating to you, like a foreign language of strange and compelling syntax.

authority

Your own authority emerges most effectively through the patterns of your thinking, writing, and speaking. When you use your mind, people pay attention. It's not that you're always right, nor that you necessarily have a unique perspective, but more that the resonance of your thoughts and the way you express them has a commanding quality. The **challenge** is to use your mind authoritatively. Our nervous systems are sensitive to the peculiar rhythms of semantics, and it is not lost on you that words carry their own magnetic impact on people. However, in your case, the power does not finally reside in the words themselves; rather, it is you who invests them with their impact.

Venus/10th

collective responsibility

Responsibility is a source of true enjoyment. The **pitfall** is that you so enjoy both the rigors and the rewards of collective responsibility that too much of your urge for pleasure is focused into work. Do not become a workaholic. On the other hand, guard against the tendency to expect your work to be more pleasant than the work required of others. If there is to be elite status, especially at the spiritual level, you must earn it with a display of grace under pressure. The **challenge** is to foster the art of love and enjoyment, to show that growing up and taking part in the collective life around us can be, and indeed should be, a beautiful experience.

professional ambition

Your most prized possession is your social image, and you love nothing better than polishing it. You're happiest when you're working, or in the public sector, dealing with the world-at-large. You know how to present yourself, how to show your best side to the camera. One might presume that linking Venus to the 10th house might correspond to a lack of ambition, but this is not usually the case. There is, however, greater flow in ambition, more pleasure than effort. You work better in tandem than alone, and your business partnerships often have a basis in affection. You're drawn to careers involving art, beauty, aesthetics, or luxury. You can be your own product, an actor or model, or you could market products designed for entertainment or leisure. Whatever profession you choose, it should bring you pleasure in doing it, or you should try something else. At the most symbolic level, your career is love, and you need to love your career.

missions and messages

It is your female qualities that stand out in our eyes. Through your living, we remember the importance of active receptivity and the power of personal magnetism. You have a radiance that puts us in touch with our sensitivity to beauty, the flow of graceful living. More than anything else, we learn about personal love from the example of your own life. You may or may not be fulfilled in love; you may or may not be beautiful, but either way, we are sparked to consider these qualities through your efforts at expressing them.

"outer-link" parent

Placement of a feminine symbol in this traditionally masculine area can indicate that the father's impact was suspended, or his power superceded by the mother, although that possibility is greater with the Moon or Neptune here than with Venus. But strong or weak, present or absent, your affection for your father is enduring. You learned to link love and work through him. His appreciation of the world was a source of inspiration for you, and you adopted that orientation for yourself. There was a reliance on keeping up appearances, putting on a face to show the world. Even if there was conflict, you imprinted on that same sense of hospitality, the ambition to be a good host or hostess.

authority

Your regard for authority is based not as much on pure respect for structure as it is on love of prestige and those who have it. Even if you're chafing at the bit of oppression, something in you still loves the contact with power. Your own authority is based on affection rather than power; on harmony rather than impact. You do not command, but instead draw people's attention magnetically. A sense of social tact and gentle order are keystones of your leadership. You understand better than most people the principle that you can catch more flies with honey than with vinegar, and it's appropriate that you cultivate these talents into a high art form.

Mars/10th

collective responsibility

You have a strong desire to push into the realm of collective responsibility. The focus is sharp, the energy is hot, and there may be many battles to gain access to cultural power. Although you want to prove your mettle, you encounter resistance. On occasion, you may be accused of irresponsibility, or more likely, you'll simply be blocked from full participation. Your approach is so urgent, that you sometimes provoke opposition. It can be a difficult paradox for you. How can you be adult and youthful at the same time? The **challenge** is to show responsibility by a consistent refusal to knuckle under. Keep moving ahead until you enter the corridors of power, but when you have, replace aggression with patience. There is a time for conquest, and a time for keeping the peace.

professional ambition

You work hard for success, confronting any obstacles that stand in the way of your ambitions. But in the course of your career life you may take occasional actions that have a detrimental effect on your public image. However, the threat of a little tarnish won't stop you from going after what you want. "Cross that line" or "knock that chip off my shoulder" are attitudes you may feel at times. Your profession must provide you with active, physical outlets for your surging energies. Don't get stuck behind a desk. You don't have to be a longshoreman, of course, but your career should allow you to move, to go from place to place and interaction to interaction in relatively quick bursts. The **challenge** is to succeed, and then to be able to relax enough to enjoy your success.

missions and messages

In your radiance, there is an assertiveness that comes across impressively. We see the archetype of the Warrior. We feel your desire, your frustrations and conflicts—the male side of your nature, and we reconsider the importance of these primal urgings. It's not that we necessarily want what you want, nor that we adopt your methods of expression. From this symbolism alone, there is no certainty that you will fulfill your desires, for Mars does not signify fulfillment. It symbolizes the basic surge of adolescence, the heightened and often brash energies of proving the self's mettle in battle with the world. This is what we learn about from you.

"outer-link" parent

Your father was very male in attitude and behavior, almost raw in his relationship with you. There was competition, an unspoken challenge, a fight for dominance. Both of you could not win, and you were at considerable disadvantage since you were small. Thus, he intimidated you considerably. Even so, you learned to fight intensely, as if your survival were at stake. The **pitfall** is long-held anger at your father, and in extreme cases hatred. But this need not be the case. Your relationship may have resulted simply in a quality of sharp and heightened energy between the two of you. Realizing full use of this energy is the **challenge.**

authority

Your authority is likely to be marked by a spontaneous, natural grasp of power, an instinctive sense of command. There may be a sense of military crispness in your attitudes, so that you take orders easily from those you recognize as clearly superior, and give orders to your subordinates with poised alacrity. But if your experience has been frustrated, if other factors in your life create complications, then you could become aggressive in the quest for power, provoking conflicts with those around you. Remember that people are not the enemy.

Jupiter/10th

collective responsibility

Though you are likely to be offered cultural power in the course of your life, amassing it is not so important. What is important is fulfillment of your responsibilities with a clear sense of conscience for the greatest good. Doing what seems most correct is not only morally right, it's also the most practical strategy for you, for it opens doors to fulfillment. However, guard against the **pitfall** of self-righteousness. Humility is the best antidote. The **challenge** is to take advantage of every opportunity to do the right thing. No one needs to tell you what that is, for every situation has subtle keys. For you, acting responsibly costs less and brings more rewards than any other course of behavior.

professional ambition

Unless other factors override this placement, your profession will be group-oriented more than one-to-one. It may require travel, but even if you're not constantly on the go, the people you deal with are spread over a wide area, both physically and philosophically. Your natural task is to organize and operate a network connecting individuals to a central whole, and set up procedures to clarify how the structure works. Putting your best foot forward is natural, as is presenting yourself in the best light possible. These factors are more significant than sustained effort. Work hard to make it look easy.

missions and messages

You seem to us very fortunate in some basic way. Whether or not you are well-endowed in personality, we see you as having good luck at all the right moments. We remember the importance of social contacts, the results of creating a broad network, and the meaning of humanitarian or group concern. Finally, we learn about universal bounty from you. If you can have even what you don't apparently deserve, then perhaps life is on our side after all.

"outer-link" parent

Your father was concerned with social evolution, with the meaning of culture, and with principles more than situations. He also impressed you as a man who loved being in social situations, one who had considerable ease and command when it came to dealing with relative strangers. With either quality, your father was probably not as close to the family as you felt he should have been. This is not to say he was uncaring, but you may have felt him to be more interested in the outside world than in his own flesh and blood, more concerned with teaching lessons of morality than with sharing the simple act of loving. On the other hand, you learned a great deal from him about how to live in the world, how move in the social realm. As an adult, your philosophy of life gradually comes to reflect his brand of optimistic conservatism.

authority

You cultivate relationships with authoritative people, for they aid you in personal growth and professional prestige. In fact, you could benefit by apprenticeship with someone in a high position. When in positions of power, your own style of authority has the natural grace of royalty, as if you were born to lead. And presuming that you don't sink into the **pitfall** of pomposity, you do indeed make a terrific boss. You command with an easygoing touch, relying on wisdom, dignity, and fairness to get your points across. The **challenge** is to inspire faith in your leadership.

Saturn/10th

collective responsibility

You are learning the significance of spiritual development, not the fantasy of enlightenment, not the rush of power, but full responsibility for creation. The higher we go up the mountain of spirit, the steeper the climb becomes. The air is thinner, the effort tougher. But the view is also more breathtaking, the atmosphere more rarified and refined. This is where the eagles live. Learn to rest when necessary, but know that each well-disciplined effort carries you closer to the summit. Don't rush, don't run. Don't ask for more than you can handle, but know that you're strong enough to bear whatever life may require of you, and expect fulfillment.

professional ambition

Ambition is immensely powerful, even if you're shackled early in life by doubt or fear of failure. And you may suffer more than one failure. But rest assured that perseverance pays off. No one succeeds without failures. Professionally, you're conventional, using well-traveled roads to success. The risks you take for advancement might sometimes be ethically questionable; it's safer in the long run if you move up the ladder by solid, enduring effort. Quick success is unnerving, even though you think you want it all now. So take the slow path, and learn to discipline your discipline. This is to say, teach yourself moderation in your work. As the old saying goes, "what profit a man to gain the world and lose his soul?" Your dogged determination can take you to the top, but remember that success, like beauty, is finally in the eye of the beholder.

missions and messages

We learn about the tough lessons of life from you. We see living proof that it is indeed a struggle, survival of the fittest. You teach us about the necessity for patient, steady effort even in the face of long-delayed gratification. You show us how important it is to mature rather than succumb to frustration or negative thinking. We see in you the basic archetype of ambition against any and all odds, the importance of fulfilling our responsibilities, and the inescapable fact that we must carry our burdens, even when they are undeserved. In you, we see the relation of fate and free will, and realize that all our dreaming will finally be tested in the crucible of real life.

"outer-link" parent

Your father could have been a very powerful and formal figure, stern and disciplined. Or he may have felt cold and unwilling to love. In the first instance, your reaction would have been respect and awe; in the second, fear and feelings of rejection. At either extreme, and anywhere in the middle, you become sensitized to patriarchal authority, experiencing a blend of respect and fear. Your father is an enduring model for all that comes later in your life around authority.

authority

As an adult, you're likely to obey authority without question, although there may be an inner backlash of submerged resentment. You see the world as an hierarchy of power, believing that each individual must prove his worth by taking orders from those above, and conveying them to those below. Obedience is expected, and discipline required. While you're willing to be a team player, your ultimate ambition is to be in the position of absolute authority. When you achieve that stature, as you almost certainly will, remember that abuse of power is a dangerous **pitfall.** The **challenge** is to wield power with the dignity your role demands, and to treat others with the respect they deserve.

Uranus/10th

collective responsibility

Your spiritual task is to stand apart, to be different from the crowd. Traditional security is not only unlikely, it is inadvisable. Individuality may on occasion feel like an onerous liability, but even with your own doubts, you willfully maintain that sense of distinction. You want to stand out in a crowd. You're supposed to be independent. This is the mark of true maturity for you, to travel a singular road, marching to the beat of a different drummer. It doesn't mean you're not permitted the ordinary pleasures of sharing. Intimacy, union, relationship—all these are available to you. But you must somehow define yourself apart from the mass. The **challenge** is to transcend the ordinary in human affairs, to embrace independence without succumbing to fear of ostracism.

professional ambition

Career is where your individuality can shine. Others may think you slightly strange, but never mind (and you won't). Just continue to follow your own course in ambition. You need to be independent, and this could mean literally working alone, or it could infer that you contract your services. Employment is not for you—you'd be a square peg in a round hole. Even if a safe career beckons, you're better off pursuing your own path, for status in and of itself is almost meaningless. Success can come suddenly, like being discovered after a long period of invisibility. Any similar but negative shifts are an indication that your life was hardening, so welcome even these, for they allow you to make important course corrections. Stay open, be aware, and roll with the punches.

missions and messages

Something about you seems strange and foreign to us, as if you were from another planet, another solar system, as if you were an alien in human trappings. This is not to say that we experience you as threatening, as a monster from outer space. But through your personality, we remember that we are all aliens in one way or another. We realize the importance of independence, of not following well-worn paths of conformity, and we see the results of willfully standing apart from others, for better or worse. We're reminded that every individual has the potential for brilliance, for connecting with a pure idea. Finally, we see how life can change completely, suddenly, without warning. We learn how security is an illusion, how we must not cling to what is seemingly safe, but must instead experiment with our lives.

"outer-link" parent

Your father was a unique person, different from other people, or different in how he related to you. He may have been erratic, or highly self-willed, but at any rate, he carved out his own unique life. It's possible that you were separated from him, either literally or figuratively. In some way, you learned through your relationship with him the necessity of standing on your own two feet, depending on no one, and that imprint formed one of the basic attitudes that will follow you into adulthood.

authority

You want to chart your own course, to discover a new world. You are probably not especially receptive to the idea of accepting responsibility for others or for the world, preferring instead to remain apart, an island in the middle of an ocean. But you have the ability to lead when you feel it necessary. The power you wield culturally comes from the uniqueness of your personality, and the success of your authority depends upon your flexibility. Your **challenge** is to be a responsible revolutionary, and that is quite a paradox indeed.

Neptune/10th

Your responsibilities are not concrete, but they bleed into every area of your life. There is no focus; your *dharma* is shown to you in every action, every situation, every life circumstance. Compassion is total and unqualified; there are not some settings where it's appropriate and others where it's not. However, this does not mean always providing comfort. Yours are not necessarily shoulders that should be offered to cry on. Try simple acceptance while letting others continue their struggle. True support is not a crutch, but an encouragement. True understanding is not an escape from responsibility, but an aid to its fulfillment. You don't need to have the answers; just have faith in the goodness of the universe. Your responsibility is to live in the flow of that faith.

*professional
ambition*

There is a gentle quality to your ambition; you are not likely to be competitive in your professional drive. You may be drawn to spiritual service, either traditionally, as in ministry, or through psychic or occult pursuits. Medicine and healing are fascinations, though you're not inclined to seek the high end of cultural stature, preferring the Mother Teresa approach. Anything involving images is good, such as graphic design. Performance art is attractive, as are music or acting. Even something as mundane as chemical engineering or pharmaceuticals is possible, since you're drawn to alchemy. This placement does incline toward things being not quite what they seem, which can result in unintentional confusion, deception, or even public scandal. But don't focus on those dubious possibilities; they're only the shadow aspect. Rather, keep your ambition focused on ideals, and learn to blend the pragmatic with the divine.

*missions
and messages*

In your living, we see that reality is not in contradiction with fantasy, for you exist in both worlds simultaneously. We discover that it is possible to experience a breadth of feeling beyond self-interest. We see that the circumstances of our lives do not bind us, for we rediscover the wonders of imagination, the power of dreams and ideals. Finally, we're reminded to develop compassion for our fellow human beings. We may learn this from your own gentle strength, the consistency of your kindness, or we may get in touch with it by seeing your delicacy crushed as your dreams are revealed to be illusions. Either way, you put us in touch with the mystery of intangible realms of existence.

*"outer-link"
parent*

Your father may have been drawn more to the spiritual than the material, a person of gentleness and compassion. If this is the case, then his idealism or artistry have left an indelible imprint on your life. However, he may have been a dreamer or an escapist who couldn't cope with the responsibilities of real life or real parenting. You may have grown up where alcoholism or other chemical abuse was present, in a family where someone was martyred. In either case, you may be somewhat confused by the lack of solidness in your early conditioning, as if there were no sure footing in the world for you.

authority

Your adult approach to authority could be either reverent or mistrustful, or both. And your own authority is based on the subtle power of compassion and gentleness. Work diligently to be trustworthy and dependable in the execution of your responsibilities. You may win others' respect, but you're more likely to win their love. Authority must come from a higher level than the ego, so keep your nose clean and you'll do fine.

Pluto/10th

collective responsibility

Collective responsibility is like the water around the fish, everpresent but never seen. Much of your life may be spent searching for ways to make it visible, to find a successful form for your longing to grow up. On occasion, you'll find yourself in a situation where all your power is called forth. When this happens, let it come. Allow ego concerns to be washed away in a flood of communion with larger issues. You are the troops held in reserve, to be used only when the battle reaches its peak and the outcome is in doubt. Then you're called forth to save the day, hurled into the fray, a cavalry charge, a secret weapon, an ace up the sleeve. Your **challenge** is to be prepared.

professional ambition

Ambition is powerful but complex. You may wander about for long periods, aware of intense ambition but unable to find suitable expression. Or you may be thrust into a position of authority in a profession for which you did not consciously prepare. Also, you may abruptly change professions at critical points in your life. It can appear that you've burned your bridges behind you. You'll know, however, that you are still being faithful to an inner calling, that you simply had to destroy old forms in search of better avenues of expression. Negatively, you can be ruthless, secretive, and underhanded in ambition, and you must guard against the tendency to become despotic. These tactics may bring you great power, but they sow the seeds for destruction of your reputation, something you could overlook. Your **challenge** is to use power rather than abuse it.

missions and messages

Your life shows us that there are deeper energies coursing through our personalities, deeper than we know or can control. We learn from your life about being driven by an emotion, obsessed by an image, compelled by an idea. We see the power latent in every human being, and we remember the importance of releasing that power in ways that transform us for the better. We see the presence of profound goodness and horrible evil, and we learn about the necessity of making conscious choices to consecrate our lives to the good in ourselves, even as we must acknowledge and occasionally succumb to the dark. Finally, we see in you evidence that life can change totally. We remember that we can rid ourselves of what is no longer vital to begin again, fresh and new.

"outer-link" parent

Your father may have been a powerful force in the community. He may have ruled with an iron hand, brooking no challenges to his authority. Or he might have been distant, driven by work and professional responsibilities. In any event, you didn't know him well, and possibly not at all. He could have changed in a fundamental way, becoming a different person as you moved through your childhood. Your imprints with him are a mystery to you. There are huge chunks of your background still buried. You need to unearth your father once you reach adulthood, to excavate your memories, and even late in life you may still have major realizations about the man and his effect on you.

authority

You're very sensitive to the issue of control over others, and their control over you. Your personal authority has great emotional depth, and others are polarized: either drawn hypnotically to obey completely or likely to resist with their full power. Either way, your effect is potent. Understand that this power is real, even if it's invisible to you. Unconscious power can indeed corrupt even the best of us, so work diligently to purify your motives, open your emotions, and monitor your behavior.

Planets
in
the
11th House

11th House

group
participation

involvement with groups, organizations, or cultural institutions

The 11th is the area of participation in the collective life of society, not as an executive or leader (10th), but rather as an equal among peers. It is the level of group reality—any group where there is a common purpose or goal, whether it's the Tuesday night bridge club or the Republican party—and it emphasizes the experience of working in tandem with others to further that goal.

The condition of the 11th reveals the relative importance of group involvement, and the characteristic qualities one brings to group endeavors.

appropriate
behavior

sensitivity toward "correct" behavior, as defined by group standards

The 11th is the area of experience where we are most sensitive to social codes of conduct, group-oriented norms of behavior. This level involves the concern for appearances which was once of overwhelming importance in culture and is even today a factor with which each of us must reckon. For some people, this concern is so powerful that it conditions everything they do. But even for those increasing numbers of people who may not always choose to comply with their perception of what others regard as appropriate, it is still important to know what others consider correct or acceptable.

The condition of the 11th house reveals the significance in an individual's life of perceptions surrounding social expectations in the complex rituals of public interaction, and in addition it shows the characteristic approach each of us takes toward integrating such perceptions into a formalized social persona.

frindship,
social circle

*the experience of identification with like-minded friends;
the sense of belonging to a coherent social community*

The 5th house is the area of emotionally-involved courtships full of passion and risk. The 11th is opposite, an area of cooler, more detached relations. This is the realm of "true friendship," where there is sympathy, understanding, and good feelings, but less intimate involvement, less ego, and less chance of codependency. A number of these relationships of warm feeling and goodwill constitute a social circle, the level of life that exists beyond one's inward struggles, beyond the security and entanglements of family or marriage. The social circle is a network of individuals unrelated except as they are connected by the self, rather like a matrix.

The condition of the 11th house reveals the type of social circle a person creates or attracts: large or small; warm or cool; spontaneous and changing, or slowly building and persistent. It also shows the basic attitudes that define friendship, the qualities one offers as a friend, and the characteristics of others that are attractive when choosing friends with whom to form a coherent social circle, a sense of community.

shared creativity

group orientation in the creative process; allegiance to a collective goal

Creativity can be personal, with an emphasis on the individual ego (5th), or it can be more literally a shared experience. Almost no artistic endeavor is truly a one-person show. A play or movie may have its star, but there are many others who contribute creatively: director, camera operator, costumer, set designer, electrician, gaffer, key grip, best boy, etc. Each of these individuals is the "star" in his or her own area of creative performance (5th), but there's also a collective level where everyone is equal (11th), for the production depends upon each artist doing his particular performance well.

Television is one example of such shared artistic creativity, where the technicians, producers, actors, writers, etc., must work together, in tandem and in harmony, for the finished product to succeed as art. Success here is defined by cooperation, originality, and meaningful group productivity.

Some art forms are thought of as singular: the author whose only partner is a typewriter, the painter alone with a canvas, the sculptor with a block of granite. But even these solitary artists need comrades to complete the creative process: the writer has an editor and a publisher; the painter and sculptor have their gallery producers.

The planetary condition of the 11th house shows the relative importance of shared creativity, and it reveals the characteristic talents an individual can offer as a personal contribution to the group.

receiving love

being loved: the qualities of others' behavior understood as loving

Giving and receiving love are vastly different experiences. We give love according to the condition of the 5th house; we receive it according to the condition of the 11th.

We are all stimulated by our environments, but we're selective in the types of stimuli we regard as "friendly" or "positive." Some we like, some we don't. It's the same with love. Only certain types of emotional attitudes or concrete behaviors are interpreted as "loving." The 11th reveals what they are for each individual. For one person, feeling loved results from perceiving others as protective. For another, it may depend on the perception that others offer freedom. Some people love being dealt with directly, almost bluntly, while others require the utmost subtlety to feel they're in the presence of one who loves them. One man's ceiling is another man's floor.

We even unconsciously interpret harmful behaviors or attitudes as loving. For instance, the condition of the 11th could imply that being in the presence of authoritative behaviors and a structured environment lead to the feeling of being loved, but due to flawed imprints or blocked development, the person has learned to interpret abusive discipline or imprisonment as if they were loving, since these are shadow aspects of authority and structure. It's a catch-22 paradox; being loved is equated with suffering at the hands of another, and the more one seeks out love, the more suffering results.

The condition of the 11th house shows the relative importance for any individual of the experience of feeling loved by another, and it shows the characteristic qualities of attitude and behavior that tend to be interpreted (or misinterpreted) as "loving."

Sun/11th

group participation

Groups are where you shine. Exercise diplomacy, however, for you may throw your weight around a little too freely, assuming a dominant or superior pose. Be equally careful to avoid identifying so strongly with a group that you create a psychological clique, an in-group/out-group, "us-versus-them" reality. These *pitfalls* may initially offer you more stability, security, and confidence, but in the long run they could sap your energy and threaten your life-purpose. Remember that everyone on the planet is a member of the same group: humanity. Your **challenge** is to ground yourself in social reality, using groups to help define and express the most important themes of your life.

appropriate behavior

You're a very social animal; you don't set your own standards, but instead absorb a sense of appropriate behavior from the milieu of those around you. As your social group changes, your sense of correctness changes with it. As always, the sign and aspects of the Sun can dramatically alter your attitudes, but in any condition, you will be aware of others' expectations. What is constant is the emphasis on dignity. The major **pitfalls** involve inordinate pride surrounding your "perfect" behavior, as well as haughtiness in reaction to criticism. The **challenge** is to find a way to merge your inner self with the best outer behavior, so that each supports the other.

friendship, social circle

You absorb life-energy through your friendships. The support of true friends is a crucial requirement in your life-purpose. No friends, no life. Your social circle is large and diverse. One or two friends are not enough to feed your demand for contact. Equally, if all your friends are of the same general mind or orientation, you limit the scope of fulfillment. It may seem that you're building a wonderful world, but you'll later discover that you've limited the potential of your own Godliness. Loyalty is essential, but there you could conflicts around dignity and power. Don't let pride get in the way. Be the best friend you know how, then watch as others are drawn to you.

shared creativity

Your power increases when you work creatively within a group setting, and this energy is then available not only for you, but for the others in your group. And though this process is, by definition, shared, you want to lead, to call the shots. Temper your ambitions with humility. **Your creative role is to provide basic fuel for the group's expression, to give it both power and purpose.**

receiving love

Being loved means being treated with respect. It also means having another's attention; if people say they love you, but then ignore you, you don't feel loved, even if you're deeply in their hearts. Expressions of care must be powerful and total, to penetrate your own power center. Curiously, to feel loved, you must love. You cannot conceive of being loved by anyone for whom you don't feel love. Equally paradoxical is the fact that you are not receptive to courtship unless you've already chosen the courtier as your beloved. Yes, you are susceptible to flattery (sometimes too much...), but unless you actively love the individual already, compliments are interpreted as simple friendship. Those who love you need to know that their love is safe with you. The **challenge** is first to be loving, then to let the love that comes in return fill your center until you glow.

Moon/11th

group participation

Something in your early imprint during childhood left a strong emotional orientation toward the security of groups. You've grown up feeling safety in numbers. It's a herd instinct, a need to belong. The **pitfall** involves loss of individuality. Remember that belonging has a cost. The **challenge** is to allow yourself to gravitate toward purposeful social groups to provide the emotional glue that holds people together.

appropriate behavior

The opinions of others are meaningful for you since you need acceptance. As a result, your first instinctive reaction to group pressure is to conform, to adopt whatever code of behavior seems most correct. As you become more secure in the group, you may alter your behavior toward more original or creative forms, but if you are criticized, you will immediately feel the urge to move back into the fold. The **pitfall** is surrender of your independence, while the **challenge** is fully feel the connection provided by common social rituals.

friendship, social circle

Friendships occur on the basis of chemical attraction more than conscious choice. You don't analyze them or choose your friends based on an intentional set of criteria. Friends satisfy your emotional need for contact. From this placement alone, there's no way to tell whether your friendships are dependable or not, but in either case, you lean on your friends and encourage them to lean on you. Friends must be sensitive to your feelings. Your social circle needs to feel like a second family to you, close-knit, linked under the surface. Changes in closeness to occur due to fluctuations of emotion. Ideally, you have enough friends that you can move between people freely as these changes occur.

shared creativity

You feel nurtured when working in harmony with others, and could easily occupy the niche of den mother in a creative group. You don't provide direction as much as you foster and protect the basic direction the group is moving, especially during the flux and uncertainty of the creative process itself. **Your creative role is to provide support for the group's expression and protection for the its survival.**

receiving love

You have sentimental attitudes about being loved. Romance is the stuff your dreams are made of: candlelight, soft music, a fire in the fireplace. You want tenderness, to be held and made secure. Feeling loved is so important it could be called an emotional hunger, and this can present various **pitfalls.** The best time to go to the grocery store is when you're not hungry, for then you buy only what's on your list. If you're hungry when you go, you might binge. It's much the same with being loved. When you're needy for love is the worst time to "go to the store," since you may end up with the romantic version of junk food. Suitors should come with a label: "Warning—Love is habit-forming and could be hazardous to your health." The **challenge** involves fulfilling your need for love in ways that enhance both integrity and awareness.

Mercury/11th

group participation

You're very curious about what other people think, and even more than that, about what's in the "collective mind" of the group. You're cross-cultural in approach, with an ever-increasing pattern of organizational affiliations. Whether you are a joiner depends upon the placement of other factors (such as the Sun and Venus), but in any case, the breadth of your associations is what's important. The **challenge** is to extend your network until you've been exposed to every kind of cultural group, so that your mind has the broadest possible base of information.

appropriate behavior

You're fascinated by the spectrum of conventions in social interaction. Which fork to use first, how to address a business letter, what clothes to wear to a cocktail party—these small details of social living are endlessly interesting to your mind. Most important of all are the conventions around communication: how to talk to a certain person, what is alright to say and what isn't. You love to interview others, to find out what they're thinking. It doesn't matter so much whether you follow your own or other's rules of correct behavior, but be sure to learn them all. The **pitfall** is gossip, while the **challenge** is to master the politics of information.

friendship, social circle

Friendship is based on intelligence and the willingness to communicate. Your friends need not be the deepest thinkers in the world, but it helps if they have quick and facile minds, and are interested in a wide range of subjects. If they don't enjoy talking, they're not really your friends. You like having numerous people from whom to choose companionship, so your social circle is large and diversified. Touching base with friends is a primary interest; you want to keep up with current events in their lives. Sensitivity is not your long suit socially, so keep an eye on your tendency to gossip without regard for the truth. Based on this placement alone, friendship could be superficial. There is, of course, nothing whatsoever wrong with that leaning, since your **challenge** as a friend is to keep life well-stirred, to expand the mental connections between people. Be active in friendship. Go somewhere, do something together. But most of all, have a good time.

shared creativity

Shared creativity is a mental event. It's not that you're necessarily the brains of the group, but rather that you take off from and expand the thoughts that float around the group head. Your presence encourages the free flow of ideas as well as debate over their relative merits. **Your creative role is to disseminate ideas and provide constructive criticism to help perfect the group's expression.**

receiving love

You want expressions of love in verbal form. Even ordinary conversation, if sufficiently engaging, can be interpreted to contain the stamp of love. You're susceptible to a good line. What's important is a sense of stimulation, the massage of the nervous system. Love can be a delightful game of hide-and-seek. It's quite possible for you to feel loved by one person, but be enamored with the possibility of affection from another. You're an acrobat, able to juggle numerous light romances at once. The **challenge** is to understand that love is expressed through the mind, but that it emanates from the heart.

Venus/11th

group participation

You love the whole experience of socialization, and very little in life is more pleasing to you than group involvement. You fit in easily, naturally, comfortably. Mediation is your natural posture in groups. But accept the inevitability of some conflict, since egos clash in even the smoothest organizations. The **challenge** is to lubricate the gears of social organizations with grace and charm, but without compromising personal values.

appropriate behavior

You enjoy the rituals of social existence, and you look forward to opportunities to demonstrate your sense of class, your flair for high society. You're especially suited to formal gatherings with elaborate rules of order, for the "politics of the court" (whether serious or soap opera) are a source of joy. You're sensitive to what others seem to want you to be, since you want to please, but avoid the **pitfall** of artificiality. The **challenge** is to be both charming and sincere.

friendship, social circle

Friendship is linked with personal affection. There is a greater-than-average likelihood of romances growing out of friendships, or vice versa. You may be drawn to artistic types, and physical beauty is very compelling, as are those devoted to beauty. Appreciation of social ritual is important. There a sweetness to your friendships, a gentle delicacy. You want your friends to be pleased with you all the time, and pleasing to you as well. The **challenge** is to make your social circle a source and an outlet for the love and beauty in your life.

shared creativity

Shared creativity is a high priority and a great satisfaction. Your talent is polishing the ideas and structures other group members provide. Being sensitive to harmony, you operate in a way that smooths over rough edges, soothes ego conflicts, and alerts the group to the necessity of allowing creativity to happen rather than straining to create it. **Your creative role is to provide beautiful forms for the group's expression.**

receiving love

You feel loved when your beauty is recognized, when you're showered with affection or gifts. You may require that you be placed on a pedestal, although you're much too sophisticated to overtly express such egotism. The question is sincerity. You love being charmed, and you're certainly charming in response. Being the beloved is a role you relish. But do your suitors really love you or are they too merely acting the part? Are you in their hearts, or simply in the script? It may not make any difference at all, though this varies according to Venus' sign and aspects. The **challenge** is to experience the archetypes of courtier and beloved in all their glory, but then to go beyond your infatuation with the rites of loving, to feel the flesh-and-blood human beings who can make love more than a dance. Finally, love is a sacrament.

Mars/11th

group participation

You want to be socially accepted, to feel a part of a group. But you also want to lead, to stand at the prow of the social ship and chart its course, and others in your groups may resent or resist this assertive tendency. Work to become a vital representative of your organizations, rather than their sole voice, and you achieve greater fulfillment. Your **challenge** is to use the spontaneity of your desires to rally and propel groups toward more concrete stands, but to do so without engendering needless infighting or pointless argument.

appropriate behavior

Although you have a natural instinct for appropriate behavior, and can act as the essence of social virtue when you want to, your high spirits sometimes get you in trouble. You overstep your bounds and end up dancing with the lampshade on your head. This may be just fine, a real kick, but be aware of the **pitfall:** social embarrassment can be extremely painful to you. Keep your assertiveness in mind; if anyone criticizes you about a certain behavior, you will tend to defend yourself very aggressively, sometimes compounding the problem. And try not to attack others for what you see as inappropriate behavior. It's their business, not yours. The **challenge** is to make your pride an ally rather than an enemy.

friendship, social circle

Your friendships go through conflicts, even passionate ones. You want to cut right to the heart of friendship, so be careful that you don't wound others or yourself in the process. If the chart as a whole reveals a gentler disposition, it may that you pick out friends who provoke disagreements. But keep in mind, whether you're on the giving or the receiving end, it's still your life. You are territorial socially, willing to fight for your friends, either through shared goals, or in defending them from outsiders. When you're close to someone, your loyalty is intense, although this can change as the friendship changes. If you occasionally lose friends, pick yourself up and make new ones.

shared creativity

You see the other group members as players in the competitive game of creation, and you work in reaction to them more than with them. You enjoy the stimulation, the challenge to your ego, but you must keep in mind that others may occasionally react negatively to the personal tone of your thrust. Remember that this is indeed a shared process, and these are your comrades in arms. **Your creative role is to push the group toward new directions and new challenges.**

receiving love

You do so want to be loved. You want to be wanted, and you're willing to extend yourself to make it possible. This is a paradox, since the very nature of the experience demands a receptive posture, and thus the action must be created subtly rather than overtly, magnetically rather than aggressively. If love can be considered a dance, you are a master of leading while seeming to follow. You feel loved when your suitor acts out your desires, when the behaviors are direct, forceful, and ardent. Urgency looks like love to you, as does assertion, and above all, passion. Even anger is sometimes interpreted as a display of affection, since you understand how closely linked these primal emotions can be. Gentleness wins no points with you. Your **challenge** is to encourage a release of the fire in others, and having initially done so, to discover a way to keep the fires burning. Mere smoke will not do; the flames must rage brightly.

Jupiter/11th

group participation

You have such a spontaneous social sensibility that groups want you around. They often come to you rather than your going to them. These opportunities are not to be taken lightly, since they offer you the **challenge** of recognition and a chance to expand your social horizons. In fact, a real **pitfall** involves presuming that since you've been asked to join in the past, you will be in the future. Don't overlook these real resources.

appropriate behavior

Appropriate behavior is very natural for you, almost like a sixth sense. You seem to instinctively know how to act in almost any social setting. You're interested in what other people think, but probably not overly concerned. At your best, criticism slides off you like water off a duck's back, but be careful of the **pitfall** of self-righteousness. Everyone screws up occasionally, including you, so have patience in bearing the gracelessness or inconsideration you sometimes have to suffer. The **challenge** is to use your relaxed social sense to make others more comfortable, thus increasing your acceptance.

friendship, social circle

Friendship requires little effort. You understand and accept people, which makes you a good friend to have, and you expect others to treat you with the same understanding and acceptance. You're willing to be friendly, even in trying circumstances, and this is communicated to others, who respond in kind. It's only when they don't that you reveal your righteous side. Your social circle is a barometer. If it's large and vibrant, it means you're addressing Saturn's placement in your natal chart. If it's unfulfilling, or if you're isolated, it indicates that you're trapped. Either you're ignoring your Saturn, which means you're not investing enough to warrant a return in friendship, or you're striving to solve those Saturnian riddles too intensely, working so hard that you have no energy left to enjoy yourself. Relax and enjoy the bounty of your friendships.

shared creativity

You repeatedly find yourself linked with organizations whose purpose is creative. Through the ability to oversee the direction of the group's thinking, you influence the creative results, while at the same time becoming recognized as an invaluable source of insight for the group. Cheerleading the whole process is not only enjoyable, but something you revel in. **Your creative role is to provide enthusiasm and perspective, to give the group renewed life.**

receiving love

Being loved is based on the positive vision of yourself reflected in another's eyes. Primary among these is wisdom. When your wisdom is recognized by others, you feel loved. If you're treated as ordinary, however, you do not recognize the presence of love, even if it exists. You like your ego to be stroked. When your lover delights in your spontaneous self-expression, you feel that he or she truly loves you. If constrained or put upon to limit yourself, you back away. When a relationship increases social contacts in your life, you experience being loved. If there is too much possessiveness, the feeling of ingrown isolation destroys the love for you. When your honesty is unquestioned, you are in the flow of love. However, any mistrust or accusation surrounding the purity of your motives or actions is offensive. You don't like being tested. The **challenge** is to find a person who shares your vision of optimism and free expression, and having found that acknowledgment, to honor your beloved with fidelity.

Saturn/11th

group participation

With Saturn in the 11th, you have great ambition to succeed in groups. In part, this stems from fear that you don't belong, that society will reject you. Do not immediately take on a lot of responsibility in group settings. Simply be in the group, not at the center, but near the periphery. Then slowly and consistently move closer to center by taking a more active role, but only as you feel secure to do so. Don't push yourself too fast. Your role in organizations is to take care of business. Even in purely social groups, there are pragmatic responsibilities to be addressed. You're perfectly suited for such tasks, and while you may resent feeling like the janitor, you can become king if you persevere.

appropriate behavior

Social conventions are very important to you. While you can develop the integrity to become a true pillar of the community, respected and admired for your accomplished sense of bearing, your precise attention to correct behavior, you must first mature by laying to rest any fears of ostracism on the basis of class or family background. You may act as if you don't care what people think about how you act, but in truth you care very much, sometimes too much. Avoid the **pitfall** of killing yourself to gain acceptance. The **challenge** is to trust that you can develop a successful social persona, and beyond that, that you're fine just as you are.

friendship, social circle

You are both serious and cautious surrounding friendship. This could be the result difficult experiences involving friends in your childhood or adolescence that left scars on your psyche. Your caution may cause you to close your heart, substituting a more calculating approach designed to gain you the security and stature you long for. Be careful not to cling too tightly to the security of your social circle. Especially, do not create a clique where you convince yourselves that you and your friends occupy an exalted social niche. Seeing your social circle as superior to other people inevitably brings a harsh fall later. Do not rush into friendships; develop them slowly. If you are forgiving of yourself and others, you'll discover the consistency you need. Finally, if you want dependable and true friends, first you need to be a dependable and true friend.

shared creativity

You take shared creativity very seriously. You feel pressure, as if you alone are on the spot. Keep in mind that others don't know this, because you downplay your anxiety over their reactions. If the group fails, you feel it as a personal failure, rather than a shared one. When the group succeeds, you may not instantly receive the credit you feel you are due. Fulfillment comes with sustained efforts over a long period of time, as you learn to work with others, yet still be yourself. **Your creative role is to provide discipline and grounding for the group's expression, to be the rock of dependability.**

receiving love

You want certainty in love, with nothing left to chance. Insecurity runs deep, so you test your lovers repeatedly, giving them every chance to reject you. Only when they've passed every test do you begin to relax and trust their love. You fear that your father didn't love you, so later you feel the presence of love when others are authoritative with you. There can be confusion of love with discipline, and in extreme cases even denial or cold rejection can perversely feel like love to you. There are conflicts between affection and ambition, between love and duty. Romance may be attractive, but you mistrust it. What you crave is safety, tangible support, and dependable affection.

Uranus/11th

group participation

With Uranus in the 11th, group participation is important but unpredictable. You join at a moment's notice, and leave with equal abruptness. Your role in organizations is to play the wild card, upsetter of the status quo. You come on the scene when a group is ripe for change. The **challenge** is to have maximum effect with minimum disruption by maintaining a clear sense of humanitarianism.

appropriate behavior

You care much more about expressing your individuality by acting as you wish than about gaining acceptance by appropriate behavior. Though you may not be especially affected by others' expectations of you, you are very aware that expectations exist. In fact, the paradox is that you believe you should be accepted without having to conform. You could relish notoriety, intentionally upsetting the social applecart just to provoke effect. So try to avoid the **pitfall** of cutting off your nose to spite your face. The **challenge** is to be unconventiona while remaining attractive to others.

friendship, social circle

You want your friends to be unusual, so you're drawn to people whose individuality stands out. They may be downright eccentric, but that makes them more fascinating to you. They can be geniuses or madmen, scientists or revolutionaries, but they must have original or unusual minds. Your social circle is dynamic, with little stability. Friends come and go, and your relationships are extremely volatile. You can become very close almost immediately, but something can disrupt the closeness just as fast. This isn't a problem as long as you remember that the purpose of friends in your life is to stimulate you toward new awareness, to awaken and even sometimes shock your life. You want your individuality to shine through your friendships, and one way or another, it will.

shared creativity

You are the outsider who bursts upon the scene, the revolutionary who upsets the status quo, the black sheep whose insights and outbursts provoke unexpected and often wild periods of new creativity for the group. Who was that masked man? **Your creative role is to to keep the group from stagnating by propelling it in new directions.**

receiving love

Expect the unexpected in love. Courtships come out of the blue with astonishing suddenness, and they awaken you into a heightened state of being, as if you'd never been alive before. This represents an altered state of consciousness, one so polarized that it can't possibly last. And it doesn't. The feeling of being loved can leave as quickly as it came, but that too is a valid part of the experience. Receiving love is on and off with equal impact, keeping you on your toes. Some of your highest experiences are brief, little more than encounters, ships passing in the night. Longer relationships go through many changes. First there is a mountain, then there is no mountain, then there is… Security has no part in your approach. Love must disconnect you from the ordinary. The *challenge* is to allow the experience of being loved to jolt your evolution, to kick it into a higher gear. You'll learn the hide-and-seek nature of peak experience, and through it emerges a greater sense of what makes you special.

Neptune/11th

group participation

You believe in the power of collective action, and you long for immersion in cultural togetherness. But beware of your gullibility. You can be seduced and used, and the seduction may be either clearly Machiavellian or totally unintentional on the part of others who turn out to be less than honest in their motives or actions. Your best quality here is the willingness to fully participate, to believe, and to trust. Your worst quality in this regard is an almost religious fervor for converting others to the group's cause.

appropriate behavior

You may have a wonderful intuitive sense of what others expect from you in the social realm. If this sense is sound and well-developed, you can flow through the demands of conformity effortlessly, flirting with the boundaries of acceptable behavior, getting away with murder, so to speak, often without even realizing it. On the other hand, you could experience great confusion and anxiety about social interaction, believing that you have an invisible donkey's tail, as if your socks didn't match or your fly were open. This **pitfall** is a quiet hysteria that others are secretly mocking you. So don't try to be someone you're not. The **challenge** is to be your authentic, gentle self.

friendship, social circle

Your approach to friendship involves an eagerness to see the best in people. You base your friendships on the highest potentials, and this makes you both inspirational and also somewhat naive, almost romantic in your attitudes toward friends. You're drawn to kindness and beauty in others, both physical and spiritual. You like your friends to be creative dreamers, for it supports your own faith. However, be aware that things are not always as they seem. Since you often deal with your friends as you wish them to be, rather than as you actually are, you may be disappointed when they don't live up to your expectations. Don't put friends on pedestals; they may fall on you. You have no trouble forgiving people for their imperfections, but keep in mind that a collection of stray dogs is not a viable social circle. Don't give yourself away. Offer your friendship, not your soul.

shared creativity

You dissolve into the group process, honoring the magical dream of fusing each member into a single creative source. Your effect is usually in one of two directions: to uplift the group through recognition of the spiritual purpose of its togetherness, or to subtly undercut its productivity through your own inner confusion. **Your creative role is to provide the group with a spiritual direction through your vision.**

receiving love

You believe in romance. You cannot see it, taste it, touch it, or smell it, but somehow the universe itself is loving you through the person of your beloved. This profound subtlety is central to the experience of being loved. You want to be treated gently, with ineffable tenderness, to be made lighter and less physical, to drown in the ocean of the heart. And you want your lover to provide the flying carpet to take you there, swept up into the heavens. Love is otherworldly, larger than life. But is it real? Are these exquisite moments happening in fact, or are they merely flickering images on the silver screen? Is this your life or a romance novel? Have you found God or lost your sanity? Typically, you couldn't care less, but your **challenge** is to differentiate between loving spirituality and escapist delusions.

Pluto/11th

group participation

You want to be involved, to work toward a collective goal, but your social course is difficult to control. At times, nothing works, as if there were nowhere you belonged. Other times, you find yourself at the heart of group activity, driven with fanatic intensity. Your natural role in organizations is to intensify group-purpose. This may mean sowing seeds of destruction to make way for new values and new coalitions. Your **challenge** is to act with maximum efficiency and minimum ruthlessness. Keep your ego out of groups; otherwise, you're asking for trouble.

appropriate behavior

You tend not to see your full effect on others, especially in social interaction. As a result, you may feel quiet and withdrawn, believing yourself to be invisible. Trust that you're not. Or you become the proverbial "bull in a china shop," amplifying and exaggerating every behavior, knocking people flat with your intensity. Others have strong reactions to your social personality, but it takes a long time for you to understand this. It seems that they don't react at all for extended periods, then suddenly they overreact. Avoid the **pitfall** of social insensitivity by considering other people's feelings, which protects your own. The **challenge** is first to see your power, then to use it cooperatively.

friendship, social circle

Friendship is intense, passionate, but curiously prone to misunderstandings. Long-held assumptions turn out to be false. Friends become enemies, and vice versa. One of the reasons for the turbulence is that friendship usually has a special purpose. When a relationship has fulfilled its purpose, one of you may terminate the association with finality. If you do this, you're surprised at the upset or animosity you face; if you're on the receiving end, you can't believe the insensitivity of your ex-friend. To avoid this **pitfall,** you need to work at cooperation in your friendships in all phases of the relationship, from the beginning through the end. A friendship could last a lifetime, but it must go through numerous deaths and rebirths, and you have to be willing to go with that **challenge,** all the way into and through the deepest recesses of your own psyche.

shared creativity

Your presence in the group works to unearth formerly unconscious energies, making them available for one of two forms of expression: to destroy the old and push the group toward a new sense of creative purpose, or to destroy the group itself if an appropriate creative form cannot be found. Either way, your energy promotes deep change, whether or not you intend it to, or are aware of your effect. **Your creative role is to provoke the fertility of the group, and to eradicate blocks to the group's expression.**

receiving love

You wonder if love will ever find you, and you may go through long phases of your life despairing of ever having the experience. But it will periodically find you, and when it does, it shakes you to the roots of your being. You understand being loved only when you are touched at your core. Love is revealed in a tidal wave of emotional force, a watershed of passion. Your lovers need not be beautiful or handsome; they needn't be athletic or graceful. They must, however, possess a powerful radiance, penetrating your every cell with their charismatic energy. They may be kind or gentle, but they're more likely to be a touch ruthless and emotionally driven. You need great intensity to feel truly loved. Nothing less will do. Love consumes you, destroys you, rebirths you, and finally, alters you forever.

Part Two/12th House

Planets in the 12th House

in 12th House*

270   *12th House Interpretive Levels*

272   *Sun*
273   *Moon*
274   *Mercury*
275   *Venus*
276   *Mars*
277   *Jupiter*
278   *Saturn*
279   *Uranus*
280   *Neptune*
281   *Pluto*

12th House

imagination

fantasies, dreams; the intersection of the personal unconscious and the collective unconscious

This is the reservoir of uncategorizable experience, the realm of intersection between the personal and collective unconscious, where reality becomes a dream, and dreams become reality. It is the experience of waking sleep, of open-eyed dreaming, where fantasy is paramount, directed from within the personal unconscious, aimed at the archetypes existing in the collective unconscious of humankind.

The 12th house can be the last stop on the road to enlightenment, the transformation of bewildering complexity into compassionate simplicity and inspirational rebirth, but it can also be the final, confusing torments of a disintegrating mind about to sink into the quicksand of illusion or deception. Enigmatically, it is often both.

unfocused intuition

nonrational knowing in its most generalized context; true mediumship

The 12th house is the third and final area of intuitive receptivity. First came the 4th, intuition for and about the self in purely emotional terms. Next was the 8th, intuition focused into a laserlike ability to probe the inner motivations of individual partners. Now in the 12th, intuition is unfocused, nonselective, and more universal in context.

Here the self is a lightning rod for anything floating through the collective, like a radio scanner, automatically searching the airwaves for signals, locking onto any transmission it discovers. This is mediumship or "channeling," where the individual consciousness functions as a screen upon which are projected all the archetypes reaching critical mass in humankind, akin to the phenomenon of the "hundredth monkey." To be a clear channel requires constant discipline over a long period of time. You must become very pure to avoid traps of misinterpretation.

The condition of the 12th shows for any individual the psychological emphasis and natural tonality of such unfocused intuitive experiences, as well as the expected directions purification must take for clarity to be maintained.

withdrawal or isolation

the experience of withdrawal from life; the sense of transparency; voluntary or enforced isolation

Does the fish recognize or "see" the water in which it lives? It's certainly there, but so evenly distributed, so "everywhere" that it's hardly anywhere at all. Each of us has this experience of transparency, where everywhere and nowhere seem to intertwine. We know it's there, but we can't get our hands on it, since it's transparent and seemingly impossible to focus.

Certain types of intangibility are divine, for instance, the subtle "presence of God" or the transcendent sense of cosmic meaning most of us experience from time to time. Other types are less uplifting. The mystery of some obsessions, compulsions, or neurotic habit imprints is their dogged persistence. They're always with us, agonizingly so since their effect on our conscious minds is so wearying, yet we can't seem to concentrate the experiences enough to work on changing the imprints.

We may seem invisible to others, or sense in ourselves a need for withdrawal from the literal world of events and people, the desire for a private space where we can vanish ourselves back into the universal womb. This too is part of the transparency process.

The condition of the 12th shows our tendency to withdraw from experience into a state of relatively invisible isolation, whether that is life-affirming or life-shattering.

selfless giving

unconditional giving in response to any need; transcendence of personal will

The 6th house involved self-perfection through service requiring discrimination and mental effort, for which we receive recognition and compensation. In the 12th, serving is again emphatic, but here it is undiscriminating: we respond to any need of any person at any level. It is emotional: healing through forgiveness, through the cleansing power of compassion. Finally, it's not a business transaction, but a pure gift.

Transcending self-interest requires surrender of personal will, and the 12th indicates where the will is irrelevant or useless. Sleep is one state of such surrender. Hospitals, prisons, and ashrams all connote experiences where the personal will is meaningless. If you've ever felt the frustration of being shuttled through a bureaucracy, you know what it's like to lose willful effectiveness. The key is to let go, to surrender the ego, to project perfect harmlessness.

The condition of the 12th house reveals the orientation toward selfless giving. It also reveals the potential for transcending personal will, for gracefully surrendering the sense of individuality in favor of compassionate acceptance through universal love.

"past lives"

***invisible conditions prior to birth that affect the life;
in occultism, the karma of alternate realities***

The 12th house represents the "echo" of other realities as they interpenetrate with this one. In the occult concept of reincarnation, such reverberations are the unfulfilled potentials of past lives, still buried in the subconscious, waiting to be understood. They are like icebergs with most of their frozen bulk invisible, lurking beneath the surface.

"Evidence" of an afterlife from people who've died and been resuscitated is suspect and can hardly be considered proof, for clinical death may not be the actual end moment of human life. Such reports could indicate merely a continuation of natural intrapsychic existence. Still, it is beyond question that certain psychics have an uncanny ability to accurately describe individuals and life circumstances through "past life scripts."

Reincarnation may be no more than a poetic language of archetypes. But even metaphor is a valid path to understanding the self. Or it may be real. Stranger things than this have turned out to be true. We cannot know for sure. What is clear is that the 12th house represents fascination with ultimate mysteries and invisible possibilities.

The 12th indicates the directions an individual must search to uncover the infinite levels of self, beyond ego, beyond will, even beyond being human, back to the center of the universe, all the way to God.

Sun/12th

imagination

Fantasy is central to your life-purpose. No dreams, no life-energy, it's that simple. Fantasies are constructed around two sets of images: monumental self-importance where the whole universe is commanded by your particular essence, or total surrender, the release of self as you dissolve into the cosmos. The difference is that one image expands ego while the other evaporates it, but the end result is identical: reunion with everything. The **pitfall** is losing the distinction between what is real and what is only possible, what's actually happening and what you imagine to be happening. Don't get lost in the Twilight Zone; you could go crazy. The **challenge** is to offer no resistance to either realm. Allow dreaming to influence and be influenced by real life, and let fantasies gently guide your development rather than blinding you to what is true.

unfocused intuition

Give intuitive receptivity high priority in your life, without controlling the specifics of what you receive, and your life sings with vibrant energy. Shut down your intuition, and you close off access to cosmic juice. Don't strain to figure out why you pick up flows of imagery and feeling, bits of information and insight. Don't strive to figure out what they mean nor what you should do with them. Your task is to remain radiantly quiet, vibrantly still, pregnantly calm. The **pitfall** is misinterpretation, creating sophisticated forms while missing the truth. The **challenge** is to become a clear channel for the universe to speak through, a prism for otherwise invisible light.

withdrawal or isolation

You require frequent periods of isolation from ordinary life. You need time away to recharge. It is when you are most isolated that your purpose is revealed. This propels you back into the world with renewed enthusiasm. You are everywhere and nowhere simultaneously, both a real person and yet a mere vessel for greater divinity. Your power comes from balancing the paradox, allowing both poles to exist simultaneously. Meditation in some form is an essential.

selfless giving

When you give of yourself with total compassion, you plug directly into your Godliness. When you act with forgiveness, you absorb life-force. When you give of yourself, you fulfill your destiny. Giving does not mean martyring yourself. Don't give yourself away. Instead, give the understanding that we're all in the same boat. Don't strive for sainthood, for too often that course boomerangs back toward egotism. Let your life respond to a power beyond that of mere human selfhood. "Not my will, but Thine."

"past lives"

Your past lives are pressing in, trying to be felt and understood. You're at the end of a life-series; it demands integration through this current life if the whole evolutionary pattern is to be made spiritually meaningful. The precise nature of the lives in question cannot be seen from the Sun's placement alone. We can suggest, however, that they focused on developing personal effectiveness through the integrity of individual power. In addition, your relationships to your father or to other authority figures have karmic rhythms. Naturally enough, the **pitfall** lies in replaying the mistakes of the past without letting go of the attachment that caused such patterns to exist in the first place. The **challenge** is to to see in every action the signature of prior momentum, and to adjust your understanding accordingly. Eventually you can achieve true spontaneity rather than be undermined by repetitive cycles of unconscious reaction.

Moon/12th

imagination

You are not entirely comfortable in your body; you need time every day to relax the ordinary effort of self-awareness. Immersion in fantasy provides you with a way to rejuvenate your willingness to be human. It's necessary, and if you don't get it, you break down emotionally. Imagine being in the womb, completely safe, with no troubles. You may not be aware of your need for release from the pressures of ordinary life, and as a result could go on autopilot, dreaming unconsciously without emotional benefit. The *challenge* is to nourish yourself with conscious fantasy. Dreams are the background source of manifestation, so go to the well often. Just don't fall in and drown.

unfocused intuition

Intuition is instinctive; how you use it is the question. Early imprints with your mother or other maternal figures fostered a high sensitivity to intangible information. Now your intuitive radar is second nature. Channelship can replace fear and confusion with safety and certainty. The **pitfall** involves boundaries. Your own emotional opinions often intertwine with intuitive messages. You may identify with feelings not really your own, or presume your feelings to be messages. The **challenge** is to identify what is truly yours in the realm of emotion, to separate personal feelings from intuitive information.

withdrawal or isolation

No matter how vibrant your personality nor energetic your life may be, you become more softly translucent in solitude away from the world. You float with the emotions that surface in withdrawal; they take you somewhere else, other than here, other than now. You need to slow down and pull off the side of the road to let yourself cool, so you can remember the mystery of things. This placement requires sleep to "knit up the ravelled sleeve of care." Rest is exquisite when you're in your natural flow, but if you encounter periods where sleep is troubled or denied, you suffer terribly, becoming run down almost immediately. Then you must consciously pull away from life.

selfless giving

Your maternal feelings are easily aroused, so much so that you may be regarded by others as a "soft touch," someone whose sympathies are easy to gain. And this is as it should be. Strength does not arise from a hard edge or steely demeanor. On the contrary, your greatest strength is your deep willingness to feel the predicaments of others' lives, and to respond gently. Avoid being overly self-effacing; false humility serves no one. Sheltering the poor, comforting the sick, and calming the disturbed are all acts of compassion. But don't be swept away by sympathy. Remain a safe harbor in the storm, an emotional beacon, like a lighthouse, guiding others to shore. It is not your task to rescue, but to provide sanctuary, so others can save themselves.

"past lives"

The pattern of your emotions and needs is strongly connected to other realities, which have bled into this life to be understood and resolved. There are significant and deep karmic connections between you and your mother, as well as other individuals who touch maternity and nourishment in your life. Examine these relationships carefully to discern any patterns "from the past." There was a tendency toward unconsciousness or habitual behavior in prior incarnations, as if you didn't really see what was unfolding as you created it. Those rhythms have been brought in this life so you can let go of them and get on with the full development of conscious choice.

Mercury/12th

imagination

Your rational mind is an open and inspirational screen for the projection of your dreams. It extends into your own unconscious and beyond, into the collective unconscious of humankind. However, communication is often confused or misunderstood. Sometimes you don't know how to express yourself in clear language, and sometimes others aren't tuned to your imagery. More often, you misinterpret what they're saying, infusing their words with images from your own unconscious. The **challenge** is to communicate your thought-dreams in as clear a way as you can. Realize that your mind is sometimes not your own, and learn methods for communication other than verbal.

unfocused intuition

Intuitions are received as thoughts, as if they were the conscious product of your own rational processes. But they're not; they're signals you convert into thought-patterns. Your own thinking tends to flow with the patterns moving through culture, so you are a bellwether for currents at the cutting edge of society. New cultural vocabularies are natural to you, and your thinking changes with the times. To maintain clarity and minimize the dangers of misunderstanding, you must learn to be quiet mentally. The **challenge** is to understand that your mind is not merely a rational machine. Listen for the signals, and locate both their origins and their destinations.

withdrawal or isolation

You need to clear out the clutter of other people's thoughts from your mind, to take out the garbage. Too much input or exchange can fry your brains. If you don't get relief from the strain, your thoughts become garbled. It's not that you need to stop thinking. It is no more possible to stop the mind than the beating of the heart. But you can take a break from attending to your thoughts. Allow your mind to go its merry way without paying so much attention. You don't need to "read" every thought. Direct the focus of your consciousness upward, beyond the cacophony of thinking. Leave it behind for awhile, and when you return, your understanding will be clarified and refreshed.

selfless giving

You love to figure out solutions for the psychological puzzles of people's lives. Be careful, however, that you don't turn into an advice machine. However pure your motives may be, there is a tendency to get carried away in trying to solve others' problems. Even when they seem to want exactly that, you're better off letting them come to their own solutions through probing conversations. Remaining neutral is an essential part of your service. Occasional periods of silence—"speech fasting"—are very beneficial, since too much talking can overwhelm your sense of order.

"past lives"

The way you perceive, think, and communicate is linked with past life patterns. Your nervous system is already programmed to interpret life in specific ways, ways that now must be made conscious. Misunderstandings with others are frequently a carryover from prior incarnations where the dissonance originated. Don't presume that communication is clear, especially if there is conflict or difficulty. Assume the opposite, that there is something beyond what meets the eye, and investigate the possibilities by visualizing images of yourself and the other person in past life settings. The more you distinguish then from now, the easier it is to reach the satisfaction of mutual agreement. The **challenge** is to work into your past lives to establish the origins of disagreement or misunderstanding, to finally reach clear awareness of the facts in any current situation.

Venus/12th

imagination

Venus in the 12th reveals that fantasy is a continuing source of pleasure for you. It may be too pleasurable, so that you prefer fantasy to reality. Dreams revolve around personal love and ideal femaleness. In real life, love has many **pitfalls.** You fall in love with undeveloped beauty, or you're seduced by comely but cosmetic images. Others are seduced by your invisible radiance. Don't become a fantasy object for individuals whose love is damaged. The **challenge** is to allow your fantasies without undue indulgence, and to communicate to the world the importance of devoted care. In shepherding this dream without succumbing to its siren lures, you add to our understanding of love.

unfocused intuition

In order for your intuition to operate effectively, you "fall in love" with whatever (or whomever) you tune into. This is not forced; it's the natural way you work. But be in love with the source of intuitive messages only while you're receiving information, then disconnect and move on to the next "romance." The **pitfall** involves fixating on the object of the transmission. You become so enamored with some intuitive messengers that you attempt to create relationships with them. This is not to your advantage, and often ends in disappointment. The **challenge** is to let your love move with the flows of your intuition, like a bee skipping from flower to flower, cross-pollinating the world.

withdrawal or isolation

You withdraw to experience satisfaction, and you've learned to enjoy your own company for long stretches. Since love comes to you not from within the world, but from beyond it, there are separations in personal relationships. Absence makes the heart grow fonder, as does time spent alone with your beloved. The **pitfall** involves the sense of being cut off from life, and when isolation or separation surrounds the issue of love, suffering becomes more private and poignant. The **challenge** is to use your withdrawals not as escapes, but as forays or explorations. Hunt for feminine receptivity in the transparency of isolation, and when you find it, bring her lovingness out into the world.

selfless giving

Personal love is subordinate to universal love—giving with no thought of return. You wish to love more than be loved, and you're more devotional than your personality may reveal. Universal love flows from higher concentrations to lower. As a conduit for this flow, you're directed toward those who lack love. If you insist on operating through attached or "chemical" love, you still have romances, but these relationships result in great pain once the purpose is fulfilled and you've been disconnected from the object of your affections. In that case, you learn about grief. The **challenge** is to love openly, fully, but lightly, with grace and style. The love you feel is real, but don't cling to specific people. Trust that your beauty will be recognized not merely by one, but by all.

"past lives"

Your relationships with women are karmic, as are the issues of care and affection. Receptivity and pleasure are not yet understood. Your own femaleness is influenced by past lives, and when women are your love objects, they are beings with whom you've had significant past life contacts. Examine your images and expectations about womanhood. Is it the source of all joy, all pleasure, all aesthetic beauty? If it is, then you're fixated, and asking for trouble. Is love subject to recurring patterns of failure through seduction and betrayal? Your **challenge** is to recognize and release karmic rhythms in love or receptivity, letting them be healed, cleansed, and grounded.

Mars/12th

imagination

Your fantasies have primitive urgency. Heat fills your dreams. They are a repository for vital images of maleness in our species' evolution. While it would be absurd to suggest that all your fantasies involve aggression or conquest, there is a tendency toward these, so even benign dreams may invoke the maleness in your psyche. Crisis, confrontation, conflict, danger, and desire are all relevant symbols in your imagination. The **challenge** is to identify and connect with this imagery, promoting more effective action in real life. The transition from dream states to ordinary consciousness is especially relevant here.

unfocused intuition

You want intuition, and you want it now. But you're like an athlete with a special function on the team. Much of the time you languish on the sidelines, waiting to get into the intuitive game, pacing back and forth along the bench like a placekicker, never knowing when he'll be called on to boot the winning field goal, but understanding that he must be ready to perform when the crisis comes. Curiously, you're at your best in crisis when you surrender to intuitive guidance. Attempt to maintain ego-control, and you are lost. The **challenge** is to let yourself go wherever demons must be slain.

withdrawal or isolation

You may experience difficulty dealing with anger, both your own, and that of others. The directness of such urgent emotions can be upsetting, so they tend to build up inside. Often, you feel them most strongly when alone. This quality can work against you in situations requiring conscious action, but it may also work for you in a crisis, providing an extra boost of energy. Physical activity can be mysterious, almost meditative. You work well on your own, behind the scenes, but schedules and deadlines are not conducive to your best performance. However, you can be brilliant at creating success from the rubble of "best laid plans." The **challenge** is to use alone time to contact your heat source. Get in touch with it, then carry it back into your real life.

selfless giving

You are repeatedly drawn to situations where energy is bubbling away beneath the surface. You may find yourself in confrontations that are not of your own making, for you're a lightning rod for the release of buried, blocked, or superconscious forces. Your own desires are often sublimated beyond the control of conscious will. This can result in floundering without direction, or equally, it may lead to extraordinary commitment, like being a commando who volunteers for a secret mission. The lead sled dog on your team listens to a higher master, and thus may take off at any moment, in any direction. and at other times might just lie down and go to sleep in spite of your yelling, "Mush!" The **challenge** is to deal with assertive energies when they come, however they come, allowing expression while remembering that the ultimate goal is peace of mind.

"past lives"

Your experience of maleness in past lives is unassimilated. You may have been male, or had relationships with men in such a way as to leave unfinished business that is now cutting into this life. Assertion, anger, heat, action, and desire are not fully understood or accepted, and the old patterns need to be revealed before you can become whole. Precisely what rhythms are held over from past lives is not clear from the house placement alone, but the sign, the ruling house, and the interplanetary aspects of Mars will help solve that riddle. The **challenge** is to befriend these stored energies, then to release them in situations requiring intense but controlled explosions.

Jupiter/12th

imagination

Fantasy means freedom, release from the constraints of personality. It is also a road to wisdom and truth. The **pitfall** involves the possibility that your dreams may not translate into reality, that they remain instead a source of illusory optimism while your real life remains blind. The **challenge** is to use your imagination to see what's possible in the human realm, and then work to infuse that goodness into your day-to-day living.

unfocused intuition

Intuition works through the conceptual mind. You see patterns of understanding, huge puzzles resolved by a single formula. Currents running through the collective imagery of humankind reveal themselves as pure ideas, or laws to live by. The more people you interact with, the more you plug into your intuitive base. Strangers trigger new insights, new ways of seeing life. New social structures galvanize your enthusiasm. Visit the ruins of ancient cultures. Feel the presence of civilization. However, avoid the **pitfall** of over-simplifying reality into a set of moral rules. Remember, life is bigger than philosophy. The **challenge** is to let higher sources guide the development of your understanding.

withdrawal or isolation

You can be filled with bountiful life, but you need isolation to stay in touch with it. Retreat is necessary to rejuvenate your positiveness about relationships. Religion has great significance for you, and you may become immersed in the study of spiritual questions. The **pitfall** involves withdrawal into an unreal world of ideals and aspiration. You may waste yourself thinking about how wonderful life can be without doing anything to create it, becoming involved with an image of yourself rather than who you really are. The **challenge** is to use privacy to connect with life's wonderful possibilities, and renewing your faith, to come back into the world ready to make life more positive.

selfless giving

To an extent, each of us is imprisoned within our human selves; we are a concentration of life-energy into a temporary package. You're more sensitive than many people to the restrictions of your cell walls. Offering yourself without consideration for gain allows you to feel the translucence of those cell walls. The **pitfall** lies in groundless help, offering this season's vintage of distilled philosophy without providing any pragmatic assistance. Also, you are occasionally too opportunistic in giving, offering yourself only when it is convenient for you to do so. The **challenge** is to show your faith in others, and to effectively convey that things have a way of working out.

"past lives"

In past lives, there's a possibility that you misunderstood social relating, and that pattern has built sufficient momentum to bleed into this life. There may have been false promises; commitments made but not honored. You took advantage of others, or were used badly by them. Now you need to learn how to communicate and relate so that no one is abused. There are also incarnational patterns involving the abstract mind. Misconceptions you drew from teachings in other lives have left you mentally out-of-round. Finally, you may have been a spiritual seeker who sought the divine through miracles. You need to understand how to ground that experience, to test it in the crucible of real life. Balance your hopes and dreams against the stricter demands of pragmatism. Let your idealism shine through, but remember the Hindu admonition: **"if you see the Guru on the road, kill him, for he's not the Guru."**

Saturn/12th

imagination

You dream of perfect structure. You want your path laid out by a higher authority than yourself; fantasy has a distinctly paternal tone. You dream of solid strength, total discipline, even restraint. Teachers and institutions have a strong effect on your life. However, looking for an authority outside the self indicates a longing to return to childhood, free from the real problem of deciding for oneself what life-form to create and how to do it. The **challenge** is to accept the importance of structure in a way that doesn't imprison or humiliate you, but instead provides you with the stability you need.

unfocused intuition

You surround yourself with mysteries to prod the development of your own intuition. But the weight of your ambition makes it a difficult achievement. You're anxious about being wrong. You want to transcend your ego, but you're more than a little nervous about giving up the security of solid personality. You may vacillate between the **pitfalls** of naive gullibility and hard cynicism, swept away by metaphysical trappings and claims of false mysticism while rejecting real intuitive messages. The **challenge** is to work steadily at intuitive development by studying the the process and the techniques. As you progress, your sensitivity decreases, and you become lighter and more subtle.

withdrawal or isolation

Your work tends to isolate you from others. This can be literal, as in the case of a scientist or researcher working in a cloistered setting, or it may be metaphorical, as with the person who doesn't really know what career to choose and feels cut off from the world as a result. Your actual work is often behind the scenes, away from public ego platforms. The **pitfall** is that in some lives the career role becomes so dominant that the person behind the career is overwhelmed, somehow obscured. The **challenge** is to understand the full ramifications of your work as the ripples of your efforts spread out into the world.

selfless giving

Selflessness is a duty. First, you fear it's your lot in life to go without, to surrender or give away what little you feel you possess. Curiously, you also fear being selfish. You could even believe that when all is said and done, all veneers stripped away, that your giving will be revealed as a sham. Caught between these poles, you force yourself to give with little possibility of return. You work overtime to purify yourself, not always at the level of motive, but certainly at the level of behavior. The **challenge** is to gradually master the art of nonmartyring selflessness, slowly teaching yourself to give in ways that are self-fulfilling rather than self-abusive. Don't give until it hurts; give until it shines.

"past lives"

You were very concerned with responsibility and cultural authority in past lives. You may have held high office, been responsible for others, or you may have been in the inferior position, subject to another's authority. In either case, something happened that caused you to feel the full weight of responsibility without true understanding. You may have "dropped the ball," so to speak, or the ball may have been dropped on you. Either way, there are unconscious patterns surrounding authority, responsibility, and blame. It's likely that you're working out karma with your father or other authority figures. It's important to reveal the subtle rhythms in these relationships—in past lives, early in this life, and now. The way you project authority or play out your ambitions needs examination to reveal any shadows of coldness, cruelty, or failure. The **challenge** is to give yourself a full pardon and mature into conscious adulthood.

Uranus/12th

imagination

Your dreams glisten with the promise of the unusual, the abnormal, the miraculous. There are no limits; anything is possible. In fantasy you express freely, with no concern for acceptance. The judgments of others are irrelevant, and even your own judgments about yourself fall away. The **pitfall** occurs when fantasies become real. In dreams you leap beyond the pull of gravity, but in real experience you're subject to the density of earthly existence. It's like the difference between stopping on a dime and running into a brick wall at eighty miles an hour. Be careful about what you transfer from one realm to the other. The **challenge** is to realize through your dreams that nothing is as it seems, that the expected norms of life are mere illusions. Everything in existence is absolutely unique and incomparable.

unfocused intuition

You're fascinated with psychic development (or research in general, for that matter). Intuition is a visit from outer space, a non sequitur leaping in to disrupt the ordinary process of logic, a neon sign flashing suddenly in the night. It's either on or off, hot or cold, but never lukewarm. The **challenge** is to awaken your superconscious, however revolutionary it may prove to be. Channelship repots you, ripping you up by the roots so you can find new, more fertile soil in which to grow.

withdrawal or isolation

Others see you as unique, even odd, but you struggle to identify what makes you different. You withdraw from life to find the "real" you. Privately, you're interested in arcane and unusual pursuits, especially mental explorations. The more in touch you are with your secret self, the more tension you feel about revealing it to others. The **challenge** is to take selected individuals into your private world. As your trust increases so you're safe to be yourself with them, gradually move your private world toward the public realm. The goal is to merge the "outlaw" self with the "normal" self, so that there is finally only one self, acceptable but special.

selfless giving

When you give of yourself freely, with no conditions, something special happens. Selflessness is your chance to step out of the mundane. The precise nature of what and how you give cannot be foreseen; it is unpredictable both in form and content. In fact, the more radical your gifts are, the fuller is the release of new perspective. The **pitfall** is stubbornness. You become like the zealous minister who is going to save souls whether or not they want (or need) to be saved. Remember that pure giving is correctly a response to need. The **challenge** is to awaken to a will higher than that of the ego.

"past lives"

Independence has come up in life after life. You may have been such a nonconformist that you alienated others. There were broken commitments, sudden separations, both personal and cultural. Or you may have been someone so concerned with acceptance by others that you sacrificed your individuality, stuffing it into your unconscious. In either case, the issue of freedom has reached a point where patterns from past incarnations are carrying over into this life. Whenever you experience unpredictable breaks in relationships, urges to shock others, or compulsive desires to overthrow the status quo, you're in the flow of karmic rhythms. The **challenge** is to integrate personal freedom without totally upsetting your own and others' lives. Study what independence means; learn the difference between productive reform and unconscious iconoclasm.

Neptune/12th

imagination

Your fantasies involve pure surrender, giving up ego identity to become one with larger universes within and beyond the ordinary self. When you dream—waking or sleeping— you dissolve into a realm where control and will have no meaning. Your fantasies run the gamut, from visions of the Second Coming to winning the state lottery. The **pitfalls** are reminiscent of Venus, but subtler. You might "overeat" on religion, stuffing yourself full of "junk-food spirituality." Also, "visualization" is no substitute for hard work. If you want something, work with the Earth, not against it. The **challenge** is to allow dreams to inspire you, so that ordinary events acquire the radiant aura of divine presence.

unfocused intuition

Everything you see, hear, taste, touch, and smell has an intuitive dimension. In fact, all your sensory receptors work at multiple levels. They pick up both tangible and ethereal levels simultaneously. So the most basic ways you experience anything blend the actual and the magical. This gives you the advantage of being able to work constantly with your intuition, since it is woven into your natural vision of life. It also saddles you with the burden of having no essential distinctions surrounding intuition. You may not even realize it's happening, since it's ubiquitous. You tend not to receive specific information, but instead to absorb fundamental meanings. The **challenge** is to see the signature of higher meaning in everything you experience, to bask in the magic of life.

withdrawal or isolation

Your withdrawals are more psychic than physical. You need not be alone to vanish; you simply leave your body and float out into the cosmos. Paradoxically, it is ordinary life that feels isolated. When you withdraw, you merge with everything beyond the self, so that even in invisibility you are one with the universe. The **pitfall** is that you may prefer withdrawal to real life. You could become a full-time escapist, whisking yourself away from the demands of living into a formless realm of nonbeing, more pleasant, no doubt, but illusory at best. The **challenge** is to replenish your faith in magic through meditative privacy. Just remember to bring back the faith to others in this world.

selfless giving

Selfless giving is a lifestyle rather than an event. Your gifts tend to be spiritual rather than physical, intangible rather than concrete. They may also be romantic or idealistic in tone. When you transcend the ego, your sense of personal boundaries evaporates. This can be frightening if you believe your essence is dissolving. Or you could achieve reunion with everything, grass and sky and earth. The **pitfall** is giving without really offering anything, being openhearted but ineffective, well-intentioned but naive. The **challenge** is to make your gifts tangible enough that the spiritual bounty can be shared.

"past lives"

In past lives, you explored the boundaries between what's real and what's not. You were a magician performing sleight of hand or a yogi stopping his heartbeat, a minister promoting salvation or a charlatan selling snake oil, a true mystic reaching for divine union or a deluded schizophrenic locked in an insane asylum. Your relationships were characterized by compassion and sincere giving, or delusion and heartbreak. One thing is common: things were never quite what they seemed. Now it's time to move out of the shadows and into the light. Every time you lean backward into your karmic past, life dissolves into confusion. Accept life's dreamlike quality without succumbing to it, knowing that there is reality behind every illusion, and illusion behind every reality.

Pluto/12th

imagination

In ordinary life, your impact often seems negligible, so you dream of omnipotence. You imagine sheer power moving through you. The **pitfalls** are twofold. First, you may rev on your fantasies of control, using dreams to satisfy frustrated ego drives. This causes the power to turn against you if it manifests in real life. Second, you may use fantasy to avoid dealing with the power buried in your unconscious. If you can get fulfillment through dreams, why work to make your real life more effective? The **challenge** is to purify your ego through your fantasies. Then, having sanctified the energy, move it toward conscious expression in the real world.

unfocused intuition

Pure intuition is powerful, deep, and mysterious to you. There is Shiva energy here, the means to wipe things out of manifestation, to erase all tapes, to obliterate what is no longer alive with relevance. The **pitfall** lies in using such intuitive power for personal ends. This energy is simply not manageable by the ego. It will destroy you like the dragon eating its own tail. The **challenge** is to let the energy go where it wants, toward the outer world, or toward parts of your own personality. Something must be destroyed. If it is gracefully surrendered, new and vital forms appear in its place.

withdrawal or isolation

You withdraw to touch the roots of your power. Isolation may be compulsive, however, even to the point of keeping secrets when there is no clear reason to do so. You're a very private person, even when you don't intend to be, for feelings are hidden from others and from yourself. Being alone is a turbulent vortex of intensity. If you approach without sufficient preparation, you may release so many powerful archetypes that you come face to face with obliteration. The **challenge** is to recognize that even then you are still in the presence of God. Have the courage to slay the dragons in your unconscious, and transform the dark energies buried there back into loving light. Become a fervent explorer of your own psyche, and triumph in your own conversion.

selfless giving

Selflessness can be awesome. When it overtakes you, it's like an earthquake swallowing up your ego. You'll experience infinite power if you operate from motives beyond survival. But recognize the **pitfalls.** You may at times refuse to give. Such defiance pressurizes the need for release, eventually causing a tremendous explosion of self-disintegrating martyrdom. Or you may be giving all along but not recognizing the experience. This cripples your growth by making you believe yourself to be selfish when you're not. The **challenge** is to cleanse yourself by offering your inner power completely and without reservation, thus liberating your spirit from ego-imprisonment.

"past lives"

In past lives, you were fascinated by the coexistence of good and evil in human affairs. At times you were the paragon of goodness, using all your power to transform the world into a better place. At other times you succumbed to profound evil, twisting others in manipulation, bending them to your will. The dual roles of dominance and submission are written in your karmic past. Such power struggles can no longer be avoided; they are seeping into this life. You must integrate the two polar forces, becoming neither good nor evil, but instead a complete human being. The angelic and the demonic have had their day in your soul's evolution. Now it is time to come to the center, embracing all extremes. No black hats, no white hats, just people striving to live in grace.

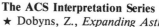